Fodor's

THIRD EDITION

# FAMILY ADVENTURES

BY CHRISTINE LOOMIS

Fodor's Travel Publications
New York • Toronto • London • Sydney • Auckland
www.fodors.com

Third Edition

ISBN 0-679-00426-2

ISSN 1528-3100

## Fodor's Family Adventures

**Editor:** Jennifer Paull
**Editorial Production:** Rebecca Zeiler
**Design:** Fabrizio La Rocca, *creative director;* Guido Caroti, *art director;* Jolie Novak, *photo editor;* Tigist Getachew, *cover design*
**Production/Manufacturing:** Mike Costa
**Cover Photographs:** Family and rafting, Warren Morgan/Westlight; cyclist, Doug McSpadden/Backcountry; girl with horse, American Wilderness Experience; skiers, David Brownell at the Balsams Wilderness

## Special Sales

Fodor's Travel Publications are available at special discounts for bulk purchases for sales promotions or premiums. Special editions, including personalized covers, excerpts of existing guides, and corporate imprints, can be created in large quantities for special needs. For more information contact your local bookseller or write to Special Markets, Fodor's Travel Publications, 201 East 50th Street, New York, NY 10022. Inquiries from Canada should be directed to your local Canadian bookseller or sent to Random House of Canada, Ltd., Marketing Department, 2775 Matheson Boulevard East, Mississauga, Ontario L4W 4P7, Canada. Inquiries from the United Kingdom should be sent to Fodor's Travel Publications, 20 Vauxhall Bridge Road, London, England SW1V 2SA.

PRINTED IN THE UNITED STATES OF AMERICA

10 9 8 7 6 5 4 3 2 1

## Author's Acknowledgments

I couldn't have completed this project without help. My thanks to Dorothy Jordon and Candyce Stapen and their families for being terrific and generous companions on and off the road; to Karin Lazarus for invaluable assistance; to Leslie Eppinger for cheerful, tireless research, and without whom there could be no new edition; to everyone at Fodor's for their thoughtful editing and Karen Cure for believing in the book; and to all the outfitters, guides, and tour operators who shared their adventures, expertise, insights, and humor with me. I also thank my own crew of family travel experts: Kira, Molly, and Hutch.

# CONTENTS

## A Note About This Book

Christine Loomis did not just write *Family Adventures*—she has lived the book. A travel writer for 16 years, she has long been an avid lover of the outdoors. After having her first child more than 18 years ago, she knew she didn't want to give up the activities she enjoyed, from rafting and hiking to cross-country skiing. Not only were they too much fun, but she also wanted to share with her family her delight in the world around her. From the time her children were very young, Christine did research to find outfitters and ranches that would accept travelers of all ages. Since then, she and her family have also logged over 25,000 miles exploring North America by RV.

As a travel writer and editor, Christine became increasingly aware she was not the only parent who wanted to continue adventuring with her family. At the same time, many outfitters, guide services, and schools noticed a growing interest in family adventure travel and began to expand their offerings. In writing this book, Christine selected her favorite sports and activities and chose the outfitters carefully. Many were people she and her family had taken trips with; others were recommended by traveling parents she knew and trusted. Still others were suggested by travelers like you. In every case, she conducted extensive interviews—asking many of the same questions listed in this book—and then decided whether to include the outfitters and schools.

Everyone who has contributed to *Family Adventures* has worked hard to make the text accurate. All prices and opening times are based on information supplied to us at press time, and Fodor's cannot accept responsibility for any errors that may have occurred. The passage of time will bring changes, so it's always a good idea to call ahead and confirm information.

Fodor's would love your feedback, positive and negative. If you have complaints, we'll look into them and revise our entries when the facts warrant it. If you've happened upon a special place we haven't included, we'll pass the information along to the writer. So please send a letter or postcard to the *Family Adventures* editor at Fodor's, 201 East 50th Street, New York, New York 10022, or send e-mail to editors@fodors.com (specifying the name of the book in the header). We'll look forward to hearing from you. And in the meantime, have a wonderful trip!

Karen Cure
*Editorial Director*

# GETTING STARTED ON THE ROAD TO ADVENTURE

The first thing you should know about adventure travel is that it's for everybody. Honest—everybody. You don't have to be a diehard daredevil or world-class athlete, you don't have to be young (though you can be), and you don't have to rough it unless you want to—even in the middle of the wilderness. In recent years travelers of every age—parents, children, and grandparents—have packed up comfortable clothing and headed into the great outdoors, where the possibilities for fun, learning, and excitement are as boundless and varied as the American landscape itself.

Outfitters, schools, and guide services have responded to the increased number of adventure-loving families by offering more family-oriented trips and activities, as well as departure dates just for families traveling with children. The choices for physical activities are many: Biking, boating, hiking, horseback riding, fishing, and snorkeling are only a few. Opportunities for learning and for expanding every family member's horizons abound as well. You and your children can work with scientists digging for dinosaur bones or aid an archaeologist uncovering ancient native ruins. You can meet, live with, and learn about present-day Native American peoples and their culture in this country and in Canada.

Whatever your family chooses to do and wherever you choose to go, all the activities in this book provide opportunities to strengthen the bonds that connect family members to each other and to the greater world. I know this has been true for my family. With no TV and no phone to pull us apart, we seem to talk more, laugh more, and take the time to discover each other and the world around us.

Even the concept of what constitutes family entertainment is expanded in the world of nature vacations. Sometimes it's the array of stars in a vast, dark sky or the music of the river or stories told by guides around a campfire. On a rainy afternoon in the Adirondacks, our family—my husband, Bill, and our children, Kira, Molly, and Hutch—played a spectacularly silly game of charades in a tent. On one ranch vacation we all paused from a fireside game of Uno to watch Hutch sleeping in his crib. He was about a year old then and hardly the focus of anyone else's good time. But for our family at that moment, he was the perfect entertainment to share and remember. It's not that such moments don't happen on other vacations or at home. It's simply that adventure vacations provide more time for such moments than any other type of travel I know.

I mentioned that Hutch was only a year old to make another point: There is no age at which you cannot enjoy adventure travel. To be sure, many trips and certain activities have age restrictions. Many don't, however, and today an increasing number of trips are available to younger children as outfitters and schools learn what families want and are capable of.

At the ripe old age of four, Molly accompanied me on a four-night, five-day float and camping trip in the Tetons. She still remembers parts of that trip vividly: her terror during the thunder and lightning on the first two nights, her bravery during the storm on the third; her first fishing lesson; and that she got to spend special time with me, alone, while her siblings spent time with their dad. She remembers the two guides who taught her about wild huckleberries and told her stories about Jackson Hole. Molly also learned about our national parks and developed a budding love of the great outdoors. These things she will carry with her for a lifetime.

Adventure travel does have an element of risk that other vacations do not. This doesn't mean families should stay home; it means they should be prepared. Talk to your kids about safety. If you give them the responsibility of listening to guides' safety talks and then ensuring that your family does what's right, you are likely to find they will take this responsibility seriously. Parents need to listen to guides, too, and to be prepared in other ways, such as using appropriate safety equipment and carrying clothing for sudden changes in weather. When you book a vacation, don't exaggerate your family's abilities in order to be accepted on a particular trip. Not only will you put them at risk for injury, your family—and the other participants—won't enjoy the trip.

On adventure vacations rules don't cut down on enjoyment; they increase it because they keep you safe even when risks are present. In addition, rules protect the environment and the wildlife you have paid to experience. Children who learn this at an early age have a world of exciting opportunities open to them.

All the outfitters, schools, and trip operators in this book are very good, but not every one of them is right for every family. The ranch that is perfect for a family with preteens may be less than ideal for a family with a two-year-old. To help you connect with the right group, here's a list of questions you should consider before signing up, as well as some general trip-planning questions. In addition, you will find adventure-specific questions at the beginning of each chapter.

## Questions to Ask

As you talk with each outfitter, you want to hear that your family will be wholeheartedly welcomed and that everything possible will be done to make this vacation work for all of you. By the same token, give the outfitter detailed information about the ages, abilities, and special needs of everyone in your family.

**Will other children be on the same trip? If not, can you recommend an alternative date?** Having peers on a trip can make a huge difference in how much fun your children have. It also lets you off the hook for entertaining them every minute. If your departure date is one for which only adults have signed up, consider traveling with another family you know or bringing along one of your child's friends. If you can be flexible about the date, you can probably find another trip on which families are already booked. Also, some adventure brokers and tour operators, as well as some outfitters, offer more than one kind of adventure, so even if there are no families on the July hiking trip, there might be kids on a canoe voyage around the same time.

**Have the trip's guides worked with children before? If so, with what ages?** Your guide should be comfortable with and knowledgeable about children the ages of yours. A guide who is used to working with children knows how to communicate information in an age-appropriate way, which both increases your kids' enjoyment and helps keep them safe.

**Do you have child-size gear and clothing that will fit my child?** Because technical and safety gear and clothing—whether it's bike helmets, Coast Guard–approved life vests, or extreme-weather clothing—are crucial for many activities, be sure to get accurate information ahead of time. Always check specific sizes of available gear and give outfitters your child's weight and height in addition to age, since the wet suit or cross-country ski boots that fit one seven-year-old may not fit another. Most outfitters send a pretrip list of required and suggested clothing and gear.

**Do you include kid-favorite meals on your menus?** Outfitters that work extensively with families know the kinds of food children like and make an effort to include some of those at all meals. However, if you have a picky eater, ask what's going to be on the menu and then see if special requests can be accommodated.

**Are there any special activities for children on your trips?** For example, do the guides tell stories to the kids about the area in which you'll be traveling? Does the naturalist line up activities that will interest children? Such activities are most common on designated family departures, so if this is important to you, book those trips.

**What if I want to participate in an activity for which my child is too young?** Some activities, such as hikes or trail rides, may be appropriate only for older kids. If that's the case, you need to know if your younger child can stay back at camp or the ranch with a responsible adult. The younger your children are, the more likely these situations will come up, so ask in advance to avoid disappointment.

**How flexible is the trip itinerary?** The hallmark of a good family guide is flexibility. When I took Molly on the Teton float, the itinerary included a long hike the first day and a change of campsites each of the four nights. With a four- and a five-year-old on the trip, the head guide changed the hike to a fishing lesson and kept us at the same campsite for two nights. It made a huge difference to the families.

**What will the group size be?** Although I believe group size is less important than the quality and attributes of an outfitter, it's still something to consider. Many outdoor enthusiasts think only in terms of small, intimate groups. Indeed, for some families that's optimal. Keep in mind, though, that larger groups are likely to have more companions for children as well as parents.

**Will you supply references from others who have taken your trips?** If possible, ask for a reference from both a parent and his or her children who were on the trip. Your child might enjoy hearing about the trip from a peer.

**Where is the nearest medical facility? What emergency training and equipment does the guide have?** When you're in the wilderness, the closest facility may be hundreds of miles away. Be prepared by bringing small amounts of normal childhood medications: acetaminophen (pain reliever), decongestant, cough medicine, and medication to prevent or cure upset stomach, diarrhea, and motion sickness. Ask your pediatrician for an antibiotic in powder form (you'll have to add water) or a type that doesn't require refrigeration—especially if you're traveling out of the country. Find out whether the guides know basic or wilderness first aid and CPR for adults and children and have wilderness training. If you'll be on the water, they should also know water safety and rescue. Also ask what medical supplies will be on hand (carry your own first-aid kit in any case) and whether there will be a radio with which to call for help if necessary.

**Are passports or other official documents needed?** If passports are required for adults, your child needs one, too; start this process well in advance of your trip. All children must have a social security number in order to get a passport. Children 13 and up must apply in person at a passport office or a designated post office; parents can apply for younger children. If only a birth certificate is required, it must be either the original or a notarized copy with a raised seal. Finally, some destinations require additional documentation. If you travel to Mexico with your child but without your child's other parent, you must bring a notarized letter from that parent stating you have permission to take your child to Mexico without him or her. Health documents proving any required inoculations are also necessary in some cases.

**Will insects be a problem?** Lots of wilderness areas have them, so be prepared. However, the most common insect-repellent ingredient, DEET, should be used with caution on children. Most health experts recommend applying DEET only on children's clothing, not directly on skin. There are some non-DEET repellents, too. Ask your pediatrician's advice.

**What is done with diapers in the wilderness?** Some outfitters accept infants on canoe voyages, but there is often no place to dispose of soiled diapers during a trip. Parents must store and carry out all diapers. Families that use cloth diapers must do the same thing because washing soiled diapers in or even near lakes and streams can contaminate the water.

**How far in advance should we book our vacation?** Adventure travel has become extremely popular, and trips—especially those designated just for families—often fill up quickly. The rule is this: Book as far in advance as possible, but don't hesitate to call at the last minute if free time suddenly comes your way.

**How much of a deposit is required, and when is the balance due?** Most schools and outfitters require a deposit well in advance of a trip. You then pay the full amount just prior to departure.

**What's the cancellation policy?** You may or may not get a full or partial refund if you cancel your reservation early enough. Policies vary from full refunds up to 30 days before the trip to partial refunds up to seven days before departure to no refunds at all. If the outfitter offers cancellation insurance, take it, or look into getting insurance from other sources. That way you'll receive a refund if for any reason your family can't take the trip.

**Are taxes and tips included in the cost?** Generally, taxes and tips aren't part of the price, and these can add substantially to a trip's cost. Be sure to ask who customarily gets tipped and how much. Guides who are exceptionally good with children are invaluable, so if you're happy with a guide, tip generously; it could encourage other guides and outfitters to work on family-friendliness, too. If you're traveling to Canada, the GST (goods and services tax) is sometimes included in the cost, and it is sometimes refundable to non-Canadians; ask in advance.

## How to Use This Book

Each chapter covers one sport or activity and profiles outfitters, companies, and schools that have great family trips. In most chapters the outfitters and schools are in alphabetical order; in a few the outfitters are given alphabetically within a region. Each profile has an age icon with the minimum age the outfitter or school accepts, but read the full description for specific requirements and occasional exceptions. The profiles have information about where the company operates and descriptions of the best trips for children of different ages. Each chapter ends with Resources, a section listing organizations, periodicals, books, and products of interest.

Families looking for adventure in a particular part of the country can use the section called Finding the Fun, which lists outfitters by the regions in which they operate. Here are the states in each region:

**Northeast:** Connecticut, Maine, Massachusetts, New Hampshire, New York, Rhode Island, Vermont

**Mid-Atlantic:** Delaware, Maryland, New Jersey, Pennsylvania, Virginia, Washington, D.C., West Virginia

**South:** Alabama, Arkansas, Florida, Georgia, Kentucky, Louisiana, Mississippi, North Carolina, South Carolina, Tennessee

**Midwest:** Illinois, Indiana, Iowa, Kansas, Michigan, Minnesota, Missouri, Nebraska, North Dakota, Ohio, Oklahoma, South Dakota, Wisconsin

**Southwest:** Arizona, Nevada, New Mexico, Texas, Utah

**Rockies:** Colorado, Idaho, Montana, Wyoming

**West Coast:** California, Oregon, Washington

The section has separate heads for trips in Alaska, Hawaii, and destinations farther afield. At the end of the book an appendix tells you the sports, activities, and outfitters in each state and country. There is also an index of outfitters.

Descriptions of outfitters and schools include a range of per-person trip prices for both adults and children, in most cases from the lowest price to the highest for each group. Sometimes adventure pricing is complex. It can depend on where you go, the number of people in your family, the accommodations you choose, and the season. It can also depend on the ages of your children. When an outfitter or school provided an age range for children's prices, this is included; when outfitters or schools did not provide this or felt different adventures would have different guidelines, no age range is mentioned. In listings where only one price range is given, there is no children's discount. Because there are so many variables, it's best to ask specific questions about trip prices. Most prices are in U.S. dollars, although we occasionally list Canadian prices only, with the designation "C$". The exchange rate at press time was US$1 to C$1.45.

Finally, most information here concerns guided trips and tours, as well as courses in various outdoor activities. Why guides and instructors? Because for the vast majority of families, that is the safest way to take children into the wilderness or onto the water, or to introduce them to these kinds of adventures. There are, of course, excellent outfitters that will provide you with all of the equipment and maps you need to find your own way. Some of those are given, too, since they can be a good option for parents who are experienced wilderness travelers.

Guided trips have appeal even for parents proficient in a sport. Leading a trip requires many skills, including child CPR and lifesaving, basic and wilderness first aid, and water safety and rescue. Moreover, a parent can be an excellent hiker, cyclist, or kayaker, but if he or she isn't thoroughly familiar with the area or the particular river, guiding is better left to those who are. Besides, with everything that outfitters are offering families these days—storytelling, special children's counselors, and the company of lots of other kids—even the most resourceful parent is hard pressed to compete. Leaving the details to someone else has its rewards. You have more time to enjoy the area through which you're traveling, the insights of those who know it well, and most important of all, the company of your children. Happy adventuring!

# ARCHAEOLOGY ADVENTURES

Digging in dirt comes naturally to most children, so it's not surprising that archaeology lends itself to family adventure. But it's not just the digging: Children are often fascinated with ancient civilizations, with the ways people lived, worked, and played long ago. Add to that interest the opportunity to experience Native American cultures—such as those studied at archaeological sites throughout the American Southwest—and you have the stuff of an exciting family adventure vacation.

Uncovering ruins and pottery is a way for families to learn not only about ancient worlds but, by extension, about themselves. Archaeology is rewarding work; however, it *is* work. When you "vacation" by volunteering at a research site, you may not come home rested, and you probably won't have had time to read that novel you've been saving for months. On the other hand, you will return home with the satisfaction of knowing that by volunteering, your family has contributed to our understanding of the earth's past, present, and future.

## Questions to Ask

**What kinds of objects have been uncovered at this site?** Although archaeology is painstaking work, the rewards from uncovering something no one else has seen for hundreds or even thousands of years are great. But because you'll want your family to have reasonable expectations about the possibility of discovering such rewards, ask ahead of time what kinds of artifacts or other material might be found and how often volunteers like you find them.

**How much time is spent digging?** Generally, days are a mix of digging and other kinds of archaeological activities, but three to six hours of digging is typical. You might dig in the morning and work in a lab in the afternoon, or you might dig eight hours straight one day and not at all on other days. Some programs give you a few choices; at other sites the itinerary is more rigid. Be assured, however, that in most cases much of your time will be devoted to digging. If you don't want to spend many hours on your knees involved in fairly painstaking work, these trips are probably not for you.

**Are there other activities?** In some cases, other activities are available. There may be recreation areas nearby or places of interest related to the project. Some programs include hikes and day trips; on other projects the opportunity to pursue recreational activities may come only at night, if at all. If you feel your family will have a hard time focusing just on archaeology, choose a site with some alternatives.

**Will I be with my children most of the time?** Volunteers are often separated, working at different activities or in different areas of a site. If this concerns you, ask ahead of time.

**What kind of housing is available?** Travelers must often share facilities (kitchen, bathrooms), and males and females usually sleep in separate quarters. This may even include lodging a single parent separately from a child of the opposite sex. That's true for spouses, too. At the least you will probably share housing with part of the group. If this is a problem, see if other lodging arrangements can be made (utilizing tent sites instead of bunkhouses, for example). If there are no alternatives, you'll need to prepare your family for the possibility of separation or choose another project.

**What are the field conditions?** These are scientific research sites, not vacation destinations. Field conditions are typically primitive—sites are hot, dusty, and dirty; and work often requires walking over uneven or rocky terrain. There may or may not be tarps or other kinds of shelter to shield you from hot sun or rain. Get all the specifics about the project you're interested in.

**Are trip costs tax deductible?** When you volunteer your time and labor on bona fide research projects, a portion of your fee is probably tax deductible, as are some of your out-of-pocket expenses and transportation costs to project sites. The tax code is complex, however, so check with your accountant or other tax expert.

**Is it possible to get college credit for this volunteer work?** In some cases, yes. However, if you are pursuing college credit, your trip may no longer be tax deductible.

**Will there be opportunities to meet local residents?** Whether you're traveling in this country or abroad, a research project can be an opportunity to meet people from another background or culture. At foreign sites, local residents often work at project sites or provide housing. Make cultural exchange part of your trip by reading about the area ahead of time. If another language is involved, try to use it as much as possible.

**What's included in the cost?** On multi-day trips lodging and meals are included unless noted otherwise. Transportation to and from the sites is not usually part of the cost. If you'll be camping or staying in dorms or bunkhouses, you may need to bring your own camping gear and bedding. Tents are provided at some sites, but ask.

## Instruction

You don't need any special skills or knowledge to participate in these trips because discussions about the project, lectures, and hands-on instruction in excavation and lab work are part of the experience. The excavation sites contain valuable and fragile materials, so you and your children will be taught the proper way to dig and to handle any finds. Advance information packets sometimes include reading lists of historical and cultural background material.

### Finding the Fun

**Southwest:** Denver Museum of Natural History, Earthwatch, White Mountain Archaeological Center. **Rockies:** Crow Canyon Archaeological Center. **Caribbean, Central America, Europe, Asia:** Earthwatch.

## Favorite Digs

### Crow Canyon Archaeological Center

12+

For more than 15 years Crow Canyon archaeologists have been working on a puzzle: Why did the Anasazi people, who flourished in the Southwest until the late 13th century, suddenly abandon the area? Their mysterious disappearance is just one aspect of the research at this facility in southwestern Colorado, where an ancient village is being excavated with the help of interested students and other lay participants. Researchers hope work here will not only provide answers about prehistoric Pueblo communities but will also yield information that will benefit contemporary society, especially Native American cultures. Like those in Mesa Verde National Park, 10 mi to the east, this important site is set among stunning, rugged cliffs and mesas. The non-profit center is renowned for its preservation and educational efforts.

**FOR FAMILIES.** Family Excavation Week, usually scheduled once or twice in August, is for parents, grandparents, and students in seventh grade or higher. Middle school students work about two half days in the field, with the rest of the time spent in the lab or in other activities and programs designed for this age group. High school students and adults alternate field work with time in the lab and experimental archaeology activities, such as learning how to use ancient tools or participating in an experiment on Anasazi farming. Everyone begins the week by examining artifacts and reconstructing the cultures and chronologies they represent. At the end of the week the group joins a guided tour of Mesa Verde. There are evening lectures throughout the week.

Accommodations are in roomy log cabins built in the style of Navajo hogans. Families are housed together. You supply your own towels and bedding. There are no private baths or showers. Meals are served cafeteria style in the dining hall.

*Crow Canyon Archaeological Center, 23390 Road K, Cortez, CO 81321, tel. 970/565–8975 or 800/422–8975. Family Excavation Week, Aug.: 7 days, $875 adults, $675 students under 18. Membership, which is required, costs $75 per family. Membership for other programs costs $20–$50, depending on age.*

### Denver Museum of Natural History

7+

The Denver Museum of Natural History, one of the finest facilities of its kind in the country, offers unusual and enlightening trips for families (see Canoeing and Rafting). One excursion is to Chaco Canyon, New Mexico. Although it's not a research-based dig in the same sense as other trips, this exploration of an ancient civilization is a learning vacation for those who love archaeology but don't necessarily want to spend days on their knees digging.

**FOR FAMILIES.** Chaco Canyon for Families, generally scheduled every other year, offers instruction in astronomy, anthropology, and archaeoastronomy (a discipline that focuses on the importance of the sky to various ancient human cultures), in addition to archaeology. The trip is led by teachers from Earth Knack, an expedition company specializing in the Stone Age. There are also guides from the Four Corners School of Outdoor Education, who help bring alive the natural and human history of the area. The setting, Chaco Canyon, is striking. This "Anasazi Capital," in a desolate area of northwestern New Mexico, was a thriving center of civilization from AD 900 to AD 1150. The Anasazi left behind a vast and complex network of roads, masonry walls, and stairways carved into cliffs, all connecting some 12 major pueblos and numerous smaller ones. Ruins of the road system and pueblos are now part of Chaco Culture National Historic Park, where the trip takes place.

Participants meet in Cortez, Colorado, then travel together to New Mexico. After settling into reserved campsites (bring your own tents and camping gear or RVs), the group tours the visitor center museum for background on Chaco Canyon. The itinerary varies from trip to trip, but typically there are lectures, discussions, and activities for different age groups, including making fire by friction, plant identification, grinding corn for ash cakes, and gathering stones for axes. The group works on a simulated dig and learns about ruins, artifacts, and other aspects of archaeology; evening programs are led by national park rangers. A highlight is the chance to experience one of Chaco Canyon's greatest archaeoastronomical phenomena, in the kiva Casa Rinconada. Researchers believe this kiva is part of an ancient astronomical observatory built so that light would enter a particular window only during the summer and winter solstices. This trip coincides with the summer solstice.

*Denver Museum of Natural History, 2001 Colorado Blvd., Denver, CO 80205, tel. 303/370–6304. June: 5 days, $625 adults, $575 children 7–12.*

## Earthwatch

16+

Earthwatch Institute, a nonprofit organization, funds research projects of all types around the globe and brings lay participants together with researchers to work on those undertakings. The benefit to each group is clear: Researchers have a pool of volunteers who provide not only labor but money to offset research costs, and volunteers can work beside some great scientists from a wide variety of fields. Earthwatch's archaeological digs are described in the Human Impacts section of its extensive catalog.

**FOR FAMILIES.** Earthwatch has many sites, so families usually make their choice based on location, historical period, and related activities. (Earthwatch leaders teach volunteers all they need to know to participate.) If Native American life interests you and your teenager, there are Hopi and Hopi-Zuni excavations in two sites in Arizona. Those who like Roman history can participate in excavations at a fort in northern England or a farm in Tuscany. A Bronze Age village in Spain, an island off the coast of Scotland, and a Belizean Maya village where civilization collapsed four centuries ago all have their own special appeal. You might also dig in Thailand, the Caribbean, and other parts of the United States.

In addition to excavating, volunteers are often called on to photograph or sketch artifacts and sites and to assist in lab work. Moreover, depending on the site, volunteers can experience other fields of interest. An anthropologist or paleontologist could be part of the team. If you work or stay with local people, you'll be exposed to another culture and language. Accommodations range from primitive campsites to modern hotels, and the group stays together unless it's being hosted by local families. The trips are very work-intensive—the team could be working 8 hours a day. Projects sometimes end and new ones begin, so catalogs may not be up-to-date. Call for current details and listings.

*Earthwatch Institute, 680 Mt. Auburn St., Box 9104, Watertown, MA 02471-9104, tel. 617/926–8200 or 800/776–0188. Year-round (all sites not available at all times): 10–14 days, $695–$1,995.*

## White Mountain Archaeological Center

9+

Raven Site Ruin, named for the many bird symbols found on ceramics and petroglyphs in the area, is in the White Mountains of Arizona, about 3½ hours southeast of Flagstaff. On a 5-acre site overlooking the Little Colorado River is a prehistoric pueblo containing two kivas and more than 800 rooms. Both Mogollon and Anasazi cultures are represented; people lived here from about AD 1000 to AD 1450. Raven Site was the scene of extensive vandalism in the 1920s and again in the 1980s, which is one reason White Mountain Archaeological Center came into existence. This nonprofit field school protects and preserves southwestern Native American sites. Since 1991, when the site opened to the public, archaeology buffs have participated in hands-on work under the center's direction.

**FOR FAMILIES.** You can sign up for a day, a few days, or a week at Raven Site. Along with field excavation, volunteers spend time working in the lab cleaning, conserving, bagging, and labeling pottery and other artifacts. Most volunteers dig at least three to four hours each day; family members may work in different areas. If you want a break one day, Lyman State Park, about 6 mi away, has boating, fishing, waterskiing, and an excellent petroglyph trail. White Mountain runs guided half-day hikes to the petroglyphs, too. If there are nondiggers in your group, it is possible to visit the center via guided or self-guided tours of the site.

Lodging for family groups of eight or more is in a bunkhouse with use of a kitchen; tent and RV sites are also available. (The bunkhouse costs an extra $12 per person per day; tent sites are $5 per person per day; RV sites are about $8.) Small family groups may make their own reservations in town. Reed's Motel in nearby Springerville has special rates for Raven Site participants. Lunch and instruction are included in the program cost. Remember that this is a mountain location and digging takes place at 6,500 ft, so be prepared for hot days, cool nights, and changeable weather.

*White Mountain Archaeological Center, HC 30, St. Johns, AZ 85936, tel. 520/333–5857 or 888/333–5859. May–mid-Oct.: 1 or more days, $60 per day adults, $40 per day children 9–17. Guided hikes: $18 adults, $12 children.*

# Resources

## Books

Children can get a general sense of archaeology and anthropology from *What Do We Know About Prehistoric People?* by Mike Corbishley (Peter Bedrick Books). Culturally oriented books for school-age children include *The Ancient Cliff Dwellers of Mesa Verde*, by Caroline Arnold (Clarion); *The Anasazi*, by David Petersen (Children's Press); and *Cities in the Sand*, by Warren Scott (Chronicle Books), which focus on the American Southwest.

For adults, Brian Fagan's *In the Beginning: An Introduction to Archaeology* (Pearson Education) is a general guide to the subject. Those digging in the Southwest will want to read *Ancient Land, Ancestral Places*, by Paul Logsdon (Museum of New Mexico Press); *In Search of the Old Ones: Exploring the Anasazi World of the Southwest*, by David Roberts (Touchstone Books); and *Chaco Canyon: A Center and Its World*, by S. H. Lekson, J. R. Stein, and S. J. Ortiz (Museum of New Mexico Press).

## Also See

If digging vacations are for your family, see Digging for Dinosaur Bones and Other Fossils. If present-day native cultures are of interest, see Native American Experiences.

# BIKING

"Have child, will cycle" could well be the motto of today's bike-loving parents. Child-friendly inventions such as carts and tandems have made multi-day cycling tours a feasible option for toddlers and preschoolers across the country. For families with older children, mountain biking is a popular vacation alternative. With all these choices, many families have begun choosing two-wheel road trips over four-wheel vacations.

The best option for families with very young children is actually an old concept. The handy cart, which attaches to the back of a bicycle, is made in deluxe versions by Burley and other manufacturers. Though carts work best on easy to moderate road tours, the range within these categories is vast. Among the trips that allow carts are road tours through Michigan's Amish country, nature-oriented treks in Washington's San Juan Islands, and scenic trips through Vermont.

A more recent invention is the child-size bike, minus the front wheel portion, that attaches to an adult's bicycle, turning the whole thing into a tandem. They're made especially for children ages 1–10. Some outfitters are starting to stock these neat bikes; if the ones you find don't, you can bring your own. There are even real tandem models, which allow one or two children to bike with you, as well as models with baby seats or support for special-needs children. The tandem device makes it possible for children to share the physical labor and also offers a safer, lighter, and more stable alternative to on-bike child seats and a less wind-resistant alternative to carts.

For families with preteens and teens, mountain biking can be a welcome physical challenge. However, since riding day in and day out strikes many in this age group as a monotonous proposition, outfitters have found great success with combination trips: biking and rafting, biking and horseback riding, biking and climbing. These trips are also good for families that enjoy bike rides but are not necessarily dedicated cyclists.

Whether you're road biking or mountain biking, it's best to search out those trips designated specifically for families. Cycling, like hiking, has a high appeal among empty-nesters and hard-core outdoor adventurers who challenge themselves by racking up the daily miles; some may feel hampered by a family's slower pace and need for more frequent stops. Moreover, some adults have little tolerance for even the best-behaved children. If your heart is set on a romantic New England inn-to-inn tour, do it when you and your spouse can get away as a couple. The good news is you won't be forced to settle for a less-than-appropriate trip. Every year there are more and more wonderful biking trips for families.

## Questions to Ask

**What ages are your trips best for?** Most outfitters have an excellent understanding of how well a child of a given age can meet the physical and mental requirements of the trip. Listen to the outfitter and go with the recommendations given.

**How experienced or physically fit should my family be for this trip?** This is an important question to ask up front. The outfitter will be able to recommend the best trips for families of all different levels, from those who cycle once or twice a year to those who bike regularly. Moreover, outfitters can also give you information about exercises to do in the weeks before the trip to get in shape.

**How many miles a day do the trips average?** Bike trips can cover as few as 8 mi a day or as many as 50. Many children can handle 25 mi a day, and those with some experience might ride as many as 35 mi. Ask very specific questions about the miles, the type of terrain, and whether there are options for shorter routes or van pickup. Make sure you choose a beginner trip if that's what you are. If hiking is included on a combination adventure, ask how many miles a day you will walk. Three to eight miles is well within the range of most children (depending on age and experience), with the exception of toddlers or preschoolers, who can be carried in a backpack, provided you can handle the extra weight.

**Do you rent children's bikes and helmets?** Some outfitters allow children but do not provide bikes or other equipment for them. Others have rental equipment but only for children of a certain age or height. If you aren't planning to bring your own bikes and helmets, this is important. If you bring your own helmets, keep in mind that they should be of high quality and not the flimsy ones available at some toy stores. When in doubt about your equipment, ask the outfitter.

**Do you allow Burleys or other pull carts?** Some outfitters may rent them; others may not even permit them on tours.

**Is there van support on the trip?** Van support allows beginners to go on tours that have some intermediate terrain, and it gives a break to any cyclist who gets tired during the day. It's a crucial option for families with young cyclists since most routes aren't chosen with only the eight-year-old in mind.

**Are guides qualified to fix bikes in case of a breakdown?** Unless you know how to fix your bike, you'll want someone along who knows what to do.

**What kind of food can we expect on our trip?** Many bike trips include overnights at fine inns and resorts where exceptional food is part of the package. If your child is a picky eater, talk to outfitters in advance to find out whether they accommodate special requests. You may want to bring some of your child's favorite foods with you—but consider that you may have to carry the load.

**Do you have children's rates?** Many bicycle tour operators have discounts for children under a certain age and for children sharing a room with parents. Rates may vary according to how many children you bring; in addition, your discount may be smaller if there is only one parent on the trip. Some special family departures give parents an even bigger break off the regular cost of the trip.

**What's included in the cost of the trip?** Generally, all accommodations and meals are included, but van transfers and travel to and from the start of the trip are not. Guides, maps, and energy-producing snacks are part of the package. Bike rentals may be included, although that's more the exception than the rule. Helmets are often but not always provided; they are usually available for rent. Rates quoted in brochures are typically per person and based on double occupancy.

## Instruction

In general, road touring companies don't offer much in the way of instruction, though some give minimal information about bike care and easy repair. Some companies have day or weekend courses devoted entirely to repair; these are especially useful for families that are considering becoming serious road cyclists (you might also find such courses at your local community college or Y). Mountain-biking tour operators are more likely to provide instruction on techniques that are helpful in off-road cycling.

## Finding the Fun

**Northeast:** Backroads, Bike Vermont, VBT Bicycling Vacations. **Mid-Atlantic:** VBT Bicycling Vacations. **South:** Backroads, Nantahala Outdoor Center. **Midwest:** Michigan Bicycle Touring. **Southwest:** Backcountry, Backroads, Escape the City Streets. **Rockies:** Backcountry, Backroads, Wilderness River Outfitters. **West Coast:** Backcountry, Backroads. **Alaska:** Backcountry. **Canada:** Backcountry, Backroads. **Central America:** Backroads, Butterfield & Robinson. **South America:** Backroads. **Europe:** Backroads, Brooks Country Cycling & Hiking Tours, Butterfield & Robinson, Ciclismo Classico. **New Zealand:** Butterfield & Robinson. **Africa:** Butterfield & Robinson.

# Favorite Outfitters

## Backcountry

**6+**

This Montana-based company knows the West. Every guide is a native or longtime resident of the area, so you're always with someone who can share insights, local history, and interesting knowledge about the land. Backcountry is also a small outfitter; personalized service and excellent support for its clients are guaranteed.

Backcountry has found that children respond well to trips that combine biking with one or several other activities, such as hiking, sea kayaking, rafting, and horseback riding. Much of the biking is on paved roads, and van support is available for anyone who needs it. Participants stay in the area's best inns, resorts, mountain lodges, and hotels, and they eat regional and international fare that will appeal to even the pickiest palates. You can choose the trip that best suits your family by activity preference or location.

**FOR FAMILIES.** Most of Backcountry's adventure trips are for families with children ages 10 and up who have some biking and outdoor experience, but there are several departure dates for families with children as young as six. Puget Sound Adventure takes place in and around coastal Washington's wildlife-rich San Juan Islands and combines biking, hiking, and sea kayaking. Arizona Adventure is centered in Sedona and includes riding, tennis, and Jeep touring in addition to biking. Grand Teton, Yellowstone, and Glacier adventures introduce you to three spectacular national parks in the Rockies: You can hike, ride, raft, and boat in Grand Teton and Glacier or ride and raft in Yellowstone. Montana Adventure, one of the easiest trips, is based in southwestern Montana's backcountry, with biking, hiking, horseback riding, and rafting through the Gallatin Range, the Spanish Peaks, and Ouzel Falls. Yellowstone, Grand Teton, and Montana adventures are the designated trips for ages six and up.

Two trips take families beyond the continental United States. Canadian Rockies Adventure shows you the breathtaking regions around Banff and Lake Louise in Alberta, where hiking and canoeing offer spectacular scenery. Another choice is Alaska Adventure, a trip in the Kenai Peninsula.

*Backcountry, Box 4029, Bozeman, MT 59772, tel. 406/586–3556 or 800/575–1540. May–Oct.: 5½ days, $1,598–$2,298; 25% discount for children 12 and under sharing lodging with parents.*

## Backroads

2+

Backroads, founded in 1979, is known for its ability to handle the details of a family trip with finesse and humor. Families can choose a bicycling-only vacation or a multi-sport adventure. Itineraries are relatively slow paced, giving youngsters time to explore tidal pools or wildflower fields. Family departures are scheduled in summer and early fall, with a choice of destinations in the U.S., Europe, and beyond. Participants stay at inns or camp out; some trips offer both options. Equipment rentals—including Burley carts for children under five—are extra.

**FOR FAMILIES.** Among Backroads's American trips are three tours in the San Juan Islands, Washington. The islands' hills and killer whales make them a favorite destination for families. One tour is biking; the other two are multi-sport. Family mountain-biking trips run in the Sedona area in Arizona and in Idaho's Sawtooth Mountains and Sun Valley. Other bike tours travel around Banff and Jasper in the Canadian Rockies and in Nova Scotia. The multi-sport adventures go even farther afield, with trips to Glacier, Yellowstone, and Teton national parks, Maine, North Carolina, the Canadian Rockies, Belize, and the Galapagos Islands. The Canada and Belize trips have a minimum age of two; the rest have a minimum age of six.

Backroads has a solid list of European family trips, too. Many, though not all, have a minimum age of either six or ten, and parents should keep in mind that these tours often include stops at historical and cultural sites that may not readily capture the interest of young children. A six-day family bike trip through the Czech Republic includes visits to Prague and southern Bohemia. Traditional cycling terrain is covered on four family trips to France. Two explore the Loire Valley, with its medieval villages and châteaux. Another winds through Brittany and Normandy on France's northwest coast, taking in villages, D-Day beaches, and Mont St-Michel, the awe-inspiring island monastery and cathedral. The fourth adventure combines biking, hiking, and kayaking in the Loire Valley. Other family biking tours are held in Denmark, Hungary, Tuscany, and the Netherlands. A trip to the Swiss Alps combines biking and hiking. (Remember to take the high altitude into account. People generally need a day to adjust to altitudes over 2,000 m/6,560 ft).

*Backroads, 801 Cedar St., Berkeley, CA 94710, tel. 510/527–1555 or 800/462–2848. June–Sept.: 5–9 days, $998–$4,598 adults; 10%–40% discount for children, depending on age.*

## Bike Vermont

10+

The heart of Bike Vermont's business is inn-to-inn cycling tours in Vermont and the Connecticut River valley. The majority of Bike Vermont's inns have interesting histories and antique furnishings; some offer fairly sophisticated menus. Many are family friendly although they aren't geared for very young children. Of particular interest to families may be the shorter tours on which riders are based in just one inn, cycling out each day to the neighboring villages and surrounding countryside. The company has also expanded its offerings with bike tours in Ireland and a few hiking explorations in Vermont. Both children's and adult bikes are available for rent.

**FOR FAMILIES.** The best trips for families are the weekend Inn at Saxtons River tour, the three-day Moose Mountain Lodge tour, and the six-day trip to Proctorsville. All three are good for beginner, intermediate, and advanced riders. (More advanced riders can take the longer, hillier route options.) The Inn at Saxtons River tour, for example, has easy riding, exemplary New England villages en route, an old-fashioned swimming hole, and a friendly, low-key village inn. The Moose Mountain Lodge tour, near Hanover, New Hampshire, is a bit more challenging than the other two. Proctorsville, in southeastern Vermont not far from Woodstock, has lakes and rivers—and one of the inns on the itinerary, the Golden Stage, has a constantly replenished cookie jar to keep children happy.

*Bike Vermont, Box 207, Woodstock, VT 05091, tel. 802/457–3553 or 800/257–2226. May–Oct.: 2–6 days, $295–$925, adults; 10% discount for children when they share parents' room.*

## Brooks Country Cycling & Hiking Tours

ALL

Brooks has no age guidelines for families, and it's had children of all ages on its tours (no seats or carts are available for rental, however). The company is based in New York City; if that's your area, you can take day trips with Brooks in the mid-Atlantic region besides the multi-day European tour recommended here.

**FOR FAMILIES.** Children are welcome on any tours; however, best for families is the Barging and Biking Holland trip—one week of blue canals, flower-filled fields, and stately windmills. This tour combines ancient cities, small villages, and some of the best cycling terrain anywhere. Holland has an exceptional network of bike paths crisscrossing its level landscape. Much of the biking is on dikes above the canals, which makes access from the barges easy for every level of rider. Barges have a sundeck for relaxed sightseeing and spacious cabins, some with private showers. Trip leaders are bilingual. Rental of a 21-speed hybrid bicycle is included in the cost of the trip. Children's bikes are available, as are Slipstreamers (like Trail-A-Bikes, see Resources *below*) and child seats.

*Brooks Country Cycling & Hiking Tours, 140 W. 83rd St., New York, NY 10024, tel.*

*212/874–5151. Apr.–Oct.: 7 days, $930–$998 adults, depending on season and whether cabin has private bath; 50% discount for children 4–11 sharing a cabin with parents; 66% discount for infants–age 3.*

## Butterfield & Robinson

3+

In 1999, Butterfield & Robinson introduced family trips for parents with children as young as three years old. As is typical of this company, family trips are well thought-out in terms of destination, itinerary, and accommodations.

**FOR FAMILIES.** B&R's inaugural three-and-up trip was in Ireland—and Ireland is nothing if not family-friendly. The group meets in Galway, then takes a ferry out to Inismor, the largest of the Aran Islands—Gaelic is still the main language there. During a day of biking and hiking you'll explore a 1,500-year-old fortress, among other sites. The next three days take you to Connemara in County Galway. Local villages, a castle, a musical instrument workshop, and turf bogs give you a real sense of life as it was—and still is—in this part of Ireland. There are several other activities available in Connemara, such as golf and horseback riding. Children can sail, fish, canoe, or just play on the grounds of your lodging, Ballynahinch Castle. The final two days are spent in Cong, County Mayo, where you'll stay in a 13th-century castle. The biking routes go along the coast of Lough Comb and near the Maumturk mountain range, though plenty of time is left to enjoy the castle itself, by exploring the grounds by horse and cart, boating on the lake, or playing golf or tennis. While daily bike rides average 25–26 mi, there's always a van to give a lift to children—or their parents—who don't want to pedal any longer. There are also supervised activities for children in the afternoons and evenings.

Other family biking trips venture into France. A second itinerary available for children as young as three goes to France's Breton coast. Famillies with children at least eight years old can join B&R's getaway to the Dordogne Valley, while those with children at least twelve years old can cycle in Normandy, the Loire Valley, and Nova Scotia, or bike from Prague to Vienna. If a mix of biking and walking sounds good, and your children are twelve or older, you could sign up for B&R's journeys to the Sahara and Atlas Mountains of Morocco, Costa Rica, or New Zealand's South Island.

Several different types of bikes are available for adults, and children's equipment includes special tandems, bike seats, and children's bikes.

*Butterfield & Robinson, 70 Bond St., Toronto, Ontario, Canada M5B 1X3, tel. 416/864–1354 or 800/678–1147. Year-round (not all trips available all months): 4–8 days, $2,795–$4,275 adults, 10%–35 % discount for children depending on age and lodging.*

## Ciclismo Classico

ALL

Ciclismo Classico is wholly dedicated to providing biking and hiking tours throughout Italy—in fact, it's the only bike touring company specializing in Italy. The owner and staff all have Italian roots and speak Italian. All tours are put together and led by staff members; the company doesn't subcontract out any guiding (something of an exception, as most tours subcontract to local companies or guides). Lauren Hefferon, who founded the company over a decade ago, has personally logged more than 15,000 mi of racing and bike touring throughout Italy. She's also taken her own young children touring with her, so she knows just what families want and need, and what they're capable of on a multi-day tour.

**FOR FAMILIES.** One of the company's cycling vacations is especially geared for families with children of all ages. Tuscan Fantasy is an eight-day, villa-based adventure in Tuscany, with its terraced and vineyard-covered hillsides, farmlands, and olive groves. The villa, Frattoria degli Usignoli (Farm of the Nightingale), has a restored 15th-century farmhouse with a pool. There are three set bike routes of varying distance to choose from each day. When you're not biking past medieval villages and castles, you'll be learning about the area's history and art, language and food. Informal cooking, art, history, or Italian lessons are offered in the afternoons or early evenings. Excursions are another learning opportunity; you could visit churches, a gelato factory, or a bike shop owned by an Italian cycling champion. You can also take advantage of the villa's tennis and horseback riding facilities. Children have the chance to join local kids in a soccer game and post-game celebration. The trip starts and ends in Florence.

If you and a couple of other families (at least 12 people) want to get together for a customized family biking trip in Italy, ask about the Umbrian Adventure. You choose a departure date and the range of activities (the company will also try to accommodate special requests). In addition to both mountain- and road-biking excursions, options include natural history walks, horseback riding, nature photography, fishing, hang-gliding, and rappelling. For lovers of Italian food (and what child isn't?) there are truffle-hunting and cheese-making demonstrations, as well as lessons in Umbrian cooking. Groups are based at the Callaccio farm complex in the heart of the Sibillini National Forest, an area of verdant mountainsides and sandstone villages. Visits to nearby Assisi and the renowned Spoleto Arts Festival round out the seven-day trip. Rome is the meeting and departure city for this trip.

In addition to the specific family trips, Ciclismo Classico has several other tours appropriate for families: The Best of Southern Italy, Villas & Gardens of Veneto, and Venice to Bologna among them. Ask about children's discounts for these trips. Child care is available on all family getaways. Rental bikes cost extra; size 14, for a child of about age 10, is the smallest rental bike. Burley carts, as well as the small bikes that are attached to a parent's bike to make a tandem, can also be rented.

*Ciclismo Classico, 13 Marathon St., Arlington, MA 02474, tel. 781/646–3377 or 800/866–7314. June–Oct.: 7–8 days, $2,375 adults, $400 ages 3 and under, $600 ages 4–7, 40 % off adult price ages 8–16 (children must share a room with two adults).*

## Escape the City Streets

**7+**

The brochure of this mountain-biking outfitter tells you immediately that this company has a sense of adventure—and humor to match. "Hey, teenagers," it says, "we love your eclectic energy." Escape the City Streets believes in playing hard, but it also understands limits. Support vehicles—44 trucks and vans—accompany every trip, and meals will satisfy even a demanding gourmet. You can rent bikes (for children and adults) and camping gear. Most trips are in Utah and the surrounding states.

**FOR FAMILIES.** There are four multi-day family tours in July and September, in addition to day hikes for families every day of the year. Children must know how to mountain-bike, and everyone should be in good physical condition. The 80-mi Brian Head–to–Bryce minitour, three days of riding and camping, starts at Brian Head Ski Resort in south-central Utah and winds through aspen groves and lava beds on the way to Bryce Canyon National Park. There's a 2,000-ft ascent, but support vehicles are always nearby. On the Grand Canyon Family Tour, a four-day camping trip, you cycle 120 mi—many of them through Arizona's Kaibab National Forest. The destination is the canyon's still uncommercialized North Rim. The five-day, 170-mi tour of Zion and Bryce national parks departs in July (camping) and

September (inn and lodge stays). Utah's Color Country has it all: mountains, lakes, rivers, multi-hue canyons, and the region's natural rock sculptures. If your family has only a day to spare, you can sign up at any time of year for the Redrock Canyon Family Bike Tour, near Las Vegas.

Family tours meet in St. George, Utah; shuttles to the trailhead are free. There's also shuttle service from Las Vegas for an extra fee (free on Redrock Canyon tours).

Ages 12 and up can join all other tours. Combination trips pair biking with hiking, riding, rafting, canoeing, rock climbing, or cross-country skiing, among other sports. *Escape the City Streets, 8221 W. Charleston, #10, Las Vegas, NV 89117, tel. 702/596–2953. Year-round: 1–5 days (family tours), $45–$819 adults, 50% discount for children 7–15 accompanied by an adult.*

## Michigan Bicycle Touring

ALL

A small family-run business, Michigan Bicycle has been guiding families through the valleys and hills of its home state since 1978. Michigan is geographically and culturally diverse: Dunes and islands, orchards, farmland, meandering rivers, quaint towns, an Amish community, and an international center for performing arts are among its attractions.

**FOR FAMILIES.** Children are welcome on most MBT tours, but some are especially family-friendly. The two-day Betsie River Pedal & Paddle trip combines biking with a short canoe trip along the Betsie River, where you're likely to see swans and herons. Lodging is at Crystal Mountain Resort. The two-day Mendon Amble takes cyclists through Amish country and to Colon, "magic capital of the world." Here magician Harry Blackstone perfected his craft and helped form Abbott's Magic Manufacturing, the world's largest producer of magic paraphernalia. Magic shows are performed in Colon throughout the summer. You'll stay at the Mendon Country Inn. For those who enjoy the performing arts, the five-day Interlochen Sightseer includes a chance to attend rehearsals and performances of music, theater, and dance.

MBT also has a two-day tour of Mackinac Island. The island has a lot to offer: the ferry ride, historic forts, awesome views of Lakes Huron and Michigan, not to mention the local fudge. It's also the site of the 5-mi-long Mackinac Bridge, the world's longest total suspension bridge, which connects Michigan's upper and lower peninsulas. Its most family-friendly aspect is that no cars are allowed on the island, which makes road biking with children a practically carefree experience. Instead of cars there are lots of horse-drawn carriages, which is another draw for families. MBT's tour lets you choose between 8 to 25 mi of biking per day, so even very young children can tour. Accommodations are at the Windermere Hotel, which offers special family rates. *Michigan Bicycle Touring, 3512 Red School Rd., Kingsley, MI 49649, tel. 616/263–5885. May–Oct.: 2–5 days, $328–$999 adults, 15%–75% discount for children, depending on trip and age.*

## Nantahala Outdoor Center

10+

Western North Carolina has great mountain-biking terrain, and Nantahala Outdoor Center (NOC) is as adept at teaching fat-tire cycling skills as it is at teaching paddling (see Canoeing *and* Kayaking).

**FOR FAMILIES.** Families with children age 13 and older can opt for a one-day sampler course that begins with a morning of instruction and ends with an afternoon trail ride at the popular Tsali Recreation Area near the school. The course includes a guide, bikes, helmets, lunch, and even a water bottle. This is ideal for families that have been leery of purchasing expensive mountain bikes. With Nantahala's sampler, you invest a minimum of money and time to find out if the sport is up your family's alley. If it is, NOC has other choices, too. Private instruction is the way to go if families want to stay together all day every day. You can opt for an intensive day of instruction, a push-the-envelope ride, or a guided bike trip. The price for this includes everything the sampler does. If parents want to kayak while children bike, there are mountain bike Kids' Camps. The three-day version is for children 10–12, the four-day for those 13–15. If you opt to put together a few days of instruction, there are a few lodging choices (motels, bunkhouses, private cabins) for an extra charge.

If a weekend adventure is what you're looking for, NOC has spring wildflower trips and fall mountain-biking getaways for families with children 16 and older. Ride through western North Carolina's blaze of colors and get some solid mountain-biking experience under your belts at the same time; you'll camp overnight. The trip includes local transportation.

*Nantahala Outdoor Center, 13077 U.S. 19W, Bryson City, NC 28713, tel. 888/662–1662. Year-round: 1–4 days, 1-day sampler, $80; private instruction, $230–$375 per family per day, depending on number of people; kids' camps, $525–$650; spring and fall weekend trips, $285.*

## VBT Bicycling Vacations

**10+**

In 1972 this company began offering inn-to-inn bicycle tours in Vermont. Today cyclists can choose from trips throughout the country and the world—from 6- to 17-day expeditions. VBT does not have any families-only departure dates; however, children 10 and up can join all domestic tours, while ages 13 and up are allowed on international trips. Most trips are better for families with some biking experience. The company does have bikes for rent, but not for children under 4 ft, 10 inches tall.

**FOR FAMILIES.** VBT's six-day Colonial Virginia & the Tidewater tour is the ultimate trip for families, thanks to its flat, easy riding and the hands-on history at Jamestown and Williamsburg where 18th-century homes and shops with costumed interpreters bring the past to life. On the first day you settle into an inn and explore James River plantations. Day 2 takes you from Jamestown along the Colonial Parkway to Williamsburg, with dinner at one of Williamsburg's historic taverns. You can return to Williamsburg on the next two days as well, as a pass is included in the price of the trip. Among other highlights are the ride through a lush landscape, with plenty of opportunities for spotting wildlife, heading to the Revolutionary War battlefields at Yorktown, and the coastal beauty of the Tidewater region viewed from easy riding paths. Each day riders have three mileage options. The shortest is generally about 20 mi, though the shortest route on day four is 30 mi.

Two other six-day tours are great for families. Martha's Vineyard & Nantucket offers easy riding and a chance to learn about the whaling and maritime history of the islands, along with a stop to watch artisans creating traditional New England crafts, such as baskets and scrimshaw. The Mad River Valley tour in central Vermont includes stays at inns with child-friendly amenities; all have a pool, hot tub, and tennis courts. It's a moderate ride and an excellent choice for families with some biking experience.

*VBT, Box 711, Bristol, VT 05443, tel. 802/453–4811 or 800/245–3868. Mid-Apr.–Nov.: 6 days, $945–$1,445 adults, 20% discount for 1 child age 10–17 when traveling with 2 adults and sharing accommodations.*

### Wilderness River Outfitters

12+

As its name implies, Wilderness River began as a rafting outfitter, but it has expanded its trip list with some of the most interesting biking and hiking trips around. Owners Joe and Fran Tonsmeire have been guiding wilderness trips since the '60s, and their knowledge and love of nature are evident.

**FOR FAMILIES.** Adults and children older than 12 can follow the trail used by the Nez Perce Indians to get to their buffalo-hunting grounds east of the Bitterroot Mountains. The Nez Perce Trail trip starts and ends in Missoula, Montana; travel is on a combination of paved and dirt roads through such exotic-sounding backcountry as the River of No Return Wilderness. You'll camp under the stars in forested meadows along the way. If you have time, this trip can also be combined with a Salmon River rafting expedition (see Rafting). The tour is suitable for beginners in good physical condition with some mountain-biking experience, as well as for more advanced riders. Bikes are included in the cost of the trip.

*Wilderness River Outfitters, Box 72, Lemhi, ID 83465, tel. 208/756–3959 or 800/252–6581. July–Aug., 6–9 days, $1,130–$1,500 adults, 30% discount for children under 13.*

## Resources

### Books

Globe Pequot Press publishes several books on bicycling in various areas of the country; one series focuses on short bike rides, another on their favorite rides. *25 Bicycle Tours in Vermont, third edition,* by John Freidin (Countryman Press), written by the founder of VBT Bicycling Vacations, describes routes, lodging, and camping facilities and includes good maps and photos as well as advice on safe and successful touring.

### Products

**Adams Trail-A-Bike** (1465 Kebet Way, Port Coquitlam, British Columbia, Canada V3C 6L3, tel. 604/552–2930 or 800/521–9088) makes a child's bike that attaches to an adult's bike, creating a sort of tandem. A number of outfitters have these for rent. If you're going with an outfitter who doesn't, contact customer service for a brochure; they can also tell you where you can buy or rent one in your area.

A number of companies make helmets for children, as well as for adults. **Bell** (1924 County Rd., 3000 N, Rantoul, IL 61866-9512, tel. 217/893–9300 or 800/456–2355) will send consumers a pamphlet on helmet use and safety, a catalog, and dealer information. **Giro Sport Design** (380 Encinal St., Santa Cruz, CA 95060, tel. 408/457–4476 or 800/294–6098) will send a catalog or give you the name of the nearest dealer, as will **Specialized Bicycle Components** (15130 Concord Circle, Morgan Hill, CA 95037, tel. 408/779–6229).

### Also See

For trips on which you can bring bikes, check out RV Adventures and Houseboating.

# CANOEING

Serenity, although elusive in everyday life, is the very essence of a flat-water canoe trip, especially one that takes your family gliding through the still backwaters and meandering rivers of North America's great wilderness areas. Sounds are few—the rhythmic dip of your paddle, rustling leaves, the occasional cry of a bird startled into flight—so even normally boisterous children often quiet down to watch and listen intently.

There's a feeling of historical continuity in canoeing, too. Many of America's early European explorers—and those native to this land before them—traveled by canoe, using the pathways nature provided. Today canoeing is an excellent way to explore protected areas without negatively affecting fragile environments.

All this said, parents should know that children from ages about 6 to 10 can have a hard time sitting for long stretches of quiet paddling. Savvy outfitters frequently suggest combination trips that pair canoeing with hiking, snorkeling, studying nature, swimming, or fishing. Base-camp trips, where you take day voyages from and return to a single camp, are an alternative to long days of paddling from camp to camp. The better multi-day trips are those where outfitters make frequent stops en route and set up camp early enough in the day for children to have time to run around. Before committing to an adventure, carefully assess your family's abilities, personalities, and needs.

Canoeing isn't only about quiet forays on mellow streams, however. White-water canoeing is fast-paced and exhilarating, and you can discover its challenges on some of the great rivers. Schools throughout the country offer courses for all kinds of families. Teens, especially, may welcome a family vacation if it entails exciting work with skilled instructors on rushing rivers. And parents may come away from such an experience seeing themselves and their teens in a whole new light. The bottom line is this: Canoeing is for everyone—from utter beginner to skillful paddler, from quiet nature lover to wild white-water enthusiast, from rambunctious toddler to adventure-addicted teen.

## Questions to Ask

**Are child-size life vests provided?** Anytime you're in a boat, you need a Coast Guard–approved safety vest that fits properly. If the company you choose doesn't have the sizes you need, purchase them before your trip.

**Are helmets needed?** On a lake or pond you probably won't need a helmet, but on any river with even a minimum of white-water, a helmet is a good idea. Ask about white-water helmets for yourself and your children. If the right sizes aren't available from the outfitter, check at an outdoor store that sells equipment for white-water enthusiasts.

**Is the guide/instructor trained in CPR, lifesaving, and first aid? What type of emergency equipment does the outfitter carry?** When it comes to water and wilderness, accidents can happen—especially with children along. If you are going into the wilderness or will be a long way from a hospital or medical help, someone should be familiar with procedures for reviving and rescuing children and adults. These days many parents themselves take classes in child cardiopulmonary resuscitation and first aid, but you should also ask about an outfitter's training and emergency supplies. Is there, for example, a radio for emergency contact with a home base or local medical personnel?

**Are instructors certified by a reputable organization, such as the American Canoe Association or the British Canoe Union?** Certification is one important point for comparison among schools and instructors. Most guides are not certified; many, however, are members of state guiding associations, another indicator of commitment to safety and of the attainment of certain quality standards. You should also always ask about experience and the number of years a guide has worked.

**What kind of canoes are provided?** Different canoes provide different experiences. Some outfitters set their rate based on the number of canoes your family needs. A family of five might all fit in one canoe, depending on the type, or they might require two canoes if only smaller varieties are available. Do you want to learn solo paddling? Do you want to put children in the middle or give them a chance to paddle, too? Do you have lots of gear? There are many options, so ask questions to avoid surprises.

**How many miles or hours does the group paddle each day?** Multi-day trips average anywhere from 5 to 12 mi a day, with participants spending from two to six hours each day on the water. Courses generally require five or six hours a day of paddling, but some have longer days. Base-camp trips are usually more flexible, with options for families to stay closer to camp and do less paddling if they wish.

**How many portages/carries are there and how long are they?** Portages (or carries, in the Adirondacks) are those places where you must cross land to get from one body of water to another or to go around an obstacle on a river such as a waterfall. When you portage, you carry the canoes and equipment by hand. Although portages are sometimes a necessity, many can be avoided by changing routes. Talk to guides about your family's abilities. Although small children can manage some portages and even help carry equipment, big people take on most of the burden. With portages ranging from a few yards to more than a mile, the route is an important consideration when you're choosing a trip.

**What's the group size likely to be?** Scheduled trips may take only from 6 to 12 people, especially in wilderness areas where permits are limited. Base-camp trips in state parks often allow for 25 or even 30 in a group. In courses, students are usually divided into groups averaging from three to six people per instructor.

**Is fishing a possible activity on the trip?** If so, and if you'd like to do a little angling, ask the outfitter for the minimum age for a fishing license in the state where you'll be vacationing and where you can pick one up before the trip starts.

**What's included in the course or trip?** Course prices listed here cover instruction, equipment, and lunch, unless otherwise noted. For a few your fee pays for lodging, too. Trips include canoes, camping gear (except that sleeping bags and pads are often not included), meals, guides, and some instruction, unless otherwise noted. Transportation costs to and from the put-in and takeout site may be included in the price or may be extra.

## Instruction

All outfitters in this chapter provide instruction in basic canoeing and general water and wilderness safety. Some teach paddling and maneuvering techniques as a matter of course, others only if asked. Schools are geared for instruction at all levels. Canoeing is appealing because you can begin to do it with almost no instruction, although there are many skills to master if you want to enjoy the sport to the fullest.

## Finding the Fun

**Northeast:** Adventure Quest, Bear Cub Adventure Tours, L.L. Bean, Sunrise County Canoe Expeditions. **Mid-Atlantic:** Outward Bound. **South:** Nantahala Outdoor Center, Wolf River Canoes. **Midwest:** Boundary Country Trekking, Gunflint Northwoods Outfitter/Gunflint Lodge, Kayak & Canoe Institute, Outward Bound, Wilderness Inquiry. **Southwest:** Outward Bound, Kayak & Canoe Institute. **Rockies:** Boulder Outdoor Center, Denver Museum of Natural History. **Canada:** Kayak & Canoe Institute, Sunrise County Canoe Expeditions, Wells Gray Chalets & Wilderness Adventures.

# Favorite Schools and Guides

## Adventure Quest

7+

A little more than 8 mi south of Woodstock in east-central Vermont, a 40-acre preserve of green woodlands and rolling hills makes an ideal classroom setting for students at Adventure Quest, one of the country's top paddling and outdoor schools. Although Adventure Quest focuses on teaching children and teens—and excels at doing just that in summer camp programs for kids 7 to 17—its family workshops are every bit as good. Because the workshops are customized, you can schedule them at your family's convenience.

**FOR FAMILIES.** If you want to learn white-water paddling, sign up for Adventure Quest's open canoeing workshop. An open canoe has special equipment for white-water use; like a kayak, the craft can be rolled, a maneuver in which the boat turns 360 degrees from right side up to upside down and back with the paddler still sitting in it. Either one or two people can paddle, using single-blade paddles, but the canoers kneel for stability and better visibility. Like all of Adventure Quest's family workshops, this one gives parents and children the knowledge and skills they need for safe outings on their own, and it's geared to the group's abilities and interests. On average, a group with some canoeing skills but no white-water experience starts on flat water and moves to white-water in one to two days. Participants spend about six hours each day on one of several local rivers—the White, the Ottauquechee, or the Connecticut.

You can book a workshop for one day, but multi-day sessions provide a continuity that will get you out on your own faster. Woodstock has plenty of lodging and Adventure Quest has both camping sites and reasonably priced rooms (ask about these in advance). *Adventure Quest, Box 184, Woodstock, VT 05091, tel. 802/484–3939. Apr.–Oct.: 1 or more days, $275 per day for up to 4 people, $50 more for each additional family member.*

## Bear Cub Adventure Tours

5+

In the 6 million acres of northern New York's Adirondack Park, you'll find outstanding canoeing opportunities and a wilderness of surprisingly rugged terrain. More than 30,000 mi of brooks and streams meander through these ancient mountains, feeding into 1,000 mi of rivers. If that's not enough, there are 2,300 ponds and lakes. Besides being enthusiastic about taking families into the wilderness, Bear Cub owner Gary Marchuk is certified in canoe instruction, water safety and outdoor emergency care, and CPR. He has studied environmental conservation and also happily shares historical anecdotes—all of which make him a terrific choice for families.

**FOR FAMILIES.** Bear Cub, based in the two-time Olympic village of Lake Placid, offers customized family canoe trips each summer. These multi-day trips mix canoeing with Adirondack history, nature studies, geology, swimming, hiking, exploring, and camping. These are usually base-camp experiences unless participants want otherwise. Bear Cub also offers scheduled half-day and one-day wilderness trips that families can join.

Adirondack Park abounds in terrific canoe routes, but Gary favors three areas for family trips. The St. Regis Canoe Area, the state's only designated canoe area, has no motorboats or crowds—just beautiful lakes and ponds in an 18,000-acre wilderness area. Remote but easy to access—and requiring only one short carry—the trip from Bog River Flow to Low's Lake makes another great family route. The 14-mi-long Low's provides exceptional lake paddling. Those who prefer rivers can opt for the Raquette, with its rushing falls, otters, and ospreys. Gary has some colorful stories about people who guided and visited here more than 150 years ago.

Canoe clinics for all levels are offered by request. A two-day clinic on calm and scenic waters teaches basic paddling skills, canoe maneuvers, self-rescue techniques, and all about safety, equipment, and outfitting. A two-day white-water training program for canoers with basic skills takes students from moving water to rapids. Paddling strokes, eddy turns, upstream ferries, wave surfing, river reading, and rescue skills are covered. The number of white-water canoes for rent is limited, so book this program well in advance. A note of caution: Black flies are ferocious from mid-May to mid-June. If you go into this area during those weeks, bring repellent and netting.

*Bear Cub Adventure Tours, 30 Bear Cub Rd., Lake Placid, NY 12946, tel. 518/523–4339. May– Oct.: ½–5 days, $55–$145 per adult per day, $45–$90 children 11 and under. The bigger your group, the less the cost per person. Ask about clinic prices. Canoe rentals, $35 per day.*

## Boulder Outdoor Center

12+

The Boulder Outdoor Center (BOC) concentrates primarily on kayaking courses and trips (see Kayaking), but it offers canoe classes as well. The Boulder/Denver area is an excellent beginning point for a variety of adventures, so families can combine canoe instruction with other activities for a multi-sport vacation. BOC has more than 15 years of experience teaching river skills to both adults and children.

**FOR FAMILIES.** All classes and clinics welcome ages 12 and up; parents must take the same class with children under 17. BOC has scheduled evening Canoe Lake Clinics at the Boulder Reservoir several times a week from May to August. The course introduces all strokes and maneuvers, braces to keep yourself upright, and information on equipment and safety, including deep water rescues. These clinics provide an excellent canoeing foundation, whether you want to pursue flat-water or white-water paddling. Private instruction is the other option for families, and a good choice if you want to concentrate on river canoeing. Your family can learn together on Boulder Creek or other local rivers; clinics are either half-day or full day.

*Boulder Outdoor Center, 2510 N. 47th St., Boulder, CO 80301, tel. 303/444–8420 or 800/364– 9376. May–Sept.: 2½ hours–1 day, $29 per person for lake clinics, $25 boat rental. Private instruction, $65–$145 per person, depending on date and length of course and number of people; 50% discount for children under 18.*

## Boundary Country Trekking

ALL

Minnesota's Boundary Waters Canoe Area (BWCA) is the premier canoeing destination in the United States. Thousands of clear blue lakes mirror the towering pines and granite cliffs of this northern wilderness that stretches across the Canadian border. Linking the lakes are well-worn trails first walked by Native Americans, then by French fur traders and other European explorers. Today families follow these same paths, carrying canoes from one pristine lake to the next on backcountry paddling adventures. Ted Young, Boundary Country Trekking's owner, has guided groups through the BWCA for more than 40 years.

**FOR FAMILIES.** The Introductory BWCA Canoe Adventure, designed for both novice canoers and families, is a three-day guided trip with two nights of camping in the BWCA. Ted shares his knowledge of local history and lore, and he's ready and willing to teach canoeing and camping skills. Routes for this adventure vary but generally require five or six portages, the longest of which is about ¼ mi. You paddle from 6 to 8 mi each day and stand a good chance of seeing moose, loons, ospreys, eagles, or even the ferocious fisher, a relative of the mink. The trip fee covers lodging the nights before and after the trip, either at the company's cabin or in a local inn along the Gunflint Trail.

Ted and his company also run longer canoe adventures for those with boating and wilderness experience, as well as one-day paddles to several lakes. And there are trips that combine paddling with mountain biking for families with older children who want to do a little of each.

*Boundary Country Trekking, 7925 Gunflint Trail, Grand Marais, MN 55604, tel. 218/388–4487 or 800/322–8327. May–Sept.: 1–5 days, $80–$895; children's discounts vary for each trip.*

## Denver Museum of Natural History

8+

The Denver Museum of Natural History, one of the country's best museums of its kind, welcomes families on a variety of outings (see Archaeology Adventures *and* Rafting), including two canoe trips in Colorado. Museum associates lead the trips with experienced canoe guides, sharing their knowledge of wildlife, astronomy, ancient civilizations, and more. One note: Do try to visit the museum itself; its exhibits are superb.

**FOR FAMILIES.** The adventures geared for families are the museum's three-day trips down either the Gunnison or Colorado rivers. The Gunnison is a 41-mi trip beginning just below Delta, Colorado, passing through the Escalante State Wildlife Area and Escalante and Dominguez canyons. While the upper Gunnison through Black Canyon is a white-water thrill-seeker's dream, the lower Gunnison, where this trip travels, is much calmer and is good for beginning and intermediate canoeists. You'll paddle past towering walls of red sandstone and hike into canyons with deep swimming holes and waterfalls. Along the way you'll see ancient petroglyphs etched into canyon walls, blue herons, hawks, and eagles. Bring a pole (and license) if you'd like to fish.

The Colorado River through Ruby and Horsethief canyons is slightly slower and wider than the Gunnison. The 26-mi journey starts south of Fruita, Colorado, in the heart of dinosaur country (see Digging for Dinosaur Bones and Other Fossils). Like the Gunnison, the Colorado flows between massive walls of red sandstone and shale. There are side canyons to explore, petroglyphs to decipher, and wildlife to spot. Plus, you'll still have plenty of time for swimming and lazing on the river's banks.

While you don't need extensive canoeing experience, both journeys have a prerequisite canoe practice session at Denver's Cherry Creek Reservoir a couple of days before the trip begins. There's more advanced instruction on the rivers. Trip cost includes canoes and canoe equipment, life jackets, meals, cooking necessities, and drinking water; participants must bring their own tents, sleeping bags, and pads. Participants must also get to Cherry Creek and the put-in site on their own, though carpooling to the put-in site is possible.
*Denver Museum of Natural History, 2001 Colorado Blvd., Denver, CO 80205, tel. 303/370– 6304. July–Aug.: 3 days, $295 adults, $205 children.*

## Gunflint Northwoods Outfitters/Gunflint Lodge

ALL

The Kerfoots excel at introducing families to the joys of the wilderness. They've been in the business for almost 70 years—guiding, outfitting, and running Gunflint Lodge in Minnesota's Boundary Waters Canoe Area. If your family already has some experience with wilderness canoeing and camping, the Kerfoots will custom design and outfit a self-guided paddling adventure for you.

**FOR FAMILIES.** In July and August scheduled guided canoe trips for families begin and end with an overnight at Gunflint Lodge. For the four nights and five days in between, families explore the waterways of the BWCA, watch beavers feeding, listen to stories and the sounds of the forest, and help set up camp at three sites. You paddle from three to five hours per day. One of the best family routes in the BWCA takes in Ham, Long Island, Winchell, and Horseshoe lakes. There's lots of wildlife (moose, otters, eagles), which is why the Kerfoots subtitle this trip Mystical Moments with Kids and Critters. The route has about nine portages, most very short, though one is nearly ½ mi. The trip price includes dinner and breakfast on the lodge nights.

Families with even a little experience can head out without guides if they wish—after Bruce Kerfoot has given them all the orientation they need to paddle and camp on their own. There's a choice of routes especially for families.
*Gunflint Northwoods Outfitters/Gunflint Lodge, 143 S. Gunflint Lake, Grand Marais, MN 55604, tel. 218/388–2296 or 800/362–5251. June–Sept.: 5–8 days, $550–$795 for scheduled trips, $295–$500 for self-guided trips; 50% discount for children 12 and under; children under 4 are free.*

## Kayak & Canoe Institute

7+

The Kayak & Canoe Institute, part of the Outdoor Program at the University of Minnesota at Duluth, sponsors some trips but really focuses on instruction. Classes range from the most basic clinic for beginners to certification courses for canoe instructors.

**FOR FAMILIES.** One-, two-, and three-day fundamentals courses teach the basics of white-water canoeing, both solo and tandem. These classes, for ages 15 and up, utilize several high-performance tandem and solo designs. White-water boats are outfitted with thigh straps, knee pads, and floatation devices for maximum control and safety. Most classes are based near Duluth (you must bring your own bag lunches), but a Fundamentals II course takes place on the Vermilion River, near the Canadian border, and includes camping and meals. Courses teach canoeing basics—equipment design, stroke technique, rescue, river reading, and safety. Their main function, though, is to prepare you to outfit your own trip, so instruction is provided on trip planning, route finding, and packing. Families with younger children, about 7 or so, can sign up for private classes in both flat water and white-water canoeing.

In terms of trips, the Institute generally offers one or two canoe outings each year. A typical itinerary is a 10-day trip on Utah's San Juan River, which combines white-water canoeing and canyon hiking. Because the rapids are mostly class I–II, this is a good river for honing paddling skills. A 14-day trip goes to Manitoba, Canada's Bloodvein River. You paddle through provincial parks, quiet lakes, rapids, and portage around several waterfalls.
*Kayak & Canoe Institute, Outdoor Program, University of Minnesota at Duluth, 121 Sports & Health Center, 10 University Dr., Duluth, MN 55812, tel. 218/726–6533. Feb.–Aug.: ½–14 days, $170–$1,173 per person, $160 for 2 people taking 4-hour private instruction.*

## L.L. Bean

8+

L.L. Bean, the outdoor store and catalog company based in Freeport, Maine, has conducted canoeing workshops for more than 15 years. The store sells canoes and gear, and classes introduce families to canoeing skills and equipment; there's no pressure on students to buy anything, however.

**FOR FAMILIES.** Look to one of the company's Parent and Child Adventures; two focus on canoeing. On the day trip you'll learn strokes for maneuvering and controlling your canoe, then take to one of Maine's rivers for a day of paddling, picnicking along the shore, and discovering flora and fauna in and by the river. The three-day Island Canoe Camping getaway gives families a chance to learn how to plan and pack for an overnight canoe trip, as well as basic paddling techniques. 'Leave no trace' camping skills are taught at your campsite on a river island, and everyone pitches in to put up tents, cook, and clean up.

Families with children age 14 and older can also join Bean's five- and seven-day paddling trips on Maine's great rivers, including the Penobscot, Moose, and Allagash. Abundant wildlife and fine scenery make these excellent canoeing adventures. Trips include all camping equipment, meals, and transportation from Freeport. On the shorter side are one-day adventures on local rivers around Freeport, as well as solo and tandem paddling workshops in which participants focus on developing a fluid paddling style. The goal is to help paddlers improve boat-handling skills and increase their "sensitivity" to the canoe, resulting in tighter turns, better steering, and better overall control. From May through September Bean offers 3½-hour Quick Start classes near Freeport in solo and tandem skills.
*L.L. Bean, Freeport, ME 04033, tel. 207/865–4761 or 888/552–3261. May–Sept.: 2 hrs–7 days, $25–$895.*

## Nantahala Outdoor Center

5+

In addition to lakes, rivers, and mountain scenery that entice canoers of every level, western North Carolina can also claim a superb paddling school. If your family is serious about learning paddling or improving its skills, Nantahala Outdoor Center (NOC) stands second to none in terms of quality and variety of courses; you can develop your skills on a number of the area's rivers. Before or after your canoeing adventure, you might visit the nearby Great Smoky Mountains, which draw families from all over the country to hike, trek with llamas, or explore Great Smoky Mountain National Park, among many other outdoor pursuits.

**FOR FAMILIES.** Participants in regular courses—including two- to seven-day sessions for novice, intermediate, and advanced paddlers—must be 16. Despite some differences based on group dynamics and the instructor's style, all classes emphasize a mix of effective paddling techniques, safety, and fun. NOC's catalog gives detailed information on assessing your skills; look at it before deciding on a class. There are also multi-day adventures that mix camping with paddling white-water rivers in the Chattahoochee National Forest of northern Georgia and the free-flowing Chattooga River, on the border of South Carolina and Georgia. Advanced paddlers who want to check out the white-water river used in the 1996 Olympic games can sign up for paddling the Ocoee, in eastern Tennessee. If you don't want to commit to longer courses, try one of NOC's samplers; the minimum age for these one-day clinics is 13. Meals and lodging, either at NOC in shared facilities or in local motels, are included in multi-day course prices.

Another alternative for families is private instruction. Children can take private canoeing classes with parents; a family with a very young child would probably stick to the lakes in the area. Families opting for private instruction pay extra for staying right at NOC (about $50–$70 per room per night, if a room is available) or at nearby lodging arranged by NOC.
*Nantahala Outdoor Center, 13077 U.S. 19W, Bryson City, NC 28713, tel. 828/488–2175 or 888/662–1662, ext. 600. Mar.–Oct.: 1–7 days, $80–$1,160.*

## Outward Bound

14+

Parents and children can choose among three locations and a number of seasons to challenge themselves and one another on the water. The Potomac and other rivers in Maryland, the Boundary Waters Canoe Area in Minnesota, and the Rio Grande in Texas each give participants a different spin on canoeing in the wilderness. Like all Outward Bound programs, these are not just about learning sports skills; they're about learning life skills, too.

**FOR FAMILIES.** Weeklong parent-child canoe courses are scheduled in Maryland and in Minnesota's Boundary Waters Canoe Area in summer and on the Rio Grande just after the Christmas holidays. These courses often involve eight-hour days on the water. Maryland courses begin and end in Baltimore. The river you paddle changes with the water level, but most courses are run on the upper reaches of the historic Potomac. In Minnesota students learn portaging techniques in addition to on-water skills, and the course includes rock climbing and rappelling. The Rio Grande course focuses on white-water canoeing on a river whose tempo changes from gentle currents to churning rapids. Families also learn the basics of canyon exploration, as well as rock climbing and rappelling. As with all Outward Bound classes, canoeing is only part of the focus. These courses are also about improved communication, mutual respect, and trust between parent and child.
*Outward Bound, 100 Mystery Point Rd., Garrison, NY 10524, tel. 914/424–4000 or 800/243– 8520. Dec.–Aug. (all courses not available all months): 7–8 days, $845–$995 adults, $695–$845 children.*

## Sunrise County Canoe Expeditions

**3+**

Sunrise County is the nickname for Maine's Washington County, in the easternmost section of the state along the Canadian border. This canoe company is headquartered there and runs many of its trips in the area. Sunrise owners Martin Brown, David Watson, and Kendra Flint are knowledgeable outfitters and guides who have personal as well as professional experience with family travel—they've taken their own school-age children canoeing with them since they were babies. Sunrise has more than 25 years of experience in guiding and outfitting, and quality technical instruction is integral to every trip.

**FOR FAMILIES.** Kendra recommends two very different rivers as terrific for families. First is the St. Croix; close to Sunrise County's headquarters, it is the company's home river. Four- or six-day trips start out at a base camp on Cathance Lake. A river of easy to moderate white water, the St. Croix flows from a chain of lakes through woodlands and meadows in an area that is a principal nesting site for bald eagles. The fishing is excellent (bring your own rod if you're serious about fishing), and there's just one short portage on the six-day trip.

Families might also choose a mellow six-day float on the Cascapedia River through Québec's Gaspé Peninsula. Black-spruce forests mix with hardwoods; moose, deer, and maybe even bears can be seen along stretches of very easy white water. The trip has no portages, and the last night's lodging at an inn in Bonaventure, Québec, is included in the price.

Sunrise doesn't offer families-only departure dates, but it does try to group families together. Customized trips are always another option; ask about prices, which vary depending on family size and requirements. Minimum ages are usually determined on a case-by-case basis.
*Sunrise County Canoe Expeditions, Cathance Lake, Grove Post, ME 04657, tel. 800/748–3730. May–Oct.: 4–6 days, $545–$895; 33%–50% discount for children (age limit varies).*

## Wells Gray Chalets & Wilderness Adventures

**ALL**

Based just outside British Columbia's Wells Gray Park, this outfitter specializes in trips to the park's rugged interior. In more than a million acres of backcountry, multi-hue flower meadows ring still lakes, and snow remains almost perpetually on the surrounding peaks. Lava canyons and ash cones—created by the long-ago volcanic activity that formed much of the area—add geologic texture and contrast. Wells Gray is a destination of extraordinary beauty that draws canoers because of the exceptional lake paddling.

**FOR FAMILIES.** You can choose between a six-day wilderness canoe trip paddling two magnificent lakes—Clearwater and Azure—or an adventure that combines three days of hiking and three days of canoeing, with one night at a bed-and-breakfast in between. Clearwater and Azure lakes are each 17 mi long, with numerous inviting campsites. None, however, is more beautiful than Azure's Rainbow Falls, a wide, white, crescent-shape beach at the spot where Angus Horn Creek tumbles into the lake. Guides try to schedule a two-night layover here to give families a respite from the normal four to five hours of paddling each day. This trip has one short portage.

On the combination trip hikers stay at either Fight or Trophy chalet (both owned by the company), heading out for three-to six-hour hikes each day. There's no need to pack much; the chalets have kitchens, baths, bedding, books, games, and even sandals to wear around. For the canoeing portion, the group goes out paddling several hours each day from a lakeside base camp.

If you don't have six days, there are three-day canoe adventures, too. Families are welcome on any and all of Wells Gray's trips. Owners Ian and Tay Briggs offer parents a wonderful opportunity to introduce children not only to Canada but to Canadian and European families, who are the majority of trip participants.

*Wells Gray Chalets & Wilderness Adventures, Box 188, Clearwater, British Columbia, Canada V0E 1N0, tel. 250/587–6444 or 888/SKITREK. June–Sept.: 3–6 days, $260–$570; 25% discount for children under 14.*

## Wilderness Inquiry

2+

Wilderness Inquiry (WI), a nonprofit organization, strives to bring all kinds of people, including those with disabilities, into the wilderness. "Our trips are shared cooperative adventures that combine the strength and positive energy of all the members in the group," executive director Greg Lais says. Whether or not disabilities are involved, this goal is exactly what many parents hope to achieve in traveling with their children. Based in Minnesota, Wilderness Inquiry offers canoeing adventures all over the country.

**FOR FAMILIES.** Of interest to parents and children are the specially designated family canoeing and camping trips. Three trips should appeal to the very youngest canoers and older paddlers alike. One is a base-camp trip with structured activities for youngsters and families throughout each day and evening, including interpretive talks by park rangers; guides provide canoeing and low-impact camping instruction. On the other expeditions families paddle from camp to camp.

At 32,000-acre Itasca State Park, the state's biggest, you can explore prehistoric archaeological sites and 500-year-old native burial areas during a four-day base-camp adventure. The highlight of any visit, though, may be a small stream just 15 steps across—the headwaters of the mighty Mississippi. When you're not jumping back and forth across America's most famous river or relaxing at base camp, paddle on beautiful Lake Itasca (rather than formal instruction, guides give you pointers), or take a hike through the pines.

Families with children age five and up can join the three-day St. Croix River family canoe trip, which departs just a two-hour drive from Minneapolis. Designated a

National Scenic Riverway, the St. Croix flows through remarkably pristine wilderness areas; a portion of the trip takes place in St. Croix State Park. Wilderness Inquiry uses 24-ft cedar-strip voyageur canoes on this trip. Each of these exceptionally stable boats holds from 7 to 10 people and has enough space for a kind of play area for children in the middle. Sandstone cliffs and stands of pine and balsam line a river that was once a loggers' highway and an important gateway for adventurers of the last century, who settled towns such as Stillwater, Taylors Falls, and Lindstrom. There are numerous small islands and sandy beaches to stop at and creek mouths to explore—but no portages. Guides teach basic canoeing techniques throughout the trip.

What better place to paddle WI's handmade voyageur canoes than in Voyageurs National Park? Travel as the fur traders did as you explore the Kabetogama Peninsula. From your campsites at Wolf Pack Islands you can paddle Rainy Lake or even cross over the border into Canada to see what can be seen on Sixdeer Island. Wildlife sightings are practically guaranteed; the park has one of the highest concentrations of river otters in the United States, and plenty of other animals make their home here, too. This is a five-day adventure.
*Wilderness Inquiry, 1313 5th St. SE, Box 84, Minneapolis, MN 55414, tel. 612/379–3858 or 800/728–0719. June–Sept.: 3–5 days, $100–$395 adults; 50% discount for children 16 and under.*

## Wolf River Canoes

**ALL**

In 1982 Joe and Jennifer Feil opened Wolf River Canoes on what they consider to be one of the world's greatest canoeing rivers. What makes the Wolf so great? World-class beaches of powdery white sand—and lots of them. If this sounds intriguing, head to the Mississippi coast, about halfway between Mobile and New Orleans. Clean and uncrowded, the Wolf winds peacefully past magnolias and cypresses, wild azaleas and cottonwoods. It is truly a river that any family, even beginners, can handle without a guide.

**FOR FAMILIES.** You can plan everything from a paddle of a couple of hours to a camping trip of several days and the Feils will set you up with all the equipment, information, and directions you need. The Wolf's sandbars are ideal for picnicking and camping, and there are swimming holes galore. Most trips float you back to your car so you can travel at your own pace. This is a river for children of all ages; the Feils impose no age limit as long as parents are responsible for their children. Teens can even paddle alone if their parents say it's okay. Joe's canoes are 16 ft long, with two seats; a child can sit comfortably in the middle. A family paddling with two small children might be able to use one canoe, but talk to Joe first. If you're on a multi-day trip, you may want to add a solo kayak for older children or travel in two canoes. As for camping, just pick your sandbar and pitch your tents (Joe will give you tips on what to bring). Then sit back, relax, swim, and enjoy what life on the Wolf has to offer. Although human sightings are rare, you may see great blue herons, ducks, wild turkeys, and otters.

This is an excellent river to tackle on your own, but if you have a group and want a guide, Joe will be happy to make arrangements with you—though you'll still have to help with the camp chores and cooking.
*Wolf River Canoes, 21652 Tucker Rd., Long Beach, MS, tel. 228/452–3874. Year-round by reservation: 1–4 days, $25–$75 per canoe or kayak, $120 per day extra for a guide.*

# Resources

## Organizations

Several organizations set standards and guidelines for outfitters and guides. **America Outdoors** (Box 10847, Knoxville, TN 37939, tel. 423/558–3595 or 800/524–4814) is the national association for river guides. Ask for its magazine listing outfitters and guides. The **American Canoe Association** (7432 Alban Station Blvd., Suite B226, Springfield, VA 22150, tel. 703/451–0141) publishes a newsletter, *The American Canoeist.* The **Professional Paddle Sports Association** (Box 248, Butler, KY 41006, tel. 606/472–2202) will send consumers information on U.S. guides and outfitters.

## Periodicals

*Canoe & Kayak Magazine* (Box 3146, Kirkland, WA 98033, tel. 800/692–2663) prints an extensive list of schools and outfitters in the back of the magazine and has several stories each year about family paddling.

## Books

Globe Pequot Press has a veritable library of books on canoeing, among them *Basic Essentials: Canoeing, Basic Essentials: Canoe Paddling, Canoeists Q & A,* and *Complete Book of Canoeing,* as well as canoeing guides to specific areas and rivers. *Paddle America,* by Nick Shears (Starfish Press, tel. 202/244–7827), represents one man's effort to provide a central place for paddlers to get all the information they need about waterways and outfitters in various regions of the country.

## Also See

If your family loves paddling rivers, lakes, and coastal waterways, check out the adventures in Kayaking *and* Rafting. Some trips in Wildlife Encounters combine boating and animal watching.

# CATTLE DRIVES

My friend David, an attorney in Washington, D.C., has traveled throughout this country and much of the world. Of all his adventures, the cattle drive he went on tops his list of great vacations. Why? Because, he says, his abilities and endurance were tested, and he was able to meet the challenges head-on. He discovered, in fact, that he was capable of more than he ever thought possible—and it was fun.

That, in a nutshell, is what a cattle drive is about for modern-day families. You work hard, play hard, and fall into your sleeping bag exhausted at night—but you feel great about yourself and your day. What better gift to give children than positive reinforcement about their abilities and accomplishments? And that's not the end of it, for you get to nurture this self-esteem in places of awesome beauty. You also have the opportunity to learn about American history, modern-day ranching, and wilderness ecology.

There's another important aspect to cattle drives, too. Many third-, fourth-, and fifth-generation ranchers have entered the tourism business because they believe it's a way to preserve both their ranches and a unique way of life that's fast disappearing. When your family goes on a cattle drive with an honest-to-goodness rancher, you will hear a heartfelt account of a way of life that shaped America's history and economy for years. *City Slickers* notwithstanding, cattle drives are an excellent mix of adventure, education, hard work, and old-fashioned fun.

## Questions to Ask

**How experienced do we have to be?** In most cases, not very. Some drives take folks who have never ridden horses; others require riding experience. Generally it depends on the terrain or sometimes on the livestock. Always ask so you choose the right drive for your family.

**Is the drive walking only? Can experienced riders go faster?** Ranchers tend to put inexperienced riders in the back or on the sides of the drive. If you want to work hard, stay up at the front. There's usually a place for riders of any ability, but some drives are more suited to very good riders.

**How many hours a day are spent in the saddle?** Six or seven hours is the average for the drives listed here, with some as few as four and some as many as 10. Whatever the specific length, the bottom line is it's plenty long enough to make you sore if you aren't used to it. Bring acetaminophen or another pain reliever for aches, as well as adhesive bandages and antibiotic cream for saddle sores. A little adversity is part of the adventure.

**If someone gets tired of riding, are there options?** On ranch-based drives or on those with a base camp, you may be able to quit early. On drives accompanied by a wagon, you can probably trade your horse for a wagon seat. On trail drives, though, there are few options. Anyone considering a cattle drive should think carefully about whether the family can handle a single-activity vacation for between four and seven long, hard days in a row. Kids, in particular, may get bored on drives that offer no breaks and no other activities.

**Is this a real drive—that is, one moving cattle for a purpose—or is it simulated?** There are outfitters that move cattle solely to entertain tourists, but they are not among those listed here. A ranch with real needs will provide you with a real experience.

**How many guests go on the drive?** From 10 to 20 is average, plus wranglers and a whole lot of cattle.

**Are cowboy boots necessary? What about gloves?** Most drovers recommend boots—and not brand-new ones. Get everyone in the family a pair, and break them in well before the drive. Why? Cowboy boots are designed to keep your feet from slipping through the stirrups. If that happened and you fell, you'd probably be dragged by the horse. As for gloves, a pair of decent leather ones will protect your hands from sores and allow you to handle a rope better. Everyone should have a pair.

**Do you have helmets?** When we asked this question, the answers ranged from "Yep, but no one wears them" to utter amusement. No one will require you or your child to wear a riding helmet, so you have to decide on your own. The bottom line: A helmet is the safe way to go. You can purchase riding helmets at a store that sells riding apparel and equipment.

**Where will we sleep?** On ranch-based drives guests generally stay in cabins or lodge rooms. Drives that use a permanent or semipermanent cow camp might have wall tents or cowboy tepees. On trail drives a campsite is set up each night, and guests sleep either in tents or cowboy style—under the stars.

**Are there showers?** Some drives do offer this amenity. I wouldn't pick a cattle drive based on the presence or absence of showers, but if you care about this, ask.

**What kind of food is served?** Hearty and delicious chow is typical. Besides all the steaks and barbecue and Dutch-oven desserts, most drives also have salads and fruit. Some outfitters can even accommodate vegetarians if asked ahead of time.

**Will there be women and girls?** Every rancher in this chapter said at least half the participants in its drives are female. In some cases, there are many more women than men. One outfitter speculated that this is because women are often better riders. Whatever the reason, cattle drives are not just a man's world, although men still outnumber women among the wranglers and drovers.

**What's included in the cost?** Drives include everything from the first day of the adventure to the last, meaning tents or cabins, meals, a horse, some instruction, and stock to move, unless otherwise noted. Some also include lodging the night before the drive starts and transportation to and from the nearest airport. You have to bring your own sleeping bag on some drives but not on others. Airfare to the ranch or meeting site is not included.

## Instruction

All ranchers provide riding instruction to anyone who wants or needs it. Children as well as adults have their riding ability checked before the drive starts, and there's discussion of basic safety issues and how to handle life on the trail. If you're a good rider, you'll be taught more advanced techniques of herding, trailing, and rounding up cows. On some ranches you learn to brand, provide health care for livestock, check fence lines, or even help castrate calves. Roping is taught on every drive. Beyond that, most ranchers want to teach participants about the complexities of modern-day ranching and about the cultural and natural history of the land.

## Finding the Fun

**Southwest:** Cottonwood Ranch, Hunewill Circle H Guest Ranch, Off the Beaten Path, Rockin' R Ranch. **Rockies:** American Wilderness Experience/GORP Travel, Cheyenne River Ranch, Cowboy Crossing, Hargrave Cattle & Guest Ranch, High Island Ranch and Cattle Company, Laredo Enterprises, Montana High Country Cattle Drive, Off the Beaten Path. **West Coast:** Hunewill Circle H Guest Ranch.

# Favorite Cattle Drives

## American Wilderness Experience/GORP Travel

(8+)

American Wilderness Experience/GORP Travel represents many ranchers and other outfitters and has several choices for cowpokes hoping to fulfill their western dreams. The two best for families are along the Wyoming–Montana border and in eastern Idaho.

**FOR FAMILIES.** Double Rafter Cattle Drives has been operating in the Big Horn Mountains on the Wyoming–Montana border for more than 100 years. The ranch was homesteaded in 1887, and the same family has been working it ever since. Double Rafter offers two different experiences. The first is on a seven-day drive, each taking cattle to different pastures as part of the normal grazing cycle (meaning you aren't moving them for the sake of moving them). You generally trail the herd from 6 to 16 mi each day, rising early and arriving back at your camp at about noon, which leaves time for fishing, hiking, swimming, learning to rope, playing cards, or just resting your weary bones. Lodging is in wall tents except the last night, when everyone gathers at a motel in Sheridan, Wyoming. Participants don't need riding experience (the ranch will match you to a horse you can handle), but you should be in at least average physical condition and be capable of following orders quickly. You might, for example, have to dismount your horse suddenly in rugged terrain. For these reasons the suggested minimum age on the seven-day drives is 12.

Double Rafter's second adventure, the five-day Summer Cow Camp, fills the bill for families with younger children as well as anyone who wants an authentic cattle experience but one that's somewhat flexible. Once the herds are in the mountains, families can join wranglers on the range as they cut out strays, rope and doctor sick cattle, scatter salt by pack horse, and perform all the normal chores of wrangling in high pastureland. You can also fish and play cards, listen to stories about the history of the area (Custer made his infamous last stand near here), and be as much of a cowpoke as you want. Fly into Sheridan, Wyoming (30 mi from the ranch), or Billings, Montana (125 mi away), for either adventure; ranch hands will meet you at the airport or at your hotel by noon, and you'll be in the saddle by 6 PM the first day.

Butch Small, arguably one of the best saddle bronc riders in professional rodeo history, invites families to learn about authentic ranch life and cattle moving on his family's 130-year-old ranch. Spread across 6,000 acres between the Bitterroot and Grand Teton mountains in eastern Idaho, the ranch is family-operated today, just as it has been for five generations. Small's operation is for approximately seven participants ages 12 and older, and for riders of all abilities. No previous experience is required.

The adventure begins when ranch hands pick up guests in Idaho Falls for the hour drive to the ranch. From there it's a 16-mi, four-wheel trek up to the rolling foothills and base camp, home for the next five days. Cowpokes-to-be are carefully matched with horses appropriate for their ability, and Small teaches all guests the basics of saddling, riding, and a little horse psychology to boot. A typical day of working with the approximately 700 head of cattle includes six to eight hours in the saddle, though shorter routes are available for those who can't manage that. Still, this is a working ranch, and there are daily chores—finding and sorting strays, riding the fence lines, hauling salt, or dealing with any of the myriad unexpected problems that might arise. The group is generally divided up each day according to both ability and interest, so participants are assigned to work they like and can handle. (Parents can help with easier chores in order to stay with their kids.) At the end of the day, there's a hearty dinner and plenty of time for storytelling, playing poker or horseshoes, and listening to some cowboy guitar picking. Those who haven't had their fill of exercise can hike in the country around base camp, or practice their roping skills on the wooden 'steer.'

Cow camp itself consists of a large, hand-hewn log lodge and several rustic cabins equipped with propane heaters and double or bunk beds. Guests who'd rather rough it a little more can opt for tepee tents in the warmer summer months. All meals are served at the lantern-lit lodge, which has a sundeck for relaxing outside. The woodstove is fired up on cold nights, and after a trail ride you can dip your feet in a nearby creek. There's a shower house with two separate bathrooms for washing up, as well as flush toilets. The cost includes transfers to and from Idaho Falls.

*American Wilderness Experience/GORP Travel, Box 1486, Boulder, CO 80306, tel. 303/444–2622 or 800/444–0099. June–Oct.: 5–7 days, $995–$1,685 adults, $495–$1,685 children.*

## Cheyenne River Ranch

8+

Fifty miles north of Douglas, in eastern Wyoming, the Cheyenne River Ranch spreads over 8,000 acres in the Thunder

Basin National Grassland. This is grassland by Wyoming standards—rolling hills covered in sagebrush, cactus, and—yes—some grass. The Pellatz family, low-key and friendly, runs both sheep and cattle on the ranch. They also drive the cattle of a niece and brother-in-law, which is why they can have three authentic drives a year.

**FOR FAMILIES.** Betty Pellatz says eight-year-olds are welcome on the spring and summer drives if they have some riding experience and are completely comfortable around horses; a child with no experience at all should be at least 11. Guests help drive between 75 and 250 head of cattle (depending on the month) from the rolling prairie through the Rochelle Hills and Cow Creek Buttes.

The land is arid—even the Cheyenne River and Antelope Creek, beside both of which you camp, are dry except during flash floods. Up in the hills, stands of pine offer shade and shelter for camping. At each site there's a big tent for men and another for the women; married couples can have a smaller tent to themselves. Children generally like to stay in the big tents, but the other option would be a second small tent next to their parents. The "prairie loo" is a trailer affair with a hot shower on one side and a potty on the other. At night everyone practices roping and eats well, but most guests, Betty says, really want to visit and get to know one another and the wranglers. Cattle drive rates include pickup from and return to the Casper, Wyoming, airport.

*Cheyenne River Ranch, 1031 Steinle Rd., Douglas, WY 82633, tel. 307/358–2380. May–Oct.: 3–6 days, $195 per person per day.*

## Cottonwood Ranch

8+

For five generations the Smith family has raised cattle in Elko County, Nevada, on a ranch 6,200 ft up in the high desert. Twelve hundred head of cattle and 100 horses roam some 40,000 acres of ranch property and thousands of additional leased acres. Although many guests come just for the ranch experience, one of Cottonwood's biggest draws is its famous six-day horse drive in June, as well as cattle work throughout the summer.

**FOR FAMILIES.** If you've never experienced the staggering beauty of a herd of horses on the run over wild and rugged land, sign up for Cottonwood's spring drive. After meeting at the ranch, the group of no more than 16 travels by van to the Jackpot or Elko area, where 100 horses are corralled and ready to move. You'll drive the horses 40 mi on the trail along rimrock canyons, over the North Fork of the Little Salmon River, and on to the ranch. Horses move a lot faster than cattle, so the drive requires some riding experience and a minimum age of 12.

In order for your family to try cattle work—gathering, rounding up, and moving the herd to new pastures—your children only have to be eight years or older, and you don't need a lot of experience. You work mostly at the ranch (on some summer days cattle work is based at a high camp), though you can be out all day working hard if you choose. Accommodations are in a seven-bedroom lodge, with both private and shared baths. There are hayrides, cookouts, and occasional singalongs, but the scenery and wildlife make up most of the trip's entertainment.

*Cottonwood Ranch, HC 62, Box 1300, O'Neil Rte., Wells, NV 89835, tel. 775/752–3135 or 775/755–2231. June: 6 days (horse drive), $995. May–Sept. (ranch stay only): $145 per day; 20% discount for children under 16.*

## Cowboy Crossing

6+

The Hewitt family ranch covers 25,000 acres on the Wyoming–Montana state line in the Powder River area. It's an easy drive to Devil's Tower National Monument, the Custer Battlefield National Monument, and the Black Hills of South Dakota, so plan on spending some time in the area before or after rounding up cattle. The ranch has three creeks that drain into the Powder River, and ridges of river breaks ranging in elevation from 3,500 to 4,500 ft. It's a land of clean air, cedar trees, and ponderosa pines, and you're likely to see a number of four-footed creatures—including deer, antelope, and coyotes—other than the cattle you work. The working ranchers use the help of novice cowhands and in return offer a very personalized experience. Activities and dates are flexible according to the desires and needs of the family group.

**FOR FAMILIES.** Being able to stay in comfortable quarters at the ranch and to pick your own dates are two things that make Cowboy Crossing a great summer activity for families with younger children. During the day you help move parts of the herd from one grazing area to another, brand animals, or perform other chores; time in the saddle varies. You can also help in the morning and stay around the ranch in the afternoon or even opt to spend one whole day at the ranch, hiking or relaxing. Evening highlights are card games, and plain old camaraderie, all against a backdrop of fiery sunsets. You'll see historical carvings on some of the cliffs you pass, as well as old homesteads and cabins. Local history, range management, and ranch life are popular topics of discussion here, so you leave Cowboy Crossing with a real understanding of life in the '90s for American ranchers. Lodging is in a separate three-bedroom, one-and-a-half bath house at ranch headquarters. The Hewitts strive to create a wholesome family atmosphere on their ranch; there is no alcohol, smoking is very limited, and prayers are said before the home-cooked meals, which feature their own ranch-raised beef.

*Cowboy Crossing, Julie and J. D. Hewitt, Recluse, WY 82725, tel. 406/427–5056 or 888/643–9488. Apr.–Oct.: 1 or more days, $120 per day adults, $60 per day ages 6–12.*

## Hargrave Cattle & Guest Ranch

10+

Forty miles west of Kalispell, Montana, the Thompson River creates a valley of broad green meadows and cool pine forests. Native Americans trapped and fished in the area, and homesteaders made a living growing hay. The Hargrave Cattle & Guest Ranch, with its main buildings tucked at the head of the valley, spreads out over 88,000 acres of mostly leased land. There are only from 15 to 19 guests at a time even in the busy summer season, and Ellen Hargrave makes every one of them feel at home. Take time to visit nearby Glacier National Park while you're here; if you don't have a car, the Hargraves will lend you one.

**FOR FAMILIES.** This adventure is not a cattle drive or roundup in the traditional sense—you won't be on the trail camping out. The Hargraves offer an honest-to-goodness cattle experience during the day and hot showers and a cozy comforter on your bed at night. If you want to test out being a cowhand, this is an excellent place.

In calving season (April and May), guests help with a variety of chores. Mothers-to-be need to be checked every three hours throughout the day and night before they give birth, and you can get up with the wranglers to do it. There's also branding, ear tagging, riding herd, or even giving the calves their first vitamin shots.

May and June mean cattle drives to pastureland 10 or so mi from the main ranch. In September and October the pastured cattle are rounded up and brought back. During those drives guests are on the trail as long as eight hours a day. Lunch is usually a picnic out of the saddlebag, beside a stream or up on the mountain. Sometimes you're moving moms and calves; other times it's bulls. The opportunities for experiencing real ranch life are endless here; the more you do, the more you'll learn. Families can opt for all the traditional ranch-stay activities, too: swinging off the rope over the lake, singing cowboy songs, canoeing, fishing, and getting up close and personal with the ranch animals. A counselor called a Kid's Buddy is on staff in July and August to care for the younger children while parents and older children ride the range with cattle during the day.

*Hargrave Cattle & Guest Ranch, 300 Thompson River Rd., Marion, MT 59925, tel. 406/858– 2284 or 800/933–0696. Year-round (Apr.–Oct. for most cattle work): 7 days, $1,095–$1,620 adults, $1,095 children ages 7–12, $990 children ages 3–7. Non-riders receive a $200 discount.*

## High Island Ranch and Cattle Company

12+

High Island in Wyoming is not anywhere near water. But when you stand and look around at the high peaks, you feel almost as if you're on an island, which is how the ranch got its name. Your family can come here to help brand and care for cattle, or you can join a trail drive—one that's traditional or one that's a complete, authentic re-creation of a drive in the 1800s.

**FOR FAMILIES.** The 130,000-acre ranch has several drives and one spring branding week. Ages 12 and up can participate in branding week at the ranch, where accommodations are in rustic cabins. The drives, which cover about 15 mi per day over rough sage and prairie high country, are for ages 16 and up only. Fly into Cody, and someone from the ranch will pick you up.

On drives plan on spending the better part of the day in the saddle chasing and pushing cattle from winter pasture to summer pasture on the vast ranch land. Depending on the season, the drive moves cattle from a lower lodge at about 6,000 ft to an upper lodge at 9,000 ft, or the reverse. The group camps on a different part of the trail each night; although tents are available, almost everyone sleeps in the open unless the weather is really bad. You stay in rooms in the very simple lodges at both ends of the drive. There is sometimes entertainment—a cowboy poet and singer or someone to teach you clog dancing—but most wranglers are happy just to crawl into their sleeping bags and sleep the deep and peaceful sleep of someone who's done a hard day's work and done it well. If you want to learn roping, buy a rope from the ranch, and one of the wranglers will be glad to teach you.

Once each summer High Island re-creates an 1800s drive, in which period clothing is worn and all cooking and sleeping arrangements are as they would have been before the turn of the 20th century. The ranch provides shirts, armbands, dusters, and silk "wild rags" (a bandanna). Don't wear watches or newfangled gear—everyone tries to be as authentic as possible. The biscuits are legendary, and the traditional sweet-and-sour cider vinegar drink is popular. They do use coolers to keep the food safe, but they're covered in canvas, and, yes, outhouses are still available. This is an experience of a lifetime for history buffs; 16 is the minimum age.

*High Island Ranch and Cattle Company, 346 Amoretti, Suite 10, Thermopolis, WY 82443, tel. 307/867–2374. June–Sept.: 7 days, $1,250, $1,550 for 1800s-style drive.*

## Hunewill Circle H Guest Ranch

9+

One of California's top guest and cattle ranches, the Hunewill Circle H is in the eastern Sierra Nevada, near the northeastern border of Yosemite National Park. It's often booked far in advance for the popular summer months, but one of the great experiences here is working the cattle in the fall.

**FOR FAMILIES.** The big drive takes place the second week of November, when the herd travels from the Hunewill's summer ranch to the winter ranch 50 mi away in Nevada's Great Basin area. It's a good choice for families that don't want to sleep out every night. You move the herd over five days, spending anywhere from five to nine hours a day in the saddle. Your route goes through sage and piñon desert, up into the Sweetwater Mountains, and down into the wide, high desert of Nevada; ask about the Paiute cemetery that you pass on the way. Each night vehicles drive you back to the ranch and your comfortable cabin. The maximum number allowed is 25 participants, who must be intermediate to advanced riders and at least 12 years of age.

In September regular ranch guests can help round up the herd of about 300 and move it from high pastures down to the ranch. You'll be out one full day, returning to the ranch that night. Adult beginning riders and experienced children as young as nine can go on this one. There are other activities, such as roping lessons and Border collie and sheep demonstrations, but riding is the main focus, with horsemanship instruction, swim rides, cavalry maneuvers, and the like. Children six and up can ride the trails at the ranch. It's very much a family operation, run by several generations of Hunewills, including kids. Welcoming and relaxing, it's a terrific experience. Many guests fly into Reno, 120 mi away, and drive a rental car to the ranch.

Hunewill also offers special focus weeks at the ranch during the year. Cattle Work Week, typically in May or June, is for intermediate and better riders ages 12 and older. You ride with a Hunewill family member and help with branding, cutting, and moving the cows. In addition to the big fall drives, there are cattle moves during the regular summer ranch season as well, and guests can participate in any of those if they choose to.

*Hunewill Circle H Guest Ranch, in summer: Box 368, Bridgeport, CA 93517, tel. 760/932–7710; in winter: 200 Hunewill La., Wellington, NV 89444, tel. 775/465–2201. Sept. (ranch stay, including roundup): 5–7 days, $866–$919, depending on cabin; Nov. (drive): 7 days, $950; 25% discount for children 10–12; 50% discount for children under 10.*

## Laredo Enterprises

4+

Lifelong ranchers Bob and Judy Sivertsen own and operate Laredo Enterprises. Although their own Montana ranch isn't conducive to an authentic drive because of farming and development in the area, the Sivertsens wanted to give families an understanding of today's cattle business. To do this, they teamed with ranchers in both the eastern and western parts of the state to offer six cattle drives each year.

**FOR FAMILIES.** Families with young children should consider the X Hanging H, in eastern Montana near Glendive. Any child six or older who can ride (nine is the minimum for youngsters who've never ridden) is welcome on the trail; those under six and nonriders can still go along in one of the covered wagons. On the June drive between 300 and 500 head of cattle are moved over rolling hills from the ranch to summer pastures. You ride from 8 to 12 mi a day and set up new campsites most, but not all, evenings. This drive finishes with fun back at the ranch: barrel racing and tests of other cowhand skills. The trip includes transportation between the ranch and the airport in Billings.

At the Rumney Ranch all children must be experienced riders, and adults should have some experience, too. This terrain is a little more challenging—50,000 acres of ranch right up against the Rockies. Fly in and out of

Great Falls for these five drives in May, June, and September. (Some packages include transportation to and from the airport.) Rumney runs more than 4,000 head of cattle, and you participate in all forms of ranch work. Guests stay in the bunkhouse as a rule. Plan on covering from 10 to 25 mi a day; despite these long hours moving cattle to different pastures, you do return to the ranch each night. If you have any energy left, there's good fishing. You'll probably hear tall tales around the campfire, but the most spectacular evening entertainment at Rumney is viewing the abundance of stars above.

Although cattle drives are scheduled on specific dates, the Rumney Ranch will take guests on other weeks as well, and there's a guest house in which families can stay. Because this is a working ranch and not a traditional guest ranch, there's no entertainment—in fact, families will probably need to entertain themselves at times during their stay. But there are also opportunities for families to join in with the real work of the ranch, including riding with cowboys and cattle. Families who want to skip ranch work one day can explore Glacier National Park, just 25 mi away.

*Laredo Enterprises, Box 2226, Havre, MT 59501, tel. 406/357–3748 or 800/535–3802. May– Sept.: 7 days, $1,000–$1,330 on horseback, $775–$1,000 by wagon with no riding; parents with 2 or more children get 12% discount off adult rate; also ask about day rates.*

## Montana High Country Cattle Drive

12+

This organization of five Montana ranchers and outfitters is trying to diversify in order to keep their ranches as they've been for generations. John Flynn, whose family came into the area in the 1860s as miners and horse traders, is the group's point man. Soft-spoken but passionate about ranching and what that life has to offer, he believes those who have participated in a working cattle drive go home with a new perspective on life. John's into perspective—he's also a novelist (*see* Resources, *below*).

**FOR FAMILIES.** You spend the first and last nights of the week at a ranch in Townsend and four days out on the trail about halfway between Bozeman and Helena, 30 mi from the source of the Missouri River. Each of the 35 participants is assigned to a wrangler who will assist you throughout your stay. There's also a safety and riding clinic the first morning. Whether you're beginning or experienced, there's a place for you—five or six can even just ride in the wagon.

Depending on the drive, cattle travel from a 4,000-ft valley up to 7,000 ft, through sagebrush, juniper, yucca, and alpine meadows to lodgepole pine and spruce forests, or back down to the ranch. Views of Old Baldy rising nearly 10,000 ft in the Big Belt Range remind you that this is Rocky Mountain country. Plan on four to six hours a day on the trail to move between 400 and 1,200 head of cattle 8 or so mi. This is a big drive; the herd is 1½–2 mi long. If you've never seen real cow dogs (usually Border collies and Australian shepherds) hard at work, here's your chance. They're remarkable animals.

In addition to a regular cook, the procession usually includes an authentic restored chuck wagon from which desserts—cobblers, cinnamon rolls, and homemade ice cream—are served. The outfitter can accommodate vegetarians with advance notice; otherwise there's lots of barbecue. You sleep in tent camps along the trail. Entertainment might be a singer-poet or the "rattlesnake guy," who brings his snakes out for everyone to see and touch. John Flynn's brother, who has a master's degree in range management, shares his knowledge and demonstrates which high-mountain plants are edible.

*Montana High Country Cattle Drive, 674 Flynn La., Townsend, MT 59644, tel. 406/266–3534 or 800/345–9423. June–July: 7 days, $1,400.*

## Off the Beaten Path

ALL

Off the Beaten Path's Bill and Pam Bryan work with many of the West's best outfitters. Because their company specializes in customized vacations and small-group departures, they've had the opportunity to find out from both guests and outfitters exactly what makes a successful western vacation. They recommend two cattle outfits as terrific for families.

**FOR FAMILIES.** The rangeland of the All 'Round Ranch in Jensen, Utah, flanks the Blue Mountains and Dinosaur National Monument. All 'Round offers several cattle drives from March to September, but the July Family Course remains the best bet for parents and children. Al and Wann Brown, former Outward Bound (OB) leaders who run the program, say this adventure is the outgrowth of an OB course—"but geared more for fun." The minimum age is 12, and although the emphasis is on horsemanship, participants work with cattle, too, doing whatever needs to be done: moving cattle to new pastures, branding, and doctoring sick animals. The amount of time spent in the saddle varies quite a bit, depending on the day's work.

On this educationally oriented week, participants split their time between two campsites; there's a pond at one and a creek at the other and you can take a dip at either camp. Both setups have tepees. You don't need to bring a thing—even sleeping bags and foul-weather gear are provided. Ask about other courses and drives; the minimum age for those is 16.

Another good family option is a week on one of the three ranches owned by the Bassett family. Depending on the season and the work, your family will be at one or more of these ranches. Spring drives start out at the Lovell Ranch in Wyoming, where the cattle winter. Summer ranch weeks and fall drives are based about 50 mi away in Montana at the Schively or Dryhead ranch. The Bassetts enjoy having children around and don't have rigid age restrictions.

Ranch weeks, offered throughout the summer, are especially appealing because even babies are welcome as long as parents take turns riding with the cattle. If you bring young children and are willing to watch them closely, the Bassetts can find something on the ranch for them to do. Ranch-week guests help with chores such as pregnancy testing on cows, branding, rounding up strays, taking care of sick animals, moving the herd, and weaning calves. Your family stays in cabins or a bunkhouse with shared showers.

On the big drives, which move from 250 to 300 cow/calf pairs over six days, kids as young as five or six can join the action if they are good riders. Wranglers stay in a cow camp with tepee tents and a chuck wagon. *Off the Beaten Path, 27 E. Main St., Bozeman, MT 59715, tel. 406/586–1311 or 800/445–2995. Mar.–Oct.: 4–7 days, $850–$1,200.*

## Rockin' R Ranch

12+

Thirty-seven miles north of Bryce Canyon National Park, the 1,000-acre Rockin' R is in a stunning area of Utah where red-rock canyons open onto wide green valleys. The ranch lodge has 41 rooms, but even with a large number of guests you still experience the land in a very personal way. People tend to be in different areas doing different things. The cattle drives take a maximum of 20 guests at a time.

**FOR FAMILIES.** The ranch leases 50,000 acres from the forest service; drives take place within the borders of Dixie National Forest. The group stays at one of the ranch's two permanent cow camps. Sweetwater, at 7,000 ft, is set in the foothills of the Boulder Range among the pines, close to a natural spring. The Griffin Springs camp edges a meadow at 10,000 ft; if you can brave cold water, you can take a swim in the nearby lake and spring. The camps have wall tents and mattresses.

Cowhands can stay in the saddle about seven hours a day, moving the cattle, helping doctor any sick stock, and checking miles of fence. Even when the 1,000 head of cattle split into two drives, the herd can still be as much as 2 mi long. Everyone is pretty tired at night, but there are singing around the campfire and entertainment by a cowboy poet and cowboy singer/guitarist. Deer, antelope, and elk are often seen on the trail. The Rockin' R also offers horse-packing trips (see Horse Packing).

*Rockin' R Ranch, Reservation Office, 10274 S. Eastdell Dr., Sandy, UT 84092, tel. 801/733-9538. June–Oct.: 4–6 days, $625–$1,250 (includes 1 night at ranch before drive begins).*

# Resources

## Organizations

The **Dude Ranchers' Association** (Box 471, LaPorte, CO 80535, tel. 970/223-8440) has information on more than 100 guest ranches in 13 western states. Not all the ranches are working cattle ranches, but the association can identify these and help your family choose an appropriate one.

Besides the booking agents mentioned in this chapter, you can use **Pat Dickerman's adventure travel advisory service** (7550 E. McDonald Dr., Suite M, Scottsdale, AZ 85250, tel. 602/596-0226 or 800/252-7899) to set up a cattle drive vacation. Pat has been in the adventure travel business for several decades.

## Books

*The Arbuckle Cafe: Classic Cowboy Stories* by V. S. FitzPatrick (Yellow Cat Publishing) is a fascinating collection of turn-of-the-20th century cowboy tales, transcribed by a cowpuncher. *Montana Pursuit*, by J. T. Flynn (Aegina Press, tel. 304/429-7204), is Montana cattleman John Flynn's novel. He calls it "an adventure hunting mystery," with lots of local geography and color. If you're driving cattle with him, pick up a copy first.

## Also See

If you want a western riding experience that is generally a bit slower and more relaxed than a cattle drive, turn to the Horse Packing chapter. The chapter on Ranches lists ranches where you may work with cattle.

# COVERED WAGON ADVENTURES

Few experiences give families a feel for the Old West and pioneer life in the way a wagon train can. Some "modernization" to wagons (such as rubber tires and padded seats) means you'll be more comfortable than pioneers were, yet wagon masters today take great care to preserve the authenticity of the experience by following wagon train traditions and, in many cases, historic routes. Education is mixed with fun as guides spin stories about the men, women, and children who persevered in the face of tremendous difficulties to reach the West and about the mountain men, Native Americans, and Pony Express riders who sometimes appeared on the trail.

Because wagon trains are easygoing adventures, they can accommodate a variety of ages in a way many western experiences cannot. In most cases members of your family can ride saddle horses in addition to traveling in the wagons, but you certainly don't have to, so no special skills are necessary. All you need is a willingness to suspend disbelief and for a few days to imagine you are traveling across the United States 150 years ago.

## Questions to Ask

**Can guests help?** Guests are often encouraged to help with camp chores and to learn traditional skills such as cooking over an open fire and driving the wagons. In some cases you are responsible for taking care of the horses and helping set up camp each night. Find out what's expected of your family and especially what the children are allowed to do. Pitching in helps you re-create the real experience.

**Are there horses to ride?** Typically guests take turns riding a few saddle horses brought along for that purpose. On one particular wagon train all guests have the option to ride for half of each day, but it's not a requirement. Some guests choose to walk part of the way, too, which is in keeping with what pioneer wagon trains were really like. The minimum age for riding horses may be higher than that for riding in the wagons.

**What are the sleeping arrangements?** Guests on most wagon train adventures sleep in tents provided by the outfitter, though on some trips you may sleep in the wagons. On still others, guests opt to sleep under the stars, the way cowboys and pioneers did. If your children have never slept in sleeping bags or tents before, borrow equipment in order to try this experience or let them test sleeping bags and tents at an outdoor store.

**What kind of food is served?** Hearty meals are the norm on these trips, with most offering standard chuck-wagon fare—beef, beans, and biscuits are typical.

Some outfitters go farther, with near- gourmet meals, including fresh salads and fruit, as well as fresh-baked desserts.

**What kinds of bathroom facilities are provided?** Several wagon trains pull a separate wagon with a chemical toilet or other toilet facility. Those that camp on forest service land have access to regular toilets or outhouses. Young children going into the wilderness for the first time may be reluctant to use unfamiliar kinds of toilets. Ask ahead of time so you can prepare your youngsters if necessary. Showers on the trail are rare, but a minimal amount of water for washing up is generally available.

**How many miles are covered each day?** Traveling between 6 and 12 mi is typical. Wagons are not a speedy means of transportation; instead, they let you settle into a slower mode and take in the country and history in a relaxed way.

**Will there be other recreational activities on the trip?** Some trips do allow for hiking, swimming, or other activities at the campsites. On many trips, though, it takes an hour or two to set up camp once you arrive; then it's time for dinner and evening activities such as campfire programs and other western-style entertainment. This is why some outfitters think a child should be at least six for this experience. If you don't ride horses and if you get bored sitting, this may not be the trip for your family.

**Are the guides knowledgeable about wagon train history and local lore and about the area's plant and animal life?** History—both human and natural—is a big part of a wagon train experience, so make sure guides are going to provide that.

**Will there be surprise "attacks" during the trip?** Although this is fun entertainment for most, young children may be scared by these re-creations of wagon train experiences. Even though outfitters don't like to ruin the surprise, explain that you need to prepare your child ahead of time.

**What's included in the cost?** Wagons, food, tents, and use of horses for at least part of the time are included on the trips, unless otherwise noted. In some cases you must bring your own sleeping bags. Some outfitters will pick up guests at a local airport or other location; others require you to get to the trailhead on your own. Because wagon trains generally start first thing in the morning and return in the afternoon, you'll probably have to arrange local lodging the night before the trip starts and possibly at the end of the trip, too.

## Instruction

A covered wagon adventure requires no prior experience or ability: If you don't know how to set up a tent, the crew will teach and help you. If you or your children don't know how to ride, you'll get some pointers. You'll only be traveling at a walk on the horses, so even the inexperienced should be just fine. On some wagon trains young children may not ride or may have to be led by parents. Take the opportunity to learn a new skill out on the trail, whether it's cooking over a fire or taking care of the horses: The majority of wagon masters and guides really want to share their knowledge with you.

### Finding the Fun

**Midwest:** Grandtravel, Oregon Trail Wagon Train. **Rockies:** American Wilderness Experience/GORP Travel, Grandtravel, Myers Ranch Wagon Trains, Teton Wagon Train and Horse Adventure.

## Favorite Wagon Trains

### American Wilderness Experience/GORP Travel

**5+**

Old logging roads through Bridger-Teton National Forest, just outside the town of Jackson, Wyoming, provide ideal trails on which to relive a piece of American history. The Grand Tetons and the Gros Ventre and Wind River ranges form an inspiring backdrop. Wagons West, the outfitter with whom American Wilderness Experience/GORP Travel contracts for this trip, will meet your family in Jackson and drive you to the trailhead, which is north of town toward Grand Teton and Yellowstone national parks.

**FOR FAMILIES.** Pioneers never had it quite so good. These wagons are cushioned with rubber tires and foam-padded seats that convert into deluxe bunks at night. You can expect four or five wagons on this train and a maximum of 25 people. One benefit of traveling with this group is that they're happy to let guests help drive the wagons. Each guest also rides horseback for half of each day. Children as young as seven or eight can ride, but they must have some experience; those 10 and up don't need previous experience. Most days there's time for fishing and hiking, and guests visit a historic homestead, too. At night plan on singing cowboy songs around the campfire. *American Wilderness Experience/GORP Travel, Box 1486, Boulder, CO 80306, tel. 303/444–2622 or 800/444–0099. June–Aug.: 4–6 days, $595–$795 adults, $510–$695 children under 14.*

### Grandtravel

**7–17**

Grandtravel's Western Parks, Western Space trip attempts to bring the romance and adventure of the West alive for grandparents and grandchildren. This itinerary, like all of Grandtravel's trips, is specifically designed to meet the needs of both senior citizens and children; travel is primarily by motor coach. But that doesn't mean coddling: Grandtravel is for active people who love new experiences. There's a lot to take in on this journey from Rapid City, South Dakota, to Jackson, Wyoming—including a ride in a covered wagon.

**FOR FAMILIES.** Two trips—one for grandparents with grandkids ages 7 through 11, one for grandparents with grandchildren from 12 to 17—are offered each summer. The amount of time spent in the bus each day varies quite a bit. The groups visit important landmarks, natural wonders, and national monuments and parks, and participants have a chance to meet Native Americans and cowboys who share their perspective on the West, past and present.

In Rapid City members of the Lakota tribe give a presentation. In Cody, Wyoming, the groups visit the impressive Buffalo Bill Historical Center, which is four museums in one: the Buffalo Bill Museum, the Whitney Museum of Western Art, the Museum of the American Indian, and the Winchester Arms Museum. You also stop at Mt. Rushmore, in South Dakota, and Devil's Tower, in eastern Wyoming. There's lunch at Old Faithful in Yellowstone, and in Sheridan, Wyoming, you make a visit to a historic ranch to see what life was really like during the early 1900s. On the day of a float trip on the Snake River, the group climbs into covered wagons, accompanied by cowboys and mountain men, for a dinner trip in Cache Canyon outside Jackson.

There is no camping on this adventure (lodging is in hotels with private baths), but you can still appreciate the heart of this experience: the rugged beauty of the West and the strength and courage of its people. *Grandtravel, 6900 Wisconsin Ave., Suite 706, Chevy Chase, MD 20815, tel. 301/986–0790 or 800/247–7651. July–Aug.: 10 days, $3,490–$3,690, depending on number of family members sharing accommodations.*

## Myers Ranch Wagon Trains

6+

Sharon and Wayne Myers have a unique piece of property in southeastern Montana. It includes a portion of General Custer's last route from North Dakota to Miles City, Montana, and a section of the old Deadwood Stage route. Hills, pine forests, prairie, and badlands give families a taste of the varied terrain pioneers encountered. One highlight is the climb up a 3,000-ft hill for a view of four states: Montana, Wyoming, North Dakota, and South Dakota.

**FOR FAMILIES.** The Myerses will consider children younger than six, but talk to them first to decide if this is something your child will handle well. To keep the trip small and personal, there are generally five or six wagons for up to 25 people. You can ride in the wagons (some are more comfortable than others, so guests are encouraged to exchange places) or spend some time riding a saddle horse. Although you don't need to be an advanced rider, you should have some experience—and you must have riding boots.

Along the way you see an old stagecoach stop with a barn and other buildings, and you visit a cave in which pioneers from the 1800s scratched their names and the date on the walls. At night there are cowboy poetry, music, and a chance to dance around the campfire under a billion stars. This country is beautiful at all times, but Sharon Myers believes June—when the grass is green and the deer and antelope, along with coyotes and wild turkeys, are out and about playing—is the best. *Myers Ranch Wagon Trains, HC 80, Box 70, Ismay, MT 59336, tel. 406/772–5675. June–Aug.: 3–5 days, $660–$1,100.*

## Oregon Trail Wagon Train

5+

The 2,000-mi-long Oregon Trail was the pioneer wagon route from Independence, Missouri, on the Missouri River, to the Columbia River region of the Pacific Northwest. In the 1840s alone at least 10,000 pioneers made the arduous trek through northeastern Kansas, up along Nebraska's Platte River, and on to Fort Laramie in Wyoming. From there they crossed the Rockies at South Pass, journeyed through Snake River country, and if they made it all the way, stopped finally in the Willamette Valley in Oregon. Today, as people rush across I–80 in minivans and RVs, it's hard to imagine what this journey was really like. If your family wants to know, though, you can find out with the Oregon Trail Wagon Train.

**FOR FAMILIES.** Starting from a base camp in Bayard, just north of the Platte River in western Nebraska, the wagon train makes a circular tour through rolling hills and prairie along portions of the original Oregon Trail. Five wagons for 40 people is typical. Some wagons carry 16 passengers; some hold only four. All of the guides—current or former cowboys or retired farmers—are well versed in the history of the Oregon Trail and the area.

Participants can ride in a different wagon each day to get a different perspective, and many choose to walk much of the route, as the original pioneers did. The group takes turns riding the saddle horses, too.(Children must be at least six and have some previous riding experience.) At night, before turning in to your tent and sleeping bag (both supplied), you might be surprised by a Pony Express "delivery" or an "Indian attack," after which the visitors will share stories and historical information. Guests are encouraged to participate in camp chores and to lend a hand with open-fire cooking.

A noon-to-noon mini-version of this trek, called 24 Hours of 1850, doesn't include as many experiences but still gives you lots of trail history and adventure. Before or after your trip, visit nearby Chimney Rock National Historic Site, the famous landmark on the Oregon Trail that marked the end of the prairie.

*Oregon Trail Wagon Train, Rte. 2, Box 502, Bayard, NE 69334, tel. 308/586–1850. June–Sept.: 1 and 4 days, $150 and $479, respectively for adults, $125 and $379 respectively for children under 12.*

## Teton Wagon Train and Horse Adventure

4+

When the wagon master shouts "Roll the wagons!" the train rumbles onto the back roads of Targhee National Forest, between Grand Teton and Yellowstone national parks in Wyoming. These modern- day prairie schooners, as they were originally named because of their resemblance to "sails on a sea of grass," have rubber tires and padded seats but are otherwise authentic. Gentle riding horses are also available for adventurers who would like to ride from camp to camp, or trail ride farther into the backcountry. Riders have access to waterfalls and viewpoints inaccessible to the wagons.

**FOR FAMILIES.** Three wagons and up to 40 guests travel to a different area each day, forming a circle once camp has been reached. Two camps are on the shores of alpine lakes, where loons, trumpeter swans, moose, elk, and deer are likely to be seen. The wagon train arrives early enough that guests have time to hike, swim, canoe, or just relax. This range of recreational activities makes the trip perfect for younger children, who may need a change of pace.

Cowboys from the Double H Bar Ranches run the train and provide western-style amenities and entertainment. Meals are cooked in Dutch ovens over an open fire, and evenings are spent around the campfire, singing and listening to cowboy yarns. Mountain men, "Indians," and Pony Express riders will probably pay surprise visits during the trip.

There are U.S. Forest Service outdoor toilets at all campsites. All camping gear, including tents and comfortable sleeping bags, is provided. And remember: This is high country. You need lots of sunscreen during the day and warm clothes at night.

*Teton Wagon Train and Horse Adventure, Box 10307, Jackson Hole, WY 83002-0307, tel. 307/734–6101 or 888/734–6101. June–Aug.: 4 days, $745 adults, $695 children 9–14, $645 children 4–8.*

# Resources

## Organizations

You can get information about the history of the Oregon Trail, as well as a reading list and other materials for families, from two groups: the **Oregon-California Trails Association** (524 S. Osage, Independence, MO 64050, tel. 816/252–2276) and **Jefferson National Expansion Memorial** (11 N. 4th St., St. Louis, MO 63102, tel. 314/655–1700).

## Software

Your children may have played **Oregon Trail** (Mecc) on the computer at home or school. You'll want to join them before your wagon adventure. It gives insights into trail life as well as good background information.

To spark children's interest in wagon trains, look up a copy of Ellen Levine's *If You Traveled West in a Covered Wagon* (Scholastic Trade). Another good choice is Kristiana Gregory's *Across the Wide and Lonesome Prairie: The Oregon Trail Diary of Hattie Campbell* (Scholastic Trade), a diary- style, detailed book describing a young girl's wagon train journey in the mid-1800s.

## Also See

For more adventures that can take your family back to the days of the Old West, *see* Cattle Drives, Horse Packing, and Ranches.

# CROSS-COUNTRY SKIING

Cross-country, or Nordic, skiing has gained in popularity in this country recently—and for good reason. The sport gives families a wonderful workout in the wintry outdoors, often at a lower cost than a downhill-skiing vacation. Although it may not hold the thrill of downhill skiing, it doesn't suffer from the noise or the often crowded slopes of downhill. There's also less chance for injuries with this slower, more easygoing sport. Cross-country skiers stride and glide through silent, snowy forests; their skis can carry them into the heart of nature—to backcountry wilderness areas where they are more likely to encounter deer and all kinds of other wildlife than to see other humans.

Although most cross-country ski lodges and day-use areas do not yet have the extensive children's programs found at downhill resorts, many do carry some child-size equipment. Some even have special sleds that parents can use to tow their youngest children behind them as they ski. Lessons and other children's activities are most available during holidays, though some family activities may be offered throughout the ski season. Besides ski lodges, multi-day tours with outfitters and even single-day ski classes are opportunities for cross-country ski adventures. Most lodges and outfitters have both groomed and ungroomed terrain, which is nice if your family has skiers of differing abilities.

The listings in this chapter are an eclectic mix of backcountry wilderness possibilities, courses, ranches, and those inns and lodges that have either new or innovative programs for families. This selection is by no means exhaustive: There are also hundreds of day-use lodges and ski centers throughout North America where cross-country skiing is available, as well as countless trail systems in national forests and parks, used primarily by families that feel comfortable skiing without a guide. Also not here are some very well-known lodges that have been offering cross-country skiing for years because the listings focus on less publicized establishments. Once your family gets into the sport, you will find thousands of miles of trails on which to hone your skills and enjoy serenity and winter beauty far from the madding crowds.

## Questions to Ask

**What kinds of skiing do you teach?** Instruction in the traditional diagonal cross-country stride is commonly available and is most appropriate for families, because even fairly young children can master it. Skating, a style used by more experienced skiers, and telemark, a sort of cross between downhill and cross-country technique, may also be taught.

**Are instructors certified by the Professional Ski Instructors Association?** Some terrific skiers may not necessarily be great teachers of skiing. PSIA-certified instructors not only know how to ski, they've been taught how to teach. This can be especially important when it comes to children. Ask the lodge, school, or outfitter if instructors are certified and particularly if they are trained to work with children; you want an instructor who will use age-appropriate language and have expectations that are on a par with young students' skill and stamina levels.

**What kind of clothing and equipment are needed?** You work hard and get warm when you cross-country ski, so wearing layers of clothing is important. It's not generally necessary to invest in the expensive outerwear downhill skiers require. Fleece and wool garments and wind-resistant shells are good choices; all clothing should be breathable. Beyond this, the weather will dictate specific clothing needs. Skis, cross-country boots, and poles are pretty much all the equipment you'll need. Many skiers like to take backpacks with them to carry extra clothing, water, and snacks. One tip for parents: If you ski with your children and they're slower than you are, wear extra clothes; you'll get cold going at their pace.

**Is equipment available for rent? For children, too?** Lodges and ranches usually rent skis, poles, and cross-country boots, but outfitters may not. If gear isn't available, ask for the name of a reputable rental shop in the area. In either case, be sure their children's equipment will fit a child the size of yours—ask specific questions about what you need. Supplies of child-size items are often limited, so try to make reservations for equipment when you make your trip arrangements.

**Are trails groomed or ungroomed?** Groomed trails—those on which machines have packed down the snow and sometimes even preset tracks—are easier to ski. Families with beginner or intermediate skiers should look for a high ratio of groomed to ungroomed trails. In most cases you'll find a mix of trails, a plus if your family has skiers of different skill levels.

**Is there terrain for all abilities?** Look for ski territory with a combination of flat, open land—such as meadows—along with steeper, more challenging terrain. It's typical for areas to cover a variety of landscapes.

**How long are the trails? Do they connect to other systems?** Most trail systems have a number of shorter loops and longer routes, so you can get away from the main area without committing to an all-day venture. Lodges and ranches often border national or state forests or recreation areas, and their trails may connect to a larger network of trails, usually ungroomed, where you can ski for long distances and have the wilderness practically to yourself.

**What other activities are available?** You will sometimes find sledding, hiking, wildlife viewing, riding, sleigh riding, and other outdoor winter activities in cross-country ski areas. Families who don't want to spend all of their time skiing will probably do best at a ranch or lodge.

**What's included in the cost?** Accommodations, meals, trail passes (if required), and activities are included in the fee for ranches and lodges, unless otherwise noted. Equipment is occasionally part of a package, as is instruction, but more often they cost extra. There may or may not be an extra charge for tours. Outfitters usually include lodging and meals on multi-day trips, guide service, and permits (if necessary); equipment is generally extra. The price for schools covers instruction only, unless otherwise noted.

## Instruction

Most guides and tour leaders will teach the basics of cross-country skiing, but if you want to develop more than a passing knowledge of the sport, choose a lodge, ranch, or school where instruction is the focus. That doesn't mean you have to spend a lot of time in classes before you can explore the great outdoors. Unlike beginning downhill skiers, who usually require a considerable amount of instruction before they can venture to most areas of the mountain, cross-country novices can ski many trails while they're still learning. Know your limits, though. Don't tackle long routes unless you have the stamina to finish—there may be no shortcuts back.

## Finding the Fun

**Northeast:** Appalachian Mountain Club, L.L. Bean, Telemark Inn. **Midwest:** Gunflint Northwoods Outfitters/Gunflint Lodge. **Rockies:** Adventures to the Edge, C Lazy U, Izaak Walton Inn, Lone Mountain Ranch, Off the Beaten Path. **Canada:** Backroads, Off the Beaten Path, Wells Gray Chalets & Wilderness Adventures.

# Favorite Outfitters and Lodges

## Adventures to the Edge

**ALL**

Jean Pavillard, the former director of the Crested Butte Ski School, is well qualified to guide families into the Colorado backcountry. As a native of Switzerland, where Alpine activities are part of daily life, Jean brings a perspective not often found among American-born guides: that skiing and mountaineering can be shared by all ages. As the father of two young skiers, he is also well versed in finding innovative ways to take children into wilderness areas. Jean and his partners will custom-design a backcountry experience in which your family will both learn and push the limits of your collective imaginations and abilities.

Customized trips are the company's specialty but by no means its only offering. One unusual activity, common in Europe, is Alpine ski touring, with gear that resembles a cross between downhill and cross-country skis. The heels of touring bindings can be freed for ascending slopes (like those on cross-country skis) and snapped down for downhill terrain (like those on downhill skis).

**FOR FAMILIES.** The fondue-lunch ski tour is a popular option for families. You ski a 2-mi route out to a wilderness hut and eat next to a roaring fire; if you have children too young to ski, Jean or his guides will pull them in a cozy sled. If your family wants a longer adventure, the company uses several huts and yurts in the mountains around Crested Butte, and guided hut-to-hut adventures can be arranged for all abilities and for any length of time—from a day to a week.

Even though instruction is part of every adventure, some tours and routes are still best for families with older children or for those who already have considerable ski experience. Beginners should take a lesson and go on a half-day outing before heading out on longer excursions.

*Adventures to the Edge, Box 91, Crested Butte, CO 81224, tel. 970/349–5219 or 800/349–5219. Nov.–May: ½–7 days, $280 for tour and lunch for a family of 4, $180–$225 for all-day ski tour and lessons, $280–$300 per day for private guide on custom trip, depending on group size and destination.*

## Appalachian Mountain Club

5+

The Appalachian Mountain Club (AMC) is perhaps best known for its hiking programs and other summer activities (*see* Fishing, Hiking and Backpacking, *and* Trekking with Llamas and Burros), but it does offer a few winter courses. AMC's Catskill campus—near Phoenicia, New York, in the heart of the Catskill Mountains—is just 8 mi from Frost Valley Ski Center, an excellent cross-country area. You can bring your own skis or rent equipment at Frost Valley; lodging and meals for families are in the Valley View Lodge, AMC's Catskill center.

**FOR FAMILIES.** AMC generally holds its Cross-country Skiing for Families courses each February. Typically there are two instructors for the class of about 20 students, made up of parents or grandparents with children ages 6 to 12. Whether your family includes accomplished skiers or never-evers, this course is for you. Families are taught together; learning games keep children interested, but the instruction meets the needs of all ages. Instructors cover techniques for negotiating both uphill and downhill terrain, as well as skiing flat terrain using the traditional diagonal stride. Another option is AMC's Winter Family Fun weekend, also in February. Besides cross-country skiing, parents or grandparents with children ages 5 to 10 go tubing, sledding, skating, and animal tracking; there are also winter nature studies. When the sun goes down the group gets together around a campfire and explores trails on a night hike.

*Appalachian Mountain Club, Box 366, Longlake, NY 12847, tel. 518/624–2056 for Catskill campus. Feb.: 2 days, $180–$185; 50% discount for children under 10, 10% discount for AMC members. Price does not include nominal day-use fee for Frost Valley.*

## Backroads

14+

Backroads has a six-day cross-country ski vacation in the Canadian Rockies that, like its stellar biking, hiking, and multi-sport tours, is a mix of adventure and pampering, with tough workouts on skis during the day and relaxing stays in elegant country lodges at night. Beyond the luxurious touches, the best thing about the company's ski program is its flexibility. The trip is geared toward beginners and intermediates but can easily accommodate advanced skiers, too. Formal and informal instruction is given daily, and there's a choice of groomed or ungroomed trails and easy or challenging terrain. Some participants ski only 3 or 4 mi a day, while others cover 10 or more—a range that allows families to ski together or apart as they choose. Rental equipment is available.

**FOR FAMILIES.** Although Backroads does not offer families-only periods, teens are always welcome with their parents. Groups generally consist of 18 to 20 guests accompanied by two leaders certified in cross-country instruction. The trip begins and ends in Banff, Alberta, a winter terrain of dense, snow-laden forests and frozen alpine lakes. On the first day the group skis the scenic trails of Lake Louise and settles into the famous Chateau Lake Louise, with its whirlpool spa and exceptional dining. Days two and three you continue to explore the snowy expanses of the area, from peaceful woodland trails to those in the Valley of the Ten Peaks. At night there are swimming and more fine food at the Post Hotel. On the final days of the trip, you take in the pristine pine forests surrounding Emerald Lake on snowshoes or skis, warming up each evening around the stone fireplaces of the turn-of-the-20th-century Emerald Lake Lodge.

Cross-country skiing and snowshoeing are, of course, the focus of this trip, yet other, optional activities draw families into the magnificent winter landscape of Alberta: a sleigh ride, skate skiing, dogsledding, downhill skiing, and ice skating. Because each of the lodges is a world-class destination in its own right, teens will probably find plenty to do and may even find skiing buddies.

All lessons are included in the price of the trip. Van transfers from Calgary Airport and equipment rental are available for an extra charge, and there's an additional fee for some optional activities, including dogsledding and downhill skiing at Lake Louise.

*Backroads, 1516 5th St., Suite L102, Berkeley, CA 94710, tel. 510/527–1555 or 800/462–2848. Feb.–Mar.: 6 days, $1,595; 10% discount for ages 14–16.*

## C Lazy U

3+

This ranch, tucked high in the Colorado Rockies in a valley carved by Willow Creek, has been hosting guests since 1925. Its summer family programs are excellent, but C Lazy U is also a winter wonderland, a paradise for cross-country skiers looking for backcountry adventure in the daytime and serious pampering at night. You can wander over 15 mi of groomed trails and 5,000 acres of unspoiled wilderness (of which the ranch owns 40%). Instructors and guides will help you make the most of your skiing, whether you prefer diagonal style, skating, or telemark. Downhill skiers are not forgotten—the ranch provides shuttle service to nearby Winter Park and Silver Creek.

**FOR FAMILIES.** The ranch's comprehensive children's program is divided into three age groups (3–5, 6–12, and teens) and runs for the two weeks around Christmas and New Year's and over the Presidents' Day weekend. Group sizes vary widely, depending on the number of guests with youngsters. While adults are on the trails, children receive daily ski instruction and participate in other winter activities. Ski games, tubing on the hill, sledding, broomball hockey, and being pulled on an inner tube behind a snowmobile are favorite snow sports, and the ranch offers indoor crafts as well. A skating pond is lighted at night, and the ranch has skates in all sizes.

Families can also head out together to ski the groomed trails or the backcountry. At the ranch's Nordic center, cross-country ski gear (included in the price) comes in many sizes—there are even strap-on skis for very small children.

For horse lovers, C Lazy U has a winter riding program. You can use the 10,000-square-ft indoor arena or wander through the valley and mountains on silent, snowy trails for a riding experience that's unique to the season. The ranch's Belgian draft horses can also take you for a whirl in an old-fashioned sleigh.

*C Lazy U, Box 379, Granby, CO 80446, tel. 970/887–3344. Dec.–Mar.: 2 days (minimum stay), $130–$225 per night per adult; 40% discount for children under 18. Weekly rates during holidays, $1,700 per adult; 20% discount for children under 18.*

## Gunflint Northwoods Outfitters/Gunflint Lodge

ALL

At this four-season resort on Gunflint Lake in northern Minnesota, families can take guided and self-guided ski adventures along more than 60 mi of groomed and tracked trails through Superior National Forest, which borders the Boundary Waters Canoe Area. Trails range from a flat, easy 3-mi loop to longer routes over more challenging terrain.

**FOR FAMILIES.** Families booking the Best of the North package can take advantage of guided ski trips, a day-long dog sled ride, and a one-hour skijoring lesson. (Skijoring, or dog skiing, resembles dogsledding on cross-country skis.) The lodge doesn't have formal ski lessons, but if you need instruction, a staff member will fill you in on the basics. Equipment is available for both adults and children. The Kerfoots, owners of Gunflint Lodge, recommend eight years as a good minimum age for children to be able to accompany parents on the trails, though good skiers often carry babies in backpacks. The four resorts on Gunflint Lake work together, a convenient feature in this area. Families are welcome to stop at any of the four to call for a pickup if the children—or their parents—get too tired to make it back on skis. Out on the trails, three warming huts with radiant propane heaters make convenient rest stops; the heaters are on timers, so you don't even have to remember to turn them off when you leave.

Although the wilderness skiing is superb, not everyone in your family has to be a cross-country skier to enjoy the lodge. You can relax in a sauna or hot tub or accompany your children on a stroll to search for wildlife. Be sure to head to the main lodge every day at 3:30, when the Kerfoots put 50 pounds of corn out in the yard, and dozens of wild deer arrive for an afternoon snack. At night you can bundle the family up and walk out on the lake for some amazing stargazing.

*Gunflint Northwoods Outfitters/Gunflint Lodge, 143 S. Gunflint Lake, Grand Marais, MN 55604, tel. 800/362–5251. Dec.–Mar.: 4–7 days, $636–$954, 50% discount for children 4–12, children under 4 free. The 7th night is free on a week-long stay.*

## Izaak Walton Inn

3+

One of the great cross-country ski inns, Izaak Walton is about 60 mi from Kalispell, just outside Glacier National Park in Montana. Now listed in the National Register of Historic Places, the inn was built in 1939 by the Great Northern Railroad to house snow-removal crews. Memorabilia and authentic furnishings carry you back to the romantic era of early train travel, and four renovated cabooses have been converted into guest quarters. Amtrak still stops practically at the door.

**FOR FAMILIES.** The inn has long been recognized for its superb lessons and tours for adults and experienced skiers, but its innovative children's program is equally deserving of recognition. Games and fun activities help build skills and get children used to the winter outdoors. Depending on how many children are present, lessons may be on an individual or group basis. The inn has trails and areas for young children just learning to ski and rents equipment for ages three or four and up (depending on the child's size); snowshoes are also available.

Package trips are the best way to go here. Families staying on the inn's five- or seven-day plan are entitled to a guided ski tour of Glacier National Park. This all-day tour is best for teens and adults, but groups that include younger children can take half-day tours over Glacier's easier trails. Kick sledding, another activity for families, uses Scandinavian sleds that work something like those used for mushing—but with no dogs. You balance on the runner with one foot and push with the other; since the action is similar to skiing, it's an easy way to get a feel for the sport while having fun.

*Izaak Walton Inn, Box 653, Essex, MT 59916, tel. 406/888–5700. Nov.–Mar.: 3–7 days, $265–$755 per person for family of 3; children's rates on 5- and 7-day packages only.*

## L.L. Bean

6+

L.L. Bean, the famous outdoor and catalog store in Freeport, Maine, has long stocked winter gear and clothing for families, so it's not surprising that its education department—well known for canoeing and fly-fishing courses—also provides instruction in cross-country skiing and snowshoeing.

**FOR FAMILIES.** Families can choose the parent-and-child courses or Bean's traditional beginner courses. The parent-and-child courses, for parents with kids between the ages of 6 and 13, puts most of the emphasis on fun. Through games like pizza tag, hand soccer, and dodge ball, families learn the basics of gliding, turning, and stopping. L.L. Bean's beginner courses, which ages eight and older can take with parents, have a stronger focus on technique. Lessons are conducted on groomed terrain—often on a golf course in Freeport that has groomed tracks—with a mix of easy, moderate, and challenging trails. You'll be taught both diagonal skiing and skating techniques. Instructors stress learning how to get your balance, sliding, and feeling confident on skis; they also discuss proper clothing and ways to stay warm while skiing. You must arrange your own lodging, but the school will supply a list of local accommodations. These courses are just 1½ hours long, but instructors may take an additional 15 minutes at the end of class to answer students' questions about specific problems. For intermediate and advanced skiers, there are Level II and Level III courses, which are each about two hours long. Courses are scheduled most Saturdays throughout the ski season. Although equipment isn't provided, you can rent or buy it at the L.L. Bean store.

Bean also has some overnight programs, including a wilderness winter getaway over a February weekend for skiers with some experience. Adults and children at least 10 years old stay in heated log cabins at a traditional Maine sporting camp, skiing or snowshoeing with guides on trails through the deep woods surrounding Spencer Lake during the day. Meals, lodging, and transportation from Freeport to and from the cabins is included in the price.

*L.L. Bean, Freeport, ME 04033, tel. 888/552–3261. Jan.–Feb.: 1½ hours– 2 days, $30 per parent/child pair, $10 each additional family member in parent-and-child courses, $20–$25 per person for regular courses; $325 per person for 2-day program.*

## Lone Mountain Ranch

3+

Lone Mountain is a year-round family guest ranch near Montana's Gallatin Canyon, down the road from Big Sky Resort and a short drive from the northernmost border of Yellowstone National Park. The ranch's renowned naturalists don't stop working in winter; instead, they lead cross-country ski tours, including treks into the Spanish Peaks region and Yellowstone's backcountry, that meld excellent skiing with education about the winter environment and the area's natural history. And lunch on the trail is an impressive gourmet affair. The 23 roomy one- and two-bedroom log cabins at the ranch have rock fireplaces or Franklin stoves in addition to electric heat; the outdoor hot tub is popular with all ages; and no one skips the fantastic meals in the tremendous log-and-stone dining lodge.

**FOR FAMILIES.** There's no formal children's program at Lone Mountain during the winter, but children are always welcome. Group lessons are an option if enough youngsters are at the ranch; otherwise, individual instruction can be arranged. Rental equipment fits ages three and older. Lone Mountain has nearly 50 mi of tracked and groomed trails that wind through meadows, up along ridges, down into mountain valleys, and through portions of the Gallatin National Forest. Miles of ungroomed trails give you access to exceptional backcountry skiing.

A particular favorite with families is the groomed Ranch Loop, a 3½-mi trail across rolling terrain that takes you through aspen groves and open meadows. Ermines, moose, coyotes, and a variety of winter birds may be seen along the trail. Because the trail goes into wilderness areas but also passes near ranch buildings, you feel both miles away and close to home, which can be comforting for children and beginners.

Among the backcountry tours with naturalists (all at an extra charge), Spanish Peaks is appropriate for teens and adults with skiing experience. Yellowstone is less technical, and older children with good skiing skills are welcome on the shorter (four- to five-hour) tour over moderate terrain. Before joining a tour, every guest must take one lesson or be otherwise evaluated by the staff.

Families also have the option to snowshoe, go sledding, or head for the downhill slopes at Big Sky, 7 mi away. Horse-drawn sleighs can carry guests to a lantern-lighted log cabin for dinner.

*Lone Mountain Ranch, Box 160069, Big Sky, MT 59716, tel. 800/514–4644. Dec.–Apr.: 7 days, $1,105–$2,360 adults, $740 children 2–12. Price does not include rentals and lessons.*

## Off the Beaten Path

12+

Although Pam and Bill Bryan of Off the Beaten Path are known primarily for their customized summer vacations in the Rockies, Southwest, and Alaska, their organization also offers a variety of winter escapes, including cross-country ski adventures. Yellowstone on Skis, Tetons/Absarokas Adventure, Canadian Rockies in Winter, and Colorado Ski Ranches are four of the company's popular ski excursions. Typical of the accommodations from which you can choose are the historic Mammoth Hot Springs Hotel, in Yellowstone; Brooks Lake Lodge, near Jackson, Wyoming; Canada's Banff Springs Hotel; and Vista Verde Ranch (see Horse Packing), 25 mi from Steamboat Springs, Colorado.

**FOR FAMILIES.** Although the scheduled cross-country ski trips are not geared toward children, the company works with many families on a custom basis, so you can adapt one of the trips with regard to timing, destination, and the amount and level of activity. Custom trips are definitely pricey, but every detail—accommodations, food, guide services, and daily skiing—is taken care of. Your guide can take you on a variety of trails, from groomed to pure untracked backcountry powder, and instruct you on skiing techniques. You'll also learn about the diverse ecosystems through which you venture.

Access to Yellowstone is limited, so you must book a custom trip there at least nine months in advance. The other destinations are more flexible—even last-minute arrangements may be possible. The com-

pany can also arrange all travel and ski rentals (at an extra charge) if you wish.
*Off the Beaten Path, 27 E. Main St., Bozeman, MT 59715, tel. 406/586–1311 or 800/445–2995. Dec.–Mar.: 6–8 days, $2,000 and up; custom nonguided trips available for less.*

## Telemark Inn

ALL

A range of adjectives fits the turn-of-the-20th-century Telemark Inn, 10 mi from Bethel in southwestern Maine: Rustic, elegant, intimate, remote, and historic all accurately describe the wood-paneled retreat, which has hand-built cabinetry and a huge stone fireplace. Well known for its llama treks in summer (*see* Trekking with Llamas and Burros), the inn becomes a winter mecca for families that like to cross-country ski. Six rooms sleep two to four guests each, and everybody likes the wood-fired sauna. Many lodging packages are available, some with breakfast only, some with three meals. You can also get hearty home-cooked meals packed for the trail.

**FOR FAMILIES.** Fourteen miles of groomed trails surround the inn; most are wide and tracked for both traditional diagonal skiing and the more difficult skating style. Families with ski experience may want to head into the maintained trails beyond the inn, which are part of the backcountry system of the White Mountain National Forest. At night there's skating on a pond lighted by kerosene lanterns and gatherings in the lighted tepee out on the meadow. Parents can choose a romantic ride in a horse-drawn sleigh built for two or a family outing in the six-seater.

Instruction in both traditional skiing and telemark is available for an extra charge. Families have the option to rent equipment even for very young children; you should request it when you make your reservation. Parents can strap on a pulk—a ski sled that can be used to pull toddlers—if their stamina and skiing ability allow. Small children learn to ski by holding on to a nylon rope with a handle (like those used for waterskiing) while being pulled by parents or instructors; this gives them the feel of ski movements.

Families that want to try something really cool should ask about skijoring, a sport that originated in Norway. Skijoring, also known as dog skiing, resembles dogsledding on cross-country skis. A dog (or dogs) pulls you, using a specially designed nylon rope and harness. There's no minimum age—six- and seven-year-olds have skijored successfully at Telemark—but you do need to be at least an intermediate Nordic skier and have a good rapport with animals. Young skiers can practice on the close-in flat areas; more experienced skiers can tackle the extensive trail system. Telemark Inn has 28 dogs trained in skijoring, and guests are welcome to bring their family dog (which should weigh at least 35 pounds) to learn the sport; however, families considering this should be serious about the sport, check first with the inn, and be aware that dogs stay in a kennel, not inn rooms. If you're on a Sunday–Friday five-day ski package, skijoring is included.

The inn is beginning a program for handicapped skiers, so ask about it if someone in your family is physically challenged.
*Telemark Inn, RFD 2, Box 800, Bethel, ME 04217, tel. 207/836–2703. Dec.–Mar.: 2–5 days, $220–$550 adults, $150–$375 children under 15. Weekends and holidays, $120 per day per adult, $85 for children, which includes lodging, meals, and activities.*

## Wells Gray Chalets & Wilderness Adventures

12+

Of the three chalets owned and operated by this group, only Fight Meadow Chalet is really suitable for family cross-country skiing. If you're up to the challenge of a helicopter flight to get there and several days of skiing in wilderness areas inaccessible to the less adventurous, this Canadian company, based eight hours from Seattle, Edmonton, and Calgary, will provide a memorable guided experience for your family. Once you have plenty of experience and knowledge of backcountry safety and survival skills, you can book the chalets on your own, including the two that require heavy ski-touring and ski-mountaineering equipment.

**FOR FAMILIES.** The guides don't give lessons in cross-country skiing, but they do educate families on wilderness travel, ski mountaineering, and avalanche safety. Fight Meadow Chalet is surrounded by a large alpine meadow system that is ideal for novice skiers in spite of its remoteness. More advanced slopes are also easily accessible, so there's something for everyone. Families take a helicopter in; the inbound flight is part of the trip cost. Unless they're up for a four- to eight-hour trek (depending on skiing ability), most are also flown out (an extra C$110). The road out is the only marked trail; the rest of your skiing is on unmarked, ungroomed, untracked backcountry snow. Scheduled trips to the chalet are limited, but groups of 6 to 12 can arrange their own trip on the dates of their choice.

*Wells Gray Chalets & Wilderness Adventures, Box 188, Clearwater, British Columbia, Canada V0E 1N0, tel. 250/587–6444 or 888–SKITREK. Dec.–Apr.: 5 days, C$770; 25% discount for children under 13.*

# Resources

## Books

*The Hut Handbook*, by Leigh Girvin Yule and Scott Toepfer (Westcliffe Publishers, tel. 303/935–0900), is an excellent guide for any family considering a backcountry hut experience. Whether you ski or snowshoe in, stay for a night or longer, there's much good information here, including a chapter just for parents and children.

## Organizations

The **Cross Country Ski Area Association** (259 Bolton Rd., Winchester, NH 03470, tel. 603/239–4341) has information on the importance of lessons, how to dress properly, how to get started in the sport, and great places to do it.

## Periodicals

*The Best of Cross Country Skiing* is a directory of more than 200 member areas, primarily in North America, published by the Cross Country Ski Area Association (*see above*). Listings have general and technical information, as well as notes on things of special interest to families, such as whether the area has equipment rentals for children, day care, programs for youngsters, and specially tracked trails for children or other child-oriented trails. You must mail in for the directory; the cost is $3. *Cross-Country Skier* (Box 83666, Stillwater, MN 55083, tel. 800/827–0607), published October–February, is an excellent publication for beginning skiers and those interested in the latest gear, cross-country getaways, or even racing. Among the many articles of interest to parents are some on children's gear and cross-country ski vacations for families.

## Also See

For more winter adventures check out Dogsledding. Many of the adventures also include some cross-country skiing.

# DIGGING FOR DINOSAUR BONES AND OTHER FOSSILS

Dinosaurs may be extinct in the real world, but they're alive and well in the hearts and minds of children everywhere. Long before that purple phenomenon, Barney, dinosaurs were a formidable presence in children's books, games, TV shows, movies, and imaginations. Ask your average five-year-old how to pronounce *hadrosaur,* and she'll tell you without stumbling over a syllable. When my own daughter, Kira, was five, she would quiz her father and me about dinosaurs endlessly, but we never reached her level of expertise. If Dinamation International Society's Family Dino Camp had existed then, I would have taken her in a flash.

Today families can choose among places all over the world where they can dig for bones and help in paleontology labs. Most of these digs are dinosaur related; however, whale fossils, mammoth and saber-toothed tiger bones, as well as plant fossils, are found at working digs, and you or someone in your family might be the first to uncover them for all the world to see.

Paleontology is mostly painstaking, slow, hot, and tedious work. Consider in advance whether your child has a real interest in and the personality to enjoy this type of multi-day vacation. Even Dino Camp, which offers a variety of child-friendly activities, is best for youngsters who already appreciate the subject. Of course, some children do discover a love of paleontology once they get involved, but it could just as easily turn out the other way. Teens and parents as well should fully discuss the itinerary, accommodations, hours, and location of a particular trip before committing. These experiences are definitely work. They're also great fun—if you're into it—and always an incredible learning experience. Because multi-day digs can be too much for some families, I've included one-day dig opportunities as well. These can also be a good way of trying out the experience before signing up for a longer trip. Whichever type of adventure you choose, you just might find that at the end of the trip, you'll be able to match your offspring's knowledge, if not their all-embracing love, of these prehistoric wonders.

## Questions to Ask

**Is it possible to talk directly to the expedition coordinator or leader?** In many cases this is a prerequisite. The trip leader wants to make sure that you are right for the trip and that you're aware of what the expedition entails. For parents it's especially important to discuss a child's ability, experience, and interest with someone who's been out in the field.

**What are the typical conditions?** Some work sites are extremely primitive; others are in towns with modern conveniences and amenities. You might be in the desert or by the ocean. Knowing the conditions can help you find the expedition that meets your family's needs.

**What accommodations are available?** Tents, dorms, hotel rooms, condos, government or university housing—all these are possibilities. What can your family handle? How well will you fit into community housing? This is an important consideration for any trip.

**Has an expedition uncovered an important fossil lately?** Dreams of a big find are part of the draw for this kind of vacation. Ask in advance how many bones or fossils have been uncovered at that particular site and how many have been uncovered by trip participants like you. Neither you nor your children should have unreasonable expectations, but dreams are definitely in order.

**Is there lab work or other work related to digging?** You might have a chance to assist in a real paleontology lab; you might be asked to record, sketch, or keep notes out in the field; or analyzing soil samples or amber could be part of your duties. Paleontology encompasses a variety of skills.

**What kind of clothing is appropriate?** Much digging work is hot and dirty. You may also hike long distances, and digs may or may not provide shade or shelter from the elements. Even in the desert the best clothing may be long-sleeve cotton shirts and long pants. Boots are probably preferable to sandals on many sites, and hats can be an important accessory. Review clothing lists carefully, paying particular attention to sun protection.

**Will my child and I spend all our time together?** Usually this is the case, but at places such as Dinamation International Society's Dino Camp, you do not.

**Are other activities available?** Is there anywhere to swim? Does the schedule allow time to hike or bike or eat out or shop? Does the area have museums or other local points of interest? Some trips provide opportunities for such activities; other digs, particularly those in remote areas, are strictly geared toward accomplishing work. If this matters to you, choose accordingly.

**What does the expedition cost include?** Accommodations, food during the trip (participants often help with cooking), and local transportation are included, unless otherwise noted. Transportation to and/or from the expedition site is usually extra. Expeditioners who will be camping out will probably need to bring their own sleeping bags and, perhaps, tents. Because accommodations vary greatly, be sure to find out what you're paying for. Day dig fees generally include lunch and sometimes snacks.

## Instruction

It's assumed that most people do not know a great deal about the intricacies of digging for fossils, so lectures, talks, and hands-on lessons are very much part of the fun on this type of adventure. Reading lists of books and other materials about paleontology are often part of the pretrip information for expeditions. Any advance reading you do will definitely enhance your family's experience.

## Finding the Fun

**Midwest:** Earthwatch Institute. **Southwest:** Dinamation International Society. **Rockies:** Dinamation International Society, The Mammoth Site, The Wyoming Dinosaur Center. **Canada:** Royal Tyrrell Museum. **Mexico:** Dinamation International Society, Earthwatch Institute.

# Favorite Expeditions

## Dinamation International Society

6+

Dinamation International Society (DIS) is a nonprofit organization that promotes education, research, and preservation in the biological, earth, and physical sciences, with a special emphasis on dinosaur paleontology. If the name Dinamation sounds familiar, that's because another branch of the outfit manufactures the robotic dinosaurs that DIS has toured at various museums. DIS works with universities, museums, and public land management agencies on projects including the identification and protection of important fossil sites. One of the society's main contributions to research and education, however, is the Dinosaur Discovery Expeditions program, which helps fund research work and creates ongoing public awareness of important work in paleontology.

**FOR FAMILIES.** Family Dino Camp, for ages six and up, is probably the best known of DIS's expeditions. The camp, based in Fruita and Grand Junction, Colorado, mixes learning fun and games, serious digging, lab work, and hikes. Children don't actually dig at the Mygatt-Moore Quarry, where loads of fossils have been found, but parents do. Young Dino Campers excavate fossil replicas, do simulated lab work, and hike the Trail through Time to see fossils embedded in area rocks. They join parents for a variety of dino-related activities, from studying plant fossils to solving a dinosaur murder mystery. The camp runs in the summer only, and accommodations are at local motels. A few, but not all, meals are included.

One recent major discovery at the Mygatt-Moore Quarry was an egg—the only egg of an armored dinosaur (a nodosaur, to be exact) ever found. It was uncovered not by a renowned paleontologist but by a 14-year-old girl on a DIS expedition. She was participating in the five-day Colorado Canyons Expedition, which runs in summer and is open to ages 13 and up. You or someone in your family just might be lucky enough to discover another fossil that will make its way into paleontological history.

Ages 16 and up can choose among expeditions with digs in Colorado, Utah, Wyoming, and Arizona. A trip in Mexico, once open only to those over 17, is now available for families with younger children on a case-by-case basis. Jonathan Cooley, DIS's director of expeditions, has an excellent sense of how children and teens will do on a particular trip. Talk to DIS if you have a dino-maniac. They'll find you a dig that will both satisfy those prehistoric obsessions and open the door to the world of scientific research. Accommodations for these adventures range from camping to first-class hotels. *Dinosaur Discovery Expeditions, Dinamation International Society, 550 Jurassic Ct., Fruita, CO 81521, tel. 800/344–3466. Year-round (all trips not available at all times): 5–8 days, $925–$5,895 adults, $625 children 12 and under.*

## Earthwatch Institute

16+

Earthwatch helps fund several fossil-finding programs, in addition to dozens of other types of scientific projects around the world. As part of that funding, Earthwatch arranges for adventurous participants to join scientists on site and work as assistants. Your fee partially defrays the cost of running the project. As scientists find it increasingly difficult to get funding from more traditional sources such as the government and universities, organizations such as Earthwatch become even more valuable.

**FOR FAMILIES.** In light of increased evidence of global warming and changes in the level of the world's oceans, it is all the more important to learn about the effects of protracted climate change on habitats and animals. In Tecolatlan, Mexico, a rugged volcanic landscape of the Sierra Madre, and Guanajuato, east of the Sierra Madre range, two paleontologists have been studying an animal migration that occurred when the sea fell, opening up a land bridge between South and North America. Doctors Oscar Carranza Castaneda and Wade Miller have 56 years of field experience between them. You can join their team, surveying the desert hills for fossils, chiseling out bones, gluing found fragments, and screen-washing sediment for teeth, seeds, and bones that are the keys to past environments. What makes this area so important is a mass migration north and south that began 3.5 million years ago. Camels, giant ground sloths, mastodons, glyptodonts Volkswagen-size armadillos), early horses, and carnivores, including the infamous saber-toothed cats, traveled through the isthmus of Central America, leaving an amazingly rich fossil record of their journey. Since 1990, Earthwatch teams have collected some 5,000 specimens at these sites, including the most complete fossil horse ever found in Mexico. Volunteers share rooms in hotels at both destinations; the Parador del Cortijo Hotel in San Miguel de Allende, the base for the Guanajuato digs, even has a pool.

Closer to home is an Earthwatch dig in Hot Springs, South Dakota, a site famous for mammoth remains. Here, in the southwest corner of the state, locals are justifiably proud of the relics of these woolly creatures. They've raised money to fund continued research and helped build a complex over the site that shades workers from the sun and allows tourists to watch the digging. Expedition participants stay in local homes and can expect a warm welcome from Hot Springs residents. *See also* The Mammoth Site, *below.*

Scientists ask Earthwatch for funding throughout the year, so sites do change. Ask for the latest information when you call. *Earthwatch Institute, 680 Mt. Auburn St., Box 9104, Watertown, MA 02471-9104, tel. 617/926–8200 or 800/776–0188. Year round (not all digs at all times): 13–15 days, $1,495–$1,695.*

## The Mammoth Site

7+

In 1999 The Mammoth Site celebrated the 25th anniversary of its discovery during excavation for a housing project. Happily, the housing project was forgotten when the first mammoth bones and tooth were inadvertently unearthed, and The Mammoth Site in Hot Springs, South Dakota, became one of the nation's most important paleontological digs and one of the world's largest exhibitions of excavated Ice Age mammal remains in situ. While only day digs are offered here, Hot Springs is the southern gateway to the Black Hills, an area where family adventures and learning experiences of all kinds abound (*see* Covered Wagon Adventures, Rock Climbing, *and* RV Adventures).

**FOR FAMILIES.** A visitor center covers the sinkhole where mammoths were trapped and died 26,000 years ago. Because it's covered, the site is open year-round and in poor weather. Walkways allow you a close-up view of scientists and volunteers working at the site (including Earthwatch volunteers here in June and July, *see above*), making it a particularly child-friendly excavation. Parents and children of all ages can watch paleontologists and marvel at the huge size of 'Sinbad,' a life-size replica of a Columbian mammoth, or check out the area where 'Napoleon Bone-A-Part,' the most completely articulated skeleton uncovered here, was found lying on his back. While going from the parking lot to the main building you'll get a 'sidewalk geology' lesson, which outlines the geologic formation of the Black Hills area. There's also a touch-screen exhibit in the visitor center explaining the geology of the Black Hills, the Ice Age, and plate tectonics. There are informative guided tours of the site leaving every 15 minutes during the summer up until 45 minutes before closing time, which is 8 in the evening from mid-May through most of August. (These tours are given less frequently off-season and not at all between November and February.)

Each summer the site runs a Junior Paleontologist Excavation program. Interested children from age 7 to 15 can practice excavation techniques using real tools, learn to identify fiberglass replicas of mammoth bones, take field notes, and map areas. The program runs every afternoon at 3.
*The Mammoth Site, Box 692, 1800 Hwy. 18 Truck Rte., Hot Springs, South Dakota, tel. 605/745–6017, 800/325–6991 for lodging and general information on the Hot Springs area. Museum: daily year-round $5.13–$5.40 adults, $3.51 children 6–12, free children 5 and under. Junior Paleontologist Excavation program: mid-June–mid-Aug. daily, $6.48.*

## Royal Tyrrell Museum

7+

Alberta's Royal Tyrrell Museum, the first Canadian institution devoted entirely to paleontology, is in Drumheller, about 90 mi northeast of Calgary and 180 mi south of Edmonton. The museum is named for Joseph Burr Tyrrell, who found the first dinosaur skeleton in the Drumheller area in 1884. It's an area rich in fossils, which is reflected in the museum's expansive collection of more than 200 dinosaur fossils, most of which were found in the Drumheller vicinity and in Dinosaur Provincial Park, 120 mi to the southeast. The museum is worth a visit on its own—the dinosaur specimen collection is the largest under one roof anywhere—but it also has family and children's dig programs that vividly bring to life the era of the dinosaur and the work of paleontology.

**FOR FAMILIES.** Day Digs are for adults and for children ages 10 and older accompanied by parents. Available weekends in June, daily in July and August, the one-day digs give families the opportunity to work with museum staff excavating real bones and recording scientific data at a site in the Red

Deer River Valley, only minutes from the museum. Advance reservations are required. The day starts at 8:30 with a behind-the-scenes tour of the museum's fossil collection. After a 15-minute van ride and an easy 10-minute hike to the site, participants (limited to just 12) work digging most of the day. You're back at the museum by about 4, and as the dig fee includes museum admission, you'll probably want to spend the remaining hours of the afternoon exploring the museum and viewing the many fossils that were mapped and collected just as you did it on your dig.

Children too young for Day Digs or who would rather spend time with peers can opt for Vacation Day Camps, designed for ages 7 through 12. The camps, which run in the afternoon from about 1 to 4:30, offer a mix of activities. Campers hike in the surrounding badlands, dig in the fossil beds, create a cast of a fossil to take home, and play a dinosaur survival game (apparently the dinos who met their demise in this area 65 million years ago were unaware of how to play). Families can get back together at day's end to see the museum or to explore Drumheller. For family members of all ages who'd rather not dig, there's the two-hour Dig Watch—a guided tour of the quarry, with lots of information about the dinosaurs who lived in Alberta and a chance to talk to the museum's working paleontologists.

Summer in Alberta's badlands can be hot (typically 86°F–100°F), but with clouds and wind the area can be cool, too. So be prepared for a range of temperatures. As for lodging, Drumheller has everything from campsites and hostels to hotels and bed-and-breakfasts. And when you've seen all the dinosaurs Drumheller has to offer, head to Dinosaur Provincial Park for more.

*Royal Tyrrell Museum, Box 7500, Drumheller, Alberta, Canada T0J 0Y0, tel. 403/823–7707 or 888/440–4240, 403/823–8100 for lodging and general area information. May–Aug.: Day Dig, C$85 adults, C$55 children 10–15; Vacation Day Camp, C$22 children 7–12; Dig Watch, C$30 for a family of 4. The museum is open year-round.*

## Wyoming Dinosaur Center

**ALL**

The Wyoming Dinosaur Center dig site in Thermopolis has unearthed one of the largest dinosaur finds in recent history. What makes it particularly unusual is the number of species uncovered in this one area. For instance, they discovered one of the most complete camarasaur skeletons ever found, along with the remains of apatosaurs, allosaurs, stegosaurs, diplodocus, and others. Lots of human types come to Thermopolis, too: some to see the mineral hot springs and surrounding park, some to enjoy the Wyoming Dinosaur Center's excellent museum, some to participate in real paleontology work—and some come for it all!

**FOR FAMILIES.** There's no minimum age for Dig-for-a-Day, where families work beside paleo-technicians. It's demanding work, though, and children and adults should be prepared both physically and mentally. This is not a re-created site but one in which scientists are still making important discoveries. Typically diggers are on site from about 8:30 to 4; however, buses come and go throughout the day, so it's possible to leave earlier if someone in your group is unable to work that long.

If you want to split up for part of your stay, there are several options. Kids' Dig is for children from 8 to 12, while Teens' Dig is for those from 13 to 15. While these younger groups are involved in activities of their own, parents and older teens can try Dig-for-a-Day. Kids' Dig is typically offered once each month in summer. The two-day program includes digging for bones at the working site, taking dino art classes, going on geology walks in Hot Springs State Park, and learning answers to such questions as "How many Big Macs could a T. rex eat?" (The answer, in case you can't wait, is several thousand, assuming the meat-loving rexes spit out buns and lettuce.) Teens' Dig runs once in July, once in August. It's a 1½-day program giving teens a chance to dig for dinosaurs, prepare bones in the lab, and cast dinosaur bones. Families get back together at about 4.

Nondiggers can explore the center's excellent museum, with its life-size dino skeletons and other displays and dioramas. The museum has a prep lab, too, where visitors can watch paleo-technicians working on bones found at the dig site. Family members who don't want to dig but do want to see where the bones are can take a bus from the center for a site tour. There's a combination ticket that includes the museum and dig site tour. At day's end families can regroup and head to the park to soak their own bones in the hot springs.

For multi-day trips, families make their own lodging arrangements in town at one of the many motels, hotels, bed and breakfasts, campgrounds, or RV parks.

*The Wyoming Dinosaur Center, Box 868, Thermopolis, WY 82443, tel. 307/864–2997 or 800/455–3466; 307/864–3192 for general Thermopolis information. Year-round (weather-permitting for digs): Dig-for-a-Day, $250 per day for a family of 4; discounts for multi-day digs; Kids' and Teens' Digs, $50; museum and site tour ticket combination, $36 for a family of 4.*

# Resources

## Books

Many children's book publishers have dinosaur books, but Dorling Kindersley offers one-stop shopping for dinosaur lovers. Titles for younger children include *The Big Book of Dinosaurs* and the *Ultimate Dinosaur Sticker Book*. Older children and adults can check out *Dinosaurs and How They Lived, Prehistoric Life, The Ultimate Dinosaur Book, The Visual Dictionary of Dinosaurs,* and *The Visual Dictionary of Prehistoric Life*. *Dinosaurs,* a title in the Reader's Digest Pathfinder series, includes an excellent section on how fossils are found, cleaned, preserved, and how scientists reconstruct dinosaur skeletons. There's also information on Dinosaur Provincial Park and the Royal Tyrrell Museum.

*Dinosaur Safari Guide,* by Vincenzo Costa (Voyageur Press, tel. 651/430–2210 or 800/888–9653), lists more than 160 dinosaur quarries, museums, parks, and trails throughout the United States and Canada. Costa also provides an excellent pronunciation guide and solid introductory material about dinosaurs, as well as a discussion of current extinction theories. The book is now out of print, but you could get it through an online bookseller, in some stores, and in libraries.

## Products

Coop's Maps (Lone Mountain Designs, tel. 800/259–3139) publishes a series of four regional map guides to North American dinosaur sites and museums. They can be found in bookstores.

## Also See

If digging is what you love to do, look into family camps at ancient Native American ruins and other types of digs described in Archaeology Adventures.

# DOGSLEDDING

Dogsledding may well be on the farthest edge of "soft" adventure. This is not a sport for timid spirits; it's not for the adventurer who wants excitement but who doesn't want to push his or her limits. Working with the dogs is physically demanding and involves spending a lot of time in the cold—bone-chilling cold. Temperatures as low as -40°F are common, and if you are miles out in the wilderness, you can't suddenly change your mind about the trip. You must be prepared, and you must really want to go. That goes for your children, too. They need to be ready for cold, hard work, including caring for the dogs, and real wilderness.

But if the thrill and romance of dogsledding appeal to your family, you'll find it to be one of the all-time great adventures. Dogs run at a fairly fast pace—it's not uncommon to travel between 30 and 40 mi a day—so you can cover a good amount of wintry territory. By the end of your trip you'll feel a closeness to your dogs, to your guides (some of whom may be natives whose people have traveled this way for generations), and to the raw and wild land through which you'll dash. Ask anyone who's ever done it—they'll tell you the experience changed them and that they are the better for it.

## Questions to Ask

**Will we mush our own sled and dogs?** Some trips give every participant a sled to work; on other trips you share sleds with a family or staff member and spend time snowshoeing and cross-country skiing in addition to mushing (as traveling by dogsled is called). Decide what activity your family wants most and go with the outfitter that provides it.

**How many miles are covered each day?** Typically, anywhere from 15 to 35 mi traveled over a four- to eight-hour period make up a day of mushing, though there are variations. Ask before you sign up, and consider how strenuous the itinerary is and how strong your family's abilities are before making a final decision.

**What is the temperature going to be on the trip?** The temperature in northern Canada will likely be well below zero in March but a relatively balmy 15°F–20°F in May. If you have a 12-year-old, you might choose the warmer May trip. A cold child is definitely a miserable child, and if your children are unhappy, in truth, you will be, too.

**What outerwear or gear is provided?** Some outfitters supply nothing; others offer traditional caribou clothing, parkas, special boots, and gloves, in addition to sleeping bags and tents. Check and recheck the clothing lists outfitters send you and ask questions about gear. If you're depending on the outfitter to provide severe-weather outer clothing, make sure it's available in your child's size as well as yours. If you bring your own, do not skimp and do not deviate from the outfitter's suggestions. The winter wilderness is a deadly place without proper clothing and equipment.

**How much camp and dog work is expected?** On some trips clients and guides work equally, setting up camp, harnessing and unharnessing the dogs, feeding and caring for the dogs, and helping prepare meals. Other outfitters offer a more catered experience. If you are real doers, go with an outfitter that will depend on you to be a working member of the expedition.

**How long have you been running dogs in this area?** Knowledgeable guides are especially important when you're dealing with severe conditions and extreme temperatures. You want a company with several years' experience not only in the area but also with the particular itinerary. Before you plunk down a considerable chunk of change, you want to be sure that all possible kinks have been worked out. You're also looking for a crew that will know how to deal with emergencies small and large quickly and in a professional way.

**What kind of accommodations and meals are available?** Cabins, tents, igloos, and even hotel rooms are possibilities. Winter camping can be surprisingly cozy and comfortable, but if it's not for you, or if you have younger children who might not be up to this challenge, choose an outfitter with more permanent lodging. As for meals, some outfitters offer a selection, and much of the food is incredibly good. Even if it isn't, it tastes great in the frozen wilderness. Food is fuel out in the cold, so most meals are the real stick-to-your-ribs type: stews, chili, spaghetti, and lasagna, and snacks such as gorp and brownies. Alcohol is generally not part of the menu.

**What's included in the cost of the trip?** Most dogsledding adventures start and end in remote wilderness areas, so you'll probably pay extra for transportation there. In addition, because of the location and limited transportation, you may have to overnight at your own expense before and/or after a trip. The per-person prices for all trips listed here include lodging or camping, meals, guides, instruction, sleds, and dogs, unless otherwise noted. You may be lent some expedition clothing and supplies; however, you will have to buy, borrow, or rent quality cold-weather gear of your own, including, in some cases, sleeping bags. Local transportation or pickup at airports might be available at no cost or for a nominal fee, so ask.

## Instruction

The time spent on instruction depends in part on how involved you are in driving and caring for the dogs; much of it will take place during the trip. But no matter how many times you watched *Sergeant Preston of the Yukon* as a child, your family will need instruction in driving a sled. Good dog teams are valuable, and no musher will turn his or her team over to someone who can't drive a sled properly. Moreover, dogsledding can be dangerous; by listening to your guide and learning the proper commands, safety procedures, and techniques, you ensure your family's safety as well as that of the dogs and anyone else on the trail.

### Finding the Fun

**Northeast:** Adventure Guides of Vermont. **Midwest:** Boundary Country Trekking, Gunflint Northwoods Outfitters/Gunflint Lodge, Outward Bound, Trek & Trail, Wilderness Inquiry. **Rockies:** Telluride Outside. **Alaska:** American Wilderness Experience/GORP Travel. **Canada:** Arctic Odysseys, Boundary Country Trekking, Kanata Wilderness Adventures/Wells Gray Ranch.

## Favorite Outfitters

### Adventure Guides of Vermont

8+

Adventure Guides of Vermont (AGVT) is the customer service branch of the Vermont Outdoor Guide Association, a professional guide association and adventure travel network. Its members offer more than 70 outdoor activities throughout Vermont and New England, many with family programs. Although Vermont has no guidelines or standards for outfitters, Adventure Guides requires that its members meet any existing national standards for each specialty and that all guides be certified in CPR, first aid, and wilderness first aid. Among AGVT's members are two dogsledding guides, both perfect for families. Ed Blechner, who owns and operates Konari Outfitters, is a former teacher who still visits schools in the Northeast and educates children about winter outdoor skills and about dogs and dogsledding. He loves to work with families and knows just how to present the necessary information. Lisy Dyre, owner of Round About Dogsledding, was trained by Ed and offers the same type of trip and atmosphere.

Most of the trips are either in central Vermont—in and around Goshen and the Green Mountain National Forest—or around Lake Champlain. Goshen, once called Moosalamoo (meaning "Moose here") by the native population, doesn't have all that many moose these days, but it has rolling hills, forests, and historic Native American sites and trails. Snowmobiles like the area, too, and they pack down the trails perfectly for the sleds. You may run into some snowmobilers, and you'll certainly see cross-country skiers. Still, winter travel in Vermont forests is light in comparison to summer months. Lake Champlain stretches 120 mi and touches Vermont, New York, and Canada. Two-thirds of it lies in northwestern Vermont, and you can travel with your dogs around these shores if the snow is right.

**FOR FAMILIES.** Ed and Lisy will take children as young as eight only if they can ski moderately well. There's no riding on these trips, which range from single-day to five-day outings. You either mush (all members of the group take turns) or cross-country ski. Occasionally there's snowshoeing, too. That doesn't mean you have to be an expert, however. The guides take one family out at a time, and the trip is organized at the pace you can handle. February has the best conditions for dogsledding in either area. Don't forget to ask about skijoring, which amounts to being pulled on skis by a single dog. You might fall a lot, but the youngsters will love it. Outfitters supply tents on overnights; bring your own sleeping bags or ask Adventure Guides about renting locally.

*Adventure Guides of Vermont, Box 3, North Ferrisburgh, VT 05473, tel. 802/425–6211 or 800/425–8747. Dec.–Mar.: 1–5 days, $150–$565 per person for a family of 3 or more.*

## American Wilderness Experience/GORP Travel

12+

You can experience the power and majesty of the Brooks Range as generations of Alaskan natives have—on a traditional mushing sled, with only the sounds of your dog team racing and the swoosh of the runners over pure north-country snow. Yet dogsledding through the Arctic wilderness requires no previous experience; you need only a sense of adventure and good physical condition because you'll be traveling between 15 and 30 mi in four to eight hours each day. Depending on the trip, accommodations are in lodge rooms, tents, or communal cabins, and everyone helps with chores.

American Wilderness Experience/GORP Travel, which contracts with top outfitters, puts you in the capable hands of the Mackey family, well known in the dogsledding world since several family members have won the Yukon Quest or the Iditarod, the 1,049-mi race from Anchorage to Nome in which exhaustion and rampaging moose are just two of the difficulties racers encounter.

**FOR FAMILIES.** There are four- and five-day lodge adventures that begin with a one-hour flight from Fairbanks to Bettles in the Alaskan Arctic, with views of the Brooks Range and Gates of the Arctic National Park. The historic Bettles Lodge with its family-style meals and Jacuzzi is your base. You'll learn the art of mushing on the first day, then spend the next few days exploring the numerous surrounding trails before returning to the lodge each evening. If you wish to tour the village and meet local Eskimos, that can be arranged. Lodge trips are run in November and December.

Everyone works together on the six- and eight-day trips available January through mid-April. These trips start from Bettles and take you along the Koyukuk River and through the boreal forest, where wolves and caribou roam the high, rugged peaks. The first and last nights are spent at the Bettles Lodge; on the other nights you stay in heated wall tents along the trail. Late-spring trips have warmer temperatures (lows below zero at night but in the teens and 20s during the day) and as much as 15 hours of daylight, which is an exciting experience in itself. On clear nights you will have a chance to experience nature's pyrotechnics—the aurora borealis.

There are also two special eight-day North Slope expeditions in April. Adventurers fly into Bettles just to get outfitted, then reboard the plane for a short flight through the magnificent scenery of the Brooks Range to Galbraith Lake, a remote pump station for the Trans-Alaskan Pipeline. Here guests meet their guide and take a training run with the dogs before setting out the next morning through the treeless alpine wilderness of the North Slope of the Brooks Range. This is an all-camping trek; each evening you'll help set up the heated wall tents and create a cozy camp in the frozen splendor of this remote land. You may have a chance to fish through the ice for arctic grayling or northern pike. Otherwise you'll dine on hearty stews and pasta dishes. Trip prices include special arctic gear, such as parkas, boots, mittens, and sleeping bags and pads, as well as snowshoes. (If your child is small, ask about sizes.) Airfare between Fairbanks and Bettles is $225 per

person; the trip prices do include transportation to and from the airport in Bettles.
*American Wilderness Experience/GORP Travel, Box 1486, Boulder, CO 80306, tel. 303/444–2622 or 800/444–0099. Jan.–Apr.: $1,700–$2,845 per person.*

## Arctic Odysseys

12+

Arctic Odysseys pioneered consumer-oriented group travel in the High Arctic more than 20 years ago. Although the company changed ownership in 1994, there isn't a better outfitter with which to explore the almost unimaginable treasures of the seemingly infinite Arctic wilderness. Customized trips and small groups (between one and three people per guide) are the trademark of the company.

**FOR FAMILIES.** You and your Inuit guide will plan your family's personal odyssey; the five-day and nine-day itineraries start and end in Ottawa, in Ontario. Children and adults must be in excellent health and good physical condition. Although trips are available mid-March through May, for families with children owner Robin Duberow recommends May, when the temperature warms up to 15°F–20°F.

On this trip through Nunavut in northern Canada (formerly the Northwest Territories), you spend the first and last nights in a hotel in one of several Inuit communities on Baffin Island. Tents or traditional snow houses (igloos) provide shelter on the other nights of your journey. Itineraries vary according to weather conditions and what you and your guide decide, but you'll typically travel to an inland lake as well as to the open sea and the very edges of the ice floes. You may encounter polar bears, seals, or ptarmigans; you'll ice-fish for arctic char. The most rewarding part of the experience, however, may well be the chance to experience a world unknown to most through the eyes of a people whose ties to the land remain strong and deep. If three or six nights out in the Arctic seem too much for your family, you can opt to add extra nights in the hotel ($80 per person per night) and travel by dogsled on day trips only.

During the very cold season traditional Inuit caribou clothing is available for rent; children's sizes are available. The outfitter will send you a list of clothing and gear and give you the names of catalogs and regional chains from which you can purchase it. The trip's cost includes two nights in the hotel and the flight between Ottawa and Nunavut.
*Arctic Odysseys, 2000 McGilvra Blvd. E, Seattle, WA 98112, tel. 206/325–1977. Mid-Mar.– May: 5–9 days, $3,275–$3,850.*

## Boundary Country Trekking

9+

These folks started offering dogsled trips in 1978, and they've been giving ordinary adventurers extraordinary thrills ever since. Most trips take place in northern Minnesota's winter wonderlands— the Boundary Waters Canoe Area, the wild and scenic Brule River valley, and Superior National Forest. The company headquarters is near Grand Marais on the Gunflint Trail (Route 12), about 130 mi north of Duluth. It's here, on the rugged coast of Lake Superior, that many of the sledding trips begin. Trips are limited to no more than six participants. Accommodations vary with the particular trip but may include yurts (dome-shape tents or huts) along the trail, rustic cabins, a homey lodge, or Arctic Oven tents (which can hold a heater).

**FOR FAMILIES.** Best for families, especially those with children in the 9- to 12-year-old range, is a three-day mushing excursion through the Boundary Waters Canoe Area and Superior National Forest. BCT doesn't allow passengers in the sled baskets, but will allow children as young as nine to drive a sled, usually one with just two dogs so that it's manageable. And, of course, guides will teach everyone all they need to know to mush safely and have fun doing it. Parents should know that on family trips, mushing time may be shorter than usual because children will probably want to head back to the cabin sooner than adults might. Although family adventures vary greatly, the average mushing distance on most trips is between 20 and 25 mi per day; on some of the longer trips you may travel farther—but you won't do it on an empty stomach. Meals include such treats as grilled rainbow trout and a Mongolian firepot dinner for those overnighting in a yurt. Two nights are spent in a cabin, the third in a yurt. While there are no specific family departures, the BCT Web site posts dates families have scheduled so others can join those trips if there's room. There are two- to six-day scheduled trips in Minnesota, or you can set up your own customized camping trip for any dates between November and March as long as dogs are available. This company also offers 8- to 11-day treks through the Canadian Arctic.

*Boundary Country Trekking, 7925 Gunflint Trail, Grand Marais, MN 55604, tel. 218/388–4487 or 800/322–8327. Nov.–Apr.: 2–15 days, $695–$3,400 per person.*

## Gunflint Northwoods Outfitters/Gunflint Lodge

4+

The Boundary Waters Canoe Area wilderness (BWCA) encompasses more than a million pristine acres of forests and lakes in northeastern Minnesota. Ideal for dogsledding, the area receives an average snowfall of more than 10 ft each winter. Here you can find the kind of solitude that few modern-day families ever experience. Gunflint Lodge, on Route 12, the famous Gunflint Trail, serves as base camp. Fifteen of the lodge's 25 cabins are used in winter, as is the main lodge, which houses the reception area and dining hall. The lodge sits on the shores of Gunflint Lake, which is divided almost in half by the border between Minnesota and Canada. In winter, as in every season, families are warmly welcomed.

**FOR FAMILIES.** Mushing Week, their formal course of instruction and sledding, is for ages 16 and up. It gives you three full days working with a team of dogs, learning how to feed, care for, and harness them. You will average between 20 and 25 mi a day on your sled, rarely taking the same trail twice. You'll also get three days to explore the BWCA on cross-country skis. And if the days rev you up and give you a feeling of accomplishment, the nights, spent in a first-class cabin with fireplace, hot tub, and sauna, are all about cozy togetherness.

Children six and older may also have a chance to ride on a sled if there's room or if one parent opts to stay back at the lodge one day. Those under six will probably get too cold for a full-day adventure and will enjoy being at the lodge with a parent. If you're uncertain about committing to a week of dogsledding, you can opt for a one-hour, half-day, or full-day dogsled ride during your Skiing Adventure Week (see Gunflint Northwoods Outfitters/Gunflint Lodge *in* Cross-Country Skiing). Whichever adventure you choose, you must bring appropriate winter wear. A limited number (and limited sizes) of mukluks and anoraks are available for rent.

*Gunflint Northwoods Outfitters/Gunflint Lodge, 143 S. Gunflint Lake, Grand Marais, MN 55604, tel. 800/362–5251. Jan.–Mar.: 1 hr–7 days, $55–$1,395 adults, $55–$995 children.*

## Kanata Wilderness Adventures/Wells Gray Ranch

6+

Western Canada remains a rugged land of wild, untamed beauty, with mountain ranges that rise from deep blue lakes to piercing blue skies. You can experience it in winter with the help of Kanata Wilderness Adventures, the outfitter that does all the bookings for Wells Gray Ranch. Popular with Europeans and Canadians but less well known to Americans, this year-round guest ranch sits at the entrance to Wells Gray Park, one of British Columbia's largest provincial parks. Riding is the main summer activity, but in winter the Kanata dogs and guides are busy giving ranch guests and nonguests the thrill of sledding.

**FOR FAMILIES.** Sign up to mush or ride (a sled can hold one musher and one child riding) on five- or eight-day adventures. For the most part adults will do the mushing; however, a strong preteen or teen with an interest in learning can probably do so. Owner Mike Mueller says parents should talk to him about their child before deciding on a trip. If Mike thinks it will work out, he'll bring a lighter sled and run it with fewer dogs for a young musher.

The five-day Musher Package takes you from the ranch to Grizzly Mountain Plateau, where you'll spend two nights in a rustic log cabin at a base camp. Each day you'll mush over abandoned logging roads, along lakeshores, and over mountain ridges. Those who choose the eight-day trip spend the first few nights at the ranch. After a training day, you head out for day trips and then follow the itinerary of the five-day adventure. You have to bring your own cold-weather clothing and sleeping bag or rent from Kanata (no children's sizes are available for rent, though).

*Kanata Wilderness Adventures/Wells Gray Ranch, R.R. 1, Clearwater, British Columbia, Canada V0E 1N0, tel. 250/674–2774. Dec.–Mar.: 5–8 days, C$950–C$1,560 per musher, C$700–C$1,140 per passenger; 25% discount for children under 12.*

## Outward Bound

14+

Outward Bound's dogsledding and cross-country skiing courses, held in Minnesota, are among its most challenging. That doesn't mean your family must already be expert in or even familiar with winter skills, but you must all be physically and mentally prepared for the challenges you will face. Your reward for such hard work is the self-empowering knowledge that you can succeed in ways you never believed possible.

**FOR FAMILIES.** In December and March parents and teens can take the combination dogsledding and cross-country skiing course together. You'll spend eight days in the Boundary Waters Canoe Area, traveling the silent, snowy forests and lakes by skis and by dog team. Up to six participants mush and ski from four to six hours, covering between 2 and 10 mi a day. You don't need to be an expert skier—beginner level is fine. In addition, you'll learn how to care for the dogs and run them, how to construct a winter shelter, and how to remain safe and comfortable during winter camping. There's a chance to try snowshoeing, too. As with all Outward Bound courses, everyone helps set up camp and prepare food each evening. While they provide winter sleeping bags, gear, and parkas, you'll need to bring your own clothing, including boot inserts.

*Outward Bound, 100 Mystery Point Rd., Garrison, NY 10524, tel. 914/424–4000 or 800/243–8520. Dec., Mar.: 8 days, $995.*

## Telluride Outside

5+

The wide-open mesas above the increasingly popular Colorado town of Telluride are perfect for mushing: a mix of flat and steep terrain, drifted snow, and trails that wind through patches of forest. When you're not mushing, take to Telluride's slopes for a day of skiing. Telluride Outside offers small, personalized treks through Wintermoon Dogsled Adventures, providing half-day or full-day excursions. While children are welcome on these adventures, they must be able to handle the conditions, which include being outside in the exhilarating cold for several hours or all day.

**FOR FAMILIES.** Here's your chance to ride with a guide—you can stand on the runners and help mush or sit in the basket, where you must shift your weight to maneuver the sled around turns. There's a limit of 350–375 pounds per sled and typically two guests on a sled; four guests is the average number for each outing. Half-day trips are the most popular for families, but you can head out into the wilderness for a full day of sledding, too. Hands-on instruction is part of the tour; your active involvement is both required and encouraged. Several considerations determine the speed and distance you travel: your sense of adventure, ability, and fitness; the weather; and the well-being of the party, including the dogs.
*Telluride Outside, Box 685, Telluride, CO 81435, tel. 970/728–3895 or 800/831–6230. Dec.–Mar.: ½ day–1 day, $130–$195.*

## Trek & Trail

10+

The winter woods of northwestern Wisconsin and Lake Superior prove a dramatic backdrop for adventuring. Trek & Trail has been running dogsled trips in this area since 1989. The well-qualified instructors capably teach their winter survival skills and mushing expertise to others, and their enthusiasm for the majesty and solitude of the wilderness in winter is contagious.

**FOR FAMILIES.** One-, two-, and three-day trips are available. Best for families is the two-day Dogsledding and Cabin Base Camp Adventure, on Bayfield Peninsula within the Red Cliff Indian Reservation and the Apostle Islands National Lakeshore. This is the only overnight sledding trip on which children under age 16 are allowed; your cabin is rustic but cozy and sleeps eight. For longer trips you stay in tents, tepees, and snow shelters.

After a three-hour winter safety course, including information about ice rescue, nutrition, hypothermia, and winter camping, you'll be ready to use the cabin as a base from which to take day-long trail runs. This traditional sugaring cabin was built by the Newago family, members of the Red Cliff Tribe, which uses it at maple-sugar time, when the family is harvesting and cooking down the syrup. Family members come out to spend the evening with you Friday night, telling stories of present-day and historical "sugar bushing" and other facets of Native American life. Saturday and Sunday you'll learn a variety of winter skills and graduate from running teams of four or five dogs to 10-dog teams, if you wish. You can even try a night run. If your children are enthusiastic and comfortable with the dog teams, they can learn to mush, too; otherwise, they can ride with guides. No winter adventuring experience is necessary, but you must be in good physical condition, and you must bring appropriate clothing.

Families with children at least 16 years old can join the three-day trek in Lake Superior's Apostle Islands. No winter camping experience is required—you'll learn it all on the trip. Besides camping skills, you'll pick up cross-country skiing and snowshoeing, in addition to learning how to work with a team of sled dogs. You'll stay in log cabins, snow shelters, or tepees.
*Trek & Trail, Box 906, Bayfield, WI 54814, tel. 800/354–8735. Jan.–Mar.: 1–3 days, $89–$425 for adults; 50% discount for children under 13.*

## Wilderness Inquiry

6+

Since 1978 this nonprofit organization has been bringing people from diverse backgrounds, including people with disabilities, together in the wilderness—in this case, in Minnesota. Teaching, learning, and sharing are the foundations on which every course is built.

**FOR FAMILIES.** Families with children ages six and up can choose a five-day ski and dogsled trip into the Boundary Waters Canoe Area, where you'll follow ancient Native American trails through deep snow and pine forests and across the many frozen lakes. The outfitter will consider younger children, but call to discuss it; two-year-olds have taken this trip.

You will pick your routes and then ski, snowshoe, dogsled, and take on the challenge of winter wilderness survival. If you or your child has a disability, ask Wilderness Inquiry about its facilities for accommodating your needs. Most daily outings cover between 3 and 8 mi, though you can also choose to relax with a cup of hot chocolate in the remote but comfortable YMCA Camp Menogyn lodge (with sauna), where you spend your nights. There's an optional overnight camp-out using tents, snow shelters, or maybe just double sleeping bags under the dark, starry skies. One of the mushers who regularly works this trip taught his own children to run dogs at age four, so a child's ability isn't prejudged. If your six-year-old is ready and willing, he or she can stand on the runners with a musher and get the feel of driving a sled.

Families with teens 16 and up can head into Minnesota's rugged north country for four or six days of sledding over the frozen lakes and wooded hills of Superior National Forest. This more intense trek begins at a base camp and includes two nights out on the trail in wall tents, which have vertical sides and can hold heaters. You'll sled from 15 to 30 mi per day. You have to bring your own cold-weather gear and sleeping bags.

*Wilderness Inquiry, 1313 5th St. SE, Box 84, Minneapolis, MN 55414-1546, tel. and TTY 612/379–3858 or 800/728–0719. Dec.–Mar.: 5–6 days, $595–$945; children under 17 generally receive 50% discount. Round-trip van transportation from Minneapolis (6 hrs each way) is available for $60.*

# Resources

## Organizations

The **International Sled Dog Racing Association** (HC 86, Box 3380, Merrifield, MN 56465, tel. 218/765–4297; membership $35) will send information on the sport (an introductory brochure is available for $2) and a sample copy of its magazine, *Info*, published 10 times each year.

## Books

Gary Paulsen, whose passion for years was dogsledding in the Minnesota wilderness, writes in *Woodsong* (Orchard Books, ages eight and up) about his dogs, his home, and participation in the 1,049-mi Iditarod dogsled race. *Dogteam* (Dell), also by Paulsen, is a picture book about the beauty of a nighttime dogsled run.

## Also See

For more winter adventures, look at the trips in Cross-Country Skiing. For more adventures with animal companions, see Horse Packing *and* Trekking with Llamas and Burros.

# FISHING

City kids, country kids, small- and big-town kids—they all love to fish. Whether it's the connection with water or the lazy, Huckleberry Finn feel of floating along with no place in particular to go, I don't know. Maybe it's the challenge, or maybe it's the simplicity of the endeavor. In a high- tech, high-speed world, fishing takes you back to a simpler era when families made their own fun. Fishing requires almost nothing except patience and a little time.

Of course, there is an art to it. In particular, fly-fishing, which involves almost continuous casting with an artificial fly, is a learned skill. It has complexities (avoiding people, trees, and reeds while casting, for example) and intricacies (knowing where fish lurk and what they eat) beyond what most of us associate with fishing. There is a right and wrong way to cast—and you can bet those wily trout in streams across the country know that by now.

Today families can discover, or rediscover, the joys of fishing in a number of ways. There are schools and clinics that teach specialized skills, usually fly-fishing, and outfitters that will take you out and teach you while you vacation. You can find lodges that focus on fishing and provide instruction as well as good old-fashioned fishing fun. Children of almost any age can fish, though most outfitters agree that fly-fishing takes a level of coordination and understanding most children under 12 don't possess. For this reason lodge-based fishing and lake fishing are often best for families with young children. But the bottom line is really this: Fishing, in one form or another, is for everyone.

## Questions to Ask

**What method is taught?** Most schools concentrate on fly-fishing, but instruction in spin casting (casting a line with a worm or lure or other bait and slowly reeling it in), trolling (dragging a line behind a moving boat), and other techniques is also available. Fly-fishing is harder for young children than trolling, so consider your youngsters' ages and abilities, as well as their levels of tolerance for sitting or standing for long periods, before booking.

**Do you have equipment for kids?** Experts disagree on whether a shorter rod is necessarily better for children, but be sure there's a rod your child can use comfortably. Children older than 12 and those large for their age don't usually have a problem with the adult equipment generally available either as part of the package or for rent. Children who are younger and smaller may have problems with available rods, so buy or borrow your child's equipment before you leave home. Get detailed information from the guide or school about what kind is best, though. *Fly-Fishing* *with Children*, by Philip Brunquell (see Resources, *below*), has an excellent section on buying rods for kids.

**What kind of fish can be caught?** Trout is the primary focus at most schools and on many wilderness trips, but there are other possibilities. Bluefish, bonitos, salmon, walleyes, and northern pike also provide a challenge for anglers of all ages. Even within species there can be differences in ease of catch. Because children may have less patience than adults, picking a fish or an area likely to bring success is a good idea.

**Where does casting instruction take place?** You'll be taught how to throw a line out in such a way that a fish will take whatever lure or bait you're offering. Most schools have casting ponds stocked with trout; in some cases instruction takes place on a river or even in the surf. On a guided trip you put skills to work in real situations rather than the artificial environs of a stocked pond. However, guided trips can be expensive, and since children like the ponds, a school's simulated environment isn't necessarily a drawback. Schools also give families a chance to try the sport to see if they like it and to test equipment before investing in it. Before booking either alternative, make sure the scenario is what you want.

**How much time is spent in the classroom?** Many schools use about half the course time to give lectures on equipment and environmental concerns, present slide shows, lead fly-tying demonstrations, and discuss pretty much anything that's not directly related to casting. Be certain your children understand that the entire class will not take place near water. In some cases no time is spent by the water, so read descriptions carefully.

**Are licenses needed?** In most states adults need a fishing license, but children under a certain age do not. Sixteen is a common cutoff, but in some states 12-year-olds must have one. Check with the school or your guide. Find out if you can purchase your license from them, or if you have to stop somewhere before your class or trip begins. The cost may be anywhere from $4 to $40 or so. In a very few courses a temporary license is part of the course fee.

**Can we keep the fish?** In most cases, no. The sport lies in outsmarting the fish, and the primary goal of most schools and guided trips is to teach you to catch fish, not to keep them. "Catch and release" is the phrase you'll hear; it means once you catch your fish, you must quickly unhook it and place it back in the water. Many places recommend barbless hooks for that reason. Ask if you need to bring them.

**Are there activities for nonfishing family members?** You'll probably find more to do besides fish at lodges rather than at schools or with wilderness guides. Some guided trips, however, are perfect for photographers or wildlife artists or for anyone who simply likes relaxing in a boat. A number of schools are in towns or areas that are popular family destinations. Even if one of you isn't fishing, you can still have a family experience.

**How far in advance should we book?** For parent-child courses, which are very limited in number, booking several months in advance is a good idea. On the other hand, last-minute cancellations are always possible, so don't hesitate to call.

**What's included in the cost?** Guided trips include boats, guides, all meals, most camping equipment (you usually have to bring or rent a sleeping bag), life vests, instruction, and transportation to and from the river, unless otherwise noted. Fishing equipment is occasionally available, but check. The cost of lodge-based trips generally covers lodging, meals, and the use of a boat; private guiding is extra. School prices include equipment but reflect course costs only, without lodging or meals, unless otherwise noted. Transportation to and from schools, lodges, or guided trips is never part of the price given.

## Instruction

Instruction is the focus of a school course, but a good guide on a trip will always provide instruction, too. If you have specific interests—fly tying, casting techniques, learning about equipment—let your guide know ahead of time so he or she can prepare materials and equipment as necessary. Ask in advance whether there are charts of local fish or written materials or directions on fly tying or using equipment. Some children—and some adults, for that matter—learn better by visual clues.

## Finding the Fun

**Northeast:** Appalachian Mountain Club, L.L. Bean, Orvis Fly Fishing School. **Midwest:** Gunflint Northwoods Outfitters/Gunflint Lodge. **Mid-Atlantic:** Orvis Fly Fishing School. **South:** Orvis Fly Fishing School. **Rockies:** L.L. Bean, Montana River Outfitters, Orvis Fly Fishing School, Telluride Outside. **West Coast:** Fly-Fishing Outfitters Clinics, Trinity Canyon Fly Fishing Workshops. **Canada:** Babine Norlakes Lodge.

# Favorite Schools and Outfitters

## Appalachian Mountain Club

13+

The Catskills campus of this venerable organization sponsors a fly-fishing clinic based at Valley View Lodge, not far from Phoenicia, New York. Although the course is strictly a landlubber affair—you don't actually go out on the water or even near a stream—your family does get to enjoy a spring weekend in the Catskills while learning the techniques and skills necessary to fish for trout on your own.

**FOR FAMILIES.** Instructors, all members of the Upper Susquehanna Chapter of Trout Unlimited, have plenty of fishing experience; some are New York State–certified guides. This organization's members focus on enjoying fishing themselves and promoting fly-fishing across the country. The class is limited to

20 people and includes lodging Friday and Saturday nights, as well as all meals from Saturday breakfast to Sunday lunch.

Participants spend some time in a classroom setting, learning how to select tackle, tie flies, and read the waters (recognize the kinds of places fish like to lurk and feed); instructors also teach a bit about entomology as it relates to fly-fishing. Saturday's class runs from about 9 to 5, while Sunday's ends around noon. Casting instruction takes place in a big field, with no hooks on the rods. Equipment is available for free if you don't yet have your own.

*Appalachian Mountain Club, Box 366, Long Lake, NY 12847, tel. 518/624–2056 for Catskills campus; tel. 603/466–2721 for general AMC information and full catalog. Apr.: 2 days, $180 for adults; 10% discount for children under 10. Family membership is $65, and members receive 10% discount on classes.*

## Babine Norlakes Lodge

**ALL**

Pierce and Anita Clegg, owners and managers of the Babine Norlakes Lodge, have four children of their own. They love having families as guests, and their guides enjoy teaching kids about fishing. There aren't many activities if you don't want to fish—maybe a little volleyball or badminton. And, of course, the Cleggs' children are around for play companions.

The lodge itself, in a remote area of northern British Columbia, is accessible only by boat or floatplane. Eight hand-hewn cabins sleep two to four, and generators supply electricity; two of the cabins are larger and have kitchens, if you prefer to cook. This woodsy, isolated living does not lack nice touches: In the morning Pierce personally visits each cabin, serving coffee, tea, or hot chocolate to guests and starting up each cabin's woodstove or stove oil heating. Guests gather for a big breakfast in the main lodge and make their lunch from a buffet; then most head out onto Nilkitkwa Lake and the Babine River for some of the best trout fishing in North America.

**FOR FAMILIES.** Accommodations include a boat, with no limit on fuel, so you are free to fish as much as you like. The lodge encourages catch-and-release only (and requires all steelhead to be released) in order to preserve the population. The fish here are all wild; there's no stocking, no hatchery. Most guests bring their own equipment, though a few rods are available for guests' use, and the Clegg children generously loan their life jackets.

First-time guests receive one day of complimentary guiding; you can hire guides other days for an additional charge. With enough notice, Anita can arrange to have a mother's helper on the property (at an extra charge) so you and your spouse can spend some time fishing on your own.

In keeping with the informal atmosphere, minimum ages and pricing structures are flexible. Anita says, "Preschoolers and youngsters are free until they really start fishing." At that point they receive a 50% discount. Large families, she adds, "can usually make a deal."

*Babine Norlakes Lodge, Box 1060, Smithers, British Columbia, Canada V0J 2N0, tel. 250/847–6160. May–Aug.: 3½–6 ½ days, C$800–C$2,100 for adults.*

## Fly-Fishing Outfitters Clinics

**12+**

This group has run clinics since 1985, both in San Francisco and on streams and rivers in various parts of northern California. Because Fly-Fishing Outfitters (FFO) also owns well-regarded equipment shops, it will provide rods and reels for clinics, but you'll have to bring or rent tackle.

**FOR FAMILIES.** FFO offers clinics at its store locations. The clinics include casting, rigging, and a little fishing in the afternoon.

Fishing trips are held on a variety of Bay Area waters and California rivers, including the Sacramento, Truckee, and Stanislaus. FFO's Peter Woolley says families are welcome participants in any of the company's clinics or trips as long as the children have a real interest in angling and the attention span necessary to handle the information. And although he says 12 is generally a realistic minimum age, he'll consider younger children—but only after talking with parents. Because these lessons can have a fairly structured itinerary and adult orientation, try to be flexible with your dates. That way you can sign up for an outing on which there will be other kids. And although land-based clinics are great for learning the basic skills, trips give parents and children a sense of using those skills on scenic rivers, where you'll find the real heart and romance of the sport. Also advantageous is the chance to spend a night camping with guides who will happily talk fishing and fish stories, even after clinic hours. Bring your own camping gear. You'll fish for rainbow and brown trout, but it's strictly catch-and-release.

*Fly-Fishing Outfitters Clinics, 3533 Mt. Diablo Blvd., Lafayette, CA 94549, tel. 925/284–3474. July: 1–2 days, $140–$240.*

## Gunflint Northwoods Outfitters/Gunflint Lodge

ALL

Members of the Kerfoot family, who own the outfitting-guide service and the lodge, have been welcoming adventurers of all ages to this Minnesota wilderness retreat since 1928. The lodge itself, about 150 mi north of Duluth, sits on the shore of 9-mi-long Gunflint Lake. Many families visit the lodge for a week, taking canoeing and fishing trips into the vast Boundary Waters Canoe Area (BWCA). Others stay at the lodge only before or after a guided or self-guided adventure. Both the lodge and the guiding service will take children of any age, though different activities will have specific age requirements. Whatever your choice, one talk with Bruce Kerfoot will convince you that Gunflint and families are made for each other.

**FOR FAMILIES.** All children age six and up staying at the lodge at least seven days will be taken out on a children-only half-day guided fishing trip twice during the week. They'll learn spin casting with some live bait and some artificial lures as they try their luck on walleyes and smallmouth bass. A family with children of any age also has the option of hiring one of Gunflint's excellent guides for a full-day trip (at an extra charge) on one of the many lakes in the vast BWCA. The use of fishing equipment is included in some packages; there's gear of various sizes but families should ask about equipment for kids. Guests may decide whether to keep or free their catch, as long as it's within the legal catch-and-release guidelines. Lodge-based guests can use Gunflint's canoes and kayaks free of charge; there are child-size kayaks, too. Families on the all-inclusive package also have use of a motorboat; other guests pay extra for this. The Gunflint nature program runs from June to September, with about 30 free activities a week, such as hikes, bird-watching, moose searches, and boating to interesting sites—even evening beaver watches.

The 41 cabins at Gunflint Lodge give families various options. Sixteen rustic "canoer" cabins sleep from four to six in one big room; a bathhouse with hot showers, toilets, sinks, and a sauna is nearby. The more luxurious cabins have one to four bedrooms, bathrooms, and carpeting, and each has a sauna; the most deluxe have outside hot tubs. Among the family package options are a housekeeping plan, for those who wish to cook their own meals, and a modified plan that includes dinner daily.

You can also book camping trips of two or more days with Gunflint's regular guiding service. Smallmouth bass are easier to catch than other local fish, so they're a good choice for children to try for on these adventures. An ideal family trip takes you to Rose Lake, in the eastern portion of the BWCA along the Canadian border. It requires about a five-hour paddle the first day, and there are two portages on the trip. There's no minimum age, but the trip is a lot easier once children are out of diapers. Bruce recommends a four-night trip. "The kids come back wishing it had been a little longer, not complaining that it was a couple of days too long," he says, and that gives them the best possible introduction to the wilderness.

*Gunflint Northwoods Outfitters/Gunflint Lodge, 143 S. Gunflint Lake, Grand Marais, MN 55604, tel. 218/388–2294 or 800/362–5251. May–Sept.: 7 days, $295–$3,200 for family of 4, depending on cabin choice and meal package; less if children are under 4, more if more than 4 in your family. Guiding costs $125 per person per day, with 50% discount for ages 4–12.*

## L.L. Bean

8+

The stated mission of this renowned outdoor store and catalog company is to help people enjoy the outdoors through its products, services, and education. L.L. Bean opened a fly-fishing school in 1980 and inaugurated a parent-child introductory course at the company's Freeport, Maine, headquarters in 1993. It's been going strong ever since.

**FOR FAMILIES.** In late June and again in July, L.L. Bean schedules a two-day parent-child course that runs from 8:30 to 5 both days and includes lunch. Instruction takes place outside Freeport at Fogg Farm, which has both a natural and a stocked pond. Participants remove their shoes and wade in, picking up rocks and studying reeds in order to get to know a fish's environment—and what it eats. Once you know what the fish like to eat, you try to match it in your lure box. The dozen parent-child pairs in the course also learn fly-casting and fly-tying techniques, how to read the water, and how weather can affect fishing conditions. Ten is the minimum age, but call the school if you have a younger child who is really interested; the school is flexible. Lodging isn't part of the deal, but participants receive a list of area accommodations ranging from campgrounds to a luxury hotel. Be sure to check out L.L. Bean's store, which has quality outdoor clothing and gear for all ages, while you're in the area.

Families with fishing aficionados eight and up can join any of Bean's other fishing schools. These include introductory and intermediate schools as well as more specialized courses, such as saltwater, Atlantic salmon, and western trout fly-fishing schools. Introductory courses are held in Freeport. The intermediate and specialty courses are all in popular fishing areas in Maine and Montana; the cost for these covers lodging.

The school follows the catch-and-release policy. All graduates receive a copy of the *L.L. Bean Fly Fishing Handbook* in addition to a diploma and pin.

*L.L. Bean, Freeport, ME 04033, tel. 207/865–4761 or 888/552–3261. June–July (parent-child school): 2 days, $495 for parent and child. May–Sept. (all other courses): 3–6 days, $395–$2,500 per person.*

## Montana River Outfitters

10+

Craig Madsen of Montana River Outfitters believes that the best class in the world puts you out on a river catching wild fish with guides who love what they're doing—and that's just what this organization offers. Guides take only two anglers in a boat (two to eight guests in all on a trip) in order to personalize instruction and service. The "classrooms" are the Missouri, Smith, and Flathead rivers. Most people bring their own rods and waders, but you can rent them if necessary. The company follows the catch-and-release policy.

**FOR FAMILIES.** Craig recommends a five- to seven-day trip on the Smith, along 60 mi of river with no public access. Limestone canyons, cliffs, and meadows cradle a river so narrow here you can often cast to either side. The rainbow and brown trout are plentiful, but they're strong and smart, so patience is necessary. Instruction is informal but, thanks to the guide-to-guest ratio, quite personalized. Although the season is short (May to July is the optimum time), the Smith is one of the most reliable trout streams in Montana, which makes it a good choice for anglers of all ages. But it's a river for nonanglers and for families with mixed interests, too, because of its excellent side hikes, caves, Native American pictographs, and spectacular scenery.

Another great five- to seven-day family trip is the South Fork of the Flathead. Getting there adds to the adventure—it's two days in by horse, with all equipment and food packed along. (You don't need to be an experienced rider.) The resident cutthroat trout make the river particularly family friendly: Cutthroat are easy to catch, which can be very satisfying to children (and adults). The South Fork of the Flathead flows through the heart of the Bob Marshall Wilderness, in northwestern Montana, offering excellent fishing set against the beauty and drama of a backcountry landscape in one of the most remote areas in the lower 48 states.

There are also several trips on the wild and scenic Missouri River. Rich in the history of pioneers, steamboats, and Lewis and Clark, the Missouri can be floated by raft, kayak, or canoe as part of a partially or fully guided trip. This is generally a warm-water habitat with a wide variety of resident species, but few trout. The Missouri between Great Falls and Helena, however, is known as one of the most productive trout areas in the world. Trout populations here are measured in the thousands per mile, making this one of the best stretches for dry fly-fishing in the west. Also, because of the controlled water flow, fishing is excellent on this portion of the river year-round. You can take half- or whole-day trips, or choose a complete, guided two- to seven-day package. You can fly-fish or spin cast, so it's ideal for all ages and abilities. Three- to five-day float trips with an emphasis on history (much of it related to Lewis and Clark) and geological formations are available, too. You can see historical buildings and sites, hike, swim, and, of course, fish.

To join most of Montana River Outfitters' trips, you generally fly into and out of Great Falls. Representatives of the outfit will pick you up at the airport and take you to your pretrip lodging (not included in the price, but they can arrange it), then transport you to the start of the trip. After your adventure they'll drop you off at the airport. At the end of the Flathead trip you fly out of Kalispell; to avoid the drive to the airport, which includes 80 mi of dirt road, you can have a small plane pick your family up not too far from the river (at an extra charge) and fly you to Kalispell.

*Montana River Outfitters, 923 10th Ave. N, Great Falls, MT 59401, tel. 406/761–1677, 406/235–4350, or 800/800–8218. Mar.–Oct.: 1–7 days, $165–$3,295 adults; children's pricing on some trips.*

## Orvis Fly Fishing School

12+

Orvis, the long-established fishing-tackle manufacturer, opened the first fly-fishing school in the country; it began offering courses in 1967 at its Manchester, Vermont, corporate headquarters. It has since added corporate center campuses in Colorado, Idaho, Massachusetts, Florida, Maryland, and New York. Hundreds of Orvis retail outlets (where you can buy fishing gear and outdoor clothing) also run courses, but the individual stores choose their offerings. The clinics at the corporate centers generally remain the same from year to year.

**FOR FAMILIES.** Orvis's parent-child school is a two-day event, usually scheduled twice a year in July at the Vermont campus. The course accommodates up to 10 pairs, which split into smaller groups (parent and child stay together). You spend half the time in the classroom, the other half at the casting ponds. They follow the catch-and-release policy.

The course meets from about 9 to 4:30 both days and emphasizes basics: rigging a fly rod, tying essential knots, trying various fly-casting techniques, and learning what fish eat and what lures to use. You learn, too, how to "mend" your line by adjusting its placement in the water based on currents. Not surprisingly, Orvis schools also emphasize proper equipment and clothing, and the gear provided is strictly Orvis.

The school recommends that you sign up for parent-child courses several months in advance—January is not too early for the July school. Children 12 and up can also participate in Orvis's regular courses, but parents should note that the parent-child course has less structure and more emphasis on fun.

The popular women-only schools in Vermont are another option for mother-daughter pairs. These are run like regular courses: The class of 36 or so divides up, and lecture time is lengthier and more detailed than in parent-child courses. As with all Orvis courses, the price does not cover lodging, but reservationists give detailed information on local accommodations; one popular choice in Vermont is the Equinox Hotel.

*Orvis Fly Fishing School, Rte. 7A, Manchester, VT 05254, tel. 802/362–8513 or 800/239–2074. Apr.–Oct. (all courses not available all months): 2–3 days, $370–$430.*

## Telluride Outside

11+

The rivers of southwestern Colorado teem with trout, and the mountain town of Telluride, with the Uncompahgre National Forest to the north and the San Juan National Forest to the south, makes an enviable base from which to pursue them. Telluride Outside has been guiding and teaching fly- fishing for more than 15 years, and the outfitter welcomes parents and children who want to fish and learn together. The company is somewhat flexible on ages; call and consult with the staff before booking any family clinic or trip.

**FOR FAMILIES.** Telluride Outside lets you choose between "walk and wades" (where you fish standing on the bank or in the water) and "floats" (fishing by boat). Of the three rivers the outfitter regularly visits—the San Miguel, the Gunnison, and the Dolores—the San Miguel probably suits families best. Although its fish aren't as big, there are lots of them, so you don't have to be as exact on your cast or your drift as you do on a river with just a few big fish spread out between pools. A one-day trip with instruction covers such topics as approach (trout behavior and reading the water), presentation (equipment and fly casting), and fly selection. You're on your own for lodging each night in Telluride.

Those looking for a multi-day camping and fly-fishing trip should consider the awesome Black Canyon of the Gunnison, about a two-hour drive from town. Fly fishers come from all over the world to test their skills on the Gunnison River, which is best for ages 14 and up. The fishing is harder, but the striking Precambrian rock of the canyon and the wildlife make the trip well worthwhile. You can sign up for one- to three-day trips, and you don't need to be an experienced paddler. Participants camp along the river; tents are provided but you bring or rent sleeping bags and pads as well as fishing gear.

Consider taking Telluride Outside's half-day casting clinic before a trip to get in shape. Guides review various casts in detail, and the outfitter provides all equipment. All trips and courses are catch-and-release.
*Telluride Outside, Box 685, Telluride, CO 81435, tel. 970/728–3895. June–Sept.: ½–3 days, $95–$235 per person per day, depending on the number of people in your group, $500–$1,850 per boat (2 people and 1 guide) for float trips.*

## Trinity Canyon Fly Fishing Workshops

10+

Trinity Canyon's Joe Mercier is an avid angler and committed environmentalist. What he offers are complete ecosystem orientations of northern California's Shasta/Trinity National Forest, Trinity Alps Wilderness, and the basin of the Trinity River, all within the context of fly-fishing. "What I combine," he says, "is service and education." By his own reckoning he knows every rock within a hundred miles of Weaverville, and he likes nothing better than introducing visitors to the beauty and diversity of this area.

**FOR FAMILIES.** Workshops are for anglers and outdoor enthusiasts of all skill levels. If you have a child who is younger than 10 or if someone in your family has a disability, talk to Joe ahead of time, and he can accommodate them. Half- or full-day instruction is tailored to the needs, interests, and ages of participants, and even nonanglers will find much to learn. The initial portion of the program includes a presentation on the region's human and natural history, along with demonstrations of fly-fishing techniques and equipment. After that, participants wade into the lakes, rivers, and streams of the Trinity watershed. Joe emphasizes that what he offers is instruction, not a guide service, and catch-and-release is a condition of his workshops. Joe also specializes in instructing people about gear and letting them try different types of equipment before they make a major buying decision; he provides all tackle and equipment for the workshops.

If you're planning to overnight in the area, ask Joe about activities in addition to fishing and for accommodation suggestions. The cost of the full-day course includes lunch.
*Trinity Canyon Fly Fishing Workshops, Box 2820, Weaverville, CA 96093, tel. 530/623–3306. Year-round: ½–1 day, $180–$275 for 1–2 people; others in your group can attend with you for a small additional charge.*

# Resources

## Books

Michael J. Rosen's *The Kids' Book of Fishing and Tackle Box* (Workman) is a beginner's guide for anglers age eight and up. It emphasizes freshwater catch-and-release fishing.

*The Young Fishing Enthusiast* by John Bailey (DK Publishing) is a compendium of facts and information on everything to do with fishing, including kinds of fish, different types of fishing, how to play and land fish, tackle, flies, lures, bait, and more. Lots of photos make this accessible even to young children.

*Fly-Fishing with Children*, by Philip Brunquell, M.D. (Countryman Press), is an excellent guide, with sections on buying equipment and diagrams on casting and fly tying.

## Also See

For more river and lake adventures in which fishing is possible, see Canoeing, Kayaking, *and* Rafting. The Horse Packing chapter also lists trips during which families can fish at lake and river campsites.

# HIKING AND BACKPACKING

Hiking is one of the most popular adventure vacations, in part because of accessibility. A family can hike just about anywhere, anytime. There are treks for all ages and all abilities and for campers and noncampers alike. Some families enjoy carrying major backpacks into remote wilderness areas; others prefer the comfort of a cozy inn or lodge each evening. Hiking itself doesn't require lots of expensive equipment (although campers need gear), nor does it involve a large investment of time. Even day hikes with young children can be fun—and educational—family adventures.

So why sign up with a group or outfitter when hiking is something you can so easily do on your own? To begin with, outfitters work in the same areas year after year and really know the country—a benefit for your family's trip planning and safety. Whether you're heading into the wilderness or hiking inn to inn, there are myriad details to take care of: mapping a great route, arranging for backcountry permits, finding a campsite, booking accommodations, and so forth. Guides do all this in advance. They also provide a wellspring of facts and memorable stories, as well as a level of safety individuals usually can't match. Moreover, they can get you into some areas that might be inaccessible to you on your own—unless you have backcountry experience and are well equipped with appropriate safety and camping gear.

Outfitters also contribute to the educational aspect of your family's experience. The naturalists and outdoor educators who accompany you on many trips can share the wonders of nature with your children—and answer their many questions—in a way you probably can't. In addition, if your family has hikers of differing abilities, you may need to compromise on the route when you're on your own. Guided trips generally have two to three hiking options each day. Experienced hikers can be challenged by steep trails and long distances while beginners take shorter routes at a slower pace as they build their stamina and skills.

Traveling with an outfitter can make financial sense, too. They have up-to-date gear, which means you don't have to go out and buy it. Tents, pads, tarps, cooking equipment, fire starters, topographical maps, backcountry first-aid kits, compasses, and radios are necessary in the wilderness. Unless you're certain that camping and hiking are long-term family interests, why invest in so much equipment?

Finally, when you travel with a hiking company, especially on a trip geared for families, you're guaranteed companions, not just for yourself but for your children. You'll meet families from all over the world that share your love of the outdoors.

Most important, perhaps, children help motivate each other. This can make a big difference when you're still 2 mi from camp, and your five-year-old doesn't want to walk any farther.

Of course, you can hike on your own; there are city and state parks and recreation areas with marked and maintained trails within a short drive of most communities—even large cities. These are good trails on which to introduce children to hiking and to build your family's skills. But try a guided trip for that multi-day exploration of backcountry or unfamiliar locales or for a special adventure that integrates hiking with history, ecology, botany, marine biology, or sociology. You'll be amazed at what you see and what you can learn.

## Questions to Ask

**How far will we hike each day?** The trips listed here average from 3 to 8 mi per day for the easy options; some hikes are as short as 1.8 mi and others as long as 12 mi. Challenging options generally range between 6 and 12 mi per day. Although size and experience are factors, in general you can expect a preschooler to walk from 1 to 3 mi a day, and five- to eight-year-olds to handle between 5 and 8 mi, depending on the terrain and their experience.

**How difficult is the trip?** Most hiking companies designate trips easy, moderate, strenuous, or difficult. All the trips in this chapter are easy or moderate, unless otherwise noted. Difficulty is determined by the distance you hike, the ascent or descent, and the trail surface. One company puts it this way: An easy trip is the equivalent of a half hour of walking three times per week. Moderate and challenging routes are the equivalent of a half hour of aerobic exercise two or three times per week. These guidelines may help you decide your family's ability level, but you should also ask lots of questions and be candid about the fitness and normal activity level of everyone in your family.

**How often can we rest?** Outdoor experts know that children need to stop more often than adults, but everyone needs to rest on the trail. Taking a couple of breaks in the morning and afternoon, in addition to stopping for lunch, is good for the group. Along the trail you'll pause frequently to look at everything you're out there to see: views, bugs, interesting plants, wildlife. To rush down the trail is to miss the point. If your guide tries to hurry you or your children, ask him or her to slow down.

**Who carries the gear?** Sometimes you do; sometimes support vehicles lug the heavy stuff while you hike. In general, if the trip is a backcountry trek with a different campsite each night, everyone in the group will probably be expected to carry a backpack of at least 30 pounds. If this isn't for you, check out inn-to-inn hiking; support vehicles usually take all but what you need in your day pack. On lodge-based treks, you leave almost everything in your room while you hike each day.

**Are there any special safety precautions for kids on the trail?** Although you're with a group and guides, there's a remote chance someone might get separated from the group for a while. Carrying a whistle is a good idea. If your children can read, write safety instructions and place them in their day pack or backpack. Children should know when to blow the whistle, how to use three sticks or stones to mark the direction they've gone, and to stay in one place if it gets dark.

**What if my child is too tired to finish a hike?** A good trail strategy is to encourage children along the way, whether they are tired or not. Praise all their accomplishments—making it up hills, making it until break time, making it to the next bend in the trail. You and they will be surprised at their natural abilities. For those times children really can't go on, you should know your options. Some trips include van support; others have shorter loops you can take. Once you've committed to a trail in the wilderness, though, your choices may be limited.

**Will an experienced hiker be bored on easy or moderate hikes?** On family trips the key is to look at the experience in a new way. You won't cover the same distances you're used to, and you won't be on terrain that's as challenging. On the other hand, you will have opportunities to see the world through your children's eyes, to slow down, and to share your knowledge of the trail with them. If you feel the need for a challenge or two, take a trip that has several hiking options every day. You and your spouse can take turns between walking with the children and going on more difficult hikes.

**How many people will be in the group?** Camping trips usually accommodate from 10 to 20 people, inn-to-inn trips typically have between 15 and 25, and lodge-based trips as many as 30 or 40. Individual listings for outfitters note any exceptions to these averages. Remember, however, that the group is divided every day into two or three smaller hiking groups based on ability and preference. You will rarely hike with more than 10 or 11 people at one time.

**Do my kids need hiking boots?** In some cases and on some terrain, boots may be better than sneakers because they provide more support. Some good national outlets sell children's outdoor wear (see Resources, *below*), and hiking boots come in a range of prices. After the trip boots are useful at camp and around town.

**Are day packs needed?** Most outfitters ask each hiker to carry his or her own day pack; that goes for children, too. Even preschoolers can carry a small pack with the essentials: safety instructions, water, trail snacks, and rain gear.

**Are snacks available?** Outfitters usually provide trail snacks each day, but they may not hand them out as often as your children need them. They also may not have what your youngsters like, so pack easy-to-carry energy-producing trail snacks in your family's day packs. Good choices include dried fruit, nuts, hard salami, and trail mix. If you have hard cheese or bagels at breakfast, take leftovers on the trail. A word of caution: In wilderness areas, especially bear country, it's not safe to keep food in your tent. At night give snacks to your guides to put in safe containers.

**What's included in the cost?** On a camping trip the outfitter supplies guides, meals, tents, and sleeping pads unless otherwise noted. Inn-to-inn trips or expeditions that use lodges and hotels typically include guides, lodging, and most, but not necessarily all, meals. Participants must sometimes get to the trailhead on their own or meet at a designated spot for group transfer to the trailhead. The cost may cover airport pickup and delivery. Airfare and lodging before or after the trip dates are not part of the price, although most outfitters can help you book these.

## Instruction

Those companies or organizations that sponsor courses, such as the Appalachian Mountain Club, provide instruction as well as fun. Efficient hiking techniques, orienteering, nature studies, and lessons in packing a backpack and setting up reliable camps are typical of what your family can learn from a course. Although vacation-oriented trips aren't geared to teaching, you learn a tremendous amount anyway. Good guides and naturalists are fonts of wilderness wisdom who will share their knowledge of everything from animal prints to edible berries.

## Finding the Fun

**Northeast:** Appalachian Mountain Club, Backroads, Sierra Club. **South:** Backroads. **Midwest:** Sierra Club. **Southwest:** Sierra Club, Southwest Trekking. **Rockies:** Backroads, Sierra Club. **West Coast:** Backroads, REI Adventures, Sierra Club. **Alaska:** Alaska Wildland Adventures, Camp Denali, REI Adventures. **Hawaii:** American Wilderness Experience/GORP Travel, REI Adventures, Sierra Club. **Canada:** American Wilderness Experience/GORP Travel, Backroads, Butterfield & Robinson, Canadian Mountain Holidays, REI Adventures, Sila Sojourns, Wells Gray Chalets & Wilderness Adventures. **Mexico:** Southwest Trekking. **Central America:** Backroads. **Europe:** Backroads, Butterfield & Robinson, Ciclismo Classico, Cross Country International.

# Favorite Outfitters

## Alaska Wildland Adventures

12+

Alaska Wildland Adventures has made an effort to design trips that meet the needs of all kinds of travelers—families, seniors, those looking for a challenging trip, those looking to mix lots of activities into one vacation. What all of the company's adventures have in common, however, is that each one showcases this great northern state in all its elemental beauty and power.

**FOR FAMILIES.** The Alaska Explorer Safari is an excellent choice for families. It includes two nights of camping in Kenai National Wildlife Refuge and two nights in Denali

National Park, interspersed with stays in cozy cabins (with hot showers). From the Kenai Riverside Lodge, you'll have two days to hike and explore the wildlife refuge and Chugach National Forest. After driving north to Talkeetna and on to Denali National Park, you'll set up tents within sight of the awesome mountain from which the park takes its name and join ranger-led hikes. In addition to hiking and camping, the safari will take you rafting on the Kenai River and provide lots of opportunities for observing Alaska's famous wildlife, especially in Denali National Park and on the Kenai Fjords National Park Cruise.

*Alaska Wildland Adventures, Box 389, Girdwood, AK 99587, tel. 907/783–2928 or 800/334–8730; 800/478–4100 in AK. June–Sept.: 10 days, $2,995–$3,195.*

## American Wilderness Experience/GORP Travel

**6+**

American Wilderness Experience/GORP Travel works with a variety of outfitters, primarily in the American West but also around the world. Although there are many hiking vacations in its catalog, two in Hawaii and Canada stand out as especially good family trips.

**FOR FAMILIES.** The 10-day, three-island Hawaiian adventure for families with children ages six and up takes in Kauai, Maui, and the Big Island, combining hiking with kayaking and snorkeling in Hawaii's alluring waters. The group stays in inns and bed-and-breakfasts along the way. You hike the dramatic sea cliffs of Kauai's Na Pali Coast, visit a wildlife refuge, and swim in both the ocean and the island's serene lagoons. On Maui you trek into the jungle and swim beneath the 420-ft Waimoku Falls. No trip here is complete without a sunrise stop at Haleakala, a dormant volcano with a spectacularly massive crater at its center. This is the longest hike of the trip—9 mi down into the crater and back out. The Big Island of Hawaii is the most rugged. You explore Kilauea and the rest of Volcanoes National Park, with its still-active volcanoes, as well as snorkel along the Kona Coast and participate in a traditional luau before heading to the Kona airport. (Airport transfers are included in the cost of the trip.)

For heli-hiking in the Canadian Rockies, your family can join lodge-based trips that include helicopter transportation to the remote wilderness areas where you hike each day. This adventure, for ages eight and up, lets you choose from a number of trip lengths and itineraries. Depending on the lodge you select, the trip begins either in Banff, in Alberta, or in Kelowna, in southern British Columbia. Relaxing in whirlpools and saunas at the lodges makes a perfect end to perfect days—as long as your idea of perfection is trekking high wilderness trails with not another soul around. Up to 48 guests can stay at the lodges, but hiking groups aren't bigger than 10 or 11.

*American Wilderness Experience/GORP Travel, Box 1486, Boulder, CO 80306, tel. 303/444–2622 or 800/444–0099. Year-round (all trips not available all months): 4–10 days, $850–$1,880 adults, $640–$1,810 children (age 14 and under on the Canadian trip).*

## Appalachian Mountain Club

**ALL**

The Appalachian Mountain Club (AMC) sponsors too many hiking, backpacking, and camping courses to list all here. Four campuses in four mountain ranges—New Hampshire's White Mountains, the Berkshires in Massachusetts, New York's Catskills, and the Poconos in eastern Pennsylvania—allow AMC to develop classes that are both extensive and varied. The club's family workshops, available at all campuses except the Poconos, are particularly worthwhile. In AMC parents and children find teachers and outdoor professionals who give them the skills to go out and enjoy the wilderness on their own.

**FOR FAMILIES.** At the White Mountain campus, families have several choices, all of which include hikes and nature walks, usually in addition to other activities. Leaders of the Family Discovery Weekend (for all ages) teach forest ecology, map and compass reading, low-impact camping, and nature crafts, among other activities. You camp overnight. Curious Explorers in Zealand centers on a 2½-mi hike to AMC's Zealand Falls hut, where preschoolers (ages three to five) spend the night with their parents and guides. Curious Explorers is for ages four through eight and their parents; the overnight on that trip is at AMC's main lodge at Pinkham Notch Visitor Center. Family Overnight at Greenleaf Hut is for parents with children ages 7 through 12. The whole family can join trips to Lonesome Lake and Crawford Notch; children under 13 are free at the Crawford Notch workshop. Lonesome Lake students overnight in a hut, and the Crawford Notch group sets up a woodland base camp from which to explore the surrounding area.

Berkshires workshops center on Bascom Lodge in the middle of Mt. Greylock State Reservation. A weekend Curious Explorers program introduces parents and children ages four through eight to the outdoors.

In the Catskills a Grandparent-Grandchild Nature Weekend for ages five and up brings different generations together for a night hike and hands-on discovery of the natural environment. The group stays at Valley View Lodge in the High Peaks region of the Catskills. A workshop for all ages, Introduction to Family Backpacking and Camping, incorporates moderate hikes and overnight camping. At this campus tents and backpacks are available for rent.

*Appalachian Mountain Club, Box 298, Gorham, NH 03581, tel. 603/466–2721 for White Mountains and AMC headquarters, 413/443–0011 for Berkshires, or 518/624–2056 for Catskills. Apr.–Oct. (all courses not available all months): 2–3 days, $40–$180; 50% discount for children under 10. AMC family membership is $65; members receive 10% discount on all workshops.*

## Backroads

**ALL**

Backroads, with one of the largest selections of family trips of any adventure-travel company, seems to add more family departures every year. By the time you try all the hiking Backroads currently offers, new destinations will be beckoning families to the trails of North America and beyond. Whichever you choose, you'll never really be roughing it; the company uses only top-notch properties for its inn trips, and the group leaders and guides provide uniformly excellent service.

**FOR FAMILIES.** In total, Backroads offers 72 family walking, biking, or multi-sport vacations to points in North America, Latin America, and Europe. One of these, a trek in Costa Rica, is strictly focused on walking. All of the others that include hiking are multi-sport adventures. Among these are trips in Washington, Canada, Switzerland, the Czech Republic, California, Montana, Wyoming, North Carolina, and Maine. Some of these are inn trips, some are camping.

The family walking adventure in Costa Rica is an inn trip—using several inns as bases, you'll discover the country's incredibly diverse landscape. You'll venture to majestic Arenal, one of the world's most active volcanoes, soak in a hot springs, explore the Monteverde Cloud Forest (and search for the elusive quetzal), and sway in hammocks on the beach at Tango Mar. If you want to camp, try the Kananaskis adventure in the southeastern corner of the Canadian Rockies where you hike, raft, and mountain bike through this rugged, alpine terrain.

In 1999 two new North American multisport itineraries were added for families: Montana's Glacier National Park and the Great Smoky Mountains of North Carolina. Montana is an inn tour with stays at the historic Many Glacier Hotel on the shores of Swiftcurrent Lake and the Prince of Wales hotel looking out over Waterton Lakes Valley. Families hike in the high country, raft the Flathead River, and bike across the mountains on fat tires. The North Carolina trip is also inn-based; you'll hike in the forested ridges of the Smokies and the backcountry of Shining Rock Wilderness Area. There are plenty of other activities too, from biking a portion of the Blue Ridge Parkway to horseback riding and rafting the Nantahala river.

And among the old favorites in the Backroads list are hiking, biking, and kayaking trips in and around Puget Sound and Washington's wildlife-rich islands, and a hiking, biking, and rafting adventure in Yellowstone and Grand Teton national parks. Both trips have inn and camping options.

*Backroads, 801 Cedar St., Berkeley, CA 94710, tel. 510/527–1555 or 800/462–2848. July–Aug., 6–7 days, $898–$1,998; 10%–75% discount for children, depending on age and accommodations.*

## Butterfield & Robinson

3+

Butterfield & Robinson (B&R) believes a walking trip "should move along at a leisurely pace, like a well-told story." That analogy works well for family hikes, too. B&R hiking trips designated specifically for families may be few in number, but the destinations are exceptional. This is a luxury operation, and prices reflect the high quality of the tours, staffing, and accommodations.

**FOR FAMILIES.** B&R has recently expanded its specialty family trips, which is good news for adventurous families with kids of all ages. The majority of these are for parents with kids at least twelve years old, but there are also several trips open for children as young as three. All trips have the signature B&R combination of awesome scenery by day, first-class amenities by night.

In 1999, B&R designed its first walking trip for families with children as young as three. Family Dolomites is a five-day excursion beginning in Bolzano in northwestern Italy, ending in Venice. Some alpine routes are challenging; however, parents with very young children can utilize trams and chairlifts to give youngsters a boost up to higher elevations where they can then easily hike through the hills and valleys of this impressive range. This region, the Alta Badia ('high Abbey'), is culturally diverse as well. In Covara, where you spend the first two days, three cultures and languages come together. It is as much influenced by nearby Austria as by Italy, and most people speak Italian, German, and Ladino, a mix of Latin, Italian, and German which is heard today only in this part of Italy and in the Swiss Engadine Valley. The hotels B&R chooses for this trip—from Covara to San Cassiano—are particularly family friendly. One hotelier invites the group to the home that has been in his family for generations, where he proudly demonstrates his yodeling.

The Montreux to Gstaad bicycling and hiking combination trip now has a departure for ages three and up and another for ages eight and up. This is an ideal itinerary for family members who aren't up to the demanding work usually necessary on mountainous cycling excursions. Here you hike the mountains and bike the valleys. Families with children at least eight years old can also sign up for Bears and Whales: Walking and Kayaking in British Columbia. While destinations may change from year to year, you can be certain that wherever the company decides to take families, it will be a trip of a lifetime, as memorable for B&R's attention to detail as for the destination itself.

*Butterfield & Robinson, 70 Bond St., Toronto, Ontario, Canada M5B 1X3, tel. 416/864–1354 or 800/678–1147. July–Aug.: 5–7 days, $3,390–$4,050 adults, 10%–35 % discount for children depending on age and lodging.*

## Camp Denali

8+

Camp Denali is one of Alaska's great destinations for family vacations, especially for families that want to get away from it all. Its location in the geographic center of the 5.7 million acres of Denali National Park puts it seven hours from the nearest town. Camp Denali's commitment to the preservation of the park's unique ecosystem guides all the activities it offers. And the lodge's wilderness setting is remarkable—it's one of only two park lodges with views of Mt. McKinley. Freshly baked goods, jams, and syrups made from the tundra's bountiful supply of wild berries, and fresh greens from the lodge's innovative greenhouse (heat is made from recycled waste) mean excellent food. The camp consists of central public buildings and seventeen cabins.

**FOR FAMILIES.** There are no separate activities for children; walking and hiking take center stage for everyone. Although Camp Denali has no hard-and-fast rule about the minimum age, it's felt that children eight and older have the capability to explore the area and take in the information shared by staff naturalists. You can hike the few maintained trails or head for the backcountry. Naturalists lead hikes of varying lengths; your family can also map out a route with the help of lodge employees. Hikes can take you to see beavers at work, grizzlies digging for food, or moose and caribou silhouetted against Denali (the native name for Mt. McKinley) itself. You can also try canoeing in Wonder Lake or biking the park road.

Families have a number of other ways to learn more about Denali. Evening activities—slides and naturalist talks—attract all ages. Camp Denali's Natural History Resource Center has interactive exhibits in addition to a herbarium and extensive resource library. Throughout the season, too, experts lead multi-day special-interest sessions on topics from the aurora borealis to nature photography. There are no additional charges for these programs.

*Camp Denali, Box 67, Denali National Park, AK 99755, tel. 907/683–2290. June–mid-Sept.: 4–8 days, $975–$2,275 adults, $735–$1,715 children under 12. Price includes all meals, activities, and round-trip transportation from Denali Park rail station.*

## Canadian Mountain Holidays

ALL

The Cariboo, Purcell, Bugaboo, and Selkirk wilderness areas of southern British Columbia may be too challenging for many families to hike into on their own. With a helicopter lift from one of its lodges each day and treks for every ability, Canadian Mountain Holidays (CMH) helps hikers of all ages discover mountain landscapes that are as breathtaking as they are remote.

**FOR FAMILIES.** At the company's five lodges, groups of about 11 are divided by ability and taste, so you can hike with your family or go your separate ways and meet back at the lodge. Hikes from Cariboo Lodge, about 80 mi southwest of Jasper in the Cariboo Mountains, lead to massive glaciers and heather-filled alpine valleys. The Bobbie Burns Lodge is about 195 mi west of Calgary, deep in the Purcell Range. Trails high on Grizzly Ridge have unparalleled views of the vast Conrad Icefield and the Bugaboo and Vowell peaks. Bugaboo Lodge, across Grizzly Ridge from the Bobbie Burns, sits at the base of the Bugaboo Glacier. The terrain here encompasses sunny meadows and blue alpine lakes, forests, glaciers, waterfalls, and rushing mountain streams. Valemount is the company's newest lodge, accommodating only 20 guests. It's situated just outside the town of Valemount in the Cariboo Mountains, about 80 mi southwest of Jasper. All of the lodge's rooms open onto a deck with magnificent views of Mt. Robson, which is just one of the areas to be explored from here. In summer Valemount runs a multi-adventure trip which is especially good for families; it includes horseback riding, rafting, canoeing, and fly-fishing in addition to heli-hiking.

CMH offers a four-night family adventure once each summer at Adamant Lodge, in the Selkirk Mountains. In addition to daily heli-hiking, there are activities for children that focus on learning and playing in this magnificent wilderness area. Families may hike together, or they may spend a day going off separately on hikes with their own age group. At night in the lodge, parents and children come back together to swap stories of their adventures over a gourmet dinner. There are evening activities for the whole group, and Adamant has a climbing wall that draws all ages. Children's programs on this trip are geared for ages 5 to 14.

Children of about age eight and older are welcome on any trip. Because CMH doesn't have a strict age minimum, families with young children can enjoy these remote areas. The company requests, however, that parents with children under eight call and discuss details before booking a stay.

The lodges have from 10 to 29 rooms each, all with private baths. Local transportation is included in the price but differs for each lodge. For Bugaboo, Bobbie Burns, and Adamant, transportation from Banff is included; guests at the Cariboo or Valemount lodges meet in Jasper or Valemount. *Canadian Mountain Holidays, Box 1660, Banff, Alberta, Canada T0L 0C0, tel. 403/762–7100 or 800/661–0252. July–Sept.: 1–6 days, C$269–C$2,829 adults, C$202–C$2,122 children 14 and under.*

## Ciclismo Classico

**ALL**

Known primarily for its stellar biking adventures (see Biking), Ciclismo Classico also mixes a good deal of hiking and other activities into its family-oriented adventure in the Dolomite range of northwestern Italy. Director (and mother of two) Lauren Hefferon has been leading trips there for more than a decade. All of the staff, including Lauren's husband, are Italian or of Italian descent, and the company has a vast network of guides and hoteliers in Italy. In short, when you go to Italy with Ciclismo Classico, you're going with people who share their passion for the country and their insiders' depth of experience.

**FOR FAMILIES.** Fly into Milan, then catch a train to Bolzano, where group members are met and shuttled to the four-star Alpenroyal Inn in Selva Gardena, base for the eight-day trip. In the heart of the intensely beautiful Dolomites, the family-run Alpenroyal has a wholly relaxed atmosphere and plenty of amenities, including an indoor and outdoor pool, a spa, a wine cellar, and a fitness course. Part of the adventure for children age 2 to 12 is Camp Ciclismo, where they'll get to know farm animals, meet local children, and play on a playground.

Mornings are dedicated to guided hikes for all levels; you can expect to hike between 5 and 15 mi each day. And there are bike rides for adults and older children along some of the world's most spectacular roads and passes: Passo Sella, Passo Pordoi, and Passo Falzarego. The bicycle trips cover 30 to 50 mi a day. In the afternoon, expand your mind with natural history talks, cooking lessons, craft demonstrations, photography clinics, and excursions to nearby villages. Or you could elect to laze by the pool, play tennis or golf on the hotel's grounds, chess on the garden board, or perhaps take up bocce.

This trip is well suited for beginner and intermediate hikers and bikers. The terrain is rolling to mountainous, so there are places where the going is easy and places where you'll be challenged.

*Ciclismo Classico, 13 Marathon St., Arlington, MA 02724, tel. 781/646–3377 or 800/866–7314. June–Oct.: 8 days, $2,495 adults, 40 % discount for children 3–16 sharing accommodations with parents, $200 for children 2 and under sharing with parents. Bike rental is $150.*

## Cross Country International

8+

Cross Country International offers walking vacations across Europe. One look at CCI's catalog of trips will show you that owners Karen and Roy Lancaster choose destinations that are rich in history as well as natural beauty—wonderful, memorable classrooms without walls.

**FOR FAMILIES.** While most of CCI's vacations are suitable for families, one in particular stands out. Perhaps it's because I'm a lifelong lover of Shakespeare—a love I now share with my daughter, Molly—that Scotland's Cawdor Estates trek has such appeal. Cawdor, in the Scottish Highlands, was the home of Macbeth, and there is something magical in walking the same land that he walked a thousand years ago. (Yes, Macbeth was a real king of Scotland, not just the playwright's invention.) Yet you don't have to be a scholar to fall in love with Scotland or to be intrigued by its history. And if you haven't read *Macbeth,* there would be no better place to do it than here, exploring by day and reading the play aloud as a family at night.

Cawdor Estates, not far from Inverness, measures about 80 square mi of hills covered in heather and clear streams running with salmon and trout. You'll be able to fully absorb this gorgeous setting since you stay in a 19th-century hunting lodge on the grounds. Each day the group walks in different areas—over the wild moors, to Moray Firth, carved long ago by glaciers; through ancient forests; along the banks of the River Findhorn; or into Cawdor Castle itself. If children choose not to hike on some days, arrangements can be made for other activities. There are mountain bikes and horses, for example, and the gamekeeper will be happy to provide fishing gear along with his knowledge on the best local fishing holes. Sumptuous picnics and barbecue lunches are served outdoors each day; when you return from exploring, tea and a three-course dinner await you at the lodge.

The group is kept small—just a dozen people. The trip starts and ends at the train station in Inverness.

*Cross Country International, Box 1170, Millbrook, NY 12545, tel. 800/828–8768. June–Aug.: 7 days, $3,040 adults, 25% discount for children age 11 and under sharing a room with parents.*

## REI Adventures

11+

REI, the nationwide outdoor gear store that has been outfitting adventurers since 1938, also schedules trips in a number of sports. The company allows children on its trips on a case-by-case basis, and several of its trips are excellent for families.

**FOR FAMILIES.** The High Sierra trip is ideal for families just beginning to venture into the wilderness. The group hikes from 5 to 10 mi each day over moderate terrain in the Ansel Adams and John Muir wilderness areas on Yosemite National Park's southern border. Lodging is in comfortable mountain lodges. Participants on the Olympic Peninsula outing hike Olympic National Park and Washington's coastal area by day and overnight in historic lodges and hotels. The Hidden Treasures Camping Adventure in Alaska takes you to Denali, Wrangell–St. Elias, and Kenai Fjords national parks. Get ready to experience one of nature's most impressive auditory events when you cross Prince William Sound: the earthshaking roar of a glacier as huge chunks of it calve into the water.

Combination trips take the adventurous to Hawaii or Canada for a variety of activities in addition to hiking. Kauai's Na Pali Coast, accessible only by trail or boat, is a favorite area for kayakers and hikers. On REI's week-long trip, you'll kayak the waters off Na Pali as well as jungle rivers. The group also gets to experience parts of the wet and mountainous interior that few tourists see. You hike portions of the ancient Kalalau Trail into Kalalau Valley and end the trip in the Kokee highlands around Waimea Canyon, often called the Grand Canyon of the Pacific. Among the trails of Kokee are those in Waimea Canyon, the Na Pali–Kona Forest Reserve, and Alaka'i Swamp, the highest swamp in North America and the largest alpine swamp in the world.

The nine-day Canadian combination trip takes you hiking, canoeing, and rafting through the Canadian Rockies and the country's most famous national parks—Banff, Jasper, and Yoho. You also have a chance to tour Calgary.

*REI Adventures, Box 1938, Sumner, WA 98390, tel. 253/437–1100 or 800/622–2236. Mar.– Dec.: 7–14 days, $995–$1,395.*

## Sierra Club

**ALL**

Of the Sierra Club's 30 family trips, 18 focus primarily on hiking. The majority of these explore western states, but you'll find several eastern destinations each year, too. Sierra Club leaders are highly experienced in guiding families. All trips, family and otherwise, emphasize respect for and preservation of America's wilderness areas. This is one of the few organizations of its kind to welcome children on some service trips as well—expeditions that involve clearing and maintaining trails or doing other projects to assist the park service.

**FOR FAMILIES.** There are family trips for all ages, but not all trips are suitable for every age. Families with toddlers (ages two and up) have a choice of two camping trips: the Fiery Furnace and Devil's Garden family adventure in Arches and Canyonlands national parks in Utah or the Acadia Toddler Tromp in Acadia National Park, Maine. Both trips highlight age-appropriate activities such as bug collecting, tidal pool explorations, easy hikes, and nature education by trip leaders and park rangers.

The club's outings for all ages—including babies in backpacks—explore the Hawaiian island of Kauai and Rocky Mountain National Park in Colorado. On the Kauai itinerary are intriguing natural sites: the Na Pali Coast, Waimea Canyon, Alaka'i Swamp with its dwarf trees and wild pigs, and glorious beaches sloping down to a blue-green sea. In addition to hiking, families can snorkel and sightsee. Rustic beachside lodging provides a base for these adventures. The Rocky Mountain Ramble in Colorado focuses on daily hikes of varied difficulty in alpine meadows, around high-country lakes, and to waterfalls, glaciers, and Longs Peak. You stay in a comfortable lodge, with programs for children ages 2½ through 17, fishing, and a swimming pool.

Children as young as five are welcome on an easy hiking trip among California's coastal redwoods in Redwood National Park. The giant trees are a prime attraction, but this area also has a rich mix of wildlife, both on land and offshore—gray whales, seals, sea lions, dolphins, and orcas. Families have a base camp in an established campground with hot showers and other facilities. A similar base-camp format is offered on the Mt. Lassen Family Camp trip in Lassen Volcanic National Park in California. Children will climb a giant cinder cone, crawl through a lava tube cave, and explore the (smelly) mud pots of the Sulphur Works Thermal Area. Swimming and possibly a climb up Lassen Peak itself are other activities. A grandparents and grandchildren outing in Tahoe National Forest in the Sierra Nevada is also for those five and up. Using the club's Clair Tappaan Lodge as a base, children and adults can hike, swim, and do some exploring away from the group, too.

Another group of trips targets children ages 6 through 12 and their parents. In Washington, families travel by ferry to a base camp of rustic cabins on Lake Chelan in the northern Cascades. Hikes on Stehekin Valley's glaciated terrain vary from easy to strenuous. Another grandparents and grandchildren trip (for children age six and older) offers backpacking in the Carson-Iceberg Wilderness between Yosemite National Park and Lake Tahoe, in the High Sierra. The group backpacks 5 mi to a lakeside base camp, after which everyone can swim, take day hikes, fish, and relax for three days. Grandparents should have some backpacking experience for this trip; children need nothing but a willingness to learn.

Families with children ages eight and up have a number of choices. They can explore Vermont's Groton State Forest by hike and bike, as well as visit a nearby cheese factory; museums; and Montpelier, the state capital. No camping trip is complete without singing songs around a campfire, and that's part of this base-camp trip, too. The packer-assisted 6-mi backpack trip in the John Muir Wilderness of California is one with vigorous hiking and peak climbing, along with plenty of opportunities for swimming, fishing, photography, nature study, and exploration of the high base-camp area on Lake Genevieve, at 10,000 ft.

For families that want to combine their vacation with outdoor work, three trail service trips give children a firsthand understanding of what it means to volunteer. Pick your destination: Coconino National Forest in Arizona (two trips) or Ritchey Woods Nature Preserve in Indianapolis, Indiana. One of the Arizona outings is a base-camp trip for ages four and up; the other is a backpack experience for ages 10 and older. On both, volunteers work to improve the trails. The Environmental Family Fun trip in Ritchey Woods lets you share the joy of the outdoors with your children as you work to upgrade trails. Various age-appropriate projects keep volunteers ages six and up busy.

Sierra Club's outings change annually, and the ones listed here are typical of its family trips but may not be offered every year. However, you can choose from a roster of fun, challenging, and educational trips, whether your children are toddlers or teens, whether you are parents or grandparents. Participants bring their own tents and gear on camping trips.

*Sierra Club, 85 2nd St., San Francisco, CA 94105, tel. 415/977–5522. Apr.–Sept.: 4–8 days, $380–$895 adults, $285–$775 children 16 and under. All participants 18 and up must be Sierra Club members; application and fees ($35 per person, $42 per couple) can be sent in with the trip reservation form.*

## Sila Sojourns Wilderness and Creative Journeys

**10+**

*Sila* is an Inuit word for nature and free-spiritedness. To the people of the Arctic, it signifies a mysterious power in the universe. A walk through Canada's Yukon wilderness will help you understand why Joyce Majiski and Jill Pangman gave their company this name. Nature's scale here is immense, giving a sense of an undefinable force. Joyce and Jill, longtime Yukon residents, have considerable wilderness experience as guides. They bring another dimension to their company as well: Both are biologists, naturalists, and fine artists. Their trips challenge adventurers to stretch their physical and creative limits.

**FOR FAMILIES.** Although Sila has some scheduled expeditions for up to 10 hikers, the company specializes in personalized trips. All journeys start and end in Whitehorse; any wilderness flights are included in the trip cost. Joyce recommends two areas for custom family treks. In either, a hiking trip can be combined with a four- to six-day rafting adventure down the Alsek River to Lowell Lake, where the calving Lowell Glacier provides a visual and auditory feast.

For ages 10 and up, Primrose Lake, a half-hour flight from Whitehorse in the southern section of the Yukon, offers moderate hikes that follow game trails across rolling hills and past clear lakes and streams. The land changes from alpine meadows to northern boreal forests of spruce, poplar, and lodgepole pine. With some of the hiking above tree line, there are uninterrupted views of the landscape and opportunities to see Dall sheep, grizzlies, black bears, and moose. You spend two nights of the trip in a wilderness lodge; on the rest you camp out.

Bordering Alaska in the southwest corner of the Yukon, Kluane National Park encompasses 8,500 square mi, with glaciers, river valleys, and mountains that are dramatic and untamed. Challenging hiking terrain makes this trip best for ages 16 and up; the park contains both Mt. Logan and Mt. St. Elias, the second- and third-highest peaks in North America. An astonishing variety of wildlife inhabits the park: moose, wolves, foxes, lynx, wolverines, otters, and black bears, as well as a large grizzly population. You camp in alpine areas or by rivers and glaciers.

Some multi-activity trips for women focus on the creative process. Mothers and teenage daughters who want to experience the wilderness and explore perspectives on creative writing, journal keeping, and other means of artistic expression should ask about these camping or lodge-based trips. Depending on the location, participants hike from a lodge, kayak on Atlin Lake in northern British Columbia, or even canoe or raft.

*Sila Sojourns, Box 5095, Whitehorse, Yukon, Canada Y1A 4Z2, tel. 867/633–8453. June–Sept.: 3–12 days, C$100–C$250 per day; 10%–20% discount for children under 18.*

## Southwest Trekking

**ALL**

John Heiman Jr. founded Southwest Trekking because he wanted to be outdoors and to share the natural world with anyone who wanted to come along with him. A father himself, he especially likes to help families experience what nature has to offer. "I respect the children's place in the outing," he says, meaning every individual in his groups, adult or child, counts. John's tours are highly customized—no big-group departures with this company. Treks can be all-inclusive (he'll provide everything you need, including camping gear) or on an as-needed basis (if you have your own tents and sleeping bags, why pay him for his?). A native Tucsonian, John specializes in treks in pristine areas of Arizona and Mexico.

**FOR FAMILIES.** Families can explore one of John's favorite destinations, the Dragoon Mountains and an area known as Cochise Stronghold, east of Tucson. In the mid-19th century Cochise, a Chiricahua Apache chief, held off the U.S. cavalry for six years, in part because of the remoteness and ruggedness of this land. It's fully accessible for car camping, though, making it an ideal family destination. Beauty, history, legend, challenge, accessibility—what could be better?

Committed to ecotourism, Southwest Trekking has been working with the local people of the Colorado River delta and upper Gulf of California region in Mexico to establish a program for visitors that would benefit the area's farmers. The result, Spatial Journeys, opens a sensitive, remote, and fragile environment to visitors and gives you a unique opportunity to learn about the culture, social history, and flora and fauna of the region, as well as the environmental concerns its residents face. You visit the homes of local families and have a chance to meet farmers, fishers, schoolteachers, biologists, and children. The trip's educational aspect makes it appropriate for families with older children. You also hike through volcanic formations, snorkel and swim on beaches to the south of the Gulf of Santa Clara, and canoe through the Cienega de Santa Clara—49,400 acres of wetlands.

Southwest Trekking works on a custom basis, and you can talk to the company about your family, how much time you have, where you want to go, and what you want to do. John and his staff will put together a trek that suits everyone in your family.

*Southwest Trekking, Box 57714, Tucson, AZ 85732, tel. 520/296–9661. Year-round: ½– multiple days, $60–$150 per day adults, $30–$75 per day children under 12. Outfitter's expenses are additional on multi-day treks.*

## Wells Gray Chalets & Wilderness Adventures

8+

The Cariboo Mountains reign over the 1.3 million acres of Wells Gray Provincial Park in southeastern British Columbia, a pristine land of alpine meadows and mountain lakes. Wells Gray Chalets & Wilderness Adventures, a family business, operates two high wilderness chalets and a secluded valley cabin here; a separate guest ranch (not owned by this company) is near the entrance to the park. The chalets can be rented individually without guides or used as part of a guided hiking trek. Although there's no stated age limit, the hut-to-hut hike is very challenging—perfect for families with teens. Families with children under age eight should talk to staff members before booking a vacation. Because of increased interest, the company now designates a hiking trip in August just for families.

**FOR FAMILIES.** If you have preteens and younger or just can't decide whether you prefer land or water, ask about the Canoe and Trek Combo. Families camp along the shore of Clearwater Lake for three days of canoeing, then spend a night at Wells Gray Guest Ranch before beginning three days of trekking based at a secluded mountain hut.

Parents with teens or children with solid backcountry experience might opt for the company's premier trip, the six-day hut-to-hut trek. Although it's just a little more than 1½ mi in to Trophy Mountain Chalet, the ascent is about 1,300 ft. This area presents the most rugged terrain of the trip; you can reward yourself with a swim and glorious views. Table Mountain Cabin, the next stop, is reached by crossing the Trophy Mountains and descending into isolated Moul Valley. Fight Meadow Chalet, the third and last hut, is 6,500 ft up at the head of an expansive alpine meadow. There are no trails between huts; this is true wilderness hiking for those who want to challenge themselves and each other. Parents should be sure of their own and their children's abilities before undertaking this trek.

*Wells Gray Chalets & Wilderness Adventures, Box 188, Clearwater, British Columbia, Canada V0E 1N0, tel. 250/587–6444 or 888/SKI–TREK. June–Sept.: 6 days, $430–$565 adults, 25% discount for children under 13.*

# Resources

## Books

For solid information on taking children into the wilderness, check out *The Sierra Club Family Outdoors Guide,* by Marlyn Doan (Sierra Club Books), and *Kids in the Wild,* by Cindy Ross and Todd Gladfelter (Mountaineers Books, tel. 800/553–4453). Michael

Elsohn Ross's *The Happy Camper Handbook* (Yosemite Association, tel. 209/379–2648) comes with a flashlight and rescue whistle and is full of essential camping information for school-age children; parents can read it aloud to younger children, too. Families serious about backpacking will find good practical advice in *Basic Essentials Backpacking* by Harry Robers, revised by Adrienne Hall (Globe Pequot Press). Talk about basics—it even tells you how best to walk with a heavy pack.

## Products

The following companies sell clothing or footwear for wilderness-loving families. **Patagonia** (8550 White Fir St., Box 32050, Reno, NV 89533, tel. 800/638–6464) is an excellent mail-order source for clothing and outerwear. You can also buy the company's products in most stores that sell outdoor and camping clothing and accessories. **REI outdoor stores** (Sumner, WA 98352-0001, tel. 800/426–4840) are found nationwide; items can be ordered from their catalog, too. REI's own brand is excellent. **Nike** (1 Bowerman Dr., Beavertown, OR 97005, tel. 503/671–6453 or 800/344–6453) has hiking boots, water sandals, and aqua socks for all ages, as well as some children's sports clothing and outerwear. **Hi-Tec Sports USA** (4801 Stoddard Rd., Modesto, CA 95356, tel. 209/545–1111 or 800/521–1698) makes hiking boots and "adventure racing shoes" for children and adults. **L.L. Bean** (Freeport, ME 04033, tel. 800/221–4221) has a camping catalog that includes a section on family camping gear and equipment. There's also a children's catalog with outdoor clothing and more.

The following companies make camping gear for children and adults. **Tough Traveler** (1012 State St., Schenectady, NY 12307, tel. 518/377–8526), a parent-owned and -operated company, produces quality outdoor gear and luggage for children. Call or write for a catalog. **Mountainsmith, Inc.** (18301 W. Colfax Ave., Golden, CO 80401, tel. 303/279–5930 or 800/426–4075) manufactures day packs suitable for most ages and inner-frame backpacks for older children and adults. **Crazy Creek Products** (Box 1050, Red Lodge, MT 59068, tel. 406/446–3446 or 800/331–0304) makes camping comfortable with 12 models of take-anywhere fold-up soft chairs.

# HORSE PACKING

Like hiking adventures, horse pack trips take your family into some of the world's most incredible backcountry wilderness areas. But because these are on horseback, you don't have to walk on your own two feet to get there, and you don't have to carry a heavy backpack. Often it's not even necessary to be an expert rider. Adults and teens need no riding experience on many pack trips, although for everyone's safety and enjoyment outfitters often require that children under the age of 11 or 12 ride moderately well and be comfortable around horses. For this reason, horse packing (with a couple of exceptions) is not usually appropriate for families with very young children. Anyone else who wants to experience glorious land and a mode of travel that has been around for centuries should give it a try.

There's another nice benefit to horse pack trips. Because horses and mules are capable of carrying a lot more than a human, you can escape the spartan atmosphere of long backpacking adventures: Food and supplies are first-rate and plentiful.

## Questions to Ask

**How much time is spent riding each day?** On average, outfitters keep you in the saddle from four to six hours per day, but on some trips you may ride as long as eight hours. Depending on the group's size and whether the camp destination is specific or flexible, riding time can also change from day to day. Keep in mind that layover days are usually figured into multi-day trips, too. Remember that even if you have some riding experience under your belt, a day in the saddle can leave you aching and dealing with saddle sores. The discomfort doesn't usually last that long, but do bring acetaminophen or another pain reliever, antibiotic cream, and a bunch of adhesive bandages.

**Will the horses travel a faster gait than a walk?** Most horse pack trips are primarily walking because they often take place in hilly or otherwise challenging terrain. Although horses are very surefooted, walking is the safest way to negotiate these trails—both for horse and rider. Sometimes wranglers allow good riders to go a bit faster under controlled circumstances. If your family cares about this, speak up when you're booking. If you can't work something out, consider a cattle drive (see Cattle Drives), which often allows a faster pace.

**Are there activities other than riding?** Packers generally return to camp early enough in the afternoon to give your family time for hiking, swimming, and maybe even fishing. You usually need to bring your own fishing gear, however.

**Is there a weight limit to what we can bring?** Often, yes. A 30-pound limit per person is typical, and you should pack in duffel bags, not hard-sided suitcases.

**Are riding boots necessary?** Some packers require boots; even if they don't, everyone in the family should have them for safety and comfort. Shoes without adequate heels may allow your foot to slip through the stirrup. If that happened and you fell off as a result, you'd be dragged. Be sure to break new boots in well before the trip.

**Is a cowboy hat or a riding helmet needed?** A cowboy hat will keep the sun off your face and your hair out of your eyes, and that can be important. It won't, however, protect your head if you fall. Some outfitters provide helmets; most don't require them. To keep yourself and your children safe, you should wear them. You can buy helmets at stores that sell riding apparel and equipment.

**Should we bring a camera?** You bet. Keep it in a case for protection against dust and dirt, and talk to packers about stopping occasionally for a good shot (most, actually, will tell you when a great photo op is coming up). Don't leave the group to get a good picture without telling someone first; you could get lost. If you're not comfortable carrying a camera when you ride, it can usually go in a saddle bag with your stuff.

**What kind of food is served?** If your family likes outdoor cooking—hearty egg-and-pancake breakfasts, Dutch oven meals, barbecue, steaks, salads, fruit, and desserts—you'll like the meals just fine. Special requests can usually be accommodated, so ask.

**What kind of lodging is provided?** These are backcountry trips. Sleeping is almost always in tents—or cowboy style, under the stars, if you prefer. A few packers use cabins or lodges.

**What facilities are available for bathing and showering?** Do you like the smell of horses? You should, because it will be the predominant odor on a pack trip. At the end of the day, though, some outfitters do provide portable showers or shower trailers. If you're staying in lodges or cabins, you may have access to showers.

**What's the typical group size?** The average is from 8 to 12, though some outfitters take as few as 4 and others as many as 20. Between two and five wranglers and/or packers accompany the group. A large group isn't necessarily bad because it provides lots of companionship, and a small group isn't necessarily good if you don't want to be the only ones in the group.

**What's included in the cost?** Prices for the trips listed here include wranglers and/or packers, a horse, sleeping quarters, all meals from start to end of the actual pack trip, and local transportation to and from the trailhead, unless otherwise noted.

## Instruction

Horsemanship is part and parcel of every horse pack trip; the wranglers will give you pointers and informal instruction on the trail. Your family can also learn about feeding and caring for horses—and even saddling bags. While you're out in the wilderness, guides will teach you about the cultural and natural history of the land, as well as wildlife identification.

## Finding the Fun

**Midwest:** Dakota Badlands Outfitters. **Southwest:** American Wilderness Experience/GORP Travel, Cottonwood Ranch, Rockin' R Ranch. **Rockies:** Adventure Specialists, American Wilderness Experience/GORP Travel, Fantasy Ranch, Great Divide Guiding & Outfitters, Skinner Brothers, Vista Verde Ranch, WTR Outfitters/White Tail Ranch. **West Coast:** Mammoth Lakes Pack Outfit. **Canada:** American Wilderness Experience/GORP Travel, Spatsizi Wilderness Vacations.

# Favorite Packers

## Adventure Specialists

**10+**

Horse pack trips are just one adventure offered by this unique outfitter. Based on a 5,000-acre ranch in southern Colorado, Adventure Specialists uses what it possesses—the ranch itself and 70 Appaloosa and Paso Fino horses—and all that's in its backyard, too: the rugged Sangre de Cristo Mountains, the gentler Wet Mountains, and the Arkansas River. In addition to riding, you can hike, bike, climb, and raft, depending on the trip.

Owners Gary Ziegler and Amy Finger emphasize natural history and environmental awareness. Gary earned a doctorate in archaeology, discovered the ruins of an ancient city in Peru, and has made first ascents of several 20,000-ft South American peaks. Amy, a geologist, has studied languages, flora, and ecology extensively. She's worked with horses most of her life.

**FOR FAMILIES.** Three adventures are especially appropriate for families. The three-day pack trip into the Sangre de Cristo Mountains is best for spirited children 10 and up who are ready for a challenge. They should have some riding experience and be comfortable around horses. There's one base camp, and rides go through dense forests and up to shimmery alpine lakes. The Surf and Turf trip combines the three-day pack trip with two days of rafting on the Arkansas; because the Arkansas is Class III and IV white water, the minimum age is 13. Accommodations during the rafting portion are at the Westcliffe Inn, with cozy rooms and a hot tub.

For a completely different experience, Mountain Sports Week offers rock climbing; two days of riding the open range; two days of mountain biking, including a day on the famous Rainbow Trail in the Sangre de Cristo (or you can opt for a hike); and a day of rafting. Participants are based at the ranch in a camp with individual tents for sleeping, showers, and a large dining and kitchen tent. Children under 10 might be considered on an individual basis, but this is a physically challenging week. You can also customize your own course, choosing any of the activities.

Transportation to and from Colorado Springs, 1½ hours away, is included in all packages. Ask about trips to Mexico, Peru, and Spain.
*Adventure Specialists, Bear Basin Ranch, Westcliffe, CO 81252, tel. 719/783–2519 for ranch (year-round) or 719/630–7687 for Colorado Springs office (Dec.–Apr.). May–Oct. (all trips not available at all times): 3–6 days, $480–$965; customized courses, $125–$150 per day.*

## American Wilderness Experience/GORP Travel

6+

If you haven't picked the area in which you want to ride, take a look at the American Wilderness Experience/GORP Travel catalog. It lists more than eight pages of horse pack adventures. Some of the outfitters they use are in this chapter, and you can book directly with them. But if research isn't your thing, the company is an excellent choice. It has already evaluated the outfitters, knows which ones work best with families, and can make recommendations based on experience and solid knowledge.

If the scheduled trips don't work for you, the company will also customize a family trip for ages six and older. Your willingness to meet adventure head-on and your imagination are the only limits to the horse pack vacation of a lifetime.

**FOR FAMILIES.** One trip takes riders age eight and older across the ridges, peaks, and alpine meadows of the Canadian Rockies of Alberta, to the deep wilderness habitat of elk and bighorn sheep. June is calving season for elk, so sightings are generally plentiful then; September is rutting season, and the distinctive bugle of mature bull elk can be heard day and night. This is an active holiday; riders are expected to help with camp chores and horse care, and weather is unpredictable, so be prepared. You can choose from 5-, 7-, and 10-day treks.

In the Lower 48, children age 10 and up can explore Wyoming's Grand Teton Range, 18 mi west of Jackson. The land is unspoiled, but the guests aren't: The camp, up at 7,200 ft, has a dining tent and spacious wall tents with cots, rugs, and wood stoves. Day rides take you through old growth stands of aspen, fir, and spruce into wildflower meadows and up to summer snowfields. Two nights of the week are reserved for a trip to the Jackson rodeo. Farther south, families with children eight and up can ride through the mesas, meadows, canyons, and rugged landscape of the Gila Wilderness, part of New Mexico's 3.3-million-acre Gila National Forest. The Gila area is home to eagles, antelope, mountain lions, and elk, among other wildlife. Motel lodging before and after this trip is included; otherwise, you camp along the trail.

Families interested in the Southwest might choose instead to explore Monument Valley, a wild western landscape straddling the Arizona–Utah border. Towering mesas and sand- and wind-sculpted monoliths define the valley, which is within the Navajo Nation. At the base camp, near Thunderbird Mesa, expect spacious wall tents, sleeping cots, bedrolls, pads, sheets, pillows, a hot-shower trailer, and fine food each afternoon.
*American Wilderness Experience/GORP Travel, Box 1486, Boulder, CO 80306, tel. 303/444–2622 or 800/444–0099. Jan.–Nov.: 3–10 days, $380–$1,510 per person; custom trips average $160 per day. Children's discount available on some itineraries.*

## Cottonwood Ranch

7+

A horse pack trip with the Smiths is a gem of an adventure, far off the beaten path in

Nevada. Their family ranch, 75 mi north of Wells in the northeast corner of the state, is near nothing—except clean, quiet high desert and the exquisite landscape of the Jarbridge Wilderness. Horace Smith will share with you his love of a land that few have a chance to experience.

**FOR FAMILIES.** Guests spend the first night at Cottonwood Ranch, then take off for five days in the wilderness. Deep canyons and high peaks make this terrain appropriate for riding at a walk only. You hit the trail from about 9 to 4 each day; camps with wall tents and cook tents are set up by the wranglers before you arrive. Photo stops are numerous, and you visit abandoned mining cabins that look, according to Horace, "like the old miner just went into town for a day and forgot to come back." There's plenty of wildlife on the trail and good fishing at Emerald Lake (some gear is available); you can also swim in the lake if you can stand the cold water. On the last night you reach the old mining town of Jarbridge and stay in a remodeled barn turned hotel.
*Cottonwood Ranch, HC 62, Box 1300, O'Neil Rte., Wells, NV 89835, tel. 775/752–3135 or 775/755–2231. July–Sept.: 7 days, $995; 20% discount for children under 16.*

## Dakota Badland Outfitters

11+

John Husted, a fifth-generation South Dakota rancher, comes from a family that homesteaded in the Dakota Badlands. He and his wife, Jane, enjoy showing the state they love to visitors. Their ranch is in the state's other famous territory—the Black Hills—and before or after a pack trip you should visit that area. One neat place is the Dakota Badland Outfitters Western Heritage Livery. From the livery you can take trail rides through the Black Hills and near the work-in-progress Crazy Horse Monument. Back at the barn, blacksmiths and horse trainers may be seen working; evening team-roping demonstrations and team-penning competitions are held here, too.

**FOR FAMILIES.** Parents with children age 11 and up may join treks through the high, grassy tableland and buttes of the Badlands. This is the country of Red Cloud, Sitting Bull, and Crazy Horse, of the ghost dances at Stronghold Table that led to the massacre at Wounded Knee, and of General George Custer. It's also where *Dances With Wolves* was filmed; the fragile prairie grasslands have changed little over the centuries. Camp is set along the Cheyenne River; from there rides go up to the tabletops with panoramic views of the vast prairie wilderness. Back at camp, a chuck wagon kitchen and heated mess tent provide hearty food and a relaxing place to unwind. If you have time before or after, journey by car into lunarlike Badlands National Park, a harshly beautiful place of eroded canyons and wide-open vistas, with sunrises and sunsets not soon forgotten.
*Dakota Badland Outfitters, Box 85, Custer, SD 57730, tel. 605/673–5363. Sept.–Oct.: 4 days, $680 per person.*

## Fantasy Ranch

6+

You won't meet a harder-working outfitter than Jim Talbot of Colorado. He'll clear snow from the trails by hand if Mother Nature hasn't cooperated by the time the season's first pack trip is scheduled. Jim has a personality children can relate to, which makes learning from him easy, and he's enthusiastic and knowledgeable about the magnificent wilderness area that is his backyard. He's also flexible: Jim won't bend safety rules, but he's willing to work with families to make their pack-trip fantasies a reality.

Fantasy Ranch now has a five-bedroom lodge; overnights there include a Continental breakfast. Ask Jim about staying over and about horseback riding and hay-wagon barbecues. Families can also hike, fish, and bike in the area. When the weather turns cold, come to Fantasy Ranch for a day of winter riding through the snowy landscape.

**FOR FAMILIES.** Ages six and up can try an overnight in the Oh-Be-Joyful Wilderness northwest of Crested Butte, Fantasy Ranch's hometown. These trails are gentle, but the views and scenery—rushing waterfalls and massive rock formations—are classic Colorado. Children ages six through eight who have never ridden will be led by one of the wranglers. Children eight and up can take a two-to five-day pack trip into the West Elk Wilderness area, where the Rockies rise above the meadows and mountain lakes, which makes this superb riding country. You can camp or stay in a rustic cabin on the boundary of the wilderness area.

One of the all-time great pack trips is Jim's Crested Butte to Aspen adventure, for experienced riders age 13 and up. The three-day ride between the two mountain towns starts at 9,000 ft, just east of Crested Butte, on trails through Maroon Bells Wilderness. You camp in the mountains, then ride four or so hours the following day before descending into alpine meadows and the trailhead outside Aspen. A van takes you into town for an overnight in this world-class resort. Lodging in Aspen is included, but you're on your own for meals. The next morning you begin one of the most spectacular rides anywhere—up and over 11,800-ft East Maroon Pass, then back into Crested Butte.

You need to bring your own sleeping bag and pad; add fishing gear if you want to fish.
*Fantasy Ranch, Box 236, Crested Butte, CO 81224, tel. 970/349–5425 or 888/688–3488. July–Oct. (for pack trips): 2–5 days, $90–$150 per day per person.*

## Great Divide Guiding & Outfitters

8+

Richard Jackson, who has nearly 20 years of guiding and outfitting experience, leads every group, with his son along as a wrangler. All Richard's trips take place in Montana's Lewis and Clark National Forest, which is surrounded by Glacier National Park, the Blackfoot Indian Reservation, the Bob Marshall Wilderness, and the Great Bear Wilderness. The combination of the Jacksons' expertise and the countryside makes Great Divide's adventure and wilderness credentials impeccable.

**FOR FAMILIES.** A mixture of activities on two layover days makes one five-day trip a particularly good choice for families. On Monday morning the group is picked up in East Glacier Park for a 45-minute drive to the Jacksons' ranch, where gear is packed and guests meet their equine companions. A four-hour ride brings you to a broad mountain meadow and a clear stream, which will be your home for two nights. The next day your family can opt to spend time riding, fishing, hiking, or working with cattle pastured in the area. After breakfast Wednesday the group rides on to Two Medicine River and a campsite with views of Glacier National Park. There are the same choices of activities here.

Everyone helps set up and break down camp on this trip, and evenings center on cowboy cooking, cowboy poetry, and guitar music around the campfire. Bring your own fishing gear if you can, or rent from Richard. You can rent sleeping bags as well.
*Great Divide Guiding & Outfitters, Box 315, East Glacier Park, MT 59434, tel. 406/226–4487 or 800/421–9687. June–Sept.: 5 days, $795 adults, $695 children.*

## Mammoth Lakes Pack Outfit

7+

The old pioneer trails of the eastern Sierra Nevada and the John Muir Wilderness lead riders over high mountain passes and into hidden valleys where brilliant wildflowers dazzle the eyes and animals peer at you curiously from shaded glens and rocky outcrops. This is Mammoth Lakes Pack Outfit's third decade: Families can book scheduled and custom guided trips with confidence, knowing they're getting experience and knowledge they can count on. The many choices allow Mammoth Lakes to accommodate riders of all ages and abilities.

**FOR FAMILIES.** Mammoth Lakes sends out a brochure describing the various camping areas and the length of time it takes to get to each. Families with children ages seven or eight must book a custom guided trip; scheduled trips are for ages nine and up. People who want to spend less than three hours on the trail—such as families with young children—might choose Skelton and Woods lakes, which are available on custom trips only. You don't lose out on views by staying close to the trailhead, because this area is at an elevation of about 10,000 ft.

Families with children nine and up can ride three to four hours over 10,700-ft Duck Pass, camping along the timberline near Duck and Pika lakes. Also for ages nine and up is Purple Lake, 4½ hours away. It makes an excellent base camp for rides and hikes into the surrounding countryside.
*Mammoth Lakes Pack Outfit, Box 61, Mammoth Lakes, CA 93546, tel. 888/475–8747. June–Sept.: 4 days, $680–$750; ask about custom trips.*

## Rockin' R Ranch

8+

The southern half of Utah contains country so magnificent there are five national parks here. Rockin' R Ranch, in Antimony, is 37 mi north of Bryce Canyon National Park and not far from Zion, Capitol Reef, Canyonlands, and Arches. Adventurers could easily spend many days exploring the area any number of ways, but no one will be disappointed by a pack trip into the backcountry adjacent to the Rockin' R.

**FOR FAMILIES.** On a six-day trip you take the trail leading from the ranch up into canyons, over creeks, under quaking aspens, and onto the Aquarius Plateau, with views across the valley and down into Bryce Canyon National Park. Each night the wranglers set up camp and have dinner waiting when you come off the trail. There's time for fishing as well as a free afternoon for hiking, photography, or just plain loafing. On one of the days you take a break from trail riding to try your hand at real cowboy skills, rounding up some of the ranch's stray cattle or learning to rope.

On the last day out you can check your aim in skeet, pistol, or rifle shooting. Then you leave your horse on the plateau and head by van to Bryce Canyon National Park for an afternoon hike. Later, just outside the park, the group rides in a covered wagon and faces a staged attack on the wagon. After dinner and a local rodeo, you overnight in the ranch's comfortable quarters, which is included in the cost of the trip. Also included is one night at the ranch before the trip begins.

If your family doesn't have six days, go for the four-day version, which doesn't include Bryce or some other activities. You can also join a cattle drive here (see Cattle Drives).
*Rockin' R Ranch, Reservation Office, 10274 S. Eastdell Dr., Sandy, UT 84092, tel. 801/733–9538. June–Oct.: 4–6 days, $730–$1,255.*

## Skinner Brothers

ALL

The Skinner brothers—Robert, Monte, and Courtney—like nothing better than to share their beloved Wind River Range with families. These Wyoming mountains are not as well known as the neighboring Grand Tetons, but they are impressive in their own right. The brothers' tremendous experience with children comes from running summer wilderness camps for youngsters age 10 and up. When they're not doing that, they customize pack trips for groups as small as two. The Skinners have a few scheduled trips as well, a good choice if your family wants to ride with other families.

**FOR FAMILIES.** Customize your own trip, and the Skinners will provide everything except personal gear, sleeping pad and bag, and fishing license. You can spend as many days as you want on guided rides into the Bridger Wilderness and Wind River Range. Choose a base-camp experience (the Skinners refer to this as a stationary pack trip) or move camp each night (a moving pack trip).

The Participants Wilderness trip is a one-week scheduled group adventure. The age range for this has been from six months to 92 (though I don't advocate taking infants on horses). Guides help children take part in all activities and make it a terrific experience. You can spend time hiking, riding, and fishing, so these pack trips can meet almost anyone's needs; bring your own fishing gear if you want to fish.

Families with children age 13 and up can also join the Peak Rangers Holiday, a one-week combination pack and mountain-climbing trip. You don't need experience in either riding or mountaineering, but you should be in good shape. Experienced climbers can ascend Gannett Peak, Wyoming's highest.

*Skinner Brothers, Box 859, Pinedale, WY 82941, tel. 307/237–9138. July–Sept.: 2–7 days, $175–$350 per day for scheduled and custom trips.*

## Spatsizi Wilderness Vacations

**5+**

For the past 30 years the Collingwood family has run the only guide and outfitting service permitted to operate in Spatsizi Plateau Wilderness Park, one of Canada's truly untouched wilderness areas. Spatsizi comes from the Tahltan word meaning "red goat," a name given to the mountain goats that roll in the iron-oxide-rich soil of the park. Goats aren't the only animals at home among the peaks, plateaus, and glaciers of Spatsizi. There are sheep, caribou, and moose, black bears and grizzlies, wolves, and hundreds of species of birds. About 200 mi north of Smithers, this remote park in northern British Columbia has only about 200 human visitors each year.

**FOR FAMILIES.** The Collingwoods will help families choose among three pack trips into the Spatsizi wilderness. The first is an eight-day base-camp trip in the Eaglenest Mountains. You travel past Cold Fish Lake and onto Bug Lake and the trip's base camp. The camp has cozy log cabins and a shower house, a welcoming place to return to after riding through the rugged valleys and up into the mountains each day. You have the opportunity to hike through the Eaglenest Ecological Reserve and to test your fishing skills in some of the great trout streams of the north. Photographers can shoot most varieties of the park's wildlife in this area.

Those who want to travel deep into the most isolated regions of the park should sign up for the nine- day expedition to Buckinghorse Lake and the Fireflats, the headwaters of the Spatsizi River. This trip is probably best for children with some riding and wilderness experience. In July the area is the nursing grounds of mountain caribou and home to a large moose population. If you like fishing, try for a rainbow trout on Buckinghorse Lake; these can weigh in at six pounds. Facilities here are restricted to very rustic tent sites.

The Saddle to Paddle trip lets you experience the Spatsizi wilderness both by horse and by canoe. Start the 10-day adventure at Hyland Post, a trading post built in the 1920s on the Spatsizi River. From this base camp the group begins its three-day horse trek into the heart of the park to Laslui Lake. You overnight at Laslui Lodge with its first-class accommodations and meals, then head onto the Stikine River for five days of paddling to the confluence of the Spatsizi and Stikine rivers. It's helpful to have some riding experience for this trip, though canoeing experience isn't necessary.

*Spatsizi Wilderness Vacations, Box 3070, Smithers, British Columbia, Canada V0J 2N0, tel. 250/847–2909. July–Aug.: 8–10 days, C$2,350–C$2,930. Price includes bush-plane flights between Smithers and park.*

## Vista Verde Ranch

13+

Vista Verde is about 25 mi north of Steamboat Springs, Colorado, near Wyoming. The ranch's eight log cabins and three lodge rooms can accommodate about 30 guests. Any ranch guest can book an overnight pack trip, but Vista Verde's five-day pack trip takes no more than eight people and is booked as part of a week's ranch stay. (You can stay at the ranch for the day before and after the pack trip.)

**FOR FAMILIES.** Participants in the five-day pack trip travel through the Routt National Forest, which encompasses 1.4 million acres of wilderness. Among its trails are those used by early wranglers to move stock between Colorado and Wyoming, and these you'll follow to places such as Red Creek Ridge, Lost Ranger Peak, and Three Island Lake. One trail, known as the Outlaw Trail, was used by Butch Cassidy and the Sundance Kid to elude law officers and get in and out of their hideout just north of the ranch, up along the Wyoming border. Rides are adapted to the skills and interests of participants; you may camp out if that's what the group wants or you may use the ranch (and its hot tubs) as a base camp, riding out from there each day. From the ranch you can also hike, take trips into nearby Steamboat Springs, go mountain biking, or just relax in your cabin. This trip is offered only in the second week of September.

*Vista Verde Ranch, Box 465, Steamboat Springs, CO 80477, tel. 970/879–3858 or 800/526–7433. Sept.: 5 days, $1,795 per person.*

## WTR Outfitters/White Tail Ranch

6+

WTR Outfitters is based at an 800-acre ranch and outfitting operation in the Blackfoot Valley, about 65 mi east of Missoula, Montana. The heart of the operation is pack trips, both customized and scheduled, and riders can follow trails right from the ranch into the Bob Marshall Wilderness complex, which covers over 2 million acres.

**FOR FAMILIES.** You don't need any riding experience, and you can be practically any age: Karen Hooker, owner and operator, considers children younger than six, but you must talk to her first. What Karen cares most about is sharing with all kinds of people "a way of life worth preserving, a place of relaxation and meditation essential to American stability." If any place can have that kind of abiding effect, it's the Bob Marshall Wilderness, with a vista of incomparable beauty around every switchback. This is an area of cool streams, deep holes hiding trout, flowering meadows, and emerald lakes. And even in that soul-stirring scenery, some places stand out, such as the world-famous Chinese Wall, a rock formation 22 mi long and 1,000 ft high in parts.

State-of-the-art tents, excellent food, and a latrine with a real toilet seat secluded in its own tepee define the luxury campsites WTR provides (these are progressive trips, which means new campsites most nights). There are wildflower and bird guides to study on your trip if you wish, but much is learned—and laughed about—around the campfire each night, too.

*WTR Outfitters, 520 Cooper Lake Rd., Ovando, MT 59854, tel. 406/793–5666 or 800/987– 5666. June–Aug.: 3–11 days, $220 per day adults; 10% discount for children under 17; groups or families of 4 or more get 5% discount.*

# Resources

## Organizations

There is no national association of horse-packing outfitters; however, most states have guide and/or outfitting associations and licensing agencies. You can locate these through state tourism offices. Because many guest ranches run horse pack trips, you can also contact the **Dude Ranchers' Association** (Box 471, LaPorte, CO 80535, tel. 970/223–8440). The association represents more than 100 ranches in states throughout the West and has information on ranch activities, including pack trips.

## Also See

If multi-day riding treks and ranch work appeal to you and if you want to ride a little faster, take a look at the Cattle Drives chapter. Families with children too young for a pack trip may find the chapter on Ranches helpful. At some ranches a parent and older child may have the opportunity to join a short pack trip while the rest of the family stays at the ranch.

# HOUSEBOATING

When you step behind the wheel or in front of the tiller of a houseboat, your destiny is your own. You and your family can explore the coves you want, camp out on a deserted beach, or hike up from the water's edge when the mood strikes you. You sail as much or as little as you choose in a day, hug the shoreline to watch for wildlife, or seek the deep places where the best sport fish are found. Much of the heart and history of the nation lie along the shores of waterways that have made exploration and economic growth possible, and you can discover that, too, if you wish. On the other hand, with your houseboat as a movable feast and private lodge, your family might choose not to leave it at all (except, perhaps, by water slide when you want to cool off). Floating, relaxing, watching the scenery drift by—these are also options. The bottom line: When you are your own captain and crew, the choices are all yours.

Houseboating is a remarkably safe and roomy way to travel. Top speed is only about 6 to 9 mi per hour, so you take it easy whether you like it or not. And because activities, such as swimming, biking, hiking, and fishing, are built into a houseboat vacation, it has appeal for families with children of all ages. Babies can watch the landscape go by and feel the breezes. They can ride in backpacks or bike seats, and they sleep soundly to the rhythmic rocking. Preschoolers and school-age children love the variety of daily activities and the constantly changing scenery. Teens love the waterskiing opportunities and freedom to explore some areas on their own. Everyone loves the water slides, on which the young—and the young at heart—can zip and splash into the water.

Check to see if your boat has a running logbook. Children like to read and add to these journals, in which previous renters have jotted down the secrets and wonderful discoveries they made on their journey—the best coves and beaches, the best restaurants, the short trail that wasn't mentioned in the area brochure. Who knows, your family might even be inspired to keep a journal of its own as your trip goes on—something you can all look back on in years to come.

## Questions to Ask

**Do I need any previous boating experience to captain a houseboat?** Most companies do not require boating expertise, but some do.

**What are the other requirements?** Most companies ask that the renter and those who will be steering the boat be above a certain age and hold a valid driver's license.

**Do you have life jackets that fit my child, or will I have to bring my own?** Some companies have vests for infants; others do not. Be prepared to give your child's weight and chest measurement so you will know for sure if there is a Coast Guard–approved safety vest that will fit. Boating and sporting goods stores sell life jackets if you need to buy one.

**What are the rules regarding the use of life vests when the boat is in motion?** Some companies require that all children under a certain age wear a life vest whenever you're moving. Whether or not this is mandatory, it's a good idea. Talk to your children ahead of time about the importance of wearing a life vest. If necessary, borrow one so your child can wear it around a while and get used to it. You don't want your children to spend the vacation complaining. If you prepare them well ahead of time, it shouldn't be an issue.

**What security deposit and/or insurance is required?** All companies ask that you send a sizable deposit well in advance of your sailing date. That deposit is usually not counted toward your rental fee, and it will not be given back until you return the boat in the same condition in which you took it out. Check to see how many days prior to your trip you can cancel without forfeiting all or most of your deposit. In addition to a deposit, some companies require you to purchase damage insurance; others offer it as an option. Some have their own insurance, with deductibles that range from $250 to $1,500. Renters may be able to lower the deductible by adding a few dollars a day to the rental fee. Because you are generally responsible for paying the deductible in the event of damage to the boat, or for the damage itself if there is no accident insurance, you'll have to decide whether purchasing optional insurance is worth the extra money up front.

**How early can I arrive for my rental?** Some companies let you sleep on the boat the night before you depart; others have a very specific timetable for your arrival. If you need to be on Lake Powell, for example, at 9, you will have to arrive the previous night and make arrangements for camping or staying in a lodge.

**What are the cabin arrangements?** Houseboats differ, and depending on the makeup of your family or group, one boat may be better for you than another. Some boats come with double beds; others have a mix of queen beds, doubles, and bunk beds. Some are more luxurious but sleep fewer people. Some beds offer more privacy than others. Asking for brochures that show the various boat layouts will help you avoid disappointment with your accommodations.

**What extras do you provide?** Water slides, small power boats you can tow and use for waterskiing, dinghies, fishing gear, tubes, and other water toys are available through some rental companies, especially those operating in the western United States. These will add expense, but they can make your experience even more fun.

**Do you have maps, information about regional sights and attractions, and suggestions for where to stop?** If you are unfamiliar with the part of the country through which you'll be traveling, this is important. Almost all rental agents have navigational charts and maps on board, but you also want information and directions for the sights you shouldn't miss. There are many places to walk or bike along the popular houseboating rivers and canals, and many lakes have excellent hiking trails near their shores. You can also check out a guidebook and buy regional maps if you need to, but remember that part of the joy of this type of travel is being completely spontaneous. You don't have to be locked into a rigid itinerary.

**What's the cost of fuel and docking?** Most, but not all, houseboat rental companies work like car rental companies. They give you the boat with a full tank, and you must return it with a full tank or pay to have it filled on your return. Marine fuel prices are about 30% higher than car fuel prices. Docking charges vary greatly depending on whether you opt for a private marina or a state park. Charges for private marinas are generally by the foot and can range from 65¢ to $2 per ft per night. State parks typically charge $10–$12 per boat per night. Of course, what's great about houseboats is that in most places you don't need to tie up at established docks, so these charges will often be minimal.

**Is there some place to buy food when we arrive?** If you're arriving by car, buy your food supplies at a regular grocery store before boarding. Stores in resort towns and at marinas tend to be very expensive. If you're arriving by plane, you'll probably have to shop at the marina, but you'll save some money by bringing what you can with you and purchasing only perishables at the last minute.

**What is the rental fee and what's included?** Rental rates are affected by many things, including the size of the boat, the season, and the number of days you wish to rent. Many houseboating companies operate for three or even four seasons, and rates change dramatically during the year. Moreover, some of the things you pay extra for in summer may be part of the package in off-seasons. Amenities may also affect price or at least alter how much you get for your money. Some boats come with linens; some don't. Some have grills for cooking out on deck, but others have only galley stoves. Microwaves, generators, stereo cassette players, TVs, and VCRs all may be included, or they may be extra. There's a huge variation in what you pay and what you get, so ask lots of questions. All boats in this chapter have sleeping accommodations, a galley to cook in, a refrigerator, a bathroom, safety equipment, life vests for adults and older children, plates and pots and pans, and drinking water. Also included in the cost is parking for your car while you're houseboating. The range of rates given goes from the least expensive boat in low season to the most expensive boat in high season.

## Instruction

All houseboat rental companies give a short course—generally one to three hours—before you can take the boat out. Houseboats are so easy to steer that most, though not all, rental companies do not require previous boating experience. In addition, all rental units have extensive information and instructions posted on board for reference. Although houseboating is not difficult, it's still important to pay attention to the initial lesson and to take notes as you go through the information with the company. Docking, for example, can be tricky, especially in more congested waterways. Make certain older children listen, too, because some information given will be about safety and the use of equipment. If you're traveling with very young children, arrange in advance for a spouse or an older child to take charge of little ones so you can concentrate on crucial information during the pretrip session.

## Finding the Fun

**Northeast:** Collar City Charters, Mid-Lakes Navigation Company, Remar Rentals. **South:** Forever Resorts. **Midwest:** Forever Resorts, Seeser's Mississippi Rent-a-Cruise. **Southwest:** Forever Resorts, Lake Powell Resorts & Marinas, Seven Crown Resorts. **West Coast:** Forever Resorts, Seven Crown Resorts. **Canada:** Remar Rentals, Waterway Houseboat Vacations. **Mexico:** Forever Resorts.

# Favorite Houseboat Companies

## Collar City Charters

ALL

Once a thoroughfare of commerce but now a path for pleasure boats, the 363-mi-long Erie Canal opened in 1825. Linking Albany to Buffalo, and thus the Atlantic Ocean (via the Hudson River) to the Great Lakes, the Erie was the longest, grandest, and most ambitious canal in New York State. It was, in fact, one of the great engineering feats of its time. Today the Erie has been rediscovered and revitalized, and you can trace the history of the state and several of its canals as you travel through the picturesque New York State Canal System. There is more to see and do than a family could cover in a one-week cruise. The Canalway Trail, for example, currently encompasses 150 mi of trail segments adjoining the canal on which families can hike, bike, and view wildlife.

There are hundreds of towns at which to tie up on the canal system, and you can shape your adventure as you go. You don't have to stick to the Erie, either. From Troy, where Collar City Charters is based, boaters can travel north on the Champlain Canal all the way to Whitehall and the southernmost entry to Lake Champlain. Those who motor south on the Hudson will find natural wetlands and woods, graceful herons, villages, and sandy beaches.

**FOR FAMILIES.** Boats sleep up to six people, and there are two private staterooms, as well as a fold-out double bed in the saloon. All linens are included, and there are two bathrooms (or heads, in nautical terminology), a hot-water shower, a cabin heater for cool nights, and a marine band radio. The galley has a double sink, gas stove and oven, refrigerator with freezer, and lots of room. Collar City Charters also offers a family-friendly attitude. A call requesting information on life jackets for infants elicited this response: "If we don't have the right-size life jacket for your child, we'll find one." This is also one of the few rental companies to allow pets; the additional charge is $50 per pet.

What your children will care about most, though, are locks, locks, and more locks. There are 57 of them throughout the New York State Canal System, and they never fail to amaze. Traveling through the Waterford Flight, the first series of locks—five in all—on the Erie, your boat will be raised a whopping 169 ft in less than 2 mi. That's cool enough to intrigue children of all ages, including your normally blasé teenager.

Before or after your boating adventure on the Erie, stop in Chittenango, just east of Syracuse, to visit the birthplace of L. Frank Baum, beloved author of *The Wonderful Wizard of Oz.* There's a yellow-brick road in town. Whether it will get you to the Emerald City is uncertain, but if you visit the area in May, you won't want to leave anyway—that's the time of the annual Ozfest, with parades, games, and activities for modern-day Munchkins.

*Collar City Charters, Troy Town Dock and Marina, 427 River St., Troy, NY 12180, tel. 518/272–5341 or 800/830–5341. May–Oct.: 7 days, $1,700–$2,000.*

## Forever Resorts

**ALL**

With Forever Resorts, families have a choice of houseboat rentals on nine lakes across the country. Lake Mead, spanning the Arizona–Nevada border, and Lake Mohave, just below Hoover Dam and south of Lake Mead, offer the starkly beautiful, dramatic landscapes unique to those places where water and desert meet. The Lake Mead National Recreation Area comprises more than 3,000 square mi of desert terrain, as well as Lakes Mead and Mohave, which were both formed by the damming of the Colorado River. Hiking, rock climbing, fishing, windsurfing, and sailing bring millions of visitors to the area each year. In the northern part of California is Lake Don Pedro, 2½ hours from San Francisco and 40 mi from Yosemite National Park, in the foothills of the Sierra Nevada. Covering more than 13,000 acres with over 160 mi of shoreline, Lake Don Pedro as it is today was created in 1971 when the Don Pedro dam was built on the Tuolumne River. California's Delta region, near Stockton, offers still another view of the West from your deck: rich farmland, towns, and riverside restaurants.

Missouri's Lake of the Ozarks and Table Rock Lake are lusher and greener still. Both are in populated areas that draw visitors for a variety of sights and experiences. With more than 1,300 mi of shoreline, Lake of the Ozarks is huge—and well developed. But there are coves and wooded areas in which you can find complete privacy, if you wish. The Lake of the Ozarks Marina, where you pick up your houseboat, is near Camdenton, about 1½ hours north of Springfield, Missouri. Table Rock Lake, created in 1958 when the Table Rock Dam was completed, is 15 minutes from popular Branson, Missouri, and is surprisingly peaceful and lovely considering the well-known nightlife of that town. The lake was a destination for families looking to get away from it all long before country music stars began to call the area home, and it's still one reason many families come to the area.

Pine trees line the shore of Georgia's Lake Lanier, which is more than 63 mi long and about an hour's drive northeast of Atlanta. Lanier has excellent swimming, fishing, and waterskiing; hundreds of islands to explore make it ideal for houseboating, too. With mild spring and fall temperatures, Lake

Lanier is an excellent choice for families looking for affordable off-season getaways.

If you want to travel to foreign shores, try Lake Amistad (the Spanish word for "friendship") in the Amistad National Recreation Area, bordering Texas and Mexico, about 150 mi west of San Antonio. Lake Amistad, a joint project for the two countries, was created by the damming of the Rio Grande just below its confluence with Devil's River. The recreation area has more than 400 archaeological sites, including caves and mounds you can view along the lake. Native American pictographs dating to more than 10,000 years ago can be seen by boat at Panther Cave in beautiful Seminole Canyon. The lake is clear and blue; southwestern scuba enthusiasts call it paradise.

Farther north, way up on the Texas Panhandle, is Lake Meredith National Recreation Area and Lake Meredith itself, one of the best-kept secrets of the area. Although the surrounding landscape is desolate and windblown, the lake and the Canadian River that feeds it have canyons, sheltering cottonwoods, and some of the best walleye fishing in the state.

**FOR FAMILIES.** All boats sleep 10 people. Standard features include linens, two refrigerators, a microwave, 1½ baths, central air and heat, and a gas grill. There's excellent fishing on these lakes, and licenses are available at the marinas at all locations. The company has life jackets for all ages.

What will the children like best? *Every* boat has the all-important—and monumentally fun—water slide. And children and teens are always delighted to learn that each boat comes with a cassette player and a TV with VCR. Parents may be less enthusiastic about that.

*Forever Resorts, Box 52038, Phoenix, AZ 85072, tel. 800/255–5561. Year-round (all lakes not open all months): 3–7 days, $895–$4,500.*

## Lake Powell Resorts & Marinas

**ALL**

Nearly 2,000 mi of shoreline defined by massive red-sandstone formations and piercing blue skies make Lake Powell on the Arizona–Utah border one of the great houseboating lakes in North America. The lake is 186 mi from end to end, but you can take forever to cruise its length if you choose. There are 96 major canyons to explore, ancient pictographs and Anasazi ruins to ponder, and hiking trails, fishing coves, and beaches of shifting sands on which no footprints will be found. Nonne-Zoshi (Rainbow Turned to Stone) is the Navajo name for Rainbow Bridge, the tallest natural stone arch in the world. You can easily hike to it from the shore. The busiest season on Lake Powell is summer; if you're looking for days of solitude, book in spring or fall—when the weather is still fine, the rates are lower, and the water is still warm enough for swimming. You get your houseboat from one of the four lake marinas operated by Lake Powell Resorts & Marinas.

**FOR FAMILIES.** You can choose among seven lengths and four classes of vessels: standard, captain, sport, and admiral. Boats sleep from 6 to 12 people, and amenities vary based on vessel class, but all include life jackets for infants through adults. Depending on the boat, you'll have a queen or double bed; some have bunk beds for the children. Linens are included in the admiral category, water slides in the captain and admiral categories.

Separate small power boats are available for an extra charge at the marinas, as are fishing boats. Tow one behind your houseboat, and use it to explore small inlets or to go onshore for an overnight camp-out. Waterskiing equipment and tubes can also be rented. Carp, a mixed-review fish for most adults, are a child favorite because they're so easy to catch throughout the lake. Fishing licenses can be purchased at the marinas, but bring your own poles.

*Lake Powell Resorts & Marinas, Box 56909, Phoenix, AZ 85079, tel. 602/331–5200 or 800/528–6154. Year-round: 3–7 days, $577–$5,172.*

## Mid-Lakes Navigation Company

ALL

For the uninitiated who think New York State begins and ends in New York City, a canal cruise will be an eye-opener. Upstate New York is a land of rolling hills, farms, and historic villages. Cold Springs Harbor Marina, just a few minutes from downtown Syracuse, is the start of your houseboating adventure. From there you can travel east or west on the famous Erie Canal. You might also choose to travel the Cayuga-Seneca Canal to Seneca Falls, or head east to Oneida Lake and north on the Oswego Canal. Your family can access state parks, including the eastern border of the 6-million-acre Adirondack Park (the largest American park outside Alaska), Finger Lakes National Forest, and two wildlife refuges from the New York State Canal System.

**FOR FAMILIES.** The houseboats sleep two, four, or six passengers; families with small children might be able to fit one or two more on board, but talk to the company about your needs ahead of time. All boats come with a gas range and gas grill, bedding, and a VHF radio. Nonskid surfaces are perfect for families with younger children or grandparents, and all windows have safety glass. There's a built-in swim ladder on every boat; you'll find two bicycles, too. You can also bring along your own bikes and strap them on the roof. Ride your bike on the Erie Canal Heritage Trail Access at Palmyra, just southeast of Rochester. Families renting a boat for more than a week can also bike on the Mohawk-Hudson Bikeway (between Cohoes and Fort Hunter in New York).

If you boat on the Erie as far as North Tonawanda, near Buffalo, stop at the Allan Herschell Carousel Factory Museum (Herschell is a well-known American carousel maker). In Seneca Falls you'll find the Women's Rights National Historical Park and National Women's Hall of Fame. The biggest adventure of all in New York are the locks that raise and lower boats almost 50 ft in some places.

*Mid-Lakes Navigation Company, Box 61, 11 Jordan St., Skaneateles, NY 13152, tel. 315/685–8500 or 800/545–4318. May–Oct.: 7 days, $1,700–$2,300.*

## Remar Rentals

ALL

Long before there were people or boundaries, long before time even existed, flower petals fell from the heavens onto the St. Lawrence River, creating the Thousand Islands. The native people who told this legend called the islands Manitouana (Garden of the Great Spirit), and even today the name fits. A rich and remarkable diversity of plant and animal life thrives on these islands strung along a 50-mi stretch of the mighty St. Lawrence between New York State and Ontario, Canada. There are more than 1,800 of them—plenty to keep a houseboating family exploring for days. Some islands belong to the United States; some are Canadian. Twenty-one are part of the St. Lawrence Islands National Park, Canada's smallest national park but no less impressive because of this.

Clayton, New York, juts out into the river, giving Remar Rentals the perfect starting point for cruising the Thousand Islands, the St. Lawrence Seaway, and Canada's Rideau Canal System. Remar's steel-frame boats are similar to those used on Great Britain's canals. This is one of the few rental companies that require previous boating experience, due to the rocky shoals around the islands and the large seagoing vessels that travel parts of the river.

**FOR FAMILIES.** Boats range from 38 to 55 ft and sleep from 6 to 10 people. Guides to the islands and waterways are provided on board so you can plan the route that best meets your family's interests. Remar supplies linens, and a TV is standard equipment, too. A small dinghy comes with every houseboat, making island exploration fun and fishing in small coves a must.

*Remar Rentals, 510 Theresa St., Box 159, Clayton, NY 13624, tel. 315/686–3579. June–Sept.: 2–7 days, $550–$1,750.*

## Seeser's Mississippi Rent-a-Cruise

**ALL**

Few rivers can claim the history and romance the great Mississippi River does. Mark Twain, Lewis and Clark—these adventurous men traveled the Mississippi and made their names in part because of it. You can travel it, too, and although the wild and woolly early days of the river are long gone, there's plenty of adventure to be had and much in the way of American history to be discovered along its shores. Most houseboaters travel north from Clinton, where the river divides Iowa and Illinois. Less than 100 mi away is Dubuque and the Wisconsin border. You can see all three states simultaneously from Dubuque, which has several museums, including the National Rivers Hall of Fame. There are plenty of towns in which to stop as you travel (charming and historic Galena, Illinois, for example, is where you can see Ulysses S. Grant's home) and beaches on which to relax by day and anchor off by night. Travel midweek to avoid summer weekend crowds.

**FOR FAMILIES.** Seeser's boats are 38 ft or 40 ft and sleep six or eight people. All linens, a gas grill, deck chairs, and all the boating charts you'll need are on board, and there's air-conditioning, too. Although rentals begin at 11 AM, you're welcome to arrive between 8 and 10 the evening before your trip to spend a relaxing night on the houseboat.

Probably the most exciting part of the trip for children will be the locks found every 30 mi or so on the river. If the stoplight is red, it means a boat is in the lock and you have to wait your turn. Once in, you rise or fall to meet the river, depending on which way you're traveling. Children never seem to tire of the ingenuity and novelty of the lock system.

*Seeser's Mississippi Rent-a-Cruise, 3610 S. 54th St., Clinton, IA 52732, tel. 319/243–1111. May–Oct.: 2–7 days, $220–$1,550.*

## Seven Crown Resorts

**ALL**

On a houseboat vacation location is as important as it is in real estate. What do you want to see every day when you're sitting on deck or piloting your floating hotel? Seven Crown rents houseboats in four different areas. For summer peaks still laden with snow, towering evergreens, and wildflower meadows, you can head to Lake Shasta in northern California. Its 370 mi of shoreline offer more exploring than there's time for on one trip. Should you want to sightsee away from your boat for a few hours, Shasta Caverns, Shasta Dam, Mt. Lassen's volcano, or local fossil beds make good excursions.

Near Stockton, 80 mi west of San Francisco, is California's Delta region, more than 1,000 mi of rivers, tributaries, and channels, a meandering network of waterways with lush uninhabited islands and historic towns to explore. The fishing is good and blackberries plentiful in summer, but you can also dine at one of the riverfront restaurants you pass.

Plenty of coves and inlets provide solitude, but in the Delta you'll share the waters with oceangoing vessels heading in and out of the port at Stockton, as well as sailboats and an occasional Chinese junk.

Seven Crown also has boats on Lakes Mead and Mohave, on the Arizona–Nevada border. Mead's 550 mi of shoreline are ringed by beaches, cliffs, and dramatic rock formations; when the lake is high enough, you can see the west end of the Grand Canyon from your deck. The glassy blue waters of Mohave have long appealed to houseboaters. You can take a challenging hike to see ancient petroglyphs carved into sheer cliffs along the shore, while sandy beaches entice you to enjoy Mohave's softer side.

**FOR FAMILIES.** Boats sleep 6, 8, or 10 at all locations; the Grand Sierra style of boat, available on the lakes but not the Delta, sleeps 14. Boats are equipped with everything you need except bedding, food, drinks, and personal items; they even have a microwave and barbecue. Most boats have both a shower and tub in the bathroom, an important convenience for families with young children. The Grand Sierra, however, has two bathrooms but no tub. Pets are welcome on boats and at all marina motels used by families before or after houseboating. There's no extra charge on boats, but there is a $25 refundable deposit for pets in motel rooms, plus an additional room charge of $5 per day per pet.

Seven Crown operates seven marinas or marina-resorts; two on Lake Shasta, three on Lake Mead, and one each at the Delta and Lake Mohave. You can rent your houseboat at five of them and small take-along boats at all seven. Groceries, ice, tackle, and fishing licenses are available, too. Marina lodging varies with location; there are hotel and motel rooms and RV sites.

*Seven Crown Resorts, Box 16247, Irvine, CA 92623, tel. 800/752–9669. Year-round: 3–7 days, $550–$2,750.*

## Waterway Houseboat Vacations

ALL

Green forests, blue water, sandy beaches, quiet coves, and hundreds of miles of undeveloped wilderness are what you'll find at Shuswap Lake in southeastern British Columbia, one of Canada's best houseboating lakes. Hiking, diving, and climbing rocks are popular. You can also jet-ski and fish, and you can golf nearby. There are plenty of secluded spots for picnicking, barbecuing, and overnight camping as well.

**FOR FAMILIES.** Waterway's houseboats sleep 10 to 18 and have fully equipped kitchens, maps, and child-resistant railings. These houseboats come with water slides and AM/FM cassette stereos. Voyager and Mirage models have hot tubs on the upper deck (if children ever get out of them, parents can enjoy the hot tubs, too); Mirage 54s even have a fireplace in the living room. Waterway also has a boat equipped for passengers with special needs. It's wheelchair friendly and has a wheelchair elevator to the upper deck, two medi-beds and a special-needs bath. It's also equipped with a lift so that all passengers can use the hot tub.

*Waterway Houseboat Vacations, Box 69, Sicamous, British Columbia, Canada V0E 2V0, tel. 250/836–2505 or 800/663–4022. Apr.–early Sept.: 3–10 days, $470–$5,700.*

# Resources

## Periodicals

Every spring *Houseboat Magazine* (520 Park Ave., Idaho Falls, ID 83402, tel. 800/638–0135) publishes a special vacation guide with extensive rental and destination information, including specifics about the marinas from which you'll be renting (such as whether they have a motel or RV campground), places to leave your car or RV while you're houseboating, advice about local fishing, and more.

## Books

*The Amazing Impossible Erie Canal* (Simon & Schuster), by Cheryl Harness, a critically acclaimed picture book for ages 5 through 10, gives the history of the building of the Erie Canal from start to finish.

## Also See

For more boating adventures, turn to Sailing; Snorkeling and Diving; *and* Wildlife Encounters. You'll find a mix of small and large boats, slow and fast boats, and waters around the world to explore.

# KAYAKING

Families have taken to kayaking like, well, ducks to water. That's not surprising. Kayaks can take you anywhere from the ocean to the pristine wilderness lakes and rivers of America's heartland. You can glide through still waters or challenge yourself on rapids in almost every corner of the continent. In a kayak there's an unmistakable feeling of being not just on the water but of it, which gives an added thrill to the already fantastic opportunities to experience wildlife and nature close up.

Older children, in particular, have embraced the sport in record numbers, at least partly because kayaking allows a measure of independence other types of boating do not. As manufacturers begin to design kayaks especially for a child's size, weight, and strength, more and more youngsters can paddle their own. These child-size kayaks are easier to learn on and to handle, creating a great sense of accomplishment in young paddlers.

Kayaking promotes family togetherness, too. Two- and three-person kayaks make it possible for parents to take even young or inexperienced children with them on flat-water trips. Some kayaks are made with an extra-large cockpit opening that can accommodate up to two adults and a child. This sport also has special appeal for families with teenagers, who rarely think that family outings are cool. Kayaking is definitely cool, and it's a vacation idea that most preteens and teens will greet with an enthusiastic thumbs-up. Although kayaking is not the best choice for families with infants, toddlers, or preschoolers, almost any other family can find a boat, class, or trip that's right for them.

## Questions to Ask

**Do you work regularly with children the age(s) of mine?** Kayaking requires special skills in both paddling technique and safety practices, and it's important that instructors convey this information in an age-appropriate manner. Although instructors in children's classes probably have the requisite experience, many kayak schools say they welcome older children in adult classes. However, that doesn't mean the teacher will know how to work with this age group. Adults and children learn differently, and even preteens and teens often learn best through games. So before you put your 12-year-old in an adult class with you, make certain he or she will be taught appropriately and be welcomed.

**Are child-size life vests and clothing provided?** Any time you're in a boat, you need a Coast Guard–approved life jacket in the correct size. If the company you choose doesn't have the right-size vests, purchase them ahead of time from a marine or sporting goods store.

**Are wet suits needed, and do you have them in my child's size?** Some kayaking courses and trips take place in cold water. A child—or an adult, for that matter—who's cold will have a miserable time. Ask the company if it provides or rents suits in the sizes you need. If not, either borrow them from someone you know, or check with local dive or other marine supply stores about buying or renting suits.

**Do we need helmets?** On a lake or pond you probably won't need a white-water helmet, but on any river water, even the slow-moving variety, a helmet is a good idea. Ask about a helmet for yourself and for your children.

**Is the guide/instructor trained in child CPR, lifesaving, and first aid? What type of emergency equipment do you carry?** Child CPR requires different steps than adult CPR. If you'll be far from a hospital or medical help, someone should be completely familiar with the procedures for reviving and rescuing children. Many parents take these courses themselves—a good idea even if the outfitter is trained. Also find out whether an outfitter is equipped with a radio for emergency contact with a home base or local medical personnel and whether there is emergency equipment on hand appropriate for both children and adults.

**Are instructors certified by a reputable organization, such as the American Canoe Association or the British Canoe Union?** Certification means instructors are up on techniques and safety procedures, and it's one way to compare schools and instructors.

**What kind of kayaks are provided?** Sea, or touring, kayaks tend to be more stable than their white-water counterparts, and easier for inexperienced boaters to handle. They're used not just in the ocean and open water but on lakes, ponds, rivers, and streams. There are double kayaks with two cockpits, which are perfect for one parent and one child, and even triples (three cockpits). Ask about the pros and cons of each type with regard to the ages and abilities of your children. Many outfitters also have sit-on-tops—kayaks without the traditional cockpit. These are wonderful for the slightly claustrophobic, and they're extremely easy to steer and keep stable. Children and beginners usually love them, though they're more for fun than for serious learning.

**Are child-size kayaks available?** This isn't a requirement by any means, but it can make a difference between accomplishment and frustration, for young children especially.

**How strenuous is the course or trip?** All the courses and trips listed are for beginner or intermediate paddlers unless otherwise noted. This means you don't need a lot of paddling experience; however, you should be in good physical condition. Ask how long your family will be paddling each day and what the conditions are likely to be. Will you be paddling against wind or tides, for example (either of which can be exhausting)?

**Are there other activities on the trip?** Courses may have you out from 9 to 4, with a break for lunch, so your free time is in the evening. On extended trips, however, about six hours of paddling a day is typical before pulling into camp. With this schedule, there should be time for hiking, exploring, maybe beachcombing. These activities are often as important to children as the paddling, so find out what guides are likely to offer before you book.

**What's included in the cost of the course or trip?** Courses that take place at a school or an area near the school, whether they last one or two days, generally provide equipment, instruction, transportation from the school to a local river (if necessary), and lunch. Lodging is usually not part of the package, but schools can often help arrange it. On multi-day trips the fee includes tents and most meals—plenty of hearty, excellent food—in addition to what courses cover. The vast majority of kayaking trips are camping trips. Prices for all courses and trips include what is listed above unless otherwise noted.

## Instruction

Aside from paddling technique, Eskimo rolls (in which you rotate your kayak 360 degrees in the water, so you go from right side up to upside down and back without getting out of the cockpit), and other technical aspects of kayaking, you'll receive instruction on basic safety, water rescue and survival, and wilderness emergency information. This is especially important for parents taking children out into the wilderness and around water.

If your child is too young for regular courses or for the special children's courses, be sure to ask about private instruction. These sessions often accommodate younger children, and they allow families to learn and play together.

## Finding the Fun

**Northeast:** Adventure Quest, Maine Island Kayak Company, Outward Bound, Paddleways, Wilderness Expeditions & The Birches, Zoar Outdoor. **South:** Nantahala Outdoor Center, Outward Bound. **Midwest:** Kayak & Canoe Institute, Outward Bound, Trek & Trail, Wilderness Inquiry. **Southwest:** Kayak & Canoe Institute. **Rockies**: Boulder Outdoor Center, Dvorak's Kayak & Rafting Expeditions. **West Coast:** Cutting Edge Adventures, Outward Bound, REI Adventures. **Alaska:** Kayak & Canoe Institute, Nantahala Outdoor Center, REI Adventures. **Canada:** Outward Bound, Wilderness Inquiry. **Mexico:** Cutting Edge Adventures, Maine Island Kayak Company, Paddleways.

# Favorite Schools and Outfitters

## Adventure Quest

7+

Adventure Quest, one of the few paddling schools to specialize in teaching children and teens, holds classes in and around its 40-acre wooded preserve in south-central Vermont. Peter Kennedy, the school's founder, is among the foremost outdoors educators in the country. His work with children is built on his belief that "young people need challenges in early life to help them better cope with obstacles in their future." Like most other top outdoors instructors, Peter feels the skills learned on a river or a rock are not just sports techniques—they are life skills that will serve children and adults wherever they go.

**FOR FAMILIES.** Adventure Quest runs Family Workshops in a variety of sports, including kayaking. These courses, which take place on a number of rivers in the Woodstock area, can be booked for one day or for several days. The company now has reasonably priced, comfortable lodging for clients at its new, motel-like property near the school in Brownsville, Vermont. In the spring and fall families can probably stay at Adventure Quest's campground, but in summer it's reserved for student campers. There are plenty of inns and campgrounds in the Woodstock area, as well as restaurants; ask Adventure Quest for suggestions. When you're off the river, you can tour Woodstock with its many historic buildings or stroll over one of the area's covered bridges.

Another option is Adventure Quest's summer camp program for children, River Quest, which includes an intensive kayaking course or samplers of several outdoor sports. Sign your children up for that while you take a course aimed at adults; you can get together in the evening to talk about paddling adventures. Because Adventure Quest is nonprofit, scholarships are available for qualifying students in the children's summer program.

*Adventure Quest, Box 184, Woodstock, VT 05091, tel. 802/484–3939. Apr.–Oct.: 1 day, $275 for up to 4 people, $50 per day per additional family member. River Quest, June–Aug.: 6 days, $600.*

## Boulder Outdoor Center

8+

Nearly 20 years ago the center opened as the Boulder Kayak School. Today, as the Boulder Outdoor Center (BOC), it continues to focus on kayaking, with classes for every level and in every season. If winter doldrums get you down, you can head to Colorado and learn how to paddle and roll in one of Boulder's warm indoor pools. When you've had enough of the water, you can ski on some of the best terrain in the Rocky Mountains, only a couple of hours away. In summer Boulder and the Rockies offer hiking, rock climbing, friendly people, and good restaurants.

**FOR FAMILIES.** Children ages eight and up are welcome in novice lake clinics, which are offered in Boulder, Denver, and Glenwood Springs. Lake clinics are either all day or 3½ hours on each of two days. If you have children under the age of 12, go for the one-day lake clinics and ask about private lessons. For those with paddlers at least 12 years old, a good choice is the novice three-day clinic, which combines a day of lake learning in Boulder with two days on a nearby river, generally the Colorado through Glenwood Canyon. You can expect to paddle from 5 to 10 mi each day on the river. All children under 16 must take classes with a parent. For a dedicated kayak vacation, there are five-day river tours, the locations based on season and water levels. (The minimum age for these trips is around 12, but they're more concerned with ability.) You might experience everything from creeks to big water, from desert terrain to forested canyons; your family can sign up for these tours over and over because the experience changes with the location. The tours start and end in Boulder, and you'll need to spend the nights before and after the trip in Boulder; BOC will give you lodging suggestions.

While BOC specializes in getting paddlers ready for white-water, it also offers sea kayak and touring clinics, similar to its lake clinics. In addition, there are classes for intermediate and advanced paddlers in which you'll learn rolling, surfing, and play-paddling. You can challenge yourselves on class II to class IV rapids on almost any of Colorado's rivers, including the Cache La Poudre, Arkansas, Roaring Fork, and Colorado.
*Boulder Outdoor Center, 2510 N. 47th St., Boulder, CO 80301, tel. 303/444–8420 or 800/364– 9376. Year-round: 1–5 days, $29–$695 adults; 50% discount on lake clinics, novice river clinic, and roll classes for children under 16. 10% discount for groups of 4 or more, except with youth discount. Private instruction $95–$245 per person per day, depending on day and number of people.*

## Cutting Edge Adventures

7+

Owner Stefanie Abrishamian's contagious humor, enthusiasm, and easy way with children are just some of the reasons she and her company are an excellent choice for a family kayak course or river trip. Another is her skill and professionalism—she's been guiding, teaching, and managing river outfitters for more than 18 years. Stefanie has taught children as young as seven to do Eskimo rolls. Cutting Edge is in northern California, in the shadow of perpetually snow-covered Mt. Shasta and within easy reach of some of the nation's best rivers and lakes for family kayaking.

**FOR FAMILIES.** Cutting Edge has a five-day Kayak School that begins with a day on Lake Siskiyou near Mt. Shasta, then continues with four days down the Klamath River. You can hone your skills while watching for eagles, ospreys, blue and green herons, and other wildlife. You might also consider taking one of the lovely hikes near the river. One-day kayak roll clinics are held on Lake Siskiyou, and private instruction in both hard-shell and inflatable kayaks is available on many of the rivers in the Mt. Shasta area.

Families with teens 15 and up can travel to the Sea of Cortez (as the Gulf of California is sometimes known in Mexico) for an eight-day trip. Even novice kayakers can experience the wild beauty of Baja California.
*Cutting Edge Adventures, Box 1334, Mt. Shasta, CA 96067, tel. 530/926–4647. July–Aug.: 1–5 days, $50–$750. Baja, Oct.–Nov.: 8 days, $1,295; airfare extra but can be booked through Cutting Edge. 50% discount for children under 17 on some trips.*

## Dvorak's Kayak & Rafting Expeditions

6+

Well known for its rafting trips, especially those welcoming families, this Colorado outfitter also runs an excellent white-water paddling school and river trips. Dvorak's is in Nathrop, almost exactly in the center of the state and just a scenic three-hour drive from Denver and its great family museums. It's also an easy drive from Fruita—home of Dinamation International Society's Dino Camp and the not-to-be-missed Dinosaur Discovery Museum—and from the most popular mountain towns, including Crested Butte, Durango, Telluride, Vail, and Aspen.

**FOR FAMILIES.** Your family can sign up for courses ranging from a half-day lake session to a 12-day river trip. Dvorak's recommends a three- to five-day tour on the Arkansas

River as the best learning trip for novices. The Arkansas slices through canyons of granite and into valleys below the snow-capped Sangre de Cristo Mountains, presenting exhilarating challenges but nothing an enthusiastic family can't handle. Dvorak's guides will be there through every riffle and rapid, providing the kind of high-quality personalized experience you would expect from an outfit that has been in business for more than a quarter of a century. Hard-shell and inflatable kayaks can be used.

*Dvorak's Kayak & Rafting Expeditions, 17921 Hwy. 285, Nathrop, CO 81236, tel. 719/539–6851 or 800/824–3795 for reservations. May–Sept.: Family trips, 2–8 days, $250–$1,725 adults, $220–$1,565 children under 13. Instruction trips ½–12 days, $65–$1,745 per person. Children must weigh at least 50 lbs.*

## Kayak & Canoe Institute

**7+**

Part of the University of Minnesota at Duluth's Outdoor Program, the institute aims to "create an environment where participants can develop skills, learn about themselves, relax, enjoy, and share their gifts with others." Duluth, tucked into the western tip of Lake Superior and surrounded by protecting bluffs, is an ideal location for inner harbor expeditions. It's also near one of the country's great kayaking destinations, Wisconsin's Apostle Islands.

**FOR FAMILIES.** Families with children seven and up can participate in the three-hour safety and rescue course, the minimum training required for renting a sea kayak from the Institute. That same course is offered at a slower pace in a full-day version. These courses do provide a lot of detailed information, so children should be able to listen and participate appropriately. In terms of courses, best for families with young children is private instruction; just call to go over your interests and goals and the staff will schedule a program for your family. Ages 15 and up are welcome to join all courses and multi-day trips. White-water and sea kayaking fundamentals classes and tours run in length from three hours to four days, ranging from basic instruction to rolling, kayak 'rodeo' moves, and slalom training and racing. Intermediates who choose a four-day trip to the Apostle Islands, Lake Superior's magnificent archipelago, will see sea caves, sandy beaches, rocky inlets, lighthouses, and sunken ships. The institute also schedules multi-day summer kayaking and hiking trips for all skill levels to explore such places as Voyageurs National Park, Minnesota's inland lakes and rivers, Lake Powell, and Alaska's Kenai Fjords National Park. Trips change from year to year, so call and see what's new.

Families in the Duluth area who want to spend an afternoon kayaking in the shelter of Duluth Harbor, watching the aerial lift bridge go up and down and big freighters coming and going from the docks, can sign up for the four-hour Duluth Waterfront Tour, which even very young children can join. Do paddle right up to the docked *William A. Irvin*, former flagship of the U.S. Steel Great Lakes Fleet and look-alike of the famed *Edmund Fitzgerald*, the last big ship to sink in Lake Superior; it's an awesome view looking up from a kayak.

*Kayak & Canoe Institute, University of Minnesota at Duluth, Outdoor Program, 121 Sports and Health Center, 10 University Dr., Duluth, MN 55812, tel. 218/726–6533. May–Aug.: 3 hrs–12 days, $35–$1,575; discounts for family groups on some courses. Price does not include lunch for single-day classes.*

## Maine Island Kayak Company

**8+**

Maine Island Kayak Company (MIKCO) is oriented as much to environmental concerns and the wilderness as it is to kayaking.

What the staff likes best is taking people on multi-day tours in and around Maine's wild islands. Children must be at least eight years old to paddle in a double kayak with a parent; 10-year-olds who can swim and who have some athletic ability and enough muscle strength can paddle their own kayak. The company is based about 20 minutes by ferry from Portland, Maine.

**FOR FAMILIES.** Families have lots of choices. Scheduled three-day Family Fun trips explore Maine's islands and inlets, but if these dates don't work for you, MIKCO will design courses and expeditions for particular family groups. You can also sign up for a scheduled class or expedition. Regular course offerings include half- to three-day instruction classes, along with half- to five-day expeditions. Some expeditions are camping trips, while on others you stay in bed-and-breakfasts. For advanced paddlers, there are guide and instructor training clinics. All boats are sea kayaks—either singles or doubles (family trips usually use doubles).

MIKCO's tours take paddlers in and around Casco Bay, Jewell Island, and Penobscot Bay. One of the most popular trips goes from Stonington to Acadia National Park's Isle au Haut, with its rugged cliffs and rocky ledges. On easy trips you can expect to paddle about 5 mi per day; on moderate trips, 10 mi. For those with children ages 12 and up, there are also winter kayaking tours in international waters, but multi-day paddling experience is necessary.

Call the company to discuss the ages and abilities of your family—they'll find or design a trip for you. Wet suits are provided; a small should fit a good-size 10-year-old.
*Maine Island Kayak Company, 70 Luther St., Peaks Island, ME 04108, tel. 207/766–2373 or 800/796–2373. May–Oct.: ½–5 days, $55–$875 adults, family trips, $345 adults, $270 children in double kayak. Children's pricing available on some trips. Ask about winter tours.*

## Nantahala Outdoor Center

9+

Nantahala, in the majestic Great Smoky Mountains of western North Carolina, is one of the premier paddling schools in the country. The company is employee-owned, which may help account for the enthusiasm and high quality of its instructors. Courses begin on flat water (a lake) and move on to cover between one and four rivers, depending on the class you choose. Plan to stay in the area either before or after your trip; Nantahala is only about 30 minutes from the southern entrance to Great Smoky Mountains National Park and 1½ hours from Asheville, rich in history and opportunities for family sightseeing.

**FOR FAMILIES.** Two- to seven-day standard courses, for ages 16 and up, include novice, intermediate, and advanced levels, as well as special rolling classes. Private instruction is a more flexible alternative for families, and children can attend with parents (discuss your child's weight, size, athletic ability, and interest with the school before signing up).

Sampler courses, for ages 13 and up, are one-day minicourses designed to give beginners an introduction to the sport. There's the Kayak Sampler (white-water instruction on local rivers) and the Kayak Touring Sampler, in which you take sea kayaks onto nearby lakes and learn the basics while exploring exquisite inland waterways.

In addition to regular courses, Nantahala has special children's courses at all skill levels throughout the summer. Divided by age (9–11, 12–15, or 14–18), these emphasize learning in a high-energy, fun atmosphere. Parents can take adult-oriented classes at the same time.

Base facilities at Nantahala include a bunkhouse and two restaurants; some lodging is also available in a motel. Accommodations are limited, so book early. Day care is available for small children while parents are kayaking. Wet suits can be rented. (There's a limited amount of children's sizes.)

Nantahala's adventure travel department schedules seven- to nine-day instructional tours in North Carolina, Georgia, the Everglades, and Alaska as well as adventure tours throughout the world for various ages and abilities. A parent who's a strong paddler might be able to bring a preteen on a trip by using a double kayak. Call and discuss your skills and the ages of your children.
*Nantahala Outdoor Center, 13077 U.S. 19W, Bryson City, NC 28713, tel. 888/662–1662, ext. 600 for courses, ext. 333 for adventure travel tours. Courses, Mar.–Oct.: 1–6 days, $85–$1,100 adults, $85–$760 children. Trips, year-round: 7–13 days, $750–$2,400.*

## Outward Bound

16+

Adventure travel has become extremely popular in the past decade, but Outward Bound was way ahead of its time. After more than 50 years in adventure education, it is still a leader in the field. Outward Bound has courses all over the country and the world in a variety of sports and activities. For kayaking courses, adventurers have a choice of Maine, Florida, Minnesota, and Washington State.

As with most Outward Bound courses, which are designed to challenge you and test your limits, your family will also spend time on other activities, such as hiking, rock climbing, rappelling, negotiating a ropes course, or learning camping skills. The focus is not just on learning to kayak and sail but also on enhancing teamwork, problem-solving, and leadership skills.

**FOR FAMILIES.** Outward Bound schools have several opportunities for families. All are sea kayaking courses. The Hurricane Island Outward Bound School, based in Maine, runs courses in Florida's Canaveral National Seashore, including Indian River and the Intracoastal Waterway, and in Maine's Penobscot Bay. In Maine families can choose a sea kayaking or a sailing and sea kayaking adventure. Minnesota's Voyageur Outward Bound School takes families either to the red-sandstone cliffs and deep caves of the Apostle Islands or into the densely forested archipelago of Canada's Black Bay. Parents and teens who wish to combine sailing and rowing with kayaking should consider Oregon's Pacific Crest Outward Bound School and its seamanship–sea kayaking courses in the wildlife-rich San Juan Islands off the coast of Washington. All courses are camping trips.

In the past Outward Bound has offered kayaking courses especially for a parent and child to take together. Check its current brochure under Parent/Child listings to see if the outfit still does this.
*Outward Bound, 100 Mystery Point Rd., Garrison, NY 10524, tel. 914/424–4000 or 800/243– 8520. Maine, Minnesota, Washington, June–Sept.: 8–22 days, $895–$2,045. Florida, Dec.–Mar.: 5–8 days, $595–$995.*

## Paddleways

8+

Kevin Rose, who, with his wife, Michele, owns Paddleways, is also the founder of the Lake Champlain Paddlers' Trail and the Lake Champlain Kayak Club. He knows all of the beautiful, hidden nooks and inlets along the shore of Lake Champlain, which stretches for more than 120 mi between Vermont, New York, and Québec. He believes this lake offers some of the finest open-water paddling in North America.

**FOR FAMILIES.** Paddleways' inn-based sea kayak excursion is designed especially for families, and it's scheduled throughout the summer. You stay on the shore at The

North Hero House, a restored inn built in 1891, with sweeping views of the Green Mountains. There's a sandy beach right outside the front door; here guides teach young paddlers in shallow, protected waters. The group makes daily excursions to nearby islands, with time for picnicking, hiking, fishing, sightseeing, and swimming. The islands in this area were originally granted to Ethan Allen and his compatriots, the Green Mountain Boys, so there's plenty of intriguing history to be learned, too.

For those families who prefer to be totally outdoor-based, there's a sea kayaking camping tour as well. On either trip children can paddle with their parents in a tandem sea kayak, or, if they're ready and willing, in their own child-size kayak. Accommodations and meals are included in the price of the trip. Ask about Paddleways' other Lake Champlain tours or courses in Maine and Mexico.
*Paddleways, Box 65125, Burlington, VT 05406-5125, tel. 802/660–8606. June–Aug., 3 days: $550 adults. 20% discount for children 8–12 sharing a room with parents; 10% discount for children 13–16 sharing a room with parents; 10% discount for children 16 and under not sharing a room with two adults.*

## REI Adventures

15+

REI, the nationwide outdoor store from which many adventurers buy their gear and apparel, doubles as an excellent outfitter, with trips incorporating a number of sports, including kayaking. The best for families are around the islands off the coast of Washington State and Vancouver Island and in the dramatic waters and scenery of Alaska's Glacier Bay. Neither requires previous kayaking experience.

**FOR FAMILIES.** Naturalists lead the six-day moderate sea kayaking trip called Islands Kayaking, which has departures from June through September. Learning centers on the environment as well as on kayaking. The San Juan Islands, off the coast of Washington, are home to harbor seals, river otters, and bald eagles. Orcas also inhabit the area, and as you paddle a safe distance from them guides will tell you about their complex social structure and place in this marine environment. Nights are spent in campsites on island beaches.

On an eight-day adventure offered from June to August, you travel among Alaska's pristine islands and through tidal areas rich in marine and bird life. Kayaking, hiking, birding, wildlife viewing, and relaxing are all part of the itinerary, which is based on a comfortable small-boat cruise ship.
*REI Adventures, Box 1938, Sumner, WA 98390, tel. 253/437–1100 or 800/622–2236. June–Sept.: 6–8 days, $875–$2,435. Price does not include $15 REI membership per family; nonmembers pay an additional $100 per person.*

## Trek & Trail

10+

Trek & Trail, based in Bayfield, Wisconsin, on a peninsula at the west end of Lake Superior, has been running outdoor learning adventures in the Apostle Islands National Lakeshore and on Lake Superior since 1978. The company has a strong commitment to bringing families into the wilderness and is 100% enthusiastic about working with children.

**FOR FAMILIES.** T & T's paddling school offers courses from a basic safety class (required for all renters) to a three-day expedition preparation course. The two-hour introduction to sea kayaking is a good way to get down the basics and to try out the sheltered waters of the Bayfield harbors. There are several trips that are especially good for families. The Basswood Island Paddle is a one-day adventure with an open-water crossing from Bayfield to Basswood Island. An ideal weekend adventure is the Sand Island Overnight, which begins with a safety clinic and includes exploring sea caves and an old lighthouse and hiking to the abandoned fishing village of Shaw. One of the most popular scheduled outings is the three-day Paddle Through Time, on which you discover the mystery and richness of Lake Superior's environment, with stops at five islands and overnights on two (Oak and Sand islands).

T & T's custom-designed, four-day Island Base Camp adventure is also perfect for families of at least four paddlers. You stay in an established base camp, so there's no setting up and taking down campsites, which allows for more time to paddle. You'll also hike, learn about Ojibwa history, and fish, in addition to taking advantage of excellent paddling instruction. Sand, Oak, or Stockton islands serve well as base camps. The specific routes and itinerary are based on your family's abilities and interests. Trips depart every Monday, Memorial Day through Labor Day.

Families and children (usually ages 10 and up, but check with the company) are welcome on all other Trek & Trail trips, too. Most courses run between Memorial Day and Labor Day. Wet suits can be rented.
*Trek & Trail, Box 906, Bayfield, WI 54814, tel. 715/779–3320 or 800/354–8735. May–Sept.: 2 hrs–5 days, $30–$489; Island Base Camp, 4 days, $389 per person. Basic courses generally offer 50% discount for children under 12.*

## Wilderness Expeditions & The Birches

8+

The Birches is a rustic resort on the shores of 40-mi long Moosehead Lake in north central Maine. Set in a grove of birches in an 11,000 acre wilderness preserve, the resort and its outfitting service, Wilderness Expeditions, offer adventure opportunities with a comfortable cabin tent to return to at night. While kayaking is available, it's by no means the only activity, which makes this an ideal getaway for the family that loves to stay together, but doesn't always play together.

**FOR FAMILIES.** Family Camp is a four-day adventure vacation with something for everyone. In addition to exploring by sea kayak or inflatable 'ducky' kayak, you might go white-water rafting, hiking, biking, windsurfing, and swimming. The two-hour Moose Cruise is a must. You'll search out some of the lake's non-human residents—moose, deer, bear, bald eagles, osprey, and falcons—via pontoon boat. The resort facilities include a pool and restaurant, and there's an outside hot tub and sauna to relax in at the end of the day. You can kayak every day if you like, but the schedule is quite flexible.
*Wilderness Expeditions & The Birches, Box 41-N, Rockwood, ME 04478, tel. 207/534–7305. June–Aug.: 4 days, $349 per person.*

## Wilderness Inquiry

5+

A leader in wilderness adventure for two decades, this company places a special emphasis on making trips available to people with and without disabilities. On these trips children have the opportunity to learn new skills and appreciation for nature, along with respect for the differences among people. The company is based in Minneapolis but leads trips around the United States and in Canada.

**FOR FAMILIES.** Because these trips are in 21-ft touring kayaks, which hold two to three people, children as young as age five can go on most of them, although shorter trips may be best for younger children. There are three- and five-day Apostle Island tours in northern Wisconsin, for example, and an eight-day Isle Royale tour in Michigan, all of which include time for hiking and exploring on land. Another choice is a 12-day trip in the Queen Charlotte Islands in British Columbia, for families with children who are at least 14. Known as the Galápagos Islands of the North because of their abundant animal and ecological diversity, the Queen Charlottes offer paddling in protected bays and guaranteed wildlife sightings. On all of these trips you camp along the way.

For longer trips such as the one to the Queen Charlotte Islands, some experience and good physical condition are important. Wet suits may be required on some trips, and Wilderness Inquiry provides both adult and child sizes at no additional cost.

*Wilderness Inquiry, 1313 5th St. SE, Box 84, Minneapolis, MN 55414-1546, tel. 612/379–3858 or 800/728–0719. June–Sept.: 3–12 days, $295–$1,595.*

### Zoar Outdoor

10+

Zoar's 80-acre campus in the Deerfield River valley in northwestern Massachusetts combines everything a family needs in order to try out the sport of kayaking: a campground, bathhouse with hot showers, outfitters store, and more. Zoar Outdoor has been teaching kayaking and other outdoor sports since 1989, and it continues to grow and get better each year.

**FOR FAMILIES.** Zoar has a two-day parent-child beginner clinic in its extensive list of instructional courses. Offered in July, it's for children between ages 10 and 16 with one or both parents. Families with children ages 14 and up can take part in any of the clinics scheduled from April through October. There are beginner, intermediate, and advanced instructional clinics that run two or five days, as well as special one-day rolling clinics. Families may opt for customized classes, too. You may also choose to sign up children (ages 10 through 15) for Kids Kayak Craze, a one-day course offered during July or August, while you take a course of your own.

As for trips, two-day expeditions include kayaking among the islands of Boston Harbor and touring on Lake Champlain (camping or bed-and-breakfast accommodations are available on both).

*Zoar Outdoor, Box 245, Charlemont, MA 01339, tel. 800/532–7483. Apr.–Oct.: 1–5 days, $80– $450; price does not include lodging for some clinics.*

## Resources

### Organizations

**America Outdoors** (Box 10847, Knoxville, TN 37939, tel. 423/558–3597), a national association for outfitters and river guides, has a magazine listing outfitters and guides. The **American Canoe Association** (7432 Alban Station Blvd., Suite B232, Springfield, VA 22150, tel. 703/451–0140) publishes a newsletter and certifies guides and instructors.

### Books

Globe Pequot Press publishes the largest number of sea kayaking books in the nation. Among its excellent instructional and touring guides are *Complete Book of Sea Kayaking, Expedition Kayaking, Eskimo Rolling,* and *Basic Book of Sea Kayaking,* all by kayaker Derek Hutchinson. Another well-known name in the sport, Nigel Foster, has *Nigel Foster's Sea Kayaking* and *Nigel Foster's Surf Kayaking.* More Globe Pequot titles include *Fundamentals of Kayak Navigation* (by David Burch) and *Basic Essentials: Sea Kayaking* (by J. Michael Wyatt). They also have a regional sea kayaking series, which includes guides for southern Florida; central and northern California; Lakes Superior and Michigan; Lakes Huron, Erie, and Ontario; and southeast Alaska.

## Periodicals

*Canoe & Kayak Magazine* (Box 3146, Kirkland, WA 98083, tel. 800/692–2663) has many family-oriented articles, and most issues carry an extensive resource listing of outfitters, schools, and guides.

## Also See

Families that love the water should also check out Canoeing, Sailing, Rafting, Snorkeling and Diving, *and* Wildlife Encounters.

# NATIVE AMERICAN EXPERIENCES

Today families have wonderful opportunities to learn about the Native American peoples who are so integral to our country's cultural fabric. The importance of these firsthand encounters became clear to me on a visit a few years ago to the Cherokee Heritage Center in Tahlequah, Oklahoma. My then four-year-old kept peering intently at the Cherokee people working there. He seemed confused. Finally he asked, "But where do they keep their horses?" His sole experience of Native Americans, I'm embarrassed to say, had been obtained from reruns of the spectacularly awful television show *F Troop,* but he left the center with a different perspective.

Fortunately there are many ways for any child to be exposed to the richness of native life rather than the old stereotypes, and these trips are one of them. Although native people were once reluctant to share their culture with outsiders, that is no longer the case. In recent years tribal elders have agreed to meet with visitors to share their wisdom and knowledge, and native guides have begun to offer tours of their lands that focus as much on tribal history and cultural life as on the land itself. Native people across North America have devoted time and resources to preserving, or reestablishing if necessary, traditional languages, fine and performing arts, lore, spiritual practices, agricultural and hunting traditions, and crafts. The primary benefit of a renewal in traditional ways is, of course, a stronger native culture; but it also provides exciting learning opportunities for people outside the culture.

## Questions to Ask

**How do I know this program is legitimate?** If your family has a desire to experience authentic Native American culture, the last thing you want is a hokey, "canned" experience. By talking at length to the people running the trips, you can usually tell if there's a real interest in native culture and if they have worked closely with Native Americans to organize the trips. You can also check with the tourism departments of the states you're going to visit, and you might want to ask for references from people who have traveled with the group.

**What is the focus of this particular trip?** Is it native culture? History? Tribal lands? Crafts and artwork are featured on some trips; on others the point is to experience the present-day lifestyle of a tribe. Some experiences with native guides focus on an activity—fishing or horse packing—and native culture is secondary. Many trips combine several elements.

**Can we participate in tribal activities such as crafts or other traditional pastimes?** In many cases, yes. If this appeals to your family, talk to outfitters ahead of time to be sure native hosts and leaders at the villages know you want to try some activities. And let them know your children will be interested, too, if that's the case.

**Will there be opportunities for one-on-one discussions?** If this is important to you, choose a trip that offers a more customized or personalized experience rather than one geared to a group.

**Will there be recreational activities in addition to cultural learning?** You may be able to go horseback riding or fishing or hiking as part of some trips. Others focus almost entirely on the cultural or learning aspect. Young children have a more limited capacity for lectures and grown-up talk, so make sure there's enough action and diversity to keep your children's interest.

**If someone in the family has a particular interest, can you make arrangements beyond what is described in the itinerary?** Outfitters and tour operators that handle custom trips are the most likely to be able to arrange special activities. If you can't find what you want on a set itinerary, call some of the customization specialists in this chapter. Quite possibly you'll be able to design your own trip and still stay within your budget.

**Will my children have native children their age with whom to interact?** Trip leaders don't always give thought to this, so try to arrange it in advance. Children learn a great deal from each other through play and other activities.

**What kind of lodging is available?** Some outfitters arrange stays with Native American host families; others give you the opportunity to stay in a traditional tepee on a reservation or other land. In some cases you stay in motels, visiting tribal areas during the day. There are combinations of all of the above, too. Choose the trip that best meets your family's expectations for immersion in Native American culture.

**What kind of food will we eat?** Native foods are often part of the experience, and some may be strange to you or your children. You'll want to try everything, but do bring snack foods that your children like.

**What's included in the cost?** For the trips in this chapter, and in most other cases as well, lodging, some meals, and local transportation are included. Sightseeing, activities at reservations and villages, and participation in powwows, dances, and meetings with tribal members are also part of the package. It's up to you to get to and from the trip's starting and ending points.

## Instruction

All these trips involve learning; many include instruction in native crafts, dances, and music or in traditional activities such as fishing or tracking wildlife. Sometimes you can learn to prepare foods or make medicines. In every case tribal elders or experts will guide and teach you. Native encounters offer a rare opportunity for multicultural learning in its purest sense.

## Finding the Fun

**Northeast:** Journeys into American Indian Territory. **Midwest:** Journeys into American Indian Territory. **Southwest:** Crow Canyon Archaeological Center, Grandtravel, Off the Beaten Path, Journeys into American Indian Territory. **Rockies:** Grandtravel, Off the Beaten Path, Journeys into American Indian Territory. **Alaska:** Athabasca Cultural Journeys. **Canada:** Arctic Odysseys, Off the Beaten Path. **Mexico:** Crow Canyon Archaeological Center.

# Favorite Experiences

## Arctic Odysseys

12+

As its name implies, Arctic Odysseys specializes in introducing people of all ages and backgrounds to an area once accessible only to the most daring of explorers. This trip takes place in northern Canada with the Inuit. It still requires a special kind of family to venture into this wild and remote land, but those that do find that the rewards far outweigh the hardship or expense that Arctic travel involves.

**FOR FAMILIES.** The Summer Wildlife and Cultural Odyssey combines wildlife viewing and exposure to the traditional Inuit lifestyle. This is a totally customized experience, so you and your Inuit guide can modify the itinerary to suit your interests. For that reason, younger children can often be accommodated, but talk to owner Robin Duberow first.

You spend some time in established communities, such as Cape Dorset and Iqaluit (still shown as Frobisher Bay on some maps), on Baffin Island. During most of the trip, however, your family is traveling by 25-ft powered utility boat. (The length of the boat ride varies with your particular itinerary, but may average four or five hours each day.) You pick your way through the icebergs and stop at Inuit summer camps to visit with friends and relatives of your guide or to watch Inuit artists at work. You can usually see caribou, seals, walrus, and snow geese. If you have a license, you can learn to fish for Arctic char. A special experience is a stop at the West Baffin Co-op in Cape Dorset, which has world-renowned galleries with carvings and other work by Inuit artists. Lodging at summer camps is typically in double-wall tents. The trip begins and ends in Ottawa, Ontario, and the cost includes the flights between Ottawa, Iqaluit, and Cape Dorset. Temperatures range between 30°F and 60°F, so pay attention to clothing lists. *Arctic Odysseys, 2000 McGilvra Blvd. E, Seattle, WA 98112, tel. 206/325–1977. July–Aug.: 5 days, $3,275; 9 days, $3,850.*

## Athabasca Cultural Journeys

8+

The Athabascan people did not want their ancestral home in north-central Alaska destroyed by mining or logging, so they embarked on a commercial tourism enterprise to help sustain their tribe. The goal was to allow visitors to meet real families and see everyday Athabascan life while learning about the tribe's unique history and culture. Athabasca Cultural Journeys, owned and operated by the Athabascan people of Huslia, Alaska, describes the tours as "a wilderness and cultural adventure" in which guests "experience Alaska through the eyes of native peoples."

**FOR FAMILIES.** Huslia is remote—a 90-minute bush-plane flight northwest from Fairbanks. You pass over native villages, the Yukon River, the Trans-Alaska Pipeline, and numerous historical and working gold mines. The Athabascan host families traditionally are volunteer tribal elders, but if guests ask for host families with children, the company will try to accommodate that request. From Huslia most guests travel with their hosts by riverboat deep into the Koyokuk National Wildlife Refuge to a native wilderness camp. Only six people at a time are allowed, both to maintain the quality of the experience and to lessen the impact on the wilderness area.

The wildlife refuge, home to thousands of nesting migratory birds and birds of prey as well as to moose, caribou, bears, wolves, otters, and beavers, presents many opportunities to see and photograph wildlife. Guests can also fish, hike, and visit archaeological sites. For the trip's cultural component, tribal members teach native history, traditions, and animal lore and share traditional myths and legends. Families can try crafts and explore the use of barks and roots for eating and healing. At the primitive campsite, visitors stay in cabins or wall tents, and there is no running water. Food, however, is plentiful and includes native recipes using moose, caribou, bear, beaver, and fish.

Summer in Alaska means almost constant daylight, so there's plenty of time for all your activities. In fact, each itinerary is customized. You can spend more time in Huslia or opt for a traditional fishing camp—where you'd participate in drying and smoking salmon—instead of the wilderness camp. As with the wilderness camp, the fishing camp's facilities are quite bare bones.

*Athabasca Cultural Journeys, Box 72, Huslia, AK 99746, tel. 907/829–2261 or 800/937–0899. June–Aug.: 3 days, $1,650. Flights between Fairbanks and Huslia are included in the cost.*

## Crow Canyon Archaeological Center

9+

This prestigious, nonprofit archaeological center, whose main work is preserving, protecting, and uncovering ruins in southwestern Colorado (*see* Archaeology Adventures), also offers cultural explorations of ancient and present-day native societies in various parts of the American Southwest and Mexico. Trips change from season to season; the ones described here are representative of what Crow Canyon is likely to offer.

**FOR FAMILIES.** The eight-day Family Travel Program is the only trip aimed squarely at parents and children. Its variety of activities can keep even nine-year-olds happily busy and learning. Families travel with an archaeologist (who may bring a child along) through the Four Corners area of Arizona, Colorado, and Utah, exploring the cliff dwellings at Mesa Verde, rafting to rock art sites on the San Juan River, and horseback riding in Northern Arizona. There are opportunities to meet and learn from Navajo (or Dine) and Pueblo people, including a hike to visit with a Navajo family at their sheep camp in Canyon de Chelly.

There are several other family-appropriate trips in Crow Canyon's catalog. Because they have a stronger scholarly focus, they're best for families with teens. Monument Valley on Horseback is a journey through one of the most historic and visually stunning regions of the American Southwest, in northeastern Arizona and southeastern Utah. The Navajo people had—and have—an intimate relationship with this valley, where their hogans blend almost seamlessly into the landscape. On this tour, led by a Navajo scholar, the group learns about the natural and human history of Monument Valley, as well as the significance and story of the mesas, buttes, and jutting volcanic monoliths. Another trek for horse lovers, through the White Mountains of Arizona, is led by an Apache tribe member and an archaeologist. The Apache still live in the region today and continue to influence it with their rich culture and traditions. Or blend an interest in astronomy with a desire to learn about Native American cultures on the Solstice Markers and Puebloan Sites trip. A Native American and an astronomer will introduce you to the scientific and spiritual aspects of Chimney Rock, Chaco Canyon, and Hovenweep National Monument—all during the week of the summer solstice.

If the center has scheduled a trip to Mexico's Copper Canyon and the other canyons of the Sierra Tarahumara, where the Tarahumara people have lived for centuries, consider joining it. You can hike in the canyons—the deepest of which is more than ¼-mi deeper than the Grand Canyon—and meet Native Americans who will talk about their homeland and its recent changes. Another possibility is a journey to the state of Chiapas, where ancient Mayan and contemporary native cultures enhance a diverse landscape of forested highlands and tropical jungle lowlands. You can learn to recognize the colorful textiles worn by local Indians; each design is identified with a particular village. There's also time to explore local markets, bright with traditional weavings and embroidery.

Accommodations on Crow Canyon's trips range from tents to first-class hotels; most meals are included.

*Crow Canyon Archaeological Center, 23390 Road K, Cortez, CO 81321, tel. 970/565–8975 or 800/422–8975. Feb.–Nov.: 6–9 days, $875–$4,195, $1,375 for children in the family program. A required family membership costs $75; membership for other programs runs $20–$50, depending on age.*

## Grandtravel

**7–17**

A pioneer in intergenerational travel, Grandtravel makes available a wide variety of journeys for grandparents and grandchildren. These trips promote the discovery of new and exciting places and, perhaps most important, stimulating new ideas. The itineraries are geared for both age groups and include such activities as riding and rafting.

**FOR FAMILIES.** On the Our Native Americans trip, family members gain firsthand knowledge and understanding of Native American tribes throughout the Southwest. The trip, which starts in Albuquerque and ends in Phoenix, is run twice each summer: once for adults with grandchildren from ages 7 to 11, once for those with grandchildren from 12 to 17. The majority of travel is by motor coach and train, but the trip also has a Navajo-guided Jeep tour of Arizona's Canyon de Chelly; a train ride near Durango, Colorado; and a white-water rafting trip.

In Albuquerque the group rides the Sandia Peak Tramway to Sandia Peak's 10,674-ft summit. From the top you'll have a stunning panorama view of approximately 14,000 square mi of land that has long been important to native peoples. In Santa Fe grandchildren and grandparents attend a Pueblo Ceremonial Feast Day and take a guided "storywalk" through the historic streets of the oldest capital city in the United States. Taos, New Mexico's 800-year-old pueblo, is an important stop, as is the Jicarilla Apache Reservation. In Canyon de Chelly, the ancestral home of the Navajo people, there's a

Navajo ranger campfire program in addition to the Jeep tour. A visit to the Hopi Reservation in Arizona gives insight into how trade affected Native Americans in the 1880s; explorations of a variety of Anasazi ruins and petroglyphs add further historical perspective.

*Grandtravel, 6900 Wisconsin Ave., Suite 706, Chevy Chase, MD 20815, tel. 301/986–0790 or 800/247–7651. June–Aug.: 10 days, $3,415–$3,710, depending on number in family group.*

## Journeys into American Indian Territory

6+

For the past 12 years, anthropologist Robert Vetter and a staff of Native Americans have been giving people a chance to experience the diversity of native cultures through one-on-one contact with Native Americans around the United States. An educational consultant when not running Journeys, he is totally enthusiastic about introducing children to native cultures.

**FOR FAMILIES.** The best trip for families with younger children is the three-day Upstate New York Experience, which takes place during June and August in the lower Catskill Mountains. Vetter will consider children younger than six on an individual basis. This gathering of native people from the West and the East has separate activities for children and adults, but close interaction with native people is at the heart of everyone's experience. Unlike most other powwows, where nonnatives are spectators, this event is about participating; you learn traditional dances, games, and songs. Expect storytelling, lectures, and a chance to learn about native foods (one activity is an herbal plant walk) and crafts.

Older children—12 or 13 and up—who have a real interest in Native American cultures can join the company's other journeys. Although none has activities especially designed for children, all offer firsthand learning opportunities. A journey through New Mexico, Oklahoma, and Texas offers a wide range of experiences, including a stay at an Oklahoma guest ranch. That trip begins in New Mexico, with visits to the many pueblos of Santa Fe and Taos, and there's time to tour the family-friendly city of Santa Fe, too. (The Georgia O'Keeffe Museum makes a great, short visit.) From there it's on to Texas and the stunning Palo Duro Canyon (*see also* RV Adventures), site of the last Indian War of 1874. In Oklahoma families meet Native American families, visit spiritual and ceremonial centers important to native peoples, and attend Red Earth, one of the largest Native American festivals in the country.

Cultural places of power on the Northern Plains—the land of the Lakota, Cheyenne, Arapaho, and Shoshone peoples—are the focus of a journey through Montana, South Dakota, and Wyoming. A Cheyenne elder helps lead the group. The journey takes participants from the Custer Battlefield (observed from the Native American viewpoint) through the Cheyenne Indian Reservation and on to Bear Butte, a place of healing and pilgrimage for the Lakota and Cheyenne people in South Dakota. There's a stop at Crazy Horse Monument before venturing into the Badlands and through Pine Ridge Reservation. Devil's Tower may be Wyoming's most prominent site of Native American importance, and you'll understand why when visiting it with Native Americans. There are also stops at the hot springs in Thermopolis, Wyoming, the Northern Plains Indian Museum in Buffalo, and the Medicine Wheel of Northern Wyoming, known as the Stonehenge of the New World. The journey ends at Crow Fair, Montana's renowned powwow.

While most of the accommodations for these trips are in hotels and cabins, there are options for staying in a traditional tepee on two or three nights. The price of the Upstate New York Experience covers all meals; the fees for the other journeys include one meal a day. During the Northern Plains and New Mexico, Oklahoma, and Texas trips, you travel in vans or small buses. To allow for one-on-one contact and discussion, most trips are limited to a maximum of 20 participants.

If your schedule doesn't allow participation in these scheduled trips, ask about homestays with Native American families. Through daily routines and close interaction with your host family, you'll experience native customs, traditions, and foods and learn about native family histories. Homestays are available in Oklahoma, South Dakota, Arizona, and Montana.

*Journeys into American Indian Territory, Box 929, Westhampton Beach, NY 11978, tel. 516/878–8655 or 800/458–2632. Feb., June–Sept., and Nov.: 3–11 days, $285–$1,295 adults, $170 for children participating in the New York program.*

## Off the Beaten Path

ALL

Off the Beaten Path (OBP) excels in customized adventures for people of all ages. The company handles planning and arrangements, working with each family to put together the right trip. OBP leads many of the adventures, but sometimes contracts with outfitters and guides to lead trips, too. In addition to its customized trips, OBP has 'pre-designed' itineraries, meaning the itinerary and accommodations are already established. If your family prefers a specific itinerary, OBP will set it up at a time that works for you (keeping in mind that some things are seasonal). This cuts down on consulting time, which the company does charge for in addition to its trip prices. Owner Bill Bryan has a long personal and professional history with Native American people. He's a published authority on the tribes of Montana (see Resources, *below*).

**FOR FAMILIES.** Totally customized or predesigned encounters might include a day spent with tribal members at reservations in various parts of the West or multi-day journeys with Native American guides. You might, for example, book several nights in the hogan of a Navajo outfitter, who will guide your family around Canyon de Chelly, the Navajo homeland in northern Arizona. You can stay with natives who have ranches or fishing lodges or travel with native guides who run horse-packing and fishing trips. OBP works with Blackfeet and Flathead tribe members in Montana; Blood and Piegan natives in Alberta, Canada; and numerous tribes throughout the Southwest. Your customized trip can concentrate on spirituality, family life, history, or any aspect of native culture you may want to explore.

Each year OBP also offers its own scheduled, 8- to 10-day tour for singles, couples, and families with relatively mature children (talk to the company first about your child's interests and abilities before signing up). The trip, with about 14 participants, focuses on the history and present-day culture of tribes in Montana, southwestern Colorado, and in Alberta, Canada. The group spends time with tribal council members and reservation school principals and visits hospitals and historic sites. Some meals are with tribal members. Participants usually learn how to raise a tepee; they have the option of staying overnight in one as well. Two examples of these trips are A Journey Through Time to the Four Corners, which includes interaction with Ute and Navajo tribe members, and Tracing the Flight of the Nez Perce, which follows the 1,200 mi route through four states taken by Chief Joseph and his people in 1877. The flight of the Nez Perce is one of the most powerful and sorrowful sagas in the history of the American West, and all of it is vividly brought to life on the trail by a leading authority on the Nez Perce, who accompanies guests on this trip.

*Off the Beaten Path, 27 E. Main St., Bozeman, MT 59715, tel. 406/586–1311 or 800/445–2995. Year-round (all trips not available at all times): 7–10 days, $150–$175 per person, per day. Scheduled trip: $2,000 per person. Ask about children's discounts, offered on some trips and varying with specific circumstances. Consulting runs $200–$1,000, depending on the complexity of the trip.*

# Resources

## Organizations

For a list of reservations that allow camping or for Native American events you can attend, write to the **Bureau of Indian Affairs** (U.S. Department of the Interior, Washington, DC 20245); tell them which states you want to visit.

## Books

*Kids Explore the Heritage of Western Native Americans* (John Muir Publications), by the Westridge Writers Workshop, was written by students, many of whom live on reservations. Profiles of six families show what it means to be Native American today. Marlene Smith-Baranzini and Howard Egger-Bovet's *The Brown Paper School US Kids History: Book of American Indians* (Little, Brown) mixes historical anecdotes with stories, drawings, and projects. Bryan and Cherry Alexander's *What Do We Know about the Inuit?* (Peter Bedrick Books) has information about the ancestors of the Inuit and the Inuit people today. *North American Indians,* by Herman J. Viola (Crown), provides an introduction to native people. *They Dance in the Sky: Native American Star Myths* (Houghton Mifflin), by Jean Guard Monroe, collects stories about the constellations from tribes across North America. Travelers to the Southwest should look at *Stories on Stone,* by Jennifer Owings Dewey (Little, Brown); it's out of print but should be in libraries.

Anyone booking a trip with Off the Beaten Path should see William L. Bryan's *Montana Indians: Yesterday and Today* (American Geographic Publishing).

## Also See

Families interested in present-day Native American peoples may find the study of ancient civilizations appealing. Archaeology Adventures lists digs that focus on native cultures.

# RAFTING

My love of rafting began when I first ran the McKenzie and Rogue rivers in the early '70s as a student at the University of Oregon. My older daughter, Kira, was luckier. She had the fun of experiencing her first river—the New, in West Virginia—when she was just eight. Molly, her sister, explored Jackson Lake and the Snake River, down through Moose, Wyoming, at the age of four, and their brother, Hutch, ran the New at the ripe old age of six and at seven explored the wonders of the Salmon River Canyons. In our family, it just isn't summer if we haven't gone rafting.

Rafting is simply a great family vacation. You don't need any experience or skills, and you can choose a trip on which you paddle or one on which you sit back and watch the scenery drift by as guides wield the oars. However and wherever you do it, the combination of floating downriver under blue skies and camping at night under millions of stars is unbeatable. The roomy rafts also make it possible to carry an amount and variety of food unheard of on many wilderness trips. When my children and I joined River Odysseys West on the Salmon River, steak, tortellini salad, an awesome tomato-cilantro-onion salad, and carrot cake were all on the menu. Did we see spectacular wilderness areas and view wildlife up close? You bet. Did we rough it? Hardly.

Rafting outfitters have done more to entice children and parents onto North American rivers than any other water-sports group. Family-only raft trips seem to increase in number every season, with ever-better amenities for river-running children. Storytellers, child-oriented naturalists, and off-river activities counselors accompany some trips; excursions to historical sites are part of others. Guides on family trips are chosen as much for their ability to work effectively with children as for their rafting skills.

On the other hand, most trips that welcome families do not send you through the intense white water that sets your heart pounding and adrenaline rushing. Family trips tend to tackle rapids from Class I to Class III only, which means easy to moderate white water, appropriate for children age 12 or 13 and younger. What you trade in excitement on a family river trip with younger children, however, you make up in wildlife viewing, side hikes, and the joy of introducing your children to rivers and wilderness areas. If you are among the river-loving families with teens, you have a whole world of thrilling, chilling, and exquisitely beautiful rivers from which to choose.

Dozens of rivers throughout North America are perfect for family raft trips. A number of outfitters work the same rivers, but your experience will be different depending on which you choose. Finding the right river is important; choosing the right outfitter is crucial. Each has a distinct personality and creates a particular atmosphere on the river and in camp. Make lots of calls before you make a decision.

## Questions to Ask

**Are Coast Guard–approved life vests available for a child the size and age of mine?** Most vests are sized according to height and weight, not age, so give outfitters your child's measurements to be sure they have one that will fit. If the right size isn't available, you'll have to borrow a life vest or buy one at an outdoor or marine supply store.

**Are the guides trained in wilderness and water safety, first aid, and CPR?** Always ask. Wilderness rivers take you a long, long way from medical care or help. If an accident occurs, you want guides who know the right emergency procedures.

**How strenuous are trips, and what do the classifications of rapids mean?** The most common white-water classification system used in this country rates rapids from Class I to Class VI; Class I is barely more than a riffle, and Class VI is virtually unrunnable. Most family trips fall into Class III or below, though children eight and up are sometimes allowed on rivers with a Class IV rapid or two. Outfitters take several things into consideration: the time of year, the speed of the water, and the height of the water. A second classification system, more common among the Grand Canyon outfitters than others, has from Class I to Class X ratings. If you're uncertain which system an outfitter is using, ask.

**How many hours will we raft each day?** From five to six hours a day is average, though water level, weather, and the ability of guests and guides doing the paddling or rowing affect rafting time. Still, the pace allows for unhurried breakfasts and early enough arrivals at camp each afternoon to hike, fish, or relax. Daily stops along the way are part of all river journeys. Trips designated especially for families often have more frequent stops and shorter days on the river.

**Does the trip have scheduled activities other than rafting?** Hiking and fishing are the two most common river-camp activities, and you must usually bring your own fishing gear and arrange for licenses for teens and adults ahead of time. Family trips almost always have camp activities, such as storytelling, crafts, games, nature walks, or berry-picking hikes.

**What kinds of rafts are used on the trip?** On most but not all of the trips listed, you'll be in oar-powered rafts that the guides are primarily responsible for maneuvering and rowing. Guests almost always have the option of a paddle raft if they request it, and a couple of trips use paddle rafts only. In these, all the passengers stroke according to the guide's directions. Very few of the outfitters in this chapter use motorized rafts. Typically, the rafts hold from 6 to 12 people. Almost all outfitters will also bring along inflatable kayaks for additional fun.

**Are the rafts self-bailing?** This is by no means a requirement, but families seeking more comfort and less work may prefer self-bailers, which release water on their own. They stay drier on the bottom, so your feet and gear will be drier, too. And no one will ask you to help bail if it rains or after you go through the big splashes. A self-bailer is also more stable and easier to maneuver than a raft with water sloshing around the bottom, and when it comes to children on the river, stable is always preferable.

**Are dry bags available?** Most outfitters provide a dry bag for storing clothing and camping gear each day, but you generally can't get to your stuff until you camp. On-raft containers hold cameras and other items you want on board. A small dry bag or waterproof day pack of your own is a good idea because shared containers don't usually have room for rain gear and warm layers for the children.

**Are snacks provided on the river?** Children need to eat far more often than adults, so this is important. If the guides won't have easily accessible snacks in the rafts, bring your own on board in a day pack.

**What's the average group size?** Most outfitters listed here go out with from 10 to 20 participants, plus between two and four guides. Some trips may take only from six to eight people, however, and a few outfitters run trips with as many as 25.

**What kind of lodging is provided?** On most trips, you camp overnight—in some cases, right on a beach. In the listings below, we've noted the exceptions to this general rule.

**What's included in the cost?** All meals, guides, and local transportation to the put-in (launch site) and from the takeout (where the river trip ends) are included, as are life vests for all passengers, unless otherwise noted. Most rafting outfitters will bring along inflatable kayaks for a change of pace for adults and older children, but some charge extra for this. In most cases you must bring your own tent, pad, and sleeping bag, or rent from the outfitter for a small additional cost. A few outfitters provide this equipment as part of the basic cost. Outfitters almost always arrange a safe place for you to leave your car during the trip; it might be their own parking lot or the lot of a local motel.

## Instruction

Guides begin every trip with safety instructions for rafting and camping. These help both adults and children understand the importance of being careful around water. They also teach those who will be paddling how to do so. You'll probably be taught a bit of river lingo, too, so you can follow the guide's paddling instructions. Beyond that, all you need to do is have fun.

## Finding the Fun

**Northeast:** Northern Outdoors, Unicorn Rafting Expeditions. **Mid-Atlantic:** Class VI River Runners. **Southwest:** American River Touring Association, Arizona Raft Adventures, Canyonlands Field Institute, Denver Museum of Natural History, Dvorak's Kayak & Rafting Expeditions, Far Flung Adventures, Grand Canyon Dories/O.A.R.S. Dories, Holiday Expeditions, Sheri Griffith Expeditions, Tag-A-Long Expeditions. **Rockies:** American River Touring Association, American Wilderness Experience/GORP Travel, Canyonlands Field Institute, Denver Museum of Natural History, Dvorak's Kayak & Rafting Expeditions, Echo, Glacier Wilderness Guides/Montana Raft Company, Grand Canyon Dories/O.A.R.S. Dories, Holiday Expeditions, Hughes River Expeditions, Idaho Afloat, O.A.R.S., Outdoor Adventures, Ouzel Outfitters, River Odysseys West, Salmon River Outfitters, Wilderness River Outfitters. **West Coast:** American River Touring Association, Cutting Edge Adventures, Echo, Hughes River Expeditions, O.A.R.S., Outdoor Adventures, Ouzel Outfitters, Rogue River Raft Trips. **Alaska:** Canadian River Expeditions, River Odysseys West, Wilderness River Outfitters. **Canada:** Canadian River Expeditions, Wilderness River Outfitters. **Mexico:** Cutting Edge Adventures, Far Flung Adventures. **Europe:** River Odysseys West. **South America:** River Odysseys West. **Africa:** Cutting Edge Adventures.

# Favorite Rafting Companies

## American River Touring Association

6+

The American River Touring Association—popularly known as ARTA—donates a portion of its revenues to conservation organizations each year. The philosophy of this nonprofit organization is a belief that exposure to the wilderness benefits both individuals and the environment. Yes, ARTA is earnest about nature, safety, and environmental concerns—but it's just as serious about people having fun on its trips throughout the West.

**FOR FAMILIES.** Trips run from spring through fall, but in summer ARTA schedules numerous family departures on five rivers. You can choose from among the South Fork of the American in California, Oregon's Rogue River, two portions of the Green in Utah, and either the Salmon or the Middle Fork of the Salmon in Idaho. Each river gives rafters something special in terms of scenery and focus. The American is a great two-day escape that uses only paddle rafts; the Rogue offers excellent wildlife-viewing possibilities; the geology and history of the Green are fascinating; and the Salmon abounds in great beaches, hot springs, and swimming opportunities.

To encourage families to explore these rivers together, ARTA has a special price for children on family departures. Guides on all family trips genuinely enjoy working with youngsters, and the many side activities provided range from hiking and storytelling to pondering nature's mysteries.

*American River Touring Association, 24000 Casa Loma Rd., Groveland, CA 95321, tel. 209/962–7873 or 800/323–2782. Apr.–Sept.: 2–7 days, $199–$1,120 adults, $150–$740 children.*

## American Wilderness Experience/GORP Travel

6+

The extensive list of rafting vacations in the company's catalog shows just how much the business has grown. This trip broker represents many of the rafting outfitters in this chapter. Some standouts among its trips are a couple of vacations in Montana and Colorado that combine activities. If your family is debating which adventure to pursue, one of these may be the answer.

**FOR FAMILIES.** If you can't choose between a ranch stay and a raft trip, Glacier Raft Company and Bear Creek Ranch in Montana have put together three days at the ranch and two days of rafting. Children ages six and up can handle this one. At the ranch, near the border of Glacier National Park and Great Bear Wilderness, you can opt for exceptional riding, hiking, or fishing in a land of blue-white glaciers and high peaks. The 30-mi rafting trip down the Middle Fork of the Flathead runs through parts of Glacier National Park and the Lewis and Clark National Forest. If horse packing into the wilderness appeals more than a stay at the ranch, try the five-day ride-and-raft trip, best for ages eight and up. This adventure takes you into Flathead National Forest and ends with a raft trip on the Middle Fork of the Flathead.

Families with children eight and up can combine horse packing with rafting in south-central Colorado on a trip from Adventure Specialists. The first three days are spent packing and camping in the Sangre de Cristo range. The group then heads down to a rustic inn for showers and use of a hot tub before two days on the Arkansas River, including a wild run through Royal Gorge.

*American Wilderness Experience/GORP Travel, Box 1486, Boulder, CO 80306, tel. 303/444–2622 or 800/444–0099. May–Sept.: 5 days, $895 adults, $735–$895 children.*

## Arizona Raft Adventures

5+

I asked a rafting outfitter whom he rafts with when the season is over in his neck of the woods. His answer, without hesitation, was AzRA. That this is a river guide's river-guiding company attests to AzRA's high level of professionalism and dedication. One thing that sets this company apart is its guides, most of whom have been taking people down the Colorado and the San Juan—the two rivers in which AzRA specializes—for an average of at least 10 years. That adds up to a lot of experience and knowledge—both crucial to a good family trip.

**FOR FAMILIES.** AzRA runs dedicated family trips on the San Juan, a southwestern river that was central to the ancient Anasazi culture. Today the San Juan marks the northern border of the Navajo Nation and flows through areas of compelling geological and archaeological interest. The San Juan is also surrounded by national parks and lands important to native people: Canyonlands, Mesa Verde, Canyon de Chelly, Monument Valley, Natural Bridges, and Navajo National Monument. AzRA's San Juan voyages run from three to seven days. The shortest starts in Bluff, in southeastern Utah, and runs 27 river mi to Mexican Hat. A longer run takes families from Bluff to Lake Powell, 83 mi to the west; there's a 56-mi option, too. From remote canyons to lazy swimming holes, the San Juan is a rafting family's paradise. Children ages seven and up are welcome on any San Juan trip; ages five and up can join non-family-specific trips if they've had previous camping and rafting experience, and they're always welcome on designated family runs.

The Colorado River through the Grand Canyon is probably the classic river trip of this continent. Trips last from 6 to 15 days and cover from 89 to all 225 mi of the canyon run. The company has motorized and nonmotorized expeditions. Children as young as 10 can go on motorized trips; 12 is the minimum age for "hybrid" runs—those utilizing two types of nonmotorized rafts. On all-paddle rafting adventures (ones on which guests and a guide provide paddle power), the minimum age is 16. Grand Canyon rafting adventures are also about hiking through the awesome terrain accessible from the river and about exploring side canyons, too. The shorter trips require good physical condition and a willingness to hike a challenging and steep trail either in or out. If hiking is something you love, talk to the guides, who always customize each trip according to the wishes of the group.

*Arizona Raft Adventures, 4050 E. Huntington Dr., Flagstaff, AZ 86004, tel. 520/526–8200 or 800/786–7238. Apr.–Oct: 3–14 days, $430–$2,320; 15% discount for children under 17 on some trips.*

## Canadian River Expeditions

8+

The icy Tatshenshini River flows through the Yukon and British Columbia, empties into the Alsek, and finally spills into the sea at the Gulf of Alaska. On the way it carves through a vast wilderness landscape that humbles and awes its viewers. Canadian River Expeditions (CRE) has been guiding on the Tat and the Alsek for 25 years. The guides know and love the Tat, and they willingly share this river with the families that dare to come. The Tat is a personal favorite, but the company's trips through other parts of British Columbia are phenomenal, too.

**FOR FAMILIES.** The Tatshenshini challenges you, but the rewards are worth it—and then some. Be prepared for windy and alternately warm and chilly days, and know that fishing and swimming are not the Tat's strong suits. None of this matters, however, when you're walking on glaciers or observing wildlife such as black bears, moose, wolves, and even grizzlies. One spectacular hike with an ascent of about 3,800 ft is probably too much for anyone under age 12 or 13 (although children as young as eight are welcome on this trip), and if you have a child who wearies of just observing nature's wonders, this 12-day expedition may not be for you. On the other hand, if your family wants to travel hundreds of miles without finding one sign of human civilization, this trip will provide memories to last a lifetime.

Company owner Johnny Mikes recommends the 11-day Best of B.C. trip as ideal for families with younger children. This adventure is remarkable for both its diversity of experience and its magnificent settings. From Vancouver the group travels by boat into the Discovery Islands and the coastal region's fjords, then by seaplane over the glaciers of the Coast Mountains and on to 40-mi-long Chilko Lake. After you fish and hike among the ancient firs for two days, the rafting begins. You journey on three rivers—the Chilko, the Chilcotin, and the Fraser—passing from the mountains down through wide-open grasslands and into the arid sandstone and cactus canyons of the Fraser. With its huge volume of water, the Fraser has plenty of the big roller-coaster rapids that all rafters love. A four-hour train ride takes you back to the coast through Whistler.

Families that want to raft the great northern rivers but don't have two weeks or more to do it have two options. There's a six-day Chilcotin Fraser expedition, which basically duplicates the last six days of the 11-day Best of B.C. itinerary described above. You'll pack in fantastic landscape views—grasslands, canyons, and enormous hoodoo formations—not to mention daily runs on the best rapids. You meet in Williams Lake, spending the first two nights at Big Creek Ecological Reserve, which is a good place to hike. The second camp is opposite the Chilcotin-Fraser Junction Bighorn Sheep Reserve. Here you're likely to see impressive rams and perhaps a black bear or two. Another option is the six-day Upper Alsek adventure; on this trip, you'll experience the awesome Alsek terrain of Kluane National Park and Tatshenshini-Alsek Wilderness Park. The trip begins and ends in Whitehorse in Canada's Yukon.

*Canadian River Expeditions, Box 1023, Whistler, British Columbia, Canada V0N 1B0, tel. 604/938–6651 or 800/898–7238. June–Aug.: 6–12 days, $999–$2,825; 20% discount for children under 18.*

## Canyonlands Field Institute

8+

Canyonlands focuses primarily on its youth program, in which students from Utah, Colorado, and beyond learn about the wonders of the Colorado Plateau—its geology, wildlife, night skies, waterways, and more. Naturalists and other outdoor educators make up the institute's staff. Although family courses are limited, they are exceptional. Few river trips have an educational component as extensive as these.

**FOR FAMILIES.** Working with Elderhostel, the nonprofit organization well known for its study programs for older adults, Canyonlands sponsors an intergenerational trip that brings grandparents and grandchildren together for six days of discovery as they raft the San Juan River. Naturalists lead hands-on nature activities, teach participants low-impact camping and river-running skills, and delve into botany, geology, and a study of prehistoric rock art—all while having fun on the river. The group camps for four nights; the first night is spent at a lodge in Bluff, Utah, where the trip begins.

With three months' notice, the institute will set up customized river trips for groups of at least eight. Families with children 12 and up can run the Colorado River from Colorado to Utah, floating through Ruby and Horsethief canyons and on to the rapids of Westwater Canyon. Colorado's portion of the Dolores River through Ponderosa Gorge is another option for kids 12 and up. A naturalist leads and outfits each trip, providing the same learning opportunities found on scheduled trips.

You don't have to be an institute member to join any of the adventures, but members do get a discount on trips of 10%, to a maximum of $15.

*Canyonlands Field Institute, Box 68, Moab, UT 84532, tel. 435/259–7750 or 800/860–5262. Apr.–Sept.: 3–6 days, $415–$590 for scheduled trips; $50–$120 per day for adults and $35– $85 per day for children 18 and under for customized trips. Family membership (optional) is $35.*

## Class VI River Runners

6+

If you think all the best white water is out West, you haven't run the New or Gauley rivers in the Appalachian Mountains of south-central West Virginia. The New—which in spite of its name may be second only to the Nile in geologic age—cuts a deep and impressive gorge, with walls 1,000 ft high in places. As for the Gauley River, each fall white-water enthusiasts arrive from all over the world to test their skills against a river that drops 650 ft in 27 mi and churns up more than 100 major rapids along the way. Class VI caters equally to six-year-olds rafting for the first time and 16-year-olds looking for the ultimate adrenaline high. Parents will find in Dave Arnold and his co-owners the intelligence and spirit that characterize the very best river outfitters.

**FOR FAMILIES.** The upper New treats families with children six and up to Class I and

Class II rapids, with a Class III thrill toward the end of this one- to three-day trip. Great swimming and rock jumping along the way plus wildlife and historic points of interest make this a memorable experience. For a one-day adventure, parents and teens can raft the more difficult portions of the river while family members under 12 have their own guided adventure on the upper New. You get together again in the late afternoon at Class VI's headquarters; while there, check out the excellent barbecue at Smokey's, the outfitter's restaurant.

The lower New River Gorge is for children age 12 and up from July to Labor Day; the minimum age is 14 the rest of the season. Prepare yourself for Class III–V rapids, along with the spectacular scenery of the deeply forested Appalachians. In spite of the rapids, swimming is good here, too. Special theme adventures on both the lower and upper New, for those from age six to adult, include River Ecology, an ecologist-led trip on which families learn about the plants and creatures living in and around the New River, and birding trips to areas where herons, falcons, egrets, eagles, hawks, and songbirds may be spotted.

The Gauley is for children at least age 15. The faint of heart, out of shape, or sit-back-and-relax types should look for another river. The Gauley is work—and worth every bit of it, with a payback of world-class white water and thrills. You can choose between one- and two-day trips.

For lodging before and after trips, you can choose from among an excellent campground minutes from Class VI and a variety of motels, cabins, and bed-and-breakfasts. The elegant Greenbrier resort, with its own outstanding children's program, is about 1½ hours away. Class VI can help arrange these accommodations.

*Class VI River Runners, Box 78, Lansing, WV 25862, tel. 304/574–0704 or 800/252–7784. Mar.–Nov.: 1–3 days, $86–$316 adults, $43–$270 children.*

## Cutting Edge Adventures

3+

Stefanie Abrishamian, a co-owner of Cutting Edge, is enough of a kid at heart that children immediately relate to her, and so do parents. When you raft with Cutting Edge, you laugh—and learn—a lot on some of northern California's greatest rivers. Amazingly, one of them, the Klamath River, has sections gentle enough for preschoolers yet still delivers the thrills that rafting families want.

**FOR FAMILIES.** The Klamath River is renowned for salmon and steelhead fishing and for Hell's Corner, one of the top 10 stretches of white water in the United States. Families, however, acclaim it as an accommodating river. Beaches make terrific campsites, and Class II and III rapids provide the requisite rush. The middle and lower Klamath have exceptional wildlife-viewing opportunities; the river is on the Pacific flyway, a major migratory route for a variety of birds. Blue and green herons, bald and golden eagles, falcons, ospreys, and cormorants all travel the Klamath. River otters fish and play in the water, and in the hills above, mountain lions and bears still roam. One of California's great riverside hikes (with much splashy wading as part of the fun) follows a trail just ¾ mi long up Ukonom Creek, ending at Twin Falls. You have a choice of one- to five-day trips that cover about 12 mi a day. Storytellers come along to entertain rafters on all middle and lower Klamath trips; Cutting Edge has a bat specialist on some trips, too.

Families with children age 10 and up can try the upper Sacramento River, where Class III and IV rapids propel rafters through canyons and beautiful forested stretches. This two-day trip covers about 18 mi; you can choose camping or a lodge stay.

For the most adventurous, who must be at least 17 years old, Cutting Edge schedules a trip to Mexico that begins on the Río Jatate in the Chiapas region of southern Mexico. The Jat runs through lush jungle and canyons, with waterfalls, chutes, and slides—from Class III to Class V—to contend with. There's also a chance to visit the Maya ruins of Tonina. From the Jat the trip moves on to Río Agua Azul Park, a waterfall paradise with its own Maya ruins. The last river on the trip is the Río Shumulja, a turquoise beauty with Class III and IV white water.

Families interested in overseas adventures should ask about the Out of Africa trip, which includes river running on the Zambezi; this adventure has a minimum age of 17.

*Cutting Edge Adventures, Box 1334, Mt. Shasta, CA 96067, tel. 530/926–4647. Apr.–Jan. (all trips not available all months): 1–10 days, $75–$1,500; 50% discount for children under 17 on some trips.*

## Denver Museum of Natural History

6+

Put children, rafting, and dinosaurs together, and you have a perfect family adventure package. Among its many outdoor study programs, the museum generally schedules a family rafting trip in Utah each summer that touches on paleontology, geology, river ecology, and anthropology, in addition to plain old river-rafting fun. You do not need to be a museum member to join their trips.

**FOR FAMILIES.** The Jurassic Journey/Green River Raft Trip begins at Dinosaur National Monument, east of Vernal, Utah, where huge dinosaur fossils are being excavated. The group rafts through the 2,000-ft-deep Lodore Canyon on the Green River; off the water, hikes to native rock art sites and historic outlaw cabins, wildlife watching, and in-camp games highlight the natural environment. Scientists from various disciplines lead the trip, and all children between ages 6 and 11 receive a Dinosaur Discovery Kit, with fun activities and games.

*Denver Museum of Natural History, 2001 Colorado Blvd., Denver, CO 80205, tel. 303/370–6304. July: 4 days, $725 adults, $550 children 6–11.*

## Dvorak's Kayak & Rafting Expeditions

5+

Years ago Dvorak's was one of only a handful of outfitters promoting river running for families. They have a lot more competition these days, but their long experience has shown them what rafting can do for families. With the right leaders, the Dvoraks say, rafting helps improve communication between family members by putting children and adults on an equal playing field. Guides, rather than parents, do the leading, allowing both children and adults to try new activities and learn together.

**FOR FAMILIES.** The outfitter runs family trips on five rivers throughout the West that have varying minimum ages; in addition, Dvorak's has two different family discount programs. Kids Go Free is available on the Green River in Utah and Colorado's Dolores; the minimum age on these rivers is 5 and 10, respectively. On family departure dates each paying adult can bring a child under 13 for free. The Family Discount Program applies on the Colorado River in Colorado, the Rio Chama in New Mexico, and the North Platte, which runs in both Colorado and Wyoming. On special dates families of from three to six people receive a greatly discounted group rate. Choose a river based on the ages of your children: Children five and up can handle portions of the Colorado and Rio Chama rivers; those 10 and up are welcome on the North Platte River. All family trips emphasize camp activities that families can participate in together, as well as a terrific rafting experience.

Children can join other trips, too, so check out the catalog's extensive offerings. Teens and their parents can choose among plenty of wild rivers, but these aren't in the Family Discount Program.

*Dvorak's Kayak & Rafting Expeditions, 17921-B U.S. 285, Nathrop, CO 81236, tel. 719/539–6851 or 800/824–3795. May–Aug.: 2–6 days, $250–$935 adults, $220–$855 children. Family discount prices range from $615 for 3 family members on a 2-day trip to $2,300 for 6 people on a 4-day trip.*

## ECHO

7+

In running rivers for almost 30 years, the staff at ECHO has learned that people sign up for rafting trips for many reasons. The company caters to all ages and interests, not only in the variety of its trips—from classic white-water thrillers to special-focus music and yoga trips—but in the scope of each adventure. On its River Trips for Kids, in particular, the outfitter creates family voyages equally appealing to seven-year-olds and teens.

**FOR FAMILIES.** Family trips take place on the Salmon River in Idaho and on Oregon's Rogue River. On each expedition a Fun Director organizes educational activities and other neat stuff—whether it's looking for crawdads, skipping stones, or checking out animal tracks. Teens are encouraged to help the guides (all of whom can definitely be described as cool), or they can hang out with adults if they wish. The Kids' Raft gives children the choice of riding with new friends or with parents; some shore activities are just for children, too, so adults will have some time to themselves. These trips generally combine oar and paddle rafts and the option of inflatable kayaks. If you can't make one of the specially designated family trips, don't worry: There are always families on ECHO's regular trips.

*ECHO, 6529 Telegraph Ave., Oakland, CA 94609, tel. 510/652–1600 or 800/652–3246. May–Sept.: 3–5 days, $585–$1,025 adults, $550–$1,025 children 7–17.*

## Far Flung Adventures

5+

For more than 20 years this company has introduced rafters to the geologically diverse regions and rivers of the Southwest and Mexico. Although Far Flung Adventures doesn't market itself as a family outfitter, many parents and children sign up for these river trips—and have a great time.

**FOR FAMILIES.** Far Flung guides on seven major rivers, and the minimum age for these trips varies. One of the very best for families, the Rio Chama, flows from the Colorado–New Mexico border down toward the Rio Grande. Most of the 24-mi journey on this two-day trip is at 6,000 ft, with terrain that ranges from wide-open spaces to forests of fir and pine. It's Class II and III all the way. For an all-around great river and an excellent introduction to rafting, the Rio Grande and a series of canyons in and near Big Bend National Park in Texas provide a range of river experiences, from wide and tranquil to steep, narrow, and fast. The seven- or eight-day 85-mi run in the Lower Canyons, just east of the park, takes rafters through a maze of limestone cliffs and a stark landscape. Besides being a good rafting river, the Rio Grande is a good swimming river. Families with older children can also join trips on Arizona's Salt River and on the Arkansas in Colorado.

Very adventurous families with time in the fall or winter should consider trips to Mexico's Río Antigua, Río Actopan, and Filobobos, all in the Veracruz area. Lots of Class IV rapids on the Antigua keep everyone on edge, and native freshwater lobsters and tropical fruits satisfy the most demanding palate. The Filo and Actopan rivers are mostly Class II and III and lots of fun. Aside from one night on the Filo, these aren't camping adventures; instead, you'll stay in a lovely, restored hacienda. Mexican trips are for ages 10 and up, but make certain your children are interested in learning about a foreign culture and capable of 10 days on a river.

If you have a group of four or five and want an upscale version of the Big Bend experience, the company will help you as you plan every aspect of your trip, from menu to music. On these trips the food is top-notch and the service highly personal.

*Far Flung Adventures, Box 377, Terlingua, TX 79852, tel. 800/359–4138. Year-round (all rivers not available all months): 1–10 days, $62–$1,075; 10% discount for children under 16.*

## Glacier Wilderness Guides/Montana Raft Company

6+

Using a few of the million acres of mountains, lakes, and streams in Montana's Glacier National Park, this company guides on both land and water and has first-class combination trips. The owners have hiked, camped, rafted, fished, and explored the Glacier area for most of their lives. They love it, and they know the secret places others will love, too.

**FOR FAMILIES.** Rafting adventures take place on the Middle and North forks of the Flathead. Families can join two- and three-day rafting-only adventures, but the gems in the trip list are hike-and-raft and ride-and-raft combinations in and near Glacier. You can structure the hike-and-raft several ways: a half day of each activity, 2½ days of each, or between four and six days of hiking and two days of rafting (with a motel stay in between). Groups are small, usually from four to six guests. For the ride-and-raft, choose a one- or four-day combination with equal time for horseback riding and rafting. Glacier Wilderness Guides works with a horse pack outfitter for that portion of the trip.

*Glacier Wilderness Guides/Montana Raft Company, Box 535, West Glacier, MT 59936, tel. 406/387–5555 or 800/521–7238. May–Sept.: 1–10 days, $38–$970 adults, $29–$900 children.*

## Grand Canyon Dories/O.A.R.S. Dories

7+

If you've never thought about running a river, let alone rafting for 19 days, call and ask for the illustrated O.A.R.S. Dories brochure. Dories, four-passenger wooden boats maneuvered by oars, have a long and celebrated heritage. They provide an experience totally unlike riding in today's big synthetic rafts. They're controlled differently than synthetic rafts, so you feel the river in a unique way. If this appeals to you and if you can take the time to immerse yourself in the natural world, this is the company for you.

**FOR FAMILIES.** Most families with children over age 12 can handle O.A.R.S. Dorie's longest river journey, the full length of the Colorado from Lees Ferry to Lake Mead. For 19 days you explore the Grand Canyon's rock layers—half a billion years' worth of geologic history in shades of rose, gold, and violet. The dories shoot through mile-high walls and raging rapids. Camping experience might help, but you'll soon be old hands. Good hikers who are able to handle the near-vertical mi of the 9-mi-long trail between Phantom Ranch and the South Rim can join the group for either the 8-or 13-day partial trip, depending on whether you leave or join up at Phantom Ranch. Whether you're going up or down, it's a strenuous hike. Those who choose to can leave or join up at Whitmore Wash raft for 5 or 16 days and fly in and out by helicopter. If you travel all 19 days, you start and end in Flagstaff.

Less grand, perhaps, but equally satisfying are trips on the Salmon and Snake rivers in Idaho. These rivers are great for families with younger children and perfect for dories; the Northwest was the birthplace of the river-style dory. The free-flowing Salmon River is the largest undammed river in the American West. You can run the Middle Fork, the upper portion of the Main Salmon, or the Lower Salmon on four- to six-day trips, or combine all three in the 17-day Full Salmon Experience. Along the way are fine hikes; long, clean beaches perfect for swimming; and natural hot springs to soak in.

The 400-mi-long Salmon River empties into the Snake River at Hells Canyon, the deepest gorge in North America. On three- to five-day adventures, guides share the legends of the Nez Perce who lived here, including some tales about mythic spirits who shaped the rugged landscape and the Snake's roaring rapids. For all its wildness the Snake River also shows rafters a gentler side. In a dory you'll feel the rock and rhythm of the currents as you cannot in a raft.

*Grand Canyon Dories/O.A.R.S. Dories, Box 1119, Angels Camp, CA 95222, tel. 209/736–0811 or 800/877–3679. Apr.–Oct.: 3–19 days, $730–$4,000 adults, $668–$4,000 children.*

## Holiday Expeditions

5+

Holiday has more than 30 years' experience taking all kinds of people rafting on the great rivers of Utah, Colorado, and Idaho. Dee Holladay, the company's founder, has a passion for rivers and river history. He believes that rafting is more than the sum of its parts—scenery, wilderness, solitude, and incredible white water: It's the time of your life. The company has also discovered that when rafting is combined with mountain biking or a few days at a century-old cattle ranch, the thrills get even better.

**FOR FAMILIES.** Trips on the easiest rivers, the San Juan and the Desolation Canyon section of the Green River in Utah, take children five and up. Families with children at least eight can try such intermediate rivers as the Colorado (which is also experts-only at certain times of year), the Lodore Canyon section of the Green, and the Yampa, all of which run along the Colorado–Utah border. Idaho's great waterways, the Snake and the Salmon rivers, are other possibilities for those eight and up. Each child gets a waterproof 'kid kit' with activities related to area history, geology, and nature studies: making petroglyphs, studying plants and insects under a magnifying glass, and creating crafts. The most adventurous families with teens at least age 16 can go for an adrenaline rush on the Lochsa River in Idaho and on the Colorado and lower Salmon rivers in high-water season.

Holiday also has terrific combination adventures. A seven-day Desolation Canyon trip for families with children age five and up offers five days on the Green River with two days at Rock Creek Ranch, a century-old working cattle ranch in eastern Utah's Tavaputs Plateau. A four-day ranch-river adventure combines the Colorado River, starting just above Westwater Canyon, with a stay at Rock Creek Ranch. Because the Colorado is a more challenging river, this trip is for families with children at least eight years old.

Three rafting and mountain-biking tours give families the best of two adventures. On the White Rim Trail of Canyonlands National Park in Utah, you bike 65 mi in three days past spectacular formations. Then the group piles into rafts for a four-day run through the Colorado River's legendary Cataract Canyon. The Colorado is matched with another bike trip near the world's mountain-bike mecca—Moab, Utah. Two days of quintessential wilderness biking through 25 mi of ponderosa pine country and red-rock desert is capped with two days on the Westwater section of the Colorado.

Another trip pairs two days of biking on 46 mi of remote dirt road with five days of rafting the Yampa. All these combination trips are for ages 12 and up (except the White Rim–Cataract trips in spring, which have a minimum age of 16) and those in good physical condition. Can you and your teen keep up with each other? Find out and forge a bond you may never have thought possible.

*Holiday Expeditions, 544 E. 3900 S, Salt Lake City, UT 84107, tel. 801/266–2087 or 800/624–6323. May–Sept.: 2- to 5-day rafting trips, $350–$1,098 adults, $315–$1,010 children under 18. May–Sept.: 4- to 7-day combination trips, $685–$1,285 adults, $770–$1,075 children under 18 on the ranch combo only.*

## Hughes River Expeditions

6+

Jerry Hughes and Carole Finley, who run this company, have more than 50 years of guiding experience between them. That alone would make them a good choice for almost any rafter. But they've also explored rivers with their own three children, so they are knowledgeable about introducing youngsters to the pleasures of rafting. Jerry and Carole grew up in Idaho and specialize in the state's white water. No outfitter knows more than these two about rafting the Salmon and the Snake rivers—which is probably why they were chosen to lead trips for the National Geographic Society.

**FOR FAMILIES.** The huge beaches and warm, clear water of the Salmon River canyon make it one of the best trips for young rafters, who can build sand castles and play safely in the many shallow back eddies away from the main current. Along with untouched river wilderness, the Salmon has roller-coaster rapids that are both exciting and safe, whether you stay in the rafts or use the inflatable kayaks. Sites right on the sandbar make camping easy, too—no carrying gear over boulders and steep terrain.

The Snake River–Hells Canyon trip, with its pioneer and Native American sites, is another great choice for families, as is the Middle Fork of the Salmon River. Families with younger children that want to try the Middle Fork should pick a date after late July, when the water is warmer and flows are lower. This river runs through the 2.36-million-acre River of No Return Wilderness, the largest wilderness area in the continental United States. If early season suits your group, join the Wallowa–Grande Ronde adventure in Oregon, preferably in June. Beautiful grassy flats slope right down to the banks for exceptional camping; older children can try an inflatable kayak on this trip.

Hughes has no special family departure dates, but you're likely to find children on any summer trip. Check with the company ahead of time, and they'll be happy to tell you the dates of trips already booked by other families. If you have a child under six who's comfortable around water and likes camping, call Jerry or Carole; they sometimes make exceptions to the age limit.

*Hughes River Expeditions, Box 217, Cambridge, ID 83610, tel. 208/257–3477 or 800/262–1882. May–Sept.: 3–6 days, $750–$1,480 adults; 10% discount for children college age and under who are financial dependents of their parents.*

## Idaho Afloat

6+

Idaho Afloat is one of a number of outfitters specializing in Idaho's great family rivers, the Lower Salmon River Gorge and Main Salmon, and the Snake River through Hell's Canyon. On every trip owners Bruce and Jeanne Howard prove that rafting and pampering can coexist in a pristine wilderness area. They enjoy having families along and take more of them out each year. Bruce especially loves to help children catch their first fish, so be sure to bring the fishing gear. Because the Howards don't have minimum trip sizes, they won't cancel a trip. If just your group shows up, they'll make certain you have a vacation your whole family will remember forever.

**FOR FAMILIES.** Choose any trip on the Salmon or the Snake rivers, and the campsite you arrive at each night will have lawn chairs and a tablecloth on the dinner table; the guides will be ready with hors d'oeuvres and wine. The Howards supply all camping equipment, including sleeping bags and tents. Because your tent is set up for you, the whole family has plenty of time for guided hikes. You can explore petroglyphs, pit house ruins, and burial sites, as well as pioneer homesteads. When the guides aren't cooking feasts, leading hikes, or negotiating rapids, they share their love of storytelling with everyone. The rivers, of course, provide the lion's share of the entertainment and all the natural beauty a family could want.
*Idaho Afloat, Box 542, Grangeville, ID 83530, tel. 208/983–2414 or 800/700–2414. May–Sept.: 3–6 days, $685–$1,115; 15% discount for children under 16.*

## Northern Outdoors

8+

With two resort centers in central Maine—the Forks, 18 mi north of Bingham near the Kennebec River, and the Penobscot, 15 mi west of Millinocket by the Penobscot River—Northern Outdoors has many options for adventurers in terms of location, river, accommodations, and experience. It's a good choice for East Coast families whose members may have differing views on how to spend time on their adventure vacation.

**FOR FAMILIES.** Most of this outfitter's trips are only one day long (good for first-timers), but there are a few overnight experiences and combination-adventure possibilities. Families with children as young as eight are welcome to try the big roller-coaster waves of the Kennebec or, on selected dates, the action-packed rapids of the Dead River. Ages 15 and up can raft the Dead River anytime. Children as young as age 12 can experience the challenge of the lower Penobscot River, while those 15 and older can go for the thrills of the Penobscot's upper gorge. In addition to family dates on the Dead River, Northern Outdoors has family overnights on the Kennebec River. The East Outlet Family Overnight, scheduled every Wednesday–Thursday in July and August, combines rafting, tubing, and motoring between Moosehead Lake and the Forks. The West Outlet adventure, a raft-canoe combination, is not just for families; it's also offered Wednesday–Thursday in July and August.

The Forks resort has swimming in a pool or lake, a hot tub, platform tennis, rock climbing (minimum age 12), canoeing, fishing, volleyball, basketball, a restaurant, and a choice of accommodations including lodge rooms, condos, cottages, cabins, and tent sites. The remote Penobscot resort has a hot tub, sauna, river swimming, lake kayak touring, canoeing, fishing, a restaurant, and roomy tent cabins. Families can mix rafting with rock climbing, guided fishing, or relaxing at the resorts. Do it all together, or go for the adventure that calls to you and catch up with the rest of the family at day's end.

All trips include equipment (even wet suits when necessary), lunch, use of facilities at one resort, and a personal video of your adventure. Lodging at the resorts is extra. Overnights include tents, sleeping pads, all meals, and dry bags; you supply your own sleeping bags.
*Northern Outdoors, Box 100, Rte. 201, The Forks, ME 04985, tel. 207/663–4466 or 800/765–7238. May–Oct.: 1–2 days, $79–$224 adults; $40–$124 children under 16. Lodging costs $8 per campsite–$63 per person in a 2-bedroom cabin.*

## O.A.R.S.

(👪 4+)

The acronym stands for Outdoor Adventure River Specialists, but everyone knows this outfitter as O.A.R.S. With more than 25 years of guiding experience and an extensive selection of family-friendly programs on a multitude of rivers, O.A.R.S. is a natural choice for families. I traveled with them on Jackson Lake and the Snake River in Wyoming. Although the trip has changed somewhat since then (you travel in kayaks instead of rafts on the lake now), the high quality of the guides remains the same.

Working with a big company such as O.A.R.S. has advantages and disadvantages. You don't talk to or meet the owners as you can with small companies, and service isn't quite as personalized. On the other hand, you can take advantage of the large staff of travel specialists, who will book not only your rafting experience but also your flight, lodging, and rental car.

**FOR FAMILIES.** Family trips explore the Salmon and Snake rivers in Idaho, the lower Klamath River in California, the San Juan River in Colorado, the Rogue River in Oregon, and the Wyoming stretch of the Snake River and Jackson Lake. With so many family departures, you can pick the river and terrain you want and still be guaranteed playmates for your children. Minimum ages range from four on the lower Klamath River and Jackson Lake and the Wyoming portion of the Snake River to seven on the others. On the kayaking-rafting combination on Jackson Lake and the Snake River, four-year-olds can sit in the front of the kayak or ride in motorized skiffs, in each case with at least one parent. This trip also offers plenty of exploring right around the base camp on Grassy Island.

Guides are well attuned to children's needs and really help parents out if youngsters get restless. The company designates one guide on each family trip as Fun Director, who keeps children entertained. Each child also gets a Fun Bag of games and toys for whiling away river time.

*O.A.R.S., Box 67, Angels Camp, CA 95222, tel. 209/736–4677 or 800/346–6277. Mar.–Sept.: 2–7 days, $219–$1,398 adults, $199–$1,203 children under 18.*

## Outdoor Adventures

(👪 7+)

Outdoor Adventures believes there's a big difference between rafting trips that are just "okay for families" and designated family trips. This company has thought of every detail and is genuinely committed to making river adventures for parents and children both fun and affordable. The Salmon River in Idaho and the Kern River in California are their favorite rivers for families. The guides on these trips are specially trained in working and playing with children.

**FOR FAMILIES.** The company's Salmon River family expedition is one of the best-ever trips for families. The six-day adventure runs nine times each summer—and fills fast, so you need to book early. The river has everything a rafting family could want—from warm, lazy eddies to rolling rapids. Off-water activities have plenty of child appeal, too: bug collecting, making musical instruments out of natural objects, panning for gold, carving sticks, weaving, hiking, or fishing (bring your own gear). Wide, sandy beaches make riverside camping exceptional. The trip price covers the flight back to Boise. Ask about Kids Float Free trips—they're a great deal, although children (under 17) still pay off-river expenses, such as the flight to Boise.

Two-day lower Kern River family trips start in June. The Kern flows through Sequoia National Forest and is a river of surprising beauty and terrific white water. (And it's warm, which makes it perfect for children.) It's also the closest rafting river to Los Ange-

les, which is just three hours away. Special family rates apply for this trip. These rates, good on Monday and Wednesday only, vary with the size of your family: the bigger your family, the larger the discount.
*Outdoor Adventures, Box 1149, Point Reyes Station, CA 94956, tel. 415/663–8300 or 800/323–4234. Apr.–Sept.: 2–6 days, $298–$1,295 adults, $298–$995 children under 16; ask about Kids Float Free and Kern family discounts.*

## Ouzel Outfitters

6+

After a conversation with Kent or Beth Wickham, you'll understand why 80% of Ouzel's clients have rafted with the company before or have been referred by someone who went on an Ouzel trip. The Wickhams operate a small, very personalized business and speak to every customer themselves. Families are a big part of their business, but the company's literature doesn't advise children and families to take a particular expedition or river. Instead, the Wickhams take your family's requirements into consideration before they suggest a trip. Best of all, Ouzel runs several great family rivers in Oregon and Idaho, so you have choices as well as plenty of individual attention.

**FOR FAMILIES.** The Wild and Scenic River Act protects an 84-mi stretch of Oregon's Rogue River. Three-, four-, and five-day trips run through the 34-mi section designated "wild" (roadless wilderness), as well as a few miles of the section called "recreational" (limited road access). The Siskiyou Range, through which the Rogue runs, has deep forests and clear creeks. Wildlife is abundant: otters, eagles, ospreys, herons, deer, and bears. The cool nights make for excellent sleeping, but days can be depended on to be hot and dry. The Rogue has the thrills rafters seek in rapids such as Blossom Bar and Rainie Falls; sandy beaches in which to camp and play and good places to swim add to its appeal. If you want a touch of culture on your adventure trip, the Oregon Shakespearean Festival in Ashland is nearby.

Other rivers have a variety of attractions for families. The Deschutes, in the high desert of Oregon's eastern Cascades, combines miles of lazy drifting with treacherous white water that demands your attention. Desert canyons and excellent fishing are additional highlights on these one- to three-day trips. Families can also join Ouzel for a half day, full day, or two days on the McKenzie, a river whose exhilaratingly cool waters spill out of the western slope of the Cascade Range, less than an hour from Eugene, Oregon. It's practically all Class II and III, but hold on to your raft when you reach Martin's Rapid. If you want more choices, Ouzel schedules trips on the Salmon in Idaho, too.
*Ouzel Outfitters, Box 827, Bend, OR 97709, tel. 541/385–5947 or 800/788–7238. Apr.– Oct.: 1–5 days, $55–$ 800 adults, $50–$750 children age 17 and under.*

## River Odysseys West

5+

The Salmon River in Idaho has become the river of choice for many outfitters with family trips, including River Odysseys West (known as ROW, to rafting enthusiasts everywhere). Owners Peter Grubb and Betsy Bowen have two children of their own—in fact, Mariah and Jonah Grubb, both under 10, often come along on the summer family trips on the Salmon River. Peter and Betsy definitely know how to run an exceptional family rafting journey; their experience and approach makes them one of the best family outfitters anywhere. I've never seen guides work as well with children, nor have I seen a river activities program for children better than this one. ROW states in its brochure that it aims to run all its trips "with uncommon professionalism, unsurpassed personal service, and a commitment to protect and preserve the environment." This it does, but it also runs its trips with a lot of heart.

**FOR FAMILIES.** ROW has five-day Family Focus trips on the Salmon River geared to parents or grandparents traveling with children ages 5 through 15. Typically, from three to five families join these specially designated expeditions, which run weekly during July and August. Led by guides with degrees in environmental education, these trips give children a chance to learn about geography, geology, native and pioneer history, nature, and wildlife through hikes, nature games, campfire readings, crafts, and just floating through the magnificent canyons of the Salmon River. There's also plain old river fun, like free-for-all water fights (trust me, the adults are more dangerous than the children) and leaping off high rocks into the water below.

ROW takes both paddle rafts and inflatable kayaks on all family trips. These are great for children who can handle independence and who want to challenge themselves physically. On family trips guides stop a bit more frequently, and swimming is excellent off the Salmon River's wide, sandy beaches (with life jackets on, of course). ROW's menu, always superior, adds more children's foods; children have an early dinner, at about 6, so adults can unwind before they eat. Tents are already set up when you arrive in camp each afternoon; all you have to do is pick a tent and put your gear in it.

In addition to its rafting expeditions on a variety of western rivers, ROW welcomes families on its rafting adventures in Ecuador, and its adventure cruising explorations off the coasts of Turkey, Croatia, Greece, and in Alaska's Inside Passage. ROW also runs very family-oriented journeys on the Missouri River using 34-ft voyageur canoes, perfect for ages five and up. Even if you think some of these destinations are too far afield for your children, talk to Peter before making a decision. He's taken his own young children—and the children of clients—to all of these places with great success.

*River Odysseys West, Box 579FB, Coeur d'Alene, ID 83816, tel. 208/765–0841 or 800/451–6034. May–Sept., Family Focus trips July–Aug.: 5 days, $990 adults, $830 children under 17.*

## Rogue River Raft Trips, Inc.

5+

This outfitter has been running white-water excursions on Oregon's Rogue River since 1967. Its lodge-based trips set the company apart; you can run the river during the day and sleep in a remote wilderness lodge at night, complete with private bathrooms, hot showers, and fresh linens. Those who want just a little camping experience can choose a three-day lodge-camping combination trip, and camping enthusiasts can join the four-day all-camping trips. All trips begin at Morrison's Rogue River Lodge, about 16 mi downriver from Grants Pass, Oregon.

**FOR FAMILIES.** The Rogue, with rolling rapids, sandy beaches, and lots of wildlife, is an ideal family river. The outfitter uses both paddle boats and oar boats, depending on whether the group wants to participate or sit back and let the guides do the work. Children have opportunities to swim, hike, and pan for gold. Guides bring along inflatable kayaks, which give older children a chance to test their paddling skills. But most important, having river lodges as an option opens up this adventure to many families that might not otherwise try it.

Families should also consider combining a rafting experience with a stay at Morrison's Rogue River Lodge. Built in the '40s as a steelhead fishing retreat, Morrison's is now a terrific family destination in its own right. Set among towering pines on a lazy bend in the river, the lodge has a 5-acre lawn that slopes down to the water, where you can wade, fish, and swim. The lodge has rooms and cottages, a heated pool, a hot tub, and two tennis courts. You can visit nearby Oregon Caves National Park, Crater Lake National

Park, or the Oregon Shakespearean Festival. Lodge stays include a four-course gourmet dinner, full breakfast, and use of all facilities in the summer; in fall—when families come for steelhead fishing—rates also include evening hors d'oeuvres and a packed picnic lunch each day.

*Rogue River Raft Trips, 8500 Galice Rd., Merlin, OR 97532, tel. 541/476–3825 or 800/826–1963. May–Aug.: 1–4 days, $65–$525 adults, $45–$525 children. Lodge stays are $175–$360 per room or cabin, depending on season, accommodations, and the number of adults and children.*

## Salmon River Outfitters

5+

Steven Shephard can make rafting the Salmon River one of the best family adventures ever. He's been a guide for 30 years and has operated Salmon River Outfitters (SRO) since 1980. Steven knows everything about the Salmon and how to run it, and he believes that good service means taking care of absolutely everything—safety, well-trained guides, camp chairs, river gear, and everything you need for dining and sleeping. He even sends you a duffel bag for your personal items. You have to pack it yourself, but that's about it. When you arrive in Idaho, the SRO staff will transfer it into a waterproof bag for you. What could be easier?

**FOR FAMILIES.** The Salmon is an excellent intermediate river, with some Class III rapids. It has big beaches, few rocks, and virtually no mosquitoes. Any of SRO's expeditions is fine for families, but two specialty trips are worth noting. The Native American Indian Lore trip is generally run twice each summer. Idaho writer and herbologist Darcy Williamson leads nature walks and shares her knowledge of regional native lore, including how plants were used for food and medicine. Families gather indigenous plants and make their own sachets, tea, and ceremonial Indian sage bundles to take home. The Storyteller & Harpist trip is usually a once-a-season event featuring Patrick Ball, who has spent years in Scotland, Ireland, and Appalachia gathering stories that are part of those areas' rich oral tradition. As an accompaniment to the epic legends and folk tales, Patrick plays the Irish harp. Few river campsites are as entertaining.

*Salmon River Outfitters, Box 519, Donnelly, ID 83615, tel. 800/346–6204. June–Sept.: 6 days, $1,295 adults, $1,195 children.*

## Sheri Griffith Expeditions

5+

Sheri Griffith Expeditions runs only protected rivers in national parks and national landmarks or proposed Wild and Scenic rivers. Sheri prefers these because regulations so severely limit the number of people permitted in the water that there's never a problem with wilderness gridlock. Sheri and company, whose slogan is "With a Touch of Class," have been in business for 28 years.

**FOR FAMILIES.** Geared to families with children from ages 5 to 16, the Family Goes to Camp—Expedition Style is a five-day trip scheduled six times each summer through Desolation and Gray canyons on Utah's Green River. In spite of its name, Desolation is remarkably beautiful. Here Butch Cassidy and his Wild Bunch hid from the law among the red sandstone formations. You explore the ranch of the McPhersons, who homesteaded the grassy river bottomland and often provided assistance to outlaws, including Butch. Before the cowboys arrived, ancient native tribes carved their stories into the rocks. Today the Green River runs through the Uinta and Ouray Indian reservations; the tribes farm and ranch in these canyons. Guides point out the 300 million years of rock exposed on the canyon walls, and you're almost guaranteed to see wildlife. When not riding the river, you'll be hiking, camping, and relaxing on the white sand beaches. The guides lead special kids-only outings along the way, too. The trip starts at the Canyonlands Airport in Moab, Utah, where you fly to a mesa high above the river. The return to Moab is by van from the takeout site. Both shuttles are included in the trip price.

For families with less time and with children between ages 4 and 16, there's Family Goes to Camp: Coyote Run, a two- or three-day version of the Expedition Style family camp. This one's on a gentle section of the Colorado River, about 45 minutes from Moab. A rustic cabin on an old homestead is now a living history museum filled with tools used by pioneers. Camping is not in tents but in authentic reproductions of Plains tepees. Storytelling, interpretive history, and a campfire are all part of this family program designed to introduce young children and their parents to life on the river and to western history.

At family camp assistants lead interpretive field trips and organize games for everyone. Parents and children have time with each other and with their peers. If you're hoping to find activities that will get your family working and playing together, look no farther. These paddle raft trips require team effort and spirit. If someone really doesn't want to paddle, there's always room in the oar-powered supply boats.
*Sheri Griffith Expeditions, Box 1324, Moab, UT 84532, tel. 801/259–8229 or 800/332–2439. June–Aug.: 2–5 days, $338–$794 adults, $253–$549 children age 15 and under.*

## Tag-A-Long Expeditions

5+

Based in Moab, Utah, Tag-A-Long has been offering river and trail experiences for several decades. The company categorizes its trips three ways: Signature Expeditions (the very best), Create Your Own (customized trips), and Special Value Trips (value pricing). You can mix and match adventures with this group by adding on jetboat or jeep tours or a six-day camping and cultural journey with Tag-A-Long and Native American guides in areas of the Southwest where Navajo, Ute, and Hopi live.

**FOR FAMILIES.** The best family trip is the five-day Green River tour by raft or inflatable kayak, a 'special value trip–family style,' for ages six or seven and up. The magnificent scenery and ancient Native American sites are a draw, but what children usually like best about this river is that there are rapids every day—50 in all—which you can run in the support raft or in inflatable kayaks, which your children help paddle. You can rent sleeping bags and tents if you don't have your own. If your family wants to concentrate more on the camping and Native American experience (for ages five and up), you can add a half- or full-day rafting trip on the Colorado onto a scheduled camping trip. The age limit on this, like most rafting expeditions, is really based on weight rather than age. A child for all of these rafting trips and the jetboat excursion must be at least 40 lbs.
*Tag-A-Long Expeditions, 452 North Main St., Moab, UT 84532, tel. 800/453–3292. Mar.–Oct. (all trips not available all months) 5–6 days, $650–$1,030 adults, $560–$1,030 children. Prices for add-on jeep, jetboat adventures, ½- or 1-day rafting trips, $33–$89 adults, $26–$79 children.*

## Unicorn Rafting Expeditions

6+

Unicorn's wilderness base camps in north-central Maine–Lake Parlin Resort, near the Forks, and the Penobscot River Outpost in Millinocket, serve as headquarters for its river trips and starting points for adventures on land as well. Maine's rough-and-tumble white-water rivers have a high minimum age, often 10 or 14, making them especially good for families with teens. Unicorn has a couple of trips for younger children, too.

**FOR FAMILIES.** Families with river lovers ages 12 and up can tackle Alleyway and

Magic Falls on the upper Kennebec River; ages 14 and up test their strength and skills against Elephant Rock and Poplar Falls on the Dead River. Parents with children age six and up can choose a gentler one-day ride on the lower Kennebec. Nonrafting youngsters from ages 3 to 12 can play at Unicorn's base camps in the care of sitters (extra charge) who will take them swimming and canoeing, play games, or arrange treasure hunts. At the end of the day your family either cooks dinner in your cabin or tent or, for an extra charge, eats at the restaurants at Lake Parlin or Penobscot River Outpost.

If you and your children age 10 and up want to go for an overnight, the two-day camping and rafting trip on the Kennebec River uses small rafts and 'funyaks' in the Class I, II, and III rapids the first day, before you tackle the Class IV thrills on day two. A noontime steak barbecue and a Maine lobster dinner are included in the cost.

Families can book a four-day adventure package at Lake Parlin Resort, which includes a lakeside cabin and rafting, canoeing, mountain biking, hiking, and more. You can just hang out in the hot tub or pool, too.

On any stay with this outfitter, one of the most popular family pastimes is the evening Moose Hunt, in the woods around camp. Unicorn owner Jay Schurman says they find a moose to watch about 90% of the time. *Unicorn Rafting Expeditions, Rte. 201, Jackman, ME 04945, tel. 207/628–7629 or 800/864–2676. Apr.–Oct.: 1–2 days, $79–$214 adults, $39–$99 children under 16. The 4-day adventure package is $679 for a family of 4.*

## Wilderness River Outfitters

8+

Joe and Fran Tonsmeire started running rivers while in college during the '60s. They worked together on the Colorado River and eventually founded Wilderness River Outfitters in Salmon, Idaho. Although the company continues to evolve, rafting remains its central activity. The Tonsmeires' innovative trip list also has intriguing multi-activity adventures, especially those that combine hiking and rafting with packhorse support. This company also has bike-and-raft combination trips (*see* Biking).

**FOR FAMILIES.** The eight-day Salmon River rafting-hiking combination trip takes families with children ages 12 and up into remote backcountry for four days of trekking the high ridges that divide the Sawtooth and Salmon River mountains from the Bitterroots. The adventure starts at almost 9,000 ft in the heart of the River of No Return Wilderness, but the pace is easy—hikes average from 4 to 8 mi a day. There's plenty of time to fish in the alpine lakes (bring your own gear) and relax. You can do it all with nothing more than a day pack because horses carry the camping equipment. The last 4-mi hike down a steep trail leads to the river's edge, where the group loads the rafts for a four-day journey on the Salmon River. This trip begins in Salmon and ends in Boise; everything, including tents and sleeping bags, is provided. Another eight-day hike-and-raft trip is led in Montana; you trek through the awesome Bob Marshall Wilderness over Holland Pass and down to the South Fork of the Flathead River. This adventure starts and ends in Kalispell, Montana. Both trips are available without horse support if you want a complete backpack experience.

Families that want more horses with their rafting can opt for the nine-day ranch and Salmon River adventure, which gives you four nights at Hayden Creek Ranch, a working cattle ranch in the Lemhi Mountains 30 mi south of Salmon, Idaho, in addition to five nights on the river.

You can depend on Wilderness River for excellent rafting-only trips, too. The best for families are six-day adventures on the

Salmon River in Idaho (minimum age eight) and the Middle Fork of the Flathead River in Montana (minimum age 11). At least one Salmon River trip each summer is a designated family adventure. In recent years Denny Olson—biologist, geologist, and performer—has been on hand during family trips to entertain and enlighten both children and parents. The company also runs one of the great rivers of the north, the Tatshenshini, which flows down from the Yukon through British Columbia and Alaska. Rafters on this 11-day journey should be at least 12 years old, as the river is colder and the hikes are longer than on most other trips.

*Wilderness River Outfitters, Box 72, Lemhi, ID 83465, tel. 208/756–3959 or 800/252–6581. June–Aug.: 5–11 days, $955–$2,000 for rafting only; 8 days, $1,630–$1,775 for raft-hike trips. Families choose 1 discount option: 30% discount for children under 13 or 5% discount for families of 5 or more.*

# Resources

## Organizations

**America Outdoors** (Box 10847, Knoxville, TN 37939, tel. 423/558–3597) is the national association for outfitters and river guides. Ask for the organization's magazine listing outfitters and guides; America Outdoors cannot, however, recommend one outfitter over another. The **Professional Paddle Sports Association** (Box 248, Butler, KY 41006, tel. 606/472–2202) will send information on guides and outfitters. It also has a list of books and periodicals.

## Periodicals

*Canoe and Kayak Magazine* (Box 3146, Kirkland, WA 98083, tel. 800/692–2663) is devoted primarily to canoeing and kayaking but has many articles on equipment, technique, and environmental issues that will interest rafters. The resource section lists many rafting opportunities from schools and adventure outfitters.

## Products

The following companies make good river wear or river accessories for children and adults: Nike, Patagonia, REI outdoor stores, and Crazy Creek Chairs. Nike has river sandals and aqua socks, and Patagonia is a good source for warm, quick-drying fleece and quick-drying pants. REI has retail outlets and a catalog with reasonably priced fleeced and other warm, fast-drying apparel; it also sells life vests for children and adults. For information about these companies, see Resources *in* Hiking and Backpacking.

# RANCHES

A spirit of rugged adventure and the romance of the American West, past and present, are alive and well in guest ranches across the country. At a ranch your family can indulge its Wild West fantasies—and you can all learn a lot about riding, ranching, being a cowhand, and caring for livestock as well. Fun for everyone is almost guaranteed.

Ranch stays make perfect family vacations because they can accommodate many ages, abilities, and interests. I know this from my own family's experience. My life-long love of riding made me a natural for a ranch guest, but my husband, Bill, was uneasy around horses. On our first visit to Paradise Guest Ranch in Wyoming, Kira was 11, Molly was four, and Hutch was just a year old. Of the children, only Kira had ever even been on a horse, and Molly and Hutch were too young for the ranch's regular riding program. Nonetheless, Paradise was a resounding success for all of us. Bill lost his fear of riding and learned to lope, as did Kira. Molly thrived in the children's program, and Hutch made both human and animal friends. We took advantage of the riding program and the naturalist-led hikes; Bill carried Hutch in a backpack on these while I indulged in advanced rides in the afternoon. Sometimes we just retreated from the action and took time to enjoy each other.

There are ranches for every budget and taste, from very simple to spectacular. Riding is definitely the central ingredient of a ranch vacation, but some ranches have so many additional activities that their guest lists frequently include nonriders. Many ranches have an organized children's activity program, and a few provide infant care. Others simply include children in all ranch activities. You can find a place with rustic accommodations and hearty, basic fare, or one that has elegant, well-appointed cabins and serves meals accompanied by fine wines. Guest capacity ranges from six people to well over a hundred, and seasons vary from one- to four-season operations. Some real working ranches accept guests, but most are primarily guest operations with a bit of ranch work on the side that must be done.

Although each ranch creates its own unique atmosphere, all help bring families closer together. Sing-alongs and bonfires, hayrides, and other events give you a chance to see each other in new and wonderful ways. At the end of a family ranch stay, you may well take home, as we did, not only the requisite western bandannas and hatbands but also a renewed appreciation for each other and what you've accomplished individually and together. Who could ask for more than that from any vacation?

It's important to note, though, that although every ranch listed in this chapter is terrific, not every ranch is right for every family. And unlike most of the other adventures in this book, a ranch vacation is not a single-activity vacation, so there are more things to consider when making a choice. For families the most important criteria in choosing a ranch are its size; whether there is a children's program and, if so, for what ages; the riding program; and the activities other than riding, both for families as a whole and for adults. Because these factors are important to finding a good match, each ranch listing has a general introduction and then sections on the children's program, riding program, and activities besides riding.

## Questions to Ask

**Are all stays at least one week, or are shorter stays possible?** Almost all ranches require a minimum one-week stay during the summer high season (or winter high season for those ranches in the Southwest), but some allow briefer vacations in off-seasons. A few ranches have shorter minimum stays—or even none at all. Keep in mind, though, that in off-seasons, there may be shorter stays, but there may not be counselors or a children's program.

**Are families welcome all the time?** Many ranches have adults-only periods—sometimes just a week, sometimes a month or more—during times children are in school, such as September or October. Spring is always an off-season for ranches (except those in the Southwest), so although families may be welcome, there may be no children's activity program and probably only a few children present. Most formal children's programs run in the summer months only (or summers and holidays for year-round ranches), when college students are available to be counselors.

**What is the riding program?** These programs vary widely. Some ranches have walk-only rides; others offer slow, medium, and fast rides each day. Some have only hour-long outings; other ranches have short rides, all-day rides, and even overnight rides. Children may or may not be permitted on adult rides, although parents can sometimes join the children's rides. Some ranches provide more formal instruction than others; ask about this if it's important to your family. Rides may have as few as four participants and as many as 25. Typically, there are morning and afternoon rides each day, along with special rides—brunch, lunch, all-day, or evening cookouts—throughout the week. For safety reasons, however, guests cannot go out on trails alone but are led by a ranch's wranglers.

**Does each person get the same horse for the whole week? What if you don't like the horse?** Most ranches with minimum weeklong stays assign each guest a horse. That way, rider and horse get used to each other and become comfortable as a team, which can make a difference even to a seasoned rider. On the other hand, sometimes this doesn't work out. A ranch should be flexible enough and have enough horses to be able to make a change for members of your family who request it.

**Are guests required to have riding boots, and if so, are loaner boots available?** Most ranches prefer but do not require riding boots; they do require sturdy shoes or other boots with heels. Riding boots can be an expensive proposition if you need to get them for the whole family. Some ranches have a trunk of boots that are lent to guests, although there may be no way to guarantee your size or your child's size is available. If you decide to buy boots, break them in before your vacation.

**At what age are children permitted to ride in the regular riding program and to go out on the trail?** Six or seven is often the age given, which is usually dictated by insurance. However, some ranches won't allow kids out on the trail until they're 8, 9, or even 10. A few permit parents to put younger children in the saddle with them, which can be risky even for accomplished riders. If your children are too young for the trail, you'll probably want a ranch that has options such as a supervised children's program. Parents can also take turns staying at the ranch with younger children and taking part in other ranch activities.

**Is there an organized children's program?** If you have young children, especially children too young to ride with you, this will be important. While you are out riding, your youngsters can participate in age-appropriate activities, such as hiking, wildlife tracking, swimming, fishing, and learning Native American lore. Some ranches have corral riding sessions for children not able to go on the trail; at others, the staff may lead small children on ponies. You can usually make use of the programs in a variety of ways: just in the mornings or afternoons, or all day. You can sign the children in one day and not another. The bottom line: A good children's program is a place that they *want* to be, a place where they can meet children from other parts of the country and the world and hang out with cool counselors. When available, children's programs are almost always part of the ranch package; care for infants and toddlers, however, sometimes costs extra.

**If there isn't a supervised children's program or if there is but my child is too young for it, is baby-sitting available on an individual basis?** Families with a baby or toddler will want a ranch with something for this age group for at least part of the day so parents and older children can spend time together riding or taking advantage of other activities. Another option is to choose a ranch that allows you to bring along your own baby-sitter for free or for a nominal charge. Parents can also split up during the day, one spending time with the youngest child, the other being one on one with an older child.

**Where do we stay on the ranch?** Most ranches have cabins of various sizes; some ranches also have rooms in a main lodge, although not many of these accommodate families. Cabins often have kitchens, which are handy for families with babies and with young children who get hungry between the ranch's set mealtimes. Western decor is prevalent, as are porches, fireplaces, and grand views. You probably won't spend a lot of time in your cabin, but it's nice to know that most are roomy, cheerful places.

**What kind of food is served, and where do we eat?** Hearty, delicious, and plentiful best describe ranch food; three meals a day are usually part of the package. Breakfast and lunch are often buffet affairs—except when you eat lunch out on the trail, which is common throughout the week. Ranchers like to go all out for dinner; some even provide candles, wine, and gourmet fare. Many ranches serve meals family style: Guests sit at long tables, making it easy for families to get to know different people during the week. In general, ranches are not places to cut calories; barbecued meats and homemade pies and cobblers are often a big part of a week's menu, which also will include salads and fruit. If you do have any type of restrictive diet, however, the vast majority of ranch chefs will accommodate you.

**Do parents and children eat meals together?** At some ranches with supervised children's programs, youngsters eat lunch with counselors, either at a different time or at the same time but apart from parents. At others, families usually eat together after the morning ride. If there is an all-day or lunch ride scheduled for adults or children, however, families won't see each other again until late afternoon. Many family ranches also schedule an adults-only dinner at least once a week, during which counselors take their groups for a special children's cookout or other activity. At a few ranches children eat most or even all meals with counselors, usually at an earlier time, allowing parents to relax and meet other guests. Ask questions and know your family preferences before you choose a ranch.

**If an adult doesn't ride, is there a reduced rate? What other activities are available?** Some ranches do have a nonrider's rate; if an adult in your group doesn't want to ride at all, look for a ranch with this kind of discount. Keep in mind that ranches these days have a variety of activities besides riding. Almost all have fishing. In addition, depending on the ranch, you can also take guided nature hikes, swim, play tennis, mountain bike, picnic, go boating or rafting, or even play golf. Some ranches have hot tubs and saunas; massages are available at a few. A number of ranches are near towns with places of historical interest, museums, or fun places to shop.

**What's included in the cost?** Ranch vacations are primarily all-inclusive. Lodging, meals, riding, the children's program, and other activities are included in the cost, unless otherwise noted. If the program includes an overnight trip, the use of gear is generally included (ask ahead for specifics). Baby-sitting for infants and toddlers is usually extra, unless you bring your own baby-sitter. Off-property activities, such as rafting, guided fishing trips, and visits to museums and local rodeos, are often—but not always—an extra charge. If it's available, alcohol is generally extra as well. Most ranches will provide airport transportation for an extra charge.

Prices given here are for high season, except as noted; sometimes rates are reduced for large families. Many ranches use two or more age brackets for their children's rates, and the range of prices according to age can be quite substantial. Considering all that's included, ranch vacations can be a very reasonably priced family vacation. However, if you want to save, plan a trip early or late in the season, when rates are almos lower. Not all facilities and activities are available in the off-season, though.

## Instruction

Just about every ranch has instruction in horsemanship, although some ranches are more formal about it than others. Wranglers check all guests' abilities the first day, and progressive instruction helps riders move from walk-only rides to those that include trotting or even loping or cantering. Even if your family arrives with varying skill levels, it's likely you will be able to ride together at some point. (Advanced riders, of course, can always choose to ride with less advanced riders at any time.) Although riding is a skill that can take years to develop to its highest level, it's also a sport in which you can improve quickly with practice and good instruction.

In addition to horsemanship, some ranches teach you about caring for horses, roping, and other skills. There are fishing classes for children and adults at many ranches, as well as instruction in skeet- or trapshooting. A few ranches have courses in other types of activities, including photography, environmental issues, rock climbing, and wildflower or bird identification. In winter cross-country ski instruction may be available. Some classes may be part of the regular program; others are an extra charge.

## Finding the Fun

Because each adventure option in this chapter is in a fixed destination, the selections below are organized by region.

# Favorite Ranches

## *Northeast*

### Pinegrove Resort Ranch

ALL

A five-minute talk with Dave Ohalloran, general manager and a member of the Tarantino family that owns and operates Pinegrove, will convince you this is a place to bring your family. Although Pinegrove is in New York's Hudson Valley region, everything has been done to provide not only a family atmosphere but a genuinely western one as well. There are roping and blacksmithing demonstrations, cattle drives, and nightly cattle calls, during which guests call cattle in from the pasture to feed them. Lodging is in modern rooms with TVs and telephones, but you'll probably be too busy to make use of them. Pinegrove is a big place that can accommodate more than 300 guests, yet it's also small enough that families feel safe giving children freedom to explore on their own.

**CHILDREN'S PROGRAM.** The nursery, for ages six weeks through three years, has one staff person for every child. Activities include walks, time at the playground, visits to the baby animal farm, and indoor fun such as arts and crafts. In day camp, for ages 3 through 10, campers go swimming, play miniature golf, spend time at the playground, and have nature hikes, pony rides, and

an extensive crafts
re invited to join
the teen program,
e staff, the group
ctivities each day.
night patrol" looks in
...dren in their rooms every 15 to 20 minutes while parents attend evening entertainment. Private baby-sitting at night is also available for an extra charge.

**RIDING PROGRAM.** Daily rides meet the needs of beginner to advanced riders; groups are large, typically from 15 to 20 people. Trail riding is generally for those ages seven and up, although younger children will be permitted if they can control a horse. Children can ride with parents but don't have to; they can join any ride that suits their skill level and interest. Instructional rides at a special facility on the trail help guests progress from one ability level to the next. From Memorial Day to Columbus Day, Pinegrove also runs cattle drives (extra charge) for advanced riders. There's riding in winter, too.

**BEYOND RIDING.** You can choose from among the following, all on the property: fishing, boating, hiking, tennis, swimming indoors and out, miniature golf, boccie ball, and archery. At a nearby 18-hole golf course, ranch visitors can play one round of 9 holes at no charge. In winter there's downhill skiing geared for beginners and intermediates, as well as ice skating at the ranch, with equipment and lessons for guests included.

*Pinegrove Resort Ranch, Box 209, Kerhonkson, NY 12446, tel. 914/626–7345 or 800/346–4626. Year-round: 7 days, $275–$550; children under 4 free. Ask about the 6-day summer special for families of 3.*

800-926-6520

## Rocking Horse Ranch

**ALL**

Just 75 mi north of New York City in the historic and scenic Hudson Valley, Rocking Horse has 500 acres, its own lake, three pools (one indoors), a petting zoo, and a playground. A hot tub and two saunas give guests a break from nonstop activities. Guests stay in modern, motel-style rooms or lodge rooms with TVs, phones, air-conditioning, and carpeting. And yet the ranch has a definite western feel, as well as a focus very much on families.

**CHILDREN'S PROGRAM.** Counselors take children ages 4 through 6, 6 through 9, and 9 through 12 to swim, fish, and play a variety of sports every day from 9 to 5. Sometimes the group goes out on speedboat or banana-boat rides. Visits to the petting zoo and playground and pony rides are part of most days, especially for children under age seven. Children in the daily program eat lunch with counselors and get a snack of milk and cookies in the afternoon. There is a nursery available (extra charge) for children under age four.

**RIDING PROGRAM.** Children ages seven and older go on the trail with parents. Rides are about 1¼ hours long, and each guest is assigned to a minimum of one ride each day. If you want to go more often, you can stand by on a space-available basis for other rides. Occasionally in the fall, longer rides are offered, and this is one of the few ranches with winter riding.

**BEYOND RIDING.** The list of the ranch's family activities is so extensive you couldn't possibly get to all of them in a weeklong stay. There's everything from tennis, water skiing, miniature golf, adult and children's water slides, and hayrides in summer to skiing, tubing, skating, and sleigh rides in winter. One of the ranch's three pools is just for children.

*Rocking Horse Ranch, Highland, NY 12528, tel. 914/691–2927 or 800/647–2624. Year-round (2-day minimum): $95–$150 per day adults, $35–$55 per day children; children under 4 free. Ask about the many special family packages available throughout the year.*

## Timberlock

ALL

Part family camp, part ranch, part resort, Timberlock is a rustic, informal retreat in the Adirondack Mountains of northern New York. Only the main kitchen has electricity; guests' cabins are lighted with gas lamps. Propane creates hot water, and heat comes from woodstoves. You pay separately for riding here, and there's no structured program, no required activities—nothing, in fact, that anyone *has* to do. The Catlin family, owners since 1964, just want to give families an opportunity to spend time together in a way they can't back home. Timberlock succeeds admirably, which is why guests return year after year. Because the ranch accommodates only about 65, it's a good idea to book as early as possible.

**CHILDREN'S PROGRAM.** Timberlock has a supervised play area for children ages two through six so parents can pursue some activities their young children can't. There's no additional charge for the program, which runs three days each week. Parents can sign up at the beginning of the week for their chosen days and times. For the most part, though, families eat, play, and relax together.

**RIDING PROGRAM.** Adults and children age six and up can ride out on the trail, either English or western style. There are three trail rides each morning, beginner to advanced. Guests can also take lessons in the riding ring, and there's a weekly mountain picnic ride of about three hours. Timberlock has hard hats for children.

**BEYOND RIDING.** You can take advantage of 15-mi-long Indian Lake, along which Timberlock sits, for canoeing, sailing, fishing, and swimming. Tennis and archery are other options, or you can choose nature walks and birding. Guided hikes and canoe trips for groups of guests are an important part of any weekly stay. Don't miss the wood shop, in which you can make your own canoe paddle, birdhouse, or something else you fancy.

*Timberlock, Box 1052, Sabael, NY 12864, tel. 518/648–5494 (in season); 1735 Quaker St., Lincoln, VT 05443, tel. 802/453–2540 (rest of year). Late June–late Sept.: 7 days, $588–$735 adults, $343–$560 children; children under 2 free. Riding costs $20–$45 per ride, depending on length and destination; multi-day trail ride packages are available.*

# *South*

## Scott Valley Resort & Guest Ranch

ALL

Scott Valley's 625 acres in the Ozark Mountains are mostly lush meadows and woodlands. Guests stay in one- and two-bedroom units with air-conditioning and heating; they aren't fancy, but they're clean and comfortable. There are plenty of hiking trails to explore, as well as a playground and petting zoo. Scott Valley tries to meet the needs of a wide variety of guests: single parents, non-riders, and ecotourists among them, which is just one reason experts and guests have consistently voted this ranch, in business for more than 45 years, one of the country's great family resorts.

**CHILDREN'S PROGRAM.** The ranch has no formal program; families are encouraged to spend time together. With tennis, badminton, horseshoes, pool, and other family activities available, this isn't hard to do. If parents want to try a ride or hike that's not appropriate for younger children, babysitting is available at no extra charge.

**RIDING PROGRAM.** The ranch owns and raises its own gentle horses, the majority being Missouri Fox Trotters. Age seven is when most children start riding alone and can be assigned a horse for the week; however, if younger children show an interest and ability to follow directions, they may be given lessons and ride on the trail. Wranglers provide instruction to all guests, and there are a minimum of two rides a day for beginners to advanced riders.

**BEYOND RIDING.** When not feeding and interacting with the goats, pigs, geese, cats, or dogs, as well as a variety of wild creatures, you can try fishing on the White River, playing lawn games, swimming, or relaxing in the hot tub. Canoes are available for those who want to float down a nearby river. Dinner is served on a ferry on Lake Norfolk one evening during summer weeks, and favorite excursions for families with children of all ages are the nearby Ozark Folk Center, Blanchard Springs Caverns, and Branson, Missouri. Evening activities for families are scheduled in the summer months. Golf and guided fishing trips can be arranged (at an extra charge).

*Scott Valley Resort & Guest Ranch, Box 1447, Mountain Home, AR 72653, tel. 870/425–5136. Mar.–Nov.: $115–$145 per adult per day, $55–$125 per child per day; children under age 2 free.*

## *Southwest*

### Mayan Dude Ranch

ALL

Bandera, 47 mi northwest of San Antonio in the heart of Texas Hill Country, is home to this bighearted, hospitable ranch. Judy and Don Hicks and all 12 of their children are here to make guests feel welcome—up to 167 of them. Accommodations are in stone cottages furnished with many handmade objects. Some have fireplaces; all are air-conditioned. There are also two-story lodges with motel-like rooms. Mayan is big, but it's down-home friendly and an ideal choice for families that really want to relax, perhaps by floating in a tube on the meandering Medina River as it flows through the ranch.

**CHILDREN'S PROGRAM.** Children ages 3 through 6 and 7 through 12 are placed in separate groups; the program runs primarily in summer, although there are children's activities during holiday periods, too. The groups meet in the morning from 10 to noon and again from 1 to 3. The younger children don't ride on the trail but keep busy with arts and crafts, treasure hunts, games, and outings. The older group joins parents on trail rides. They also swim, try roping and archery, play baseball, and make leather crafts. The program is fairly flexible, and activities can change to suit the interests of the group. Children eat dinner with their group and counselors twice a week.

**RIDING PROGRAM.** In the morning and afternoon each day, there are hour-long walking rides into one of the most beautiful areas of Texas. Typically, 25 guests go on each ride. Children age seven and up can join parents on the trail.

**BEYOND RIDING.** You can swim, tube, and fish (some poles available) in the cool Medina River or use the pool and two tennis courts. For an extra charge, you have access to an 18-hole golf course. Those who wish to explore Hill Country can visit the Frontier Times Museum in Bandera, which has artifacts from pioneer days, and the late President Johnson's boyhood home, about 60 mi away in Johnson City. Sea World of Texas and Fiesta Texas, a family-oriented theme park, are in San Antonio.

*Mayan Dude Ranch, Box 577, Bandera, TX 78003, tel. 830/796–3312. Year-round (2-day minimum): $104–$125 per day adults, $55–$80 children. Children under 3 are discouraged.*

### White Stallion Ranch

ALL

The True family, which owns and runs White Stallion, believes guests get the best of two worlds on their 3,000-acre ranch. Although mountains and rugged, picturesque high desert surround the property, it is only 10 minutes around the mountain from Tucson. Longhorns graze the ranch, where up to 75 guests stay in Spanish-style adobe bungalows that have views of the cactus garden and the Tucson Mountains. Aside from the natural beauty of the area, White Stallion has much to offer families, not the least of which is plenty of time together.

**CHILDREN'S PROGRAM.** There's no formal program; parents and children of all ages are welcome to participate in activities on the ranch. With enough notice, however, baby-sitting can usually be arranged (extra charge) during the day or at night.

**RIDING PROGRAM.** One unique aspect of the program is that many rides take you into nearby Saguaro National Park to see the 50-ft cacti and abundant wildlife. Children age five and up ride the trail with their parents on their own horse. At about age eight, children can be tested to see if they meet the requirements for loping or cantering rides. There are at least two fast and two slow rides a day; during the week all-day and breakfast rides are offered, as is a hayride that takes you to a lunch cookout. For those with a little riding experience, team cattle penning is very popular. Both children and adults can help groom and saddle their horses.

**BEYOND RIDING.** You can swim in the pool, take nature hikes, use the two tennis courts, play lawn games, or relax in a hot tub. Golf is available nearby for an extra charge. The evening programs are very creative: During the busiest season, a wildlife rehabilitator stops by with rescued animals, and a local astronomer brings telescopes to the ranch once a week so you can take a closer look at the stars. Tucson is well worth exploring for an afternoon or even a full day. The Arizona-Sonora Desert Museum, a microcosm of a desert environment, has exhibits and programs that appeal to children of all ages.

*White Stallion Ranch, 9251 W. Twin Peaks Rd., Tucson, AZ 85743, tel. 602/297–0252 or 888/977–2624. Sept.–May: 7 days, $560–$1,176; children under age 3 free. Ask about daily rates.*

## Y.O. Ranch

**ALL**

One of the biggest working ranches in Texas, the Y.O. is also the largest exotic wildlife ranch in North America. Most guests come to view the more than 12,000 animals that live here, including giraffes, wildebeests, oryx, antelope, and zebras. The ranch is also famous for its herd of well over 1,000 Texas longhorns. The Y.O. can accommodate from 30 to 35 guests in century-old renovated log cabins or in rooms in a larger house on the property; the chef is a master of southwestern fare.

**CHILDREN'S PROGRAM.** The ranch welcomes families with children of all ages, but it has no children's program and no baby-sitting services. However, during the summer there are one- to three-week sessions of Ranch Adventure Camp, for ages 9 through 14, so a family could book a Y.O. vacation and camp experience at the same time. The camp emphasizes environmental learning, with minicourses in ornithology, herpetology, ecology, firearm safety, rappelling, canoeing, swimming, and riding.

**RIDING PROGRAM.** There's a separate fee for the limited horseback riding, and you must reserve times before your arrival. Rides go out for a minimum of an hour. Good riders can participate in longhorn cattle drives each spring (at an extra charge).

**BEYOND RIDING.** Safari-style vehicles take you out to observe the animals each day, and there are wildlife photographic safaris as well. These tours cost extra but are well worth the money. Although the safaris are the only scheduled programs, the Y.O. also has a swimming pool and 40,000 acres of land to hike and explore. Families have plenty of time to relax and to savor the delicious meals, too.

*Y.O. Ranch, Mountain Home, TX 78058, tel. 830/640–3222. Year-round: 1 day, $85–$95 adults, $50 children; no minimum stay required. Adventure Camp, June–Aug.: 7–14 days, $545– $995. Riding is $25 per hour.*

## *Rockies*

### Aspen Canyon Ranch

ALL

Just 70 mi west of Denver in the Williams Fork River valley, Aspen Canyon Ranch is easy to reach even though it's tucked away at 8,400 ft among the aspen and lodgepole pines. The ranch borders Arapaho National Forest and is a short drive from Rocky Mountain National Park. From 30 to 35 guests stay in cozy log cabins with fireplaces, private baths, refrigerators, and coffeemakers. Aspen Canyon is a relatively small ranch with a wide range of activities as part of its regular program. The staff is enthusiastic about providing a western experience during which you will both relax and learn.

**CHILDREN'S PROGRAM.** The ranch has day care for children from infants to age 5; the activity program divides children ages 5 through 18 into two groups by age. Five-year-olds ride on lead lines in the corral; youngsters age seven and up can go out on the trail with their group. There are also games, hiking, fishing, and crafts.

**RIDING PROGRAM.** The rides, on ranch property and through Arapaho National Forest, take small groups of similar ability. Outings range from easy trips in the morning and afternoon to a challenging all-day ride. Children ages seven and up can ride with their children's group or on adult rides with their parents. You can choose personal instruction, and the wranglers will teach you not only how to ride but also how to saddle up or rope like an old pro. For an extra charge the whole family can opt for an overnight pack trip. Winter activities include snowmobiling.

**BEYOND RIDING.** Mountain biking and skeet shooting are popular family activities here, as is soaking in the two hot tubs. Fishing, hiking with or without a guide, and wildlife viewing are also options. You can always take on a job around the ranch, such as haying. For an extra charge, families can sign up for rafting on the upper Colorado River, mountain biking (adults only), or local hot-air ballooning.

*Aspen Canyon Ranch, 13206 County Rd. 3, Star Rte., Parshall, CO 80468, tel. 970/725–3600 or 800/321–1357. May–Oct., mid-Dec.–Apr.: 7 days, $1,295 adults, $800 children 7 to 16, $650 children 3 to 6, under 3 free.*

### Breteche Creek

ALL

Part guest ranch, part wilderness learning center, Breteche Creek is a nonprofit educational institution in northwestern Wyoming that combines riding and other typical ranch vacation experiences with learning about natural history, regional history, and the arts. Each week-long session includes just 12 to 20 participants, who stay in tent cabins scattered around the property. These have wooden floors and walls with canvas roofs; bathrooms and showers are in the main building. The founders of Breteche Creek believe immersion in the natural environment helps us learn about our world.

**CHILDREN'S PROGRAM.** There's no formal program; children and adults learn together as they participate in workshops and seminars and investigate the wilderness surroundings. All ages are welcome, and workshop leaders will be glad to gear information to the children in attendance. On the other hand, parents should decide if children are too young to be engaged by these activities. Parents may want to take turns attending workshops and exploring the incredible natural setting with very young children—a path to learning in itself.

**RIDING PROGRAM.** There are horsemanship lessons and guided rides for various abilities. For an additional charge, you can take private lessons with Breteche Creek's codirector, noted horse breeder and trainer Bob Curtis. Because the center is surrounded by a 7,000-acre working cattle and horse ranch, there is also an opportunity to participate in wrangling and herding cattle. Guests of any age can join in any riding activity if they have the necessary skills. Each summer Breteche typically offers a four-day horsemanship clinic with Bob Curtis; families are welcome and it's as much for beginners as it is for advanced riders.

**BEYOND RIDING.** Each day you can choose among workshops, some of which might take place on horseback, or you can decide to kick back and explore on your own. Birding and hiking are popular with all ages here, and you have your choice of fishing in a pond, lake, or river on the ranch property. There's excellent wildlife viewing—at last count more than 200 elk and from 300 to 400 deer were living on ranch property. All seven-day sessions include a naturalist-guided tour of Yellowstone National Park. Instruction in fly-fishing, rock climbing, and windsurfing can be arranged for an extra charge, as can visits to local museums and the nightly rodeo in Cody. Families with older children might wish to sign up for the photography or author-led writing workshops offered each summer.

*Breteche Creek, Box 596, Cody, WY 82414, tel. 307/587–3844. Mid-June–Sept.: 7 days, $1,100 adults, $825 children 6–12, $425 children 1–5; nannies 50% off when accompanying children ages 1–5; daily rates are available (3-day minimum stay). Four-day horsemanship clinics, $1,200 adults, $825 children 12 and under, workshops $1,250 per person.*

## Cherokee Park Dude Ranch

ALL

One of the oldest guest ranches in Colorado, Cherokee Park was a stagecoach stop between Fort Collins and Laramie before it became a dude ranch back in 1886. Its authentic Old West character shows in furnishings and historical memorabilia from the early days, but among the many modern amenities are a heated pool and spa. Up to 35 guests stay in the main lodge or in cabins that have from two to four bedrooms. Owners Dickey and Christine Prince are renowned for their warm hospitality; their attitude carries over to the staff, too. Attentive care and enthusiasm are especially evident in the children's program.

**CHILDREN'S PROGRAM.** Children from ages 3 to 5 and 6 to 12 are in separate groups. The younger ones take pony rides around the ranch; the older ones have their own horses and a daily ride out on the trail. Other activities include hiking, fishing, nature studies, crafts, riflery, and an overnight in the ranch's tepee. Those too young for the overnight (usually the three- and four-year-olds) will be cared for in your cabin so you can participate in an adult overnight trip. The ranch schedules special hikes for teens, too, when enough are visiting. Children eat with their parents unless adults are on the trail; an exception is a weekly adults-only candlelight dinner, during which the children have a pizza party. You can bring your own sitter or nanny free of any additional charge.

**RIDING PROGRAM.** Personal instruction is available every day in the riding ring, and trail rides for different levels range from an hour in length to all day. The terrain includes open prairie as well as mountain trails. You can join one of the popular lunch rides, and no one should miss the opportunity to join an overnight pack trip (at an extra charge).

**BEYOND RIDING.** Besides swimming in the pool, from mid-May through mid-August you can take to the water for a day of rafting (at an extra charge). Ages seven and up can paddle; younger children sit in the middle of the raft. There are free fly-casting classes for novice anglers of all ages—the ranch provides equipment, and there's an Orvis-certified fishing guide each Saturday afternoon who provides fly-fishing lessons. Guided hikes are free, and there's trapshooting too.

You can take a complimentary sightseeing trip to nearby Rocky Mountain National Park, or for an extra charge visit Laramie's Wyoming Territorial Park, where the children get to reenact a prison break. Don't miss the evening activities when a "mountain man" visits the ranch to talk about trapping and western life in the mid-1800s. *Cherokee Park Dude Ranch, 436 Cherokee Hills Dr., Livermore, CO 80536, tel. 970/493–6522 or 800/628–0949. May–Oct.: 7 days, $900–$1,100 adults, $200–$850 children.*

## Colorado Trails Ranch

**5+**

The majestic San Juan Mountains in southwestern Colorado are a dramatic backdrop for Colorado Trails, which has one of the best riding programs of any ranch in the country. The managers at Colorado Trails Ranch have a straightforward goal: to "see that every guest, child or adult, has the best vacation they ever had." That has been the ranch's goal for 39 years, and children's activities have always been a focus. Up to 65 guests choose from three styles of cabins; some children's rooms have two bunk beds to accommodate large families. Also on the property are an opera house that is used for evening shows and entertainment, an old-fashioned soda fountain, and a petting zoo. The managers don't feel alcohol and children mix, so ranch policy is BYOB for consumption in your own cabin only.

**CHILDREN'S PROGRAM.** The extensive program usually has three age groups: ages 5 through 8, 9 through 12, and teens. The flexible program de-emphasizes competition but gives children a chance to participate in all ranch activities, including archery, riflery, swimming, and fishing. The 9 to 12 group and the teenage group each has its own camp-out, too. Those ages five and up take trail rides daily; the counselors who accompany the groups are adept at teaching children as they ride. Although there's no specific program for children four and under, they're welcome at the ranch and may participate in the children's activities to their level of ability. Baby-sitting is available.

**RIDING PROGRAM.** Colorado Trails offers superb instruction; even advanced riders can learn something new here. A special strength of the program is the instructors' ability to make those who have never even been near a horse feel comfortable and in control. Rides at a variety of gaits—walk, trot, cantering, and instructional—go out each day, with only about six riders to a group. Family rides are also set up during the week, if that's what children and parents want. Many forest trails are groomed.

**BEYOND RIDING.** Guests who want to learn to shoot can take instruction in archery, riflery, and trapshooting; there's an extra charge for the ammo and clay pigeons. In recent years the ranch expanded its fishing program and completed a fish habitat project on the mile of stream that runs through the property. There's fishing instruction and two stocked ponds, ideal for children and parents. Guests also have access to several lakes and streams nearby (in some waters a guide is required, which is an extra fee). Hiking and nature walks are popular as well. Those who want a change of scenery can visit Vallecito Lake, 12 mi away; the ranch provides a boat, driver, floating dock, and equipment for water skiers and power tubers. You'll probably want to see Durango, a town with great shopping and a theater offering turn-of-the-20th-century melodramas, as well as a pro rodeo. The ranch will tell you the cost of tickets for these and the popular narrow gauge railroad. Ask about guided trips to Mesa Verde National Park with its 1,000-year-old Anasazi cliff dwellings.

*Colorado Trails Ranch, 12161 County Rd. 240, Durango, CO 81301-6306, tel. 970/247–5055 or 800/323–3833. Early June–Aug.: 7 days, $3,645–$4,455 for a family of 3; $4,760–$5,560 for a family of 4, depending on size of cabin; $1,100 for each additional person in your cabin.*

## Drowsy Water Ranch

1+

"We treat your children as we do our own—with understanding, patience, love, and respect," owners Ken and Randy Sue Fosha say, and they mean it. This ranch just south of Rocky Mountain National Park in Colorado happily caters to families with children from one year old to the teens. It has one of the few programs for children under five that has activities, rather than just being a baby-sitting service. Most families will stay in the rustic but bright and cheerful log cabins that sleep up to nine people; there are lodge rooms, too. Cabins overlook Drowsy Water Creek or the ranch ponds. There's a good old-fashioned feel here and plenty of warm western hospitality for about 60 guests.

**CHILDREN'S PROGRAM.** One- to five-year-olds are kept busy while adults participate in scheduled ranch activities for part or all of the day. They have rides on lead lines, crafts, nature hikes, and games—lots of outdoor fun. Children ages 6 through 13, called Range Riders, get their own horse for the week and ride together on the ranch and out on the trail. Counselors also lead games and crafts and take the group for picnics and hikes. These youngsters can try archery or the obstacle course, too.

**RIDING PROGRAM.** Slow, moderate, and fast rides go out daily, and you can get in extra riding on all-day and cookout rides during the week. Instruction is always available. Many trails above the ranch have views of the Continental Divide and the Gore Range. Although the Range Riders can't ride with adults on the trail, parents can choose to ride with the children. For an extra charge, parents and children six and up can take an overnight pack trip.

**BEYOND RIDING.** There's fishing on the property; the ranch provides equipment for beginners. Children also love the ranch's playground. Your stay includes a rugged Jeep trip up into the mountains. You can arrange rafting, golf, and tennis nearby for an extra charge. For romantics there's an adults-only hayride at the end of the week while children have their own hayride and dinner.

*Drowsy Water Ranch, Box 147FA, Granby, CO 80446, tel. 970/725–3456 or 800/845–2292. June–mid-Sept.: 7 days, $1,020–$1,250 adults, $560–$1,100 children.*

## Elk Mountain Ranch

4+

At 9,535 ft, Elk Mountain is the highest guest ranch in Colorado, with a spectacular setting in the San Isabel National Forest. There are deer, elk, and wildflowers in abundance amid thousands of acres of unspoiled wilderness. Log cottages or a suite in the main lodge are ideal for families; the guest capacity is limited to 30. You'll always find fresh flowers and fruit in your room. Although the ranch has a full children's program, families spend a lot of time together.

**CHILDREN'S PROGRAM.** Children ages four through seven have an extensive program. Aside from riding twice a day in the ring, they go on scavenger hunts, create crafts, and fish, among other pastimes. Children eight and up are welcome in all the ranch's activities, including riding. It's especially nice that even those younger than eight can take part in brunch rides—vehicles bring them up to meet riders so the whole family can enjoy the meal and the views. The ranch has no organized program for children under age four, but they are welcome; parents should arrange baby-sitting (for an extra charge) when they book their stay.

**RIDING PROGRAM.** Riding is exceptional at Elk Mountain. Each day there are rides on and off the trails, as well as excellent instruction in riding, tack, and the care and feeding of horses. You ride in very small groups through rock canyons, across high plateaus, and on trails through stands of shimmering aspens. Children age eight and up can go out with parents on the adult rides. Don't miss the weekly brunch ride or the overnight camping trip; the overnight is included in July and August (additional charge in June and September).

**BEYOND RIDING.** Elk Mountain has free guided hikes to a nearby ghost town and high meadows filled with wildflowers. There's also archery, riflery, and trapshooting. Bring your own fishing gear, and the ranch will cook up your catch. You can also join complimentary van trips to Aspen. Parents and children age eight and up can spend a day rafting the Arkansas River with a local outfitter; this excursion is included in the price of your ranch stay.

*Elk Mountain Ranch, Box 910, Buena Vista, CO 81211, tel. 719/539–4430. June–Sept.: 7 days, $975–$1,175 adults, $675–$875 children age 12 and under.*

## Hidden Creek Ranch

**ALL**

Adventure and ecological awareness go hand in hand at this ranch in the mountainous lake country of Idaho's panhandle. Iris Behr and John Muir, who opened Hidden Creek in 1993, envisioned a place where people could reconnect with nature as well as ride horses. All products used at the ranch are natural, biodegradable, and packaged in recycled containers; none has been tested on animals. There are cabins (built of dead standing timber) with accommodations for 40, but you shouldn't think spartan just because the philosophy is harmony with nature. Food is exceptional, the children's program is extensive, and the "chocolate fairy" turns down your bed each night.

**CHILDREN'S PROGRAM.** The ranch has a full program for children age three and up from mid-June through August, although it's entirely optional; families can spend as much of their day together as they wish. The youngest guests ride at the ranch under the supervision of counselors; children six and up can join the regular trail rides. Other activities are hiking, fishing, crafts and nature studies, and picnics. Children have their own campfire with storytelling and an overnight in a tepee. Care for children under age three (at an extra charge) must be arranged in advance.

**RIDING PROGRAM.** "If you want to see what men have made, you can ride in a car. If you want to see what God has made, you have to ride on a horse." That's the philosophy of the Hidden Creek riding program, which takes you into forests, grassy meadows, and magnificent mountain settings. There are daily rides for all abilities; groups are small. No one's left out of the weekly specials either—these include everything from a walk-only dinner ride to a challenging fast ride for advanced equestrians. Families with children age six and up can ride together. Families with riders 10 and older can also sign up for a two-night pack trip; ask for details.

**BEYOND RIDING.** Among the hikes is an all-day trek to a nearby gold mine. Trapshooting, target riflery (there's an extra charge for targets and ammunition), and archery are popular; the ranch also has a stocked pond and fishing poles. Guides, equipment, and instruction are available for mountain biking. Hot tubs are an option for the muscle sore or bone weary at any time, day or night. Winter activities include snowshoeing, cross-country skiing, sleigh rides, and murder mysteries to solve; snowmobiling is available at an extra charge.

*Hidden Creek Ranch, 7600 E. Blue Lake Rd., Harrison, ID 83833, tel. 208/689–3209. May–Oct.: 6 days, $1,481–$1,790 adults, $1,431 children 3–11; Dec.–mid-Mar.: 4 days, $987 adults, $789 children 3–11. Children age 2 and under free. Pack trip, $595–$695 per rider. Ranch guests age 18 and older only May–mid-June and Sept.–Oct.*

## Lake Mancos Ranch

ALL

The Sehnerts, owners of Lake Mancos Ranch, believe that a lot of American families still want an old-fashioned vacation, without video games, cable TV, or bars. At Lake Mancos Ranch you can ride and relax in the heart of southwestern Colorado's authentic cowboy country. Up to 55 guests stay in cabins of various sizes; all have porches, two baths, and refrigerators. You can bring your own liquor for use in your cabin. This ranch is a good choice if at least one person in your family doesn't ride, as non-rider rates are available.

**CHILDREN'S PROGRAM.** Li'l Ropers is for children ages 4 and 5; Cowpokes is the 5 through 9 group; Buckaroos is for those 9 through 12; and teens are the Mavericks. Li'l Ropers have the opportunity to learn about horses while on the lead line at no extra charge. All other age groups spend time riding with their counselors if they opt to be in the riding program. The ranch also offers hiking, fishing, scavenger hunts, lawn games, hayrides, cookouts, camp-outs, and more. Teens have plenty of action of their own, including various sports and a Jeep trip.

**RIDING PROGRAM.** Adults and children (usually ages five and up) who choose to participate in the program go out on the trails in supervised groups. Parents and children generally ride separately, but there are family rides three times a week. In this rugged terrain most rides are walk-trot only, but you won't be bored; each day you explore a different area, from the ranch lands to the adjacent San Juan National Forest. Instruction takes place primarily at the beginning of your stay, but wranglers give pointers throughout the week.

**BEYOND RIDING.** Some favorite activities are guided hikes, mountain biking, gold panning, time in the pool, and guided four-wheel-drive trips up into the San Juan Mountains. Guests of all ages can fish because there's equipment even for children. You could also head off-property to ride on the Durango and Silverton Narrow Gauge Railroad or visit the famed ruins at Mesa Verde National Park, just 17 mi from the ranch; the ranch will give you a box lunch to take along. Rafting is another option for families with children from about age six and up (at an extra charge).

*Lake Mancos Ranch, 42688 County Rd. N, Mancos, CO 81328, tel. 970/533–1190 or 800/325–9462. June–Aug.: 7 days, $1,020–$1,300 adults, $810–$1,050 children under 18. Rates include gratuities. Adults only in Sept.*

## Lone Mountain Ranch

ALL

The Schaap family, which owns Lone Mountain, believes the enjoyment of nature is good for both the body and the mind. The ranch's location, high in the mountains at the northern end of the Greater Yellowstone ecosystem in Montana, provides abundant opportunity for nature discovery and learning for all ages. You have a choice of many activities and programs. Up to 70 people stay in cabins with fireplaces; ranch amenities include a massage therapist, who for an extra charge is ready to soothe sore muscles during your stay.

**CHILDREN'S PROGRAM.** Children ages 4 through 12 and teens participate in a variety of activities; there's no program for those under age four, but the ranch has information on quality day care in Big Sky, and special rates are available if you bring your own nanny. The four- and five-year-olds are given pony rides by counselors; ages six and up go on their own wrangler-led rides. Activities can include nature discovery hikes, animal tracking, panning for gold, orienteering, mountain biking, climbing wall challenges, and camp-outs, depending on the age group. Parents can join their children for any or all of these activities. Teens also take adventure hikes and participate in other special activities.

**RIDING PROGRAM.** Adults and children ages six and up are assigned their own horse. Children can ride in the regular adult program rather than on children's rides if space allows. Half-day, all-day, and instructional rides are available for every ability. First-time riders learn in the ring, building up skills and confidence before going out on the trail.

**BEYOND RIDING.** Lone Mountain has many programs for nonriders, including hiking and skiing (see Cross-Country Skiing). There's some fishing equipment and instruction for children, and Orvis-certified guides and instruction for adults; birding is popular, too. The ranch's friendly llamas will carry a picnic lunch while you and the children lead them on a day hike; you can also choose to relax in the hot tub. Guided tours of Yellowstone, best for families with children age six and up, are part of any weeklong stay. Extra-charge activities include naturalist-led canoe trips and, in nearby Big Sky, golf, tennis, gondola rides, rafting, and rock climbing. For more information on the ranch's winter activities, see the Cross-Country Skiing chapter.

*Lone Mountain Ranch, Box 160069, Big Sky, MT 59716, tel. 406/995–4644 or 800/514–4644. Year-round (riding available June–Oct.): 7 days, $1,015–$2,625 adults, $638 children; children under 2 free.*

## North Fork Guest Ranch

ALL

A mere 50 mi from Denver and yet surrounded by the Mt. Evans Wilderness Area, North Fork is a ranch that encourages families to spend time together and to try a variety of activities as part of its regular program. Lodging is in log cabins, an impressive stone building, or the main lodge; capacity is about 40 guests. The North Fork of the South Platte River runs through the property. If your children are looking for animals to pet and feed, this is the place. There are calves, pygmy goats, bunnies, and chickens.

**CHILDREN'S PROGRAM.** Counselors care for infants and children up to about age six; depending on age, children can try riding, hiking, fishing, swimming, crafts, nature studies, and camp-outs in a tepee. The program's main purpose is to provide fun for children too young to accompany parents on rides or on river rafting. The ranch has no supervised evening program or baby-sitting; nighttime activities are geared to the entire family.

**RIDING PROGRAM.** Wranglers give instruction throughout the week for those who want or need it, and each guest is assigned a horse for the entire stay. Rides for small groups go through high alpine meadows or stands of aspen and ponderosa pine. Children ages six and up can accompany parents on rides.

**BEYOND RIDING.** North Fork is unusual because river rafting and an overnight pack trip are included in the regular weekly rate, so almost all guests participate. Parents with children too young to raft can bring them along; counselors will take the children on a land-based excursion on their own while parents are on the river. The eight-hour ride up to the campsite is best for ages 12 and up, but younger children and other nonriders can travel to the campsite by vehicle and join their families. There's a weekly fly-fishing class (good for ages 10 and up), as well as hiking, trapshooting, and archery. The ranch has a heated pool and spa.

*North Fork Guest Ranch, Box B, Shawnee, CO 80475, tel. 303/838–9873 or 800/843–7895. May–Sept.: 7 days, $1,195–$1,395 adults, $400–$1,195 children.*

## Paradise Guest Ranch

ALL

The ranch brand, FUN, is the first thing you'll see when you drive into Paradise. It's a promise owner Leah Anderson attempts to fulfill for all ages over the course of the weeklong stay. Beautifully renovated but authentically rustic log cabins provide families of all sizes with comfortable lodging and views of the surrounding valley in Wyoming's Big Horn Mountains. In July and August there are often 80 guests, many of them returnees who greet each other like long-lost friends. And then there's Reba, the ranch bloodhound, who greets everybody, period.

**CHILDREN'S PROGRAM.** Children ages three through seven and those age eight and up are grouped separately, and there are programs with hiking, fishing, crafts, and nature studies to occupy those under seven and any older children who don't want to join the adult rides. A ranch nanny will watch children under the age of three in the mornings only; private baby-sitting can be arranged for an extra charge. Children have an overnight on the hill just above the ranch, and the teens have their own overnight pack trip.

**RIDING PROGRAM.** Children age six and up join their parents out on the trail. There are long, short, slow, and fast rides. Exceptional are the Learn to Lope rides high on the mesa. Paradise wranglers seem to be able to get almost everybody loping like pros before week's end. Good riders can learn team cattle penning and receive specialized instruction for a modest extra fee.

**BEYOND RIDING.** Guided and self-guided hikes, fishing instruction and guided trips for both children and adults (equipment provided), swimming, and a once-weekly town trip into Buffalo all provide a change from riding. So does the hot tub. Paradise breeds and raises mules, and learning about these intelligent, hardworking animals is surprisingly interesting. Parents have a weekly adults-only candlelight dinner while the youngsters are on their overnight, and the whole family will be intrigued by the legend of Butch Cassidy on a visit to his famous 'Hole-in-the-Wall' hideout, not far from Paradise. For an extra charge adults can arrange a pack fishing trip.

*Paradise Guest Ranch, Box 790, Buffalo, WY 82834, tel. 307/684–7876. May–Sept.: 7 days, $1,000–$1,575 adults, $300–$1,475 children. Late Sept. adults only.*

## Rainbow Trout Ranch

ALL

Located in southwestern Colorado in the rugged and remote Conejos River valley, Rainbow Trout is 185 mi from Colorado Springs and just 80 mi from Taos, New Mexico. The centerpiece of the ranch is the 13,000-square-ft main lodge, built in the 1920s without, it is said, a single nail. Cabins are a short distance from the lodge and have a variety of floor plans, though all have porches. This ranch is a family haven where 60 guests of all ages are warmly welcomed and cared for.

**CHILDREN'S PROGRAM.** There are three groups: ages 3 through 5, 6 through 11, and 12 and up. Children age six and up have a full riding program that has instruction both in the arena and on the trail. Children ages three through five are led by counselors in the arena and around the ranch. When not on horses, youngsters here are hiking, fishing, swimming, and exploring the natural surroundings. The teen program is very flexible, but hikes, basketball, and fishing are all likely activities in addition to riding.

**RIDING PROGRAM.** Small groups, divided by ability, go on a variety of rides: slow, fast, long, short, leisurely, and scenic. Adults can join the children for games and lessons in the arena if they wish, and if families want to ride together, the ranch will arrange that.

**BEYOND RIDING.** Once a private fishing retreat for wealthy businessmen, Rainbow Trout has, as its name suggests, exceptional fishing. Lessons are given for beginners in fly-fishing, and supplies can be purchased at the ranch. Get your license (mandatory for ages 15 and up) before arriving. The ranch also has a heated pool and hot tub. You can take guided hikes or use trail maps to plan your own. Families can raft on the Rio Grande (at an extra charge), combining that adventure with a tour of Taos (about 1½ hours away); rafting is for children age six or so and up. One of the thrills for most families is a chance to ride the Cumbres & Toltec Scenic Railroad (at an extra charge), "America's longest and highest narrow gauge." Ask the ranch how to go about arranging these excursions; it may be best to make reservations before you arrive.

*Rainbow Trout Ranch, Box 458, 1484 FDR 250, Antonito, CO 81120, tel. 719/376–5659 or 800/633–3397. Late May–late Sept.: 7 days, $1,200 adults, $700–$1,100 children. Ask about minimum 2-day stays in May and Sept.*

## Red Rock Ranch

6+

Here's a small horse ranch in Wyoming that loves families. "Children are an important part of Red Rock.... It wouldn't be the same without them," states the brochure, and the programs and facilities for children are indeed extensive. Set in a high valley of Jackson Hole's mountain country, the ranch gets its name from the imposing red-rock formations in the area. Lodging is in authentic log cabins that accommodate no more than 30 guests in any given week.

**CHILDREN'S PROGRAM.** There are no activities or baby-sitting services for children younger than age six. Children age six and up go on daily rides with wranglers. Along the way they might look for fossils, stop to wade in a crystal-clear mountain creek, or search for wildlife. There's also a weekly overnight. Parents can ride with their children on kids' rides, but only children age 13 and up join adult rides. Children eat dinner with their wranglers three times a week.

**RIDING PROGRAM.** Part of Red Rock's operation is the raising and care of fine horses. The staff know the horses well, which makes matching guests with the right mount that much easier. The ranch has morning and afternoon rides for all abilities, as well as all-day lunch rides on which you might see antelope, moose, coyotes, and other native wildlife. The high mountain trails yield views of the Teton, Wind River, and Absaroka ranges.

**BEYOND RIDING.** Fishing, hiking, swimming in the heated pool, and relaxing in the hot tub are ranch favorites. Slopping the pigs (when these animals are in residence) is a favorite among younger children. Almost everyone likes to visit Jackson for shopping or for the local rodeo and "shoot-out." The National Elk Refuge, just north of town, is well worth the visit, as is the Wildlife of the American West Art Museum.

*Red Rock Ranch, Box 38, Kelly, WY 83011, tel. 307/733–6288. June–Sept.: 6 days, $1,467.50.*

## Seven D Ranch

ALL

The Seven D Ranch is 50 mi northwest of Cody, Wyoming, in the Sunlight Basin, surrounded by the Absaroka Mountains and the Shoshone National Forest. Taking only 32 guests at a time, the ranch has log cabins set in a tranquil aspen grove with a crystal-clear creek meandering nearby. Few places are as peaceful as this, and few offer more for families. There are conveniences for parents with infants—cribs, babysitting, free laundry facilities, and microwaves—and a superb children's program that focuses on environmental education and western history as well as riding.

**CHILDREN'S PROGRAM.** For infants and children up to age six, there's baby-sitting at no charge during the adult rides. Younger children will have a chance to experience lead-line rides in the corral. Children ages 6 through 12 participate in an extensive program that includes environmental education, hiking, woodsmanship, and cave exploration. This group also learns about ranch life and the natural history of the area. There are opportunities for riding and riding instruction every day except Sunday.

**RIDING PROGRAM.** Each guest age six or older is assigned a horse; children ride with counselors. Instruction is available for all ages and levels. There are morning, afternoon, and all-day rides on trails with names as lovely as the Little Sunlight Trail or as evocative as the Oh My God Trail (named by a guest). Multi-day pack trips for good riders are possible with advance notice; there's an extra charge for these.

**BEYOND RIDING.** You can try world-class fly-fishing on Sunlight Creek (clinics provided), hiking, backpacking, and trapshooting at the ranch. Off-property excursions vary; you could visit the Cody Rodeo and the Buffalo Bill Historical Center in Cody, which includes the Whitney Gallery of Western Art, the Plains Indian Museum, and the Cody Firearms Museum. Most guests choose to spend all their time in the relaxing atmosphere at the ranch, but day trips to Yellowstone and the Beartooths are sometimes arranged. In the evening, everyone joins in square dancing and sing-alongs, among other activities.

*Seven D Ranch, Box 100, Cody, WY 82414, tel. 307/587–9885. June–Aug.: 7 days, $1,325– $1,485; 15% discount for children 1–12, children under 1 free.*

## Sky Corral

ALL

At Sky Corral the emphasis is on family activities and a flexible, low-key schedule. The ranch, which accommodates 32 guests, is 23 mi from Fort Collins, Colorado, in the Roosevelt National Forest, and a short drive from Rocky Mountain National Park. The main lodge has several rooms; families can also choose rustic cabins, some of which have woodstoves or fireplaces.

**CHILDREN'S PROGRAM.** Since Justin and Karen O'Connor bought the ranch a few years back, they added a full-time children's program for ages 3 to 12. Youngsters are divided into groups of ages 3 to 6 and 7 to 12. While children always have the option of being with their parents, they can also elect to join the rides, crafts, hikes, bonfires, and assorted adventures that the counselors have going each day. Guests under age seven can't ride on the trail, but they can join counselors on rides around the ranch.

**RIDING PROGRAM.** Families ride together and separately, and each guest age seven and up is assigned a horse for the week. Groups are small, just six guests and a wrangler for trail rides that wind through the Roosevelt National Forest and high into the mountains with views of the Continental Divide. An overnight camp trip is included in your stay.

**BEYOND RIDING.** The ranch has hiking, fishing in its own stocked lake, archery, and tennis. Amenities include a heated pool, sauna, gym, and hot tub. Raft trips are part of the package from June to August for everyone ages seven and up. And regardless of age, the petting zoo is a popular spot. *Sky Corral, 8233 Old Flowers Rd., Bellvue, CO 80512, tel. 970/484–1362. May–Nov.: 6 days, $1,095 adults, $800 children 6 to 12, $675 children 2 to 5; children under age 2 free. Daily rates May, Sept.–Oct., $160 adults, $95 children 6 to 12, $75 children 2 to 5; children under age 2 free.*

## Skyline Guest Ranch

ALL

Skyline, in the increasingly popular vacation town of Telluride in southwestern Colorado, is extraordinarily beautiful, with views of 14,000-ft snowcapped peaks. Owners Dave and Sherry Farny formerly ran the Telluride Mountaineering School, so it's not surprising that Skyline has all kinds of outdoor activities, including guided climbing and mountain biking. You stay in lodge rooms or cabins; beds are outfitted with down comforters and sheepskin mattress pads. Only 35 guests visit at a time, so there's both an intimacy and a wonderful sense of comfort at Skyline.

**CHILDREN'S PROGRAM.** Many activities at the ranch are designed for children and parents together. When parents are on hikes or rides more strenuous than their children can handle, youngsters join easier ones. Children age six and up learn not only riding but horse care, tack, horse anatomy, and other aspects of general horsemanship. Although the ranch welcomes all ages, most activities are best for those age six and older. However, at the all-day summer adventure program in town run by Telluride Ski & Golf Company, children ages 3 to 12 hike, bike, and explore surrounding peaks and valleys on 4x4 tours. (The 4x4 tours cost extra but are arranged by the ranch.) At the ranch baby-sitting is available for children under age three (at an extra charge), but this should be arranged well in advance.

**RIDING PROGRAM.** 'Natural horsemanship' is the focus and philosophy of the riding program here. The idea is to help humans forge a relationship with their horse for the week—a relationship based on respect and honor—with the result that even new riders will feel comfortable and safe around horses. Guests are invited to groom, saddle, and feed their horse throughout the week. There are half-or all-day rides every day; an overnight pack trip is part of a week's stay, and all ages can participate.

**BEYOND RIDING.** The ranch has a midweek trip to Mesa Verde National Park, about a 1½-hour drive away. You can also take guided and self-guided hikes to a mining town, wildflower fields, and a hot springs, among other areas. You can climb a San Juan peak—including 14,017-ft Wilson Peak—with an experienced guide, but most climbs are for adults and older children who have some hiking experience. Skyline also has guided fishing trips and fishing instruction; equipment is available. Mountain bikes are available at the ranch, and guided bike rides are offered. For an extra charge, experienced riders can join spring and fall pack trips. In winter there's cross-country skiing at the ranch (equipment available for those wearing a size 5 shoe or larger) and transportation to the Telluride ski area, 5 mi away, for downhillers. Horse-drawn sleigh rides are offered, but no horseback riding. *Skyline Guest Ranch, Box 67, Telluride, CO 81435, tel. 970/728–3757. June–mid-Oct. and mid-Dec.–Apr.: 7 days (summer only; ask about daily rates in winter), $1,400 adults; 50% discount for children 3–5, children under 3 free.*

# *West Coast*

## Coffee Creek Ranch

ALL

Coffee Creek is a river-canyon ranch on the edge of the Trinity Alps Wilderness area in California. This is the perfect ranch for families with nonriders, as you only pay for the amount of riding you really want to do. Wildflowers and wildlife abound, and all cabins have porches and wood-burning or potbelly stoves. The ranch accommodates up to 50 guests.

**CHILDREN'S PROGRAM.** Cowboys and Cowgirls are children from age 3 to 7; Junior Wranglers are from age 8 to 12; and Bronc Busters are from age 13 to 17. Although counselors don't take children riding, there's plenty to do. Depending on their age, children have pony rides, care for baby animals, pan for gold, and fish. Each child takes home at least two finished projects from the excellent creative arts program. There are also skits, lawn games, swimming, archery, and riflery. The youngest guests go in the wading pool; the older children swim, slide, and jump in Coffee Creek. During trail-ride hours, care is provided for children under age three in the Kiddie Korral.

**RIDING PROGRAM.** Rides are grouped by ability, not age. Those as young as age six can go on certain, but not all, trails, and there are all-day, breakfast, and picnic rides. Coffee Creek has a separate daily or weekly fee for rides; an overnight pack trip is included in the weekly riding fee. Private lessons are also available for an extra charge. The ranch is particularly interesting because of the international staff, part of a cultural exchange program. Wranglers from Australia and New Zealand, for example, give you a feel for cowboy life in another hemisphere. For an extra charge families can arrange multi-day wilderness pack trips.

**BEYOND RIDING.** Possibilities include visiting the health club, swimming in the heated pool or in the creek, canoeing on the pond, taking guided hikes, fishing (equipment provided for children only), panning for gold, enjoying lawn games, archery, and trying a hand at riflery or trapshooting. In the winter you can try cross-country skiing, tubing, snowshoeing, sleigh riding, ice fishing, and dogsledding.

*Coffee Creek Ranch, HC 2, Box 4940, Trinity Center, CA 96091, tel. 530/266–3343 or 800/624–4480. Year-round: 7 days, $745–$860 adults, $250–$740 children. Riding is $30 for regular ride, $60 for all-day outing, or $300 for wk.*

## Rankin Ranch

ALL

The Rankin family has been ranching in California since 1863, and their 31,000-acre spread in the Tehachapi Mountains, northeast of Bakersfield, has an old-fashioned, down-home atmosphere, from the cozy duplex cabins to the baby calves the children love to feed. The ranch is casual and western, but there are elegant touches for its 30 to 45 guests: linen tablecloths, candles, and fresh flowers on the dining room tables. Family reunions are popular here—you can book all 14 rooms—and the Rankins are proud of the fact that their ranch is a welcoming place for single women and for grandparents.

**CHILDREN'S PROGRAM.** The program is for children age four and up, but baby-sitting for younger children can be arranged in advance for an extra charge. Children ages 4 through 11 join counselors for swim meets, picnics, games, and guided nature hikes, as well as a terrific crafts program. Children eat breakfast and lunch with their families; at dinner children sit at a special table with their counselors, or they can join their parents if they like.

**RIDING PROGRAM.** You can sign up for one-hour morning and afternoon rides, which are mostly at a walk because of the terrain. A few wide-open meadows provide opportunities for advanced riders to canter and gallop. Because this is a working ranch, you can sometimes help wranglers with chores, such as moving cattle. Children under age 12 do not go on adult rides, but parents are welcome to sign up for the children's rides. There are special teen rides when enough of that age group is present, and there are two rides daily (one on Sunday) for youngsters age six and up.

**BEYOND RIDING.** You use your own equipment for fishing and tennis; archery and hiking are other options. If you bring your own bikes, you'll find plenty of paved and dirt roads on which to ride along with some exquisite scenery. One of the most popular activities is simply relaxing around the pool. Families with young children also love the petting farm with its baby calves, sheep, pigs, and chickens. In the spring, parents and children can sign up for the full-week art workshops, with classes in drawing and watercolor. These are included in the daily rate during this time period.
*Rankin Ranch, Box 36, Caliente, CA 93518, tel. 661/867–2511. Wk before Easter Sun.–Oct.: $100–$170 per day adults, $35–$100 children.*

## Rock Springs

ALL

Rock Springs sits just outside Bend, Oregon, in the foothills of the Cascade Range. About 50 guests visit at a time, staying in cabins with knotty-pine interiors and sundecks. "Family tradition is revered at Rock Springs" says owner John Gill, and there's no question that families are important here. Every detail has been thought of, down to the cookies, fresh fruit, and beverages that are always in the lodge so guests of all ages can help themselves between meals.

**CHILDREN'S PROGRAM.** Divided into groups for children ages 3 through 5 and 6 through 12, the program is available between 9 in the morning and 8:30 in the evening. Children can spend as much or as little time with counselors as they wish. In this very child-directed program, youngsters decide together what activities they would like throughout the week. Choices include riding, outdoor games, nature walks, swimming, sports, arts and crafts, an overnight, folklore, and storytelling. There are also a playground area and playhouse. Families eat breakfast together, but children generally eat lunch and dinner in their own dining room adjacent to the adult dining area.

**RIDING PROGRAM.** Twice-daily rides go out with no more than six people, grouped by age, ability, and interests. Children ages six and up can join trail rides with parents or go in groups with their counselors; younger children are helped on a lead line around the barn area. There's an all-day lunch ride, and riding instruction is available if staffing permits.

**BEYOND RIDING.** The ranch has a heated swimming pool and a boot-shape hot tub. There are two lighted tennis courts; you can ask about its special tennis weeks with free clinics by well-known coaches. Fly-fishing guides can be hired for trips off ranch property. For an extra charge families with children ages six and up can try white-water rafting on the Deschutes River, 15 mi from the ranch; families preferring calm water can canoe in a clear mountain lake. The ranch provides transportation for both adventures. There are also plenty of opportunities for day trips to nearby museums, including the High Desert Museum and Warm Springs Native People's Museum. The caves at Lava Lands State Park are another popular area attraction, as is the lift ride up Mt. Bachelor for views of the Cascades, Three Sisters, and Newberry Crater.
*Rock Springs, 64201 Tyler Rd., Bend, OR 97701, tel. 541/382–1957 or 800/225–*

*3833. Late June–late Aug.: 7 days, $1,675–$1,750 adults, $1,250 children ages 6 to 16, $1,000 children ages 3 to 5; ask about special rates for infants and nannies.*

# Resources

## Organizations

The **Dude Ranchers' Association** (Box 471, LaPorte, CO 80535, tel. 970/223–8440) has more than 100 members in western states. An excellent magazine with all kinds of information about ranches and ranch stays is available from this group. The **Colorado Dude and Guest Ranch Association** (Box 300, Tabernash, CO 80478, tel. 970/887–3128) and the **Wyoming Dude Rancher's Association** (Box 618, Dubois, WY 82513, tel. 307/455–2584) send out material about ranches.

Some tour operators or specialty travel advisers can make reservations for you at ranches as well as provide information that will help you choose a ranch. **American Wilderness Experience/GORP Travel** (2820A Wilderness Pl., Boulder, CO 80301, tel. 303/444–2622 or 800/444–3833) books vacations at ranches throughout the West and Southwest. **Off the Beaten Path** (27 E. Main St., Bozeman, MT 59715, tel. 406/586–1311 or 800/445–2995) specializes in custom western adventures and works with dozens of ranches. **Rascals in Paradise** (650 5th St., Suite 505, San Francisco, CA 94107, tel. 415/978–9800 or 800/872–7225) has organized a couple of different family weeks at ranches and has a stellar reputation as a family travel resource. **Pat Dickerman's Adventure Guides** (7550 E. McDonald Dr., Scottsdale, AZ 85250, tel. 602/596–0226 or 800/252–7899) can help you match your family to the right ranch.

## Books

**Gene Kilgore's** *Ranch Vacations* (John Muir Publications; revised 1999) is an outstanding resource that covers almost every ranch in the United States and Canada. Although there is only limited information about children's programs, the guide states clearly which ranches have children's programs and whether families are welcomed at those that don't have formal programs.

## Also See

Cross-Country Skiing lists a number of ranches that have opportunities for skiing.

# ROCK CLIMBING

A few years ago the words *rock climbing* were not part of the vocabulary of most Americans and were certainly not related to anything families might do together on a vacation. That's all changed. Today five-, six-, and seven-year-olds scramble up indoor climbing walls from Connecticut to California and every place in between. Parents are stepping into harnesses, too, joining their children in a sport that is challenging, exhilarating, and a self-esteem builder of the first order.

Rock climbing has become a relatively safe sport as equipment and technique have improved over the years. Generally you climb—in a harness attached to safety ropes—from the ground up a rock face, finding hand- and footholds as you go. After reaching the top (or however far you choose to climb) you descend, using your feet against the rocks to help you down. Those passionate about the sport think of it as a kind of natural puzzle, one that stimulates the mind as well as the body. There seems to be no single profile that fits the average rock climber. Although good physical condition is a must, you and your children of all ages might be surprised to find that working your way up a hunk of granite out in beautiful country does more for your soul than you believed possible. Happily, a variety of opportunities exists to discover the rock climber in you.

Many indoor climbing schools schedule weekend or even weeklong courses in addition to their daily classes. Several of the top outdoor schools in the country have integrated rock climbing into their programs. Both types of courses are excellent choices for families just beginning the sport, as well as for those who really want to have fun with it as a recreational pastime. America's premier alpine climbing schools, on the other hand, are for people who want to be serious climbers. Guide-training and intensive mountaineering courses are the core of what these schools offer. If you and your family want to work toward self-guided trips in the backcountry, a dedicated mountaineering and climbing school would be the best choice.

Courses vary in terms of how long you spend on the ground and how long on the rocks; from four to six hours of actual climbing is typical on the first day, with six or seven possible on days two and three. Fifty-foot climbs are typical of beginner routes. You will probably be paired with a partner, and you will take turns climbing and belaying (handling the safety ropes of the other climber) throughout the course. Children 12 and over can usually learn to belay, too. Climbers younger than that are too small and not technically skilled enough to handle belaying.

## Questions to Ask

**Is there child-size equipment, including helmets and harnesses, that can be adjusted to fit a child properly?** For safety it's imperative that helmets and harnesses fit correctly. Although climbing shoes aren't mandatory in some courses, they do provide better traction than tennis shoes and will certainly make a difference at the intermediate level. Some instructors believe these shoes make a difference for beginners, too. If rock shoes are not supplied, ask about a rental source near the school or even consider buying them.

**What is your teaching accreditation or certification, and how many years' experience do you have?** American Mountain Guides Association (AMGA; *see* Resources, *below*) is the U.S. organization that accredits schools and guide services and certifies individual guides. In Europe, Canada, and a number of other countries, an international union of mountain guides (UIAGM; *see* Resources, *below*) is the organization. Accreditation means a school has met certain standards and uses approved teaching methods. Instructors must keep up on the latest technology and safety issues and participate in a peer review process. Look for schools accredited by AMGA, not just members of it; an organization can pay to be a member but does not have to meet standards or be subjected to peer review. Individual guides certified by either AMGA or UIAGM have passed rigorous exams and technical tests. These critical guidelines can indicate someone is a good climber, but they don't tell if he or she is a good teacher. Always ask how long a guide or instructor has been climbing; then ask specifically about his or her experience with family teaching. Even on the phone you can get a feel for whether a school or a guide will be accepting and welcoming.

**What is the ratio of students to instructors?** Three students to one teacher is an excellent ratio, though in some beginner classes a slightly higher ratio is acceptable because only one or two students will climb at a time.

**What kind of emergency training do you and your staff have?** You need someone trained in basic first aid and rock rescue, at a minimum. Although rock climbing has become a safer sport, it's best to climb with someone trained to help on the spot. Moreover, if someone in your group gets halfway up the rock face and can't make it down, you want a teacher who can help that person descend.

**What happens if my children or I panic halfway up a rock?** The truth is, both children and adults may be certain they can complete a climb until they actually get stuck. You don't want an instructor who uses teasing or belittling ("My five-year-old niece can do this climb" or "Crying is what babies do") to get frightened climbers to continue. Compassion, encouragement, and positive reinforcement are the skills good teachers use, and no student should be made to feel bad for making it only halfway up. There's always a next time.

**If my children are too young for regular courses, is private instruction an option?** Regular rock-climbing courses, like those for kayaking and some other sports, are often designated for teens and older. Most schools, however, do give private instructional trips for families with children as young as six.

**At what age can my child climb in a course without me?** You may be a more advanced climber, or you may feel that your child learns better with peers; you may even think your child will have more success with instruction if you aren't there. That's okay. Some schools have courses just for children, or they'll take children in courses without parents as long as parents give permission and can be reached if necessary. You can take your own class and be with your children after your climbs. If this kind of setup seems best for your family, find a school that will accommodate you.

**If lodging isn't provided, do you have a list of options or will you help with booking?** Many multi-day courses are in wonderful camping areas, and the prices for these sessions generally, but not always, include camping. Other courses take place near inns or motels; a number of areas even have special climbers' inns, with dorm-style lodging. Some climbing outfitters will help with lodging and book rooms for you; others may just give you a list and let you make reservations.

**What's included in the cost?** The prices for courses include guides, instruction, and technical climbing gear, such as harnesses and ropes, unless otherwise noted. Some outfitters supply helmets as part of the gear; others require you rent them. Rock-climbing shoes are available for rent from outfitters or from a local store recommended by the outfitter; a few outfitters, as noted, include shoes in the course price. Many, but not all, schools and guides provide local transportation to climbing sites. Most will also give clients information on local lodging, but lodging is not included, except as noted. Lunch is sometimes supplied, but more often you must bring your own, even if you are camping. With such a wide range of possibilities, it's a good idea to ask about specifics.

## Instruction

Rock climbing is not a sport you can teach yourself; instruction is an absolute must. All the courses and trips are instructional, whether they take place on the grounds of the school or on some of the most famous rock faces in the country.

## A Note About Ages

The minimum age listed first is for regularly scheduled outdoor courses. When two ages are given, the second is for private or indoor classes, depending on the school. Younger children are often accepted for private instruction, but few schools are willing to pinpoint a specific age. Read the complete listings for details. Most schools make the decision on a case-by-case basis, taking into consideration a child's previous climbing experience, athletic ability, familiarity with the wilderness, enthusiasm for the sport, and the parents' own attitudes and abilities.

### Finding the Fun

**Northeast:** Adirondack Rock & River Guide Service, Adventure Quest, Appalachian Mountain Club, Eastern Mountain Sports Climbing School, Zoar Outdoor. **Mid-Atlantic:** Appalachian Mountain Club. **South:** Outward Bound. **Midwest:** Sylvan Rocks Climbing School & Guide Service. **Southwest:** Eastern Mountain Sports Climbing School, Fantasy Ridge Mountain Guides. **Rockies:** Adventures to the Edge, Colorado Mountain School, Eastern Mountain Sports Climbing School, Exum Mountain Guides, Fantasy Ridge Mountain Guides, Sylvan Rocks Climbing School & Guide Service. **West Coast:** Alpine Skills International, American Alpine Institute, Eastern Mountain Sports Climbing School, Joshua Tree Rock Climbing School, Outward Bound. **Canada:** American Alpine Institute, Yamnuska, Inc. **South America:** Eastern Mountain Sports Climbing School. **Europe:** Adventures to the Edge.

## Favorite Schools and Outfitters

### Adirondack Rock & River Guide Service

**14+, 6+**

Rock & River, whose core curriculum is climbing, has an unsurpassed setting—the 6-million-acre Adirondack Park, birthplace of the mighty Hudson River and depository of some of the oldest rocks known to humanity. The park, which encompasses nearly two-thirds of upstate New York, is a geologist's and rock climber's dreamscape.

**FOR FAMILIES.** Adults and teens age 14 and up can take two-day courses in beginning and novice rock climbing. The student-teacher ratio is four to one in the beginner course, two to one in the novice. Low-key and no pressure are the operative descriptions of these courses. There's a 30-ft indoor wall at the school's facility, so courses run rain or shine; the introductory courses begin here. Children age six and up can be accommodated in private classes, and the school highly recommends these for families. You can also combine excellent adventures in remote regions of Adirondack State Park with private guiding and instruction, available for between one and five days.

This school has its own reasonably priced lodging, ranging from a streamside lean-to to lodge rooms with private baths. Lunch is included in courses.

*Adirondack Rock & River Guide Service, Box 219, Keene, NY 12942, tel. 518/576–2041. Apr.–Oct.: 1–5 days, $165–$395 per person in basic courses, $180–$740 for parent-child teams privately guided, $40 per day each additional child. Group rates available for families of 4 or more.*

### Adventure Quest

**7+**

The central Vermont town of Woodstock, on the Ottauquechee River, is most noted for its historic houses and classic New

England town square. Adventure Quest, one of the country's foremost outdoor schools, is committed to helping families learn and play together in challenging workshops here.

**FOR FAMILIES.** Family workshops on rock climbing last one or several days. A maximum of eight participants can range in age from seven to, well, who knows? Adventure Quest considers rock climbing a lifetime sport, one you can enjoy until you just don't want to do it anymore. In most cases families will start on the school's climbing wall and progress to local rock faces. The student-teacher ratio is three to one, and courses include lunch and local transportation.

The company now offers reasonably priced, motel-style lodging at its new property in Brownsville, Vermont. In spring and fall you can probably book space in Adventure Quest's campground if you prefer; in summer it's used for children (from ages 7 to 17) in the school's Mountain Quest and River Quest camp programs. Rock climbing is part of Mountain Quest. Families with widely differing abilities might consider signing the kids up for camp while parents take a course of their own during the day.
*Adventure Quest, Box 184, Woodstock, VT 05091, tel. 802/484–3939. Apr.–Oct.: 1–7 days, $275 per day for up to 4 people; $50 each additional family member. Mountain Quest: 6 days, $600.*

## Adventures to the Edge

7+

Swiss native Jean Pavillard of Colorado's Adventures to the Edge is exactly the sort of person you want to have with your family on a climb: competent, steady, calm, and compassionate. He has been certified by the international union of mountain guides (UIAGM) for more than 20 years. Adventures to the Edge excels in customized trips—in this country and in Europe—for all ages and abilities, and the outfitter will put together a climb for your family that will allow each of you to discover and conquer your own "edge."

The company is headquartered in Crested Butte, Colorado, a mountain town known for laid-back skiing in winter and mountain biking in summer. Much of the town's Victorian architecture has been preserved, yet Crested Butte is neither chi-chi nor cutesy. It's friendly but still rough around the edges—and a terrific place for vacationing families to relax between adventures.

**FOR FAMILIES.** Families with children age seven and up can climb in the forested backcountry outside Crested Butte or in Eldorado or Boulder canyons near the city of Boulder. Guides—generally in a ratio of two instructors to five students when children are present—teach throughout any adventure, and they're good at accommodating differing ages and abilities within a single group, making it fun for everyone. Adventures to the Edge also runs custom Kids' Camps, which might mix hiking, mountain biking, and overnight camping with rock climbing and rappelling. While the children are learning in their supervised environment, adults can go out with guides on a challenging adventure of their own.

Pavillard and his staff will assist with all aspects of your trip, including airline reservations and lodging. If you want fine food and wine as your standard rations, they'll arrange that, too, just as they'll create a budget climbing vacation. They also run weeklong summer climbing camps in Europe, as well as guided rock climbing tours—from seacliffs in the south of France to high Alpine cliffs above glaciers—that have the benefit of a native's inside knowledge in addition to a thorough understanding of American family adventurers. For multi-day trips Adventures to the Edge provides all gear except sleeping bags.
*Adventures to the Edge, Box 91, Crested Butte, CO 81224, tel. 970/349–5219 or 800/349–5219. Apr.–Oct.: 1 day, $150 for 2*

*adults, $35 per child. Apr.–Oct.: 2–7 days, $280 per day for a group of 3, plus guides' expenses; $50 per day for each additional group member. $600 for European climbing camps, plus airfare, lodging, and meals.*

## Alpine Skills International

12+

Based high in California's Sierra Nevada, surrounded by Tahoe National Forest, Alpine Skills International (ASI) has been teaching mountaineering and other backcountry skills for more than 20 years. With a lodge at Donner Pass that serves both as a headquarters and the focal point for camaraderie among its students, ASI offers excellent climbing and a cozy bed to return to each night. You may also want to see the nearby Donner Memorial State Park, which commemorates the infamous Donner Party, stranded there in 1846 by early blizzards; those who survived resorted to cannibalism to do so.

**FOR FAMILIES.** ASI has a number of possibilities for families. Klimbing Kids Rockskills, a class for climbers ages 12 through 17, is scheduled several times each summer. Its dates coincide with the Rockskills Seminar, a five-day course that accommodates beginning and experienced climbers, who learn or refine their techniques. Both courses are lodge-based and include four nights at the lodge, as well as breakfasts and dinners.

ASI will take families with children 12 and up in other courses as well. Talk with the directors about your youngsters first, however, and let them help you choose the right course and time. The most basic course is Rock Climbing . . . the Beginning, two days of learning skills and practicing on routes that present a variety of challenges. Once you are confident about basic belaying, rappelling (a method of descending), and movement, try the Next Move, the two-day intermediate course. The student-teacher ratio ranges from two to one to eight to one, depending on the course.

Some meals and lodging are included in ASI's course prices; bring your own sleeping bags, though.

*Alpine Skills International, Box 8, Norden, CA 95724, tel. 530/426–9108 or 888/274–7325. June–Sept.: 2–5 days, $144–$578.*

## American Alpine Institute

17+

The American Alpine Institute in northern Washington has access to excellent climbing sites in both the United States and Canada. This very technical school is for people who have a serious interest in climbing, especially those who are learning rock climbing as a foundation for other alpine skills, such as ice climbing, climbing with crampons, and ascending world-class peaks. But the school is also appropriate for some beginners. "If a skill is learned the correct and safe way the first time, it needs to be learned only once," the institute's brochure notes, and the school aims to help students do exactly that.

**FOR FAMILIES.** Regular courses are for people ages 17 and up. You can take the two-day Introduction to Rock or more advanced courses at a choice of locations in the Cascades or in Canada. Camping and lodging are available in most areas; the school will give you suggestions.

The Cascades are best known for their volcanoes (Mount St. Helens is probably the most famous), but these mountains are geographically and ecologically diverse. Two favorite areas for Intro to Rock are Leavenworth, on the warm and sunny east side of the Cascades, and Index, cooler and shadier because of its west-side location; both have fine-grained granite and a range of climbs. Because the region has excellent crags for both beginners and experts, it makes a particularly good destination for families whose members have varying experience and skills.

Forty miles north of Vancouver, British Columbia, and 90 mi above Bellingham, Washington, Howe Sound cuts into the Canadian coast to create a fjord almost 30 mi long. At the head of the fjord is the logging town of Squamish and its striking white-granite walls. Mountain bikers, sailboarders, and rock climbers come here, but it's still far from any crowds. Whether you're a beginner or an expert, you'll find a pitch and a climb here. Beginners can spend days on the Smoke Bluffs perfecting the one-pitch climb. Climbers who are ready for multipitch (rock faces with a variety of angles) and steep ascents can tackle the Apron, with more than 50 separate routes, or perhaps the Chief, a 2,000-ft wall of near-vertical granite.

Beginner courses have a maximum four to one student-teacher ratio, intermediates a maximum three to one. On guided climbs the ratio can range from one on one to five students per guide. The price changes accordingly. If parents and children choose private guiding, the institute will consider climbers under 17; however, previous backpacking experience and a demonstrated willingness to work well with adults are musts. Talk with the staff about your child's skills, physical ability, and experience.
*American Alpine Institute, 1515 12th St., Bellingham, WA 98225, tel. 360/671–1570. Mid-Apr.–Oct.: 1–5 days, $260–$1,250, depending on length and level of course and ratio of students to teacher. Private instruction and guiding cost $135–$250 per day, depending on student-teacher guide ratio.*

## Appalachian Mountain Club

10+

The Appalachian Mountain Club (AMC) has climbing courses at its outdoor centers in New Hampshire's White Mountains, New York's Catskills, and in the Delaware Water Gap National Recreation Area on the New Jersey–Pennsylvania border. White Mountains workshops take place in some 700,000 acres of national forest, with the Presidential Range as a backdrop. The instructor at the Catskills location is licensed by the state and teaches for Outward Bound as well. Families choosing workshops in the Delaware Water Gap Recreation Area in the Pocono Mountains use the Mohican Outdoor Center as a base. All areas have many recreational activities for all ages.

**FOR FAMILIES.** Although there is no minimum age for the courses listed below, the club suggests children ages 10 and up will probably benefit most from the technical information. You should notify AMC in advance that children will be taking the course so the instructor will be prepared.

In May, June, August, and September families can join Introduction to Rock Climbing in the White Mountains, famous for its Cathedral Ledge and White Horse cliffs. This two-day course is designed for beginners or those with little previous experience. You'll learn the technical aspects of climbing and bouldering (moving without a harness on rocks), including rappelling, tying harness and rope knots, and belaying. The price of the class covers two nights' lodging and meals. The club's lodge at Pinkham Notch Visitor Center accommodates more than 100 overnight guests in two-, three-, or four-bunk rooms. Pillows, linens, and towels are provided; you share bathrooms and hot shower facilities. The hearty meals are served family style, and you can buy trail lunches to take to your class.

Two-day beginner courses run in June and September at AMC's Catskill center. This is a real fundamentals course with orientation to equipment, knot tying, rope handling, top rope set-up, belaying, and more. All equipment is supplied and the course fee includes two nights' accommodations at the Valley View Lodge and most meals.

A Weekend on Rock is scheduled in June, August, and September at the Delaware Water Gap center. The course focuses on basic skills, such as equipment inspection, belaying, and rappelling. Lodging in rustic cabins and a stick-to-your-ribs dinner on Saturday night are included in the price. Cabins have bunk rooms that sleep from 4 to 10 people. Pillows are provided, but you have to bring other bedding and towels.

*Appalachian Mountain Club, Box 298, Gorham, NH 03581, tel. 603/466–2727 for general information, course catalog, or to register for White Mountain courses or 908/362–5670 to register for Delaware Water Gap course. May–Sept.: 2 days, $250–$340.*

## Colorado Mountain School

**14+, 4+**

The only guide service licensed to operate in Rocky Mountain National Park, Colorado Mountain School (CMS) has a personal, flexible approach to teaching. The wide choice of scheduled classes includes one-day to seven-day courses and climbs, and you can mix and match them for the combination that works best for your family.

Rocky Mountain National Park, with its high meadows and wildflowers set against Colorado's snowy peaks and deep blue skies, is an adventuring family's playground. Besides climbing here—where some of the world's great alpine climbers test themselves on such classics as Longs Peak—you can hike on more than 355 mi of trails, attend ranger talks, ride, and fish. Camping is good, too; there are five public campgrounds in the park and numerous private ones just outside it. Your family might also take a drive on Trail Ridge Road, which at 12,183 ft is the highest continuously paved road in the United States.

**FOR FAMILIES.** Children ages 14 and up can join regular classes. Your family can be your group, or you can ask to join another family with children of compatible ages (there are no guarantees, but the school will try). CMS takes a learn-by-doing approach, so plan on plenty of climbing even in beginner courses. The best bets for families are the three-day courses at all levels, which give you information and then let you practice and reinforce what you've learned. If you know rock climbing is for you, jump right into the five-or seven-day course. At the end of it you'll be climbing rocks other people can only dream about. CMS has taught children as young as four in private instruction; if you have very young children, ask them what they recommend.

*Colorado Mountain School, Box 1846, Estes Park, CO 80517, tel. 970/586–5758. May–Oct.: 1–7 days, $160–$962 for 2 climbers, discounts for groups of 3–4.*

## Eastern Mountain Sports Climbing School

**13+**

Affiliated with the outdoor stores of the same name, this school is serious about climbing and has classes in a variety of areas. It's headquartered in North Conway, New Hampshire, in the foothills of the White Mountains, where gently sloping granite cliffs—perfect for beginners and intermediates—abound.

Classes are also held in Connecticut in the Trapp Rock region, about 20 minutes west of Hartford, and in New York's Shawangunks, near New Paltz. The Gunks, as they are called, are climber-friendly even though they're steep because they have plenty of hand- and footholds. On weekends, however, they can get pretty crowded. In Colorado you can take basic courses all along the Front Range, including Boulder and Eldorado canyons.

**FOR FAMILIES.** Standard basic and intermediate courses, for ages 13 and up, run from one to four days. These courses, which cover all of the basics from movement techniques to belaying and rappelling, are given throughout the week in all of the school's locations across the country. The student-teacher ratio is three to one.

If your family is ready for serious treks, the school also offers destination climbing in Red Rocks, Nevada; in Joshua Tree National Park in California; in Canyonlands National Park in Utah; and in Ecuador. Rock shoes are supplied for domestic courses.

*Eastern Mountain Sports Climbing School, Main St., Box 514, North Conway, NH 03860, tel. 603/356–5433 or 800/310–4504. Apr.–Oct.: 1–4 days, $90–$580.*

## Exum Mountain Guides

13+

One of the top schools in the country, Exum has been teaching and guiding since 1926. The Tetons, northwestern Wyoming's spectacular, rugged peaks, provide a dramatic landscape on which to hone your skills.

When you aren't climbing, your family will find plenty to do in Grand Teton National Park, in nearby Yellowstone, and in the town of Jackson. Don't miss the nightly "shoot-out" in Jackson or the weekly rodeo, both summertime activities.

**FOR FAMILIES.** Adults and children age 14 and up can join one-day climbing schools at basic to advanced levels. Moms and daughters may be interested in Women That Rock, a course just for women. Exum also has one- and two-day climbs in various parts of the Tetons for ages 13 and up. The student-teacher ratio can go as high as eight to one in beginner courses, but six to one is far more common. Families with younger children should book a private guide; call the school first to discuss your child's physical ability, size, and experience.

Many students stay at the American Alpine Club Climbers' Ranch, 2 mi south of Jenny Lake, which offers bunks and the companionship of other climbers. The school will help you find other lodging if you wish.

*Exum Mountain Guides, Grand Teton National Park, Box 56, Moose, WY 83012, tel. 307/733–2297. May–Sept.: 1–2 days, $90–$430.*

## Fantasy Ridge Mountain Guides

ALL

"Fantasy Ridge is about having fun . . . learning about climbing on rock, snow, and ice; achieving an understanding of mountains, nature . . . It's about calculated risk, adventure, travel, friends, and . . . life." That quote from the Fantasy Ridge brochure sums up what's great about rock climbing in general and Fantasy Ridge in particular. The positive, confident attitude of the school and its instructors is passed on to their students.

Fantasy Ridge is based in Telluride, a town tucked into the mighty San Juans in southwestern Colorado and originally made famous by such desperadoes as Butch Cassidy, who robbed his first bank here in 1889. Today celebrities have put Telluride back on the map, but their presence hasn't changed the area's enduring beauty or its historical importance.

**FOR FAMILIES.** Although the school has no minimum age, there is a requirement for joining these courses: The children must want to do it. Director Michael Covington loves to teach children, but he won't accept any whose parents seem to be pressuring them into climbing.

The best bets for families are Stage One, a five-day seminar for novices, and Stage Two, also five days but for intermediate and advanced climbers, which includes moving on to 'Big Wall' techniques. The courses take place at Telluride's Ophir Wall, a 600-ft granite cliff; Elk Park, along the Animas River (you take the Durango–Silverton narrow-gauge railway to get there); or at Indian Creek, near Canyonlands National Park in Utah. Student-teacher ratios are four to one for Stage One, two to one for Stage Two. This company hosts many families, who can participate in regular courses and climbs as their own group, a less expensive alternative to private instruction, which is also available.

All five-day courses require camping, for which you will need some of your own gear. The company will help you find lodging for other courses.

*Fantasy Ridge Mountain Guides, Box 1679, Telluride, CO 81434, tel. 970/728–3546. Apr.–Sept.: 1 hr–5 days, $25–$875 for 2 people; ask about 15% to 20% discounts for families of 3 or more.*

## Joshua Tree Rock Climbing School

**13+, 4+**

Wind, weather, and time have eroded the outcroppings of California's Joshua Tree National Park into boulder gardens of arresting beauty. The rocks draw climbers and many other visitors, although the Joshua trees that gave the monument its name are striking in their own right. From September through June this American Mountain Guides Association–accredited school holds classes in Joshua Tree. During July and August lessons take place at Suicide and Tahquintz rocks, 7,000 ft up in the cool pine forests of the San Jacinto Mountains above Palm Springs. Both areas are less than 50 mi from Palm Springs and about three hours from San Diego and Los Angeles.

**FOR FAMILIES.** Parents and teens age 13 and up can participate in any of the regular courses. The basic two-day rock seminar is most popular with beginners, but there are also four-day seminars for beginner, intermediate and advanced climbers. The student-teacher ratio is a maximum of five to one in the school's basic courses.

Families with children as young as four or five can arrange private guiding and instruction. A family of four can save money by signing up for private instruction during the week, when the cost is only $5 more per person than for a scheduled class. For groups of eight or more, Rock Climbing Experience (ages four or five and up welcome) gives you private instruction at a very family-friendly rate.

The school supplies rock shoes for students of all ages and will give you the names and numbers of motels and campgrounds near the climbing sites.

*Joshua Tree Rock Climbing School, HCR Box 3034, Joshua Tree, CA 92252, tel. 760/366–4745 or 800/890–4745. Year-round, courses: 1–4 days, $80–$295. Private guiding and instruction are $90–$110 per person per day, for a group of 3 or 4.*

## Outward Bound

**14+**

Outward Bound's goal is to help students expand self-awareness individually and as members of a working team and to have them leave a course knowing they are capable of things they never believed possible. The organization's parent-child rock climbing course begins and ends in Asheville in North Carolina's Appalachian and Great Smoky mountains. Lush and green, this region has the highest peaks in the Appalachians, as well as trails, white-water rivers, and historic sites to explore before or after your course.

**FOR FAMILIES.** The eight-day parent-child sessions for ages 14 and up combine rock climbing and backpacking, in addition to a ropes course. You have your choice of three summer dates. Aside from the basics of rock climbing—top-rope and multi-pitch techniques, rappelling, and safety skills—a good portion of the course focuses on learning how to navigate and camp in the wilderness. Outward Bound supplies some equipment. The organization doesn't feel rock shoes are a necessity.

*Outward Bound, Rte. 9D, R2 Box 280, Garrison, NY 10524, tel. 800/243–8520. Parent-child course, June–Aug.: 8 days, $945 per person.*

## Sylvan Rocks Climbing School & Guide Service

10+

Rich in history and legend, the Black Hills of South Dakota have ghost towns, craggy peaks, lakes, and, of course, the Mount Rushmore National Monument and Crazy Horse Memorial. The vast Black Hills National Forest spreads over more than a million acres. Legend says Paul Bunyan built the hills as a cairn for his huge blue ox, Babe, when Babe died after eating a red-hot stove and too many giant flapjacks. Not surprisingly, geologists beg to differ, claiming the Black Hills are the result of a massive geologic uplift that pushed a dome of ancient granite to the earth's surface.

However the hills were formed, the area is a vacationer's and climber's delight. Here Sylvan Rocks provides its students with physical and mental challenges, safe climbing, fun, and teachers who have not only extensive climbing experience but the ability and attitude to teach all ages and all levels. The school is accredited by the American Mountain Guides Association.

**FOR FAMILIES.** The two-day beginner package is for parents and children 10 and up. It focuses on building confidence on steep rock faces, safety, proper use of equipment, tying knots, belaying, and rappelling. The second day takes you out on awesome summits to reinforce the previous day's instruction. The maximum student-teacher ratio is four to one. Climbing shoes and all gear are included in beginner packages.

There are also one- to five-day classes. Those who have completed basic courses can join trips to Devils Tower (the northeastern Wyoming formation made famous in the movie *Close Encounters of the Third Kind*), and there are trips to climbing meccas such as Joshua Tree, too.

*Sylvan Rocks Climbing School & Guide Service, Box 600, Hill City, SD 57745, tel. 605/574–2425. Apr.–Oct.: 1–3 days, $115–$350, depending on length and level of course and student-teacher ratio. Devils Tower: $175–$250 per day, depending on climber/guide ratio. Call for prices on other trips.*

## Yamnuska, Inc.

14+, 6+

Canmore, on the boundary of Banff National Park in Alberta, was once a mining town supplying coal to the railroad. Now it serves as a base for many recreational activities in the nearby mountains. The majestic Canadian Rockies provide plenty of rewards for both new and experienced climbers. From the international airport at Calgary, it's an easy drive to Canmore and also to the interior ranges of British Columbia, where Yamnuska schedules some of its trips.

**FOR FAMILIES.** Parents and children age 14 and up are welcome on weekend courses. Basic Rock, Basic Rock Plus, and Advanced Rock are all two- to four-day courses. Complete Rock is six days of intensive instruction; talk to the school about your teen before signing him or her up for this more adult-oriented course. Group instruction ratios range from six to one to two to one, depending on the difficulty of the climbs. Yamnuska also has extensive private instruction, which it highly recommends for families. If your children are at least six years old, you can schedule private guiding and courses in and around Banff, Canmore, and Lake Louise, all areas with much to offer whether you're climbing or not. If you have a teen interested in mountaineering, Yamnuska also offers a week-long Intro to Mountaineering course for ages 13 to 17 in July; it's based on the Wapta Icefields just north of Lake Louise.

Banff and Canmore have reasonably priced lodging; in the mountains, Yamnuska often uses huts, which are available to its clients at nominal rates. You can rent shoes, but they are not available in very small sizes.
*Yamnuska, Inc., #200, 50–103 Bow Valley Trail, Canmore, Alberta, Canada T1W 1N8, tel. 403/678–4164. May–Sept.: 1–6 days, $115–$560, Intro to Mountaineering, C$735. Call for private guiding rates.*

## Zoar Outdoor

10+

Cool, densely forested, and green, the Berkshire Mountains of Massachusetts have several excellent climbing locations and are one of the most popular vacation destinations in the eastern United States. Zoar's 80-acre complex in Charlemont, in the far northwest corner of the state, is just a short drive from Chapel and Rose ledges, two excellent places for families to learn together. Zoar's experience working with families and children is extensive, and the school truly welcomes them in classes.

**FOR FAMILIES.** Zoar's parent-child clinic, a two-day beginner course for climbers ages 10 and up and their parents, is designed to promote communication and trust between parents and their children while they enjoy the fun and challenge of climbing. These clinics, with a student-teacher ratio of six to one, cover basic climbing skills. The center's regular rock climbing clinics are one- to five-day sessions aimed at ages 14 through adult. Beginner courses are one or two days, intermediate clinics are two-day adventures. Private instruction is also available.

You can stay in Zoar's campground for a nominal fee (using your equipment or theirs), or they'll help you book lodging at a nearby motel, inn, or bed-and-breakfast.
*Zoar Outdoor, Box 254, Charlemont, MA 01339, tel. 413/339–4010 or 800/532–7483. May–Oct.: 1–5 days, $105–$450. Private instruction runs $110–$225 per day, depending on the number of students.*

# Resources

## Organizations

The **American Mountain Guides Association** (AMGA; 710 10th St., Suite 101, Golden, CO 80401, tel. 303/271–0984) can send you a list of accredited schools and certified guides across the country.

The address of the international guides' association, **Union Internationalle Association Guide Montagne** (UIAGM), changes with each president, but you can write to the Vaud chapter president, René Pavillard (brother of Jean Pavillard of Adventures to the Edge), at Box 26, 1854 Leysin, Vaud, Switzerland. He'll answer your questions or forward correspondence.

## Periodicals

*Climbing* (0326 Hwy. 133, Suite 190, Carbondale, CO 81623, tel. 970/963–9449) publishes eight issues a year plus a gear guide and occasionally has articles on family climbing and on introducing children to the sport.

# RV ADVENTURES

When our children were 1, 5, and 11 years old, Bill and I piled them into a 27-ft motor home and traveled from Virginia to Florida and back, stopping at campgrounds each night. Since then we've logged more than 21,000 mi in various recreational vehicles (RVs) and covered most of the country, visiting national parks and monuments, national and state forests, and a variety of private and public campgrounds. My children rank these among their best vacations ever.

Recreational vehicles are ideal for family vacations, including intergenerational trips with grandparents. Young families are the fastest-growing segment of the RV population, and with good reason: RVs get you into the outdoors and the wilderness safely and easily. Very young children, who are unfamiliar with sleeping bags, latrines, and tents in the middle of the woods, may feel more at ease in an RV than at a backcountry campsite. Families with infants can take a two-week camping trip and still have a way to refrigerate and warm formula or baby food. For parents who worry that a toddler might wake up and wander away from a tent in the middle of the night, RVs have doors that lock. Many grandparents are likely to appreciate the physical comfort of an RV adventure, too.

Many campgrounds that welcome RVs have spacious wilderness surroundings and privacy; some are veritable outdoor resorts, with a restaurant, hiking trails, fishing, boating, and swimming. Some have hookups that allow you to use the campground's water and electrical supplies; others are remote sites providing only a relatively level spot in a spectacular setting.

Because different kinds of places appeal to different people, this chapter describes a range of RV destinations: national parks, forests, and monuments; state parks; and private campgrounds. The selections are based on my family's experience and the opinions of other seasoned RV travelers. Keep in mind that there's no reason a family has to stay at the same type of campground every night. You can opt for a full-service RV resort one night; the next evening you might camp in a wilderness area with nature's own amenities—a sky full of stars and a peaceful, welcoming solitude.

Note: At press time the National Park Service had a toll-free number for reservations at 16 national parks, as well as several national seashores, lakeshores, historic sites, and recreation areas. That number, 800/365–CAMP (800/365–2267), is listed for applicable parks. Call ahead to find out how far in advance you can reserve a spot. You can also check the National Park Service Web site, www.nps.gov, for latest information.

## Questions to Ask

**Where can I rent or buy an RV?** There are RV dealers across the country; many have both sales and rental departments. Look under "Recreation Vehicles—Renting and Leasing" in the yellow pages for the sources nearest you. For a complete listing of dealers, contact any of the RV organizations listed in Resources (*see below*), such as the Go RVing Coalition or the Recreation Vehicle Rental Association.

**What kinds of RVs are best?** You have many options. Some families prefer motor homes, all-in-one vehicles that range in length from 17 ft to 40 ft. In a motor home you can get snacks and use the bathroom without having to stop and search for a gas station or restaurant. (Children and adults should always be buckled into seat belts or car seats when the vehicle is in motion.) Another choice is a pop-up, which you tow with your car by day and literally pop up into a spacious and well-equipped camper at night; beds, bathroom, and often a refrigerator and air conditioner are included. Truck campers (those fitted onto the bed of a pickup truck) and full-size travel trailers (fully equipped trailer homes you tow) are also available. Prices vary greatly according to the size of the vehicle and, if you're renting, the season.

**How far in advance is it necessary to reserve?** Summer is the most popular time for RV vacations; rental companies may well be out of the vehicle you want on a particular week unless you book several months in advance.

**Are RVs allowed in all campgrounds?** No, but they are welcome in most. Some sites, especially publicly owned campgrounds, may have a size limit for RVs. Listings in campground directories and government campground publications often mention the maximum length allowed; read the specifications carefully.

**What kind of gas mileage do RVs get?** If you're driving a motor home, from 6 to 12 mi per gallon is possible; about 8 mi per gallon is typical. Pulling a car or boat behind your RV will decrease the mileage your car ordinarily gets. Other factors affecting mileage are your vehicle's engine size and capabilities, the type of terrain, and the weight of the RV. Pulling a pop-up or trailer home with your car will affect your gas mileage, too.

**What service is available in case of a breakdown?** Before your trip, find out whether your RV rental company has breakdown insurance or a roadside help policy that will cover you. You might also consider joining the Good Sam Club (*see* Resources, *below*), which offers road service for RVs.

**How is sewage disposal handled?** Dumping waste is easier than it sounds. When you pick up your rental RV, you'll learn how to attach a hose to a campground's sewer hookups and how to flush the waste by opening and closing valves. Keep a pair of gloves handy for handling the waste hose. If you stay at a campground without sewer hookups, eventually you will have to stop at a campground with a dump station and pay a fee of a few dollars to empty your waste tanks. A good campground directory (see Resources, *below*) will tell you where to find dump stations. You will always need to return your rental with the waste tanks emptied.

**What is the electrical source in an RV, and can it be tapped only when the RV is parked?** Most campgrounds have electrical hookups—outlets into which you plug the RV's heavy-duty electrical cord. If there are no hookups, you switch on the generator found in most RVs. With few exceptions, the only time you'll need your generator while driving is if you use the microwave, the water pump (either to make the sink faucet run or to flush the toilet), or the VCR, or if you need additional air-conditioning or heat. When you've stopped in a campground without hookups, you'll use the generator for all of the above and for lights. In most modern RVs the refrigerator and stove work on propane (included in rentals), so even when you're parked and the generator is off, your refrigerator will stay cool, and you'll be able to use the stove.

**If I'm renting a pop-up and towing it with my car, do I need a special hitch?** Some companies can supply what you need; others require that you purchase a low-cost part. Ask before you rent.

**What's included in the cost of a rental?** This varies widely, so shop around. Generally speaking, you get the vehicle at a daily or weekly rate plus a mileage allowance—typically 100 mi per day. Beyond these basics, there are many variations. Bedding packages, for example, are available from some suppliers; dishes, silverware, and pots and pans may or may not cost extra. Some suppliers have CD players, TVs, and VCRs, which give antsy children something to watch when they can't see out the window at night. Before renting an RV, consider the options and your needs, and then judge the prices accordingly. Also, ask whether you'll incur an extra charge if the gas and propane tanks aren't filled when you return the RV.

**What's included in the cost of a campground?** Campgrounds charge per RV site. The base rate is generally for two adults and does not include hookups (these are the rates quoted in the individual listings). Another $1 or $2 per night is added for water and electricity, and sewage hookups cost an additional $2–$3. A nominal fee is charged for children—typically $2–$4 per night. Most campgrounds let very young children stay for free, although the age cutoff varies widely. If you're camping in a national park, a national monument, or a state park, you may be required to pay a separate park entrance fee. If your family plans to visit a number of national parks and monuments, consider buying a Golden Eagle Passport, which costs only $50 and covers the entrance fees to all parks that you visit during one year. These passes are available at any park with an entrance fee. Golden Age ($10, for visitors who are at least 62) and Golden Access (free for people with disabilities) passes must be purchased in person. These have no expiration date.

## Instruction

Most rental companies will show you how to work everything before you leave in your vehicle. RVs aren't hard to drive, but they take a little getting used to. If you've never driven an RV, ask for pointers on how to back up, how to hook up the electrical and water lines at campgrounds, and how to dump waste water. Make certain you also know how the generator works, and listen to safety instructions about which switches must be shut off when you stop for gas.

## Finding the Fun

Because each adventure option in this chapter is in a fixed destination, the selections below are organized by region.

# Favorite RV Destinations

## *Northeast*

### Lake Placid/Whiteface Mountain KOA

ALL

Kampgrounds of America, known far and wide as KOA, is a national chain of campgrounds. KOAs are privately owned but must meet standards set by the national headquarters, so certain features and facilities remain consistent. All are family-friendly, and prices are reasonable—even more so if you get a KOA Value Kard (see Resources, *below*). Showers and rest rooms are clean and well maintained; you can generally find a playground and a well-stocked store and/or a snack bar; and there are almost always outdoor activities for families. Pools, lakes, or streams are quite common, and KOAs generally welcome pets. Many KOAs now have Kamping Kabins, too, so grandparents or other non-RVers can meet you on vacation and have a place of their own.

The Lake Placid/Whiteface Mountain KOA is an excellent choice for families visiting northern New York. Just 9 mi northeast of the town of Lake Placid, in the heart of Adirondack Park and the ancient Adirondack Mountains, this 85-acre campground gives you access to many outdoor adventures. Although the facility is not remote, its pine and white birch forest setting at the base of Whiteface Mountain is splendid.

**FOR FAMILIES.** In the summer you can hike or fish right at the campground along a ½-mi stretch of the Ausable River, famous for its trout. Other campground activities are canoeing, tennis, miniature golf, swimming, and in winter, cross-country skiing. A choice of full and partial hookup and non-hookup sites (144 in all) gives families plenty of options.

Adirondack Park is an excellent place for hiking, rock climbing, and multi-day canoeing; Whiteface Mountain has great skiing, too. Lake Placid has hosted the Winter Games twice, and the Olympic facilities are well worth touring.

*Lake Placid/Whiteface Mountain KOA, Fox Farm Rd., Wilmington, NY 12997, tel. 518/946–7878 or 800/562–0368 for reservations only. Year-round: $20–$32 per night.*

# *Mid-Atlantic*

## Shenandoah National Park

ALL

National parks are among the most popular RV camping destinations. All are excellent for families on adventures, but some parks have special appeal for RVers. One of these is Shenandoah, which lies along a breathtaking stretch of the Blue Ridge Mountains in northwestern Virginia. Within the park, the 105-mi-long Skyline Drive follows the crest of the mountains and is one of the most scenic roads in America and a must for anyone on wheels. Also, one hundred miles of the Maine-to-Georgia Appalachian Trail runs through the park, approximately parallel to Skyline Drive. If you want to hike a portion of it, you'll need a backcountry permit.

**FOR FAMILIES.** Big Meadows Campground, site of one of the park's two visitor centers, is among the most popular campgrounds in the park; reservations are essential between May and October, at least on weekends. There's a restaurant at Big Meadows and access to the Appalachian Trail. Three other campgrounds—Lewis Mountain, Mathews Arm, and Loft Mountain—have sites available on a first-come, first-served basis. None of the campgrounds has hookups.

The park has excellent opportunities for hiking, fishing, and bird-watching. Ranger-led family programs in summer give children and parents insight into the natural world of Shenandoah.

*Shenandoah National Park, Superintendent, 3655 U.S. 211E, Luray, VA 22835, tel. 540/999–3500 or 800/365–CAMP for reservations. Mar.–Oct.: $14–$17 per night plus $10 park entrance fee.*

# *The South*

## Chattahoochee National Forest

ALL

The many national forests scattered throughout the United States are another terrific camping option for RVing families. Although most have true wilderness settings, it's not unusual for a national forest campground to be close to a major city, near well-maintained roads; such is the case with Chattahoochee National Forest. This wild land of deep gorges and rushing water lies about 100 mi north of Atlanta, close to the Tennessee and North Carolina borders. The Appalachian Mountains in northern Georgia are untamed but remarkably accessible.

**FOR FAMILIES.** Lake Conasauga Campground is within Chattahoochee National Forest, about 20 mi north of the town of Chatsworth. An extensive network of hiking trails readily accessible from local roads makes this area ideal for RV adventures. The 35 campsites (plus overflow area) have no hookups, but the campground has what most families love—a lake. No motors are allowed on the water, so you can fish, boat, and swim in peace. This is a primitive campground with no amenities—just gorgeous scenery to explore and enjoy.

*Chattahoochee National Forest, Cohutta Ranger District, 401 GI Maddox Parkway, Chatsworth, GA 30705, tel. 706/695–6736. Apr.–Oct.: $8 per night.*

## Cherokee/Great Smokies KOA

ALL

This KOA is in Cherokee, North Carolina, at one of the gateways to Great Smoky Mountains National Park (*see below*). If you want to take a break from exploring wilderness or America's highways, you can spend a couple of days here taking advantage of all that's at your RV's doorstep. Between activities at the campground and excursions to the park and the town of Cherokee, your family will have plenty to do.

**FOR FAMILIES.** At the campground three stocked trout ponds provide a perfect outlet for the youngest anglers; you can rent fishing poles at the KOA store. Among the other facilities are a playground, tennis courts, a pool and a river for swimming, and a hot tub. Most of the 430 sites have hookups. For those who want to leave their RVs parked and set up, the campground has shuttle service into the national park and other local attractions.

Besides outdoor recreation, families can experience the cultural aspect of the area, which has long been inhabited by the Cherokee. A short drive from the campground are many Native American institutions and sites, including the Cherokee Heritage Museum and Gallery, with an interpretive center that focuses on tribal culture and history; the Oconaluftee Indian Village, a replica of a native village of about 250 years ago; and the Museum of the Cherokee Indian. All have valuable information about the Cherokee people's past, present, and future.

*Cherokee/Great Smokies KOA, Star Rte. 39, Cherokee, NC 28719, tel. 828/497–9711 or 800/825–8352 for reservations only. Year-round: $19–$34 per night; children under 18 free.*

## Everglades National Park

ALL

Not all national parks are summer destinations. In fact, although Everglades National Park in southern Florida is open year-round, the best time to visit is in late fall or winter, when insects are not a problem and the heat and humidity are quite bearable. Renting an RV is also less expensive in winter, so if savings are important to your family, a winter RV trip to Everglades National Park may be rewarding in many ways.

**FOR FAMILIES.** Encompassing 1.5 million acres, Everglades National Park is a fragile ecosystem that supports an astonishingly diverse population of plants and animals; children of all ages will find it intriguing. Though much of the park is accessible only by boat, land activities—such as hikes, bird-watching treks, and interpretive programs—are also highlights. Rangers give talks throughout the year, but these are far more frequent in the winter months.

Flamingo Campground, in the park at the southern entrance, has no hookup facilities or hot showers, but it is the site of one of the park's visitor centers. The 340 campsites are available by reservation. Campers can explore adjacent hiking trails and rent canoes or skiffs for water-based exploration. Six miles from the park's southern entrance is the 108-site Long Pine Key campground, which has no hookup facilities or showers, but does have a network of hiking trails through the pine forests around it.

*Everglades National Park, Superintendent, 40001 State Rd. 9336, Homestead, FL 33034, tel. 305/242–7700 or 800/365–CAMP for campground reservations from mid-Nov.–mid-Apr. Year-round: $14 per night plus $10 per vehicle park entrance fee.*

## Great Smoky Mountains National Park

ALL

Because the Smokies are a wonderful—and popular—family destination, it pays to know more than one camping option (see Cherokee/Great Smokies KOA, *above*). Families that want to concentrate on Great Smoky Mountains National Park, which straddles North Carolina and Tennessee, may find that staying inside the park is the best way to experience it fully.

**FOR FAMILIES.** The park's verdant deciduous forests shelter more than 1,600 types of flowering plants, as well as bears and other wildlife. If your children love flowers, and if they have even a remote interest in birds, this is the place to be. The park has nature walks and interpretive programs for all ages virtually year-round. Two facilities, The Great Smoky Mountains Institute at Tremont and The Smoky Mountain Field School, also offer programs for families, children, and adults. You can ride horses on well-maintained trails. Although the park merits a visit on its own, your family can combine a stay with other adventures that take place nearby; the Canoeing, Kayaking, Rock Climbing, *and* Trekking with Llamas and Burros chapters all list outfitters in the vicinity.

Three of the park's 10 campgrounds—Elkmont, Cades Cove, and Smokemont—can be reserved in advance. The rest take campers on a first-come, first-served basis. None of the park's campgrounds has hookups or showers; plan to fill your water tank before arriving so you can shower, cook, and use the bathroom in your RV.

*Great Smoky Mountains National Park, Superintendent, 107 Park Headquarters Rd., Gatlinburg, TN 37738, tel. 423/436–1200 or 800/365–CAMP for reservations. Year-round: $10–$15 per night; there are no park entrance fees.*

## Mammoth Cave National Park

ALL

This national park has a single focus—the Mammoth Cave. The longest cave system in the world, Mammoth extends for more than 350 mi, and much of it remains unexplored. Most parents don't feel experienced enough to take their children caving on their own, but at Mammoth you can combine an RV trip with a highly informative guided caving adventure.

**FOR FAMILIES.** If the huge vertical shafts and eerie underground rivers don't impress your children, the strange inhabitants of the caves surely will; these include eyeless fish, white spiders, and blind beetles, though you're most likely to see cave crickets and bats. Exploring the caves with park rangers is the main event here; cave walks of various lengths and varying degrees of difficulty make it possible for almost anyone to visit, and some tours are designed especially for children. You'll be equipped with hard hats and miner's lights. There's a minimum age of 10 on some cave tours. For those adventurers who prefer to stay above ground, the park has backcountry hiking trails, guided nature walks, summer interpretive programs, and boating.

None of the three park campgrounds has hookups, and only two take reservations. Headquarters Campground has 111 sites with hot showers and a laundry; Maple Springs is for groups and campers with horses. Houchins Ferry has just 12 primitive sites and does not accept reservations. Also keep in mind that although the park is open year-round, its stores and services are open seasonally.

*Mammoth Cave National Park, Box 7, Mammoth Cave, KY 42259, tel. 270/758–2328 or 800/365–CAMP for reservations. For cave tours ($3.50–$35), call 800/967–2283. Mar.–Nov.: $5–$20 per night; there's no entrance fee to park.*

# *Midwest*

## Porcupine Mountains Wilderness State Park

ALL

State parks are an excellent camping choice for families with RVs. Some are primarily back-to-nature experiences with little in the way of amenities, which suits those families looking for a great place to camp in the woods. Porcupine Mountains Wilderness

State Park is just such a place—a 60,000-acre wilderness area on the northwest end of Michigan's Upper Peninsula, not far from the Wisconsin border. It's got a visitor center with multi-media programs and exhibits.

**FOR FAMILIES.** Otters, bears, coyotes, grouse, deer, and bald eagles all make their home among the forests, streams, and mountains here. Humans, too, are in evidence, hiking the trails in spring, summer, and fall and cross-country or downhill skiing in winter. Fishing, swimming, and picnicking are other prime activities in the park, or your family can spend time simply relishing the sight of deep gorges and awesome waterfalls. Rangers offer guided hikes and programs throughout the year. Union Bay Campground has 100 sites with electrical hookups; Presque Isle Campground has 90 sites, none with hookups. Both have flush toilets and showers. For families ready for a more backcountry adventure, there are 16 hike-in wilderness cabins.

*Porcupine Mountains Wilderness State Park, 412 S. Boundary, Ontonagon, MI 49953, tel. 906/885–5275. Year-round: campgrounds, $6–$14 per night; cabins, $45 per night; vehicles, $4 per night. Children 12 and under ski free.*

## Rafter J Bar Ranch Campground

ALL

The Rafter J Bar is about as family-friendly and action-packed as a campground can get. Like many other private campgrounds, it's a destination in itself, a place traveling families can stay put for a couple of days—or longer—and enjoy a campground just as they would a hotel or resort. The area has plenty to attract families: South Dakota's Black Hills, in which the Rafter J Bar is set, are filled with history, legends, and adventure opportunities (see Rock Climbing *and* Covered Wagon Adventures). The ranch is an easy drive from Mt. Rushmore, Crazy Horse Monument, Wind Cave National Park, Mammoth Site of Hot Springs, and Custer State Park.

**FOR FAMILIES.** The Rafter J Bar sits at a 5,200-ft elevation, among wooded, rolling hills. Large meadows separate five camping areas shaded by ponderosa pines; most of the 258 sites have full or partial hookups. The campground has a pool and a hot tub, and four lakes are a short distance from the ranch. You can rent bikes and have access to the 35 mi of the George S. Mickelson Hiking/Biking Trail right from the ranch. Families can also ride horses on a trail in the Black Hills National Forest. Those too young for the trail have supervised pony rides at the campground and use of the playground. A trout stream on the property entices anglers; bring your own poles. Rental cars are available for people who want to explore while leaving their RV parked and hooked up.

If non-RVing family members or friends want to join you on vacation, this is a great place to meet. The Rafter J Bar has cabins that sleep six people.

*Rafter J Bar Ranch, Box 128, Hill City, SD 57745, tel. 605/574–2527 or 888/723–8375. May–Oct.: $21–$29 per night for 2 people; cabins start at $38 per night.*

# *Southwest*

## Lake Powell Resorts & Marinas

ALL

These campgrounds are less intriguing for their amenities than for their location—on the shores of Lake Powell. This 186-mi-long stretch of brilliant blue, banked by imposing red-rock formations and sandy beaches, starts just below the Arizona border and extends well into Utah. Families come to Lake Powell from all over the country to try their hands at piloting a houseboat (see

Houseboating) and to explore other parts of the Glen Canyon National Recreation Area, which covers more than a million acres. At nearly every campground families can combine RVing with boating and hiking adventures.

**FOR FAMILIES.** Lake Powell Resorts & Marinas operates National Park Service campgrounds as well as its own private campgrounds in the same locations: Wahweap, Bullfrog, and Hall's Crossing. The park service sites are primitive, with no hookups, and no reservations are accepted, but the campgrounds do have interpretive programs by rangers throughout the summer. The private campgrounds accept reservations and have full services and full hookups.

At the south end of the lake, near Page, Arizona, are the Wahweap campgrounds. The company runs a lodge, as well as a marina that sells groceries and camping supplies, and it's a place where you can rent a houseboat and set out to explore the lake. The park service visitor center here has exhibits that appeal to all ages.

Hall's Crossing and Bullfrog, at the lake's midpoint but on opposite shores, also have marinas; Bullfrog has a visitor center. You can rent houseboats at these marinas, and the ferry between the two takes RVs.

In addition to standard services at all the marinas, good-value RV packages combine two nights at camp with boat tours or houseboat rentals. You can also make reservations for Colorado River float trips—although there's no white water—through this company.

*Lake Powell Resorts & Marinas, Box 56909, Phoenix, AZ 85079, tel. 602/278–8888 or 800/528–6154. Year-round: $18–$25 per night.*

## Palo Duro Canyon State Park

**ALL**

In the middle of the horizon-to-horizon desolation of the Texas Panhandle, about 18 mi south of Amarillo, Palo Duro Canyon is an improbable paradise of all-encompassing beauty. At 110 mi long, the canyon is one of the largest in the country, and it will intrigue even those who thought they had no interest in geology. Its bottom layer of rock matches the top layer of the Grand Canyon; if you set Palo Duro on top of the Grand Canyon, every known geologic layer of the earth would be represented. The area has more than canyon walls of muted purple, red, and gold, though: Palo Duro State Park combines an extraordinary landscape with a multitude of services and amenities.

**FOR FAMILIES.** You can camp in a variety of places in the canyon's bottomland. Cottonwoods, grasslands, and the Prairie Dog Town Fork of the Red River create shady, pleasant spots from which to explore. Of the seven camping areas, which have a total of about 150 sites for RVs and tents, some have electricity and water, others only water.

Families can try hiking and mountain biking trails; the park's trading post rents bikes. The Lighthouse Hiking Trail is 5 mi round-trip, but very young children can walk the first part of it at least. Be alert for interesting creatures along the way—you might even see tarantulas in their native habitat. For a moderate fee you can also take a trail ride on horseback.

If you have older children who can stay up late, don't miss the summer production of *Texas!* at the amphitheater. The canyon walls serve as a backdrop, and a brilliant fireworks display ends the show.

*Palo Duro Canyon State Park, Rte. 2, Box 285, Canyon, TX 79015, tel. 806/488–2227 or 512/389–8900 for reservations only. Year-round: $9–$12 per night plus $3 per adult park entrance fee.*

## *Rockies*

### Colorado National Monument

ALL

Administered by the park service, national monuments range from natural landmarks to man-made structures and sites of historical importance. The Colorado National Monument falls under the first category: Vast canyons, towering monoliths, and unusual rock formations create compelling vistas at this often-overlooked site near Grand Junction. Hikers, bikers, and rock climbers find challenges in and near the monument. The area is also a favorite among dinosaur lovers, who come to participate in digging expeditions at nearby Mygatt-Moore Quarry and to visit the superb Devil's Canyon Science & Learning Center (*see* Digging for Dinosaur Bones and Other Fossils). Families will enjoy the monument for its own sake, however, and for its campground high above the canyon floor, on the scenic rim drive.

**FOR FAMILIES.** Peace and quiet abound at the 5,800-ft-high Saddlehorn Campground, a relatively primitive campground with 80 sites, but only a few can accommodate RVs, depending on the size of the vehicle. None have hookups. The campground does not accept reservations. Hikers of all abilities will find plenty of trails leading down from the canyon rim; the hardy can hike from the canyon floor up. For families with very young children, an excellent, easy nature walk of about ½ mi begins at the visitor center, just down the road from the campground on the rim drive. Another hike popular with families ends at Devil's Kitchen, a canyon formation that looks like a huge red-rock kitchen, complete with appliances. You can reach that trail from the lower road. There's also a junior ranger program.

*Colorado National Monument, Superintendent, Fruita, CO 81521, tel. 970/858-3617. Year-round: $10 per night plus $4 per vehicle entrance fee.*

### Great Sand Dunes National Monument

ALL

At the base of the jagged Sangre de Cristo Mountains in south-central Colorado are the 750-ft-high dunes of the Great Sand Dunes National Monument. Because they rise from a base of more than 8,000 ft above sea level, these are the highest dunes in North America—and a unique playground for families. The campground of the monument provides a very different perspective from that at Colorado National Monument (*see above*), one from which you look up, not down, for the best views.

**FOR FAMILIES.** You can hike for miles, find places to be alone, and play in Medano Creek at the monument—but you probably won't be able to get your children to do anything but jump like crazy around the dunes. Although interpretive talks and nature activities are given throughout the summer, the ideal time to visit is in late spring and early summer, because the creek dries up by August. It's best to walk on the dunes in the early morning and late afternoon—they're often too hot in the middle of the day.

Pinyon Flats Campground, the only one in the monument, has nearly 90 RV sites, but not all the spaces can accommodate vehicles of every size. Although the campground has no hookups and no reservations, being inside the monument makes up for it. On many weekends Pinyon Flats fills; if this happens you'll be directed to Great Sand Dunes Oasis, a campground and lodge just outside the monument that's nearly as good an option. For more information on other activities within the monument, check out the visitor center on U.S. 150.

*Great Sand Dunes National Monument, 11999 U.S. 150, Mosca, CO 81146, tel. 719/378–2312. Year-round: $10 per night plus $3 per adult entrance fee.*

## West Coast

### Big Bear Shores RV Resort & Yacht Club

**ALL**

Big Bear Shores is an excellent example of a private RV resort and campground right in the middle of a national forest. California's huge San Bernardino National Forest stretches from the city of San Bernardino to Palm Springs and encompasses several wilderness areas, ski areas, mountains, and lakes. The facility is in Big Bear Lake, a resort town that has become a year-round community with an emphasis on outdoor activities.

**FOR FAMILIES.** At Big Bear Shores RV Resort, on the shoreline of Big Bear Lake and 6,700 ft up in the San Bernardino Mountains, you can indulge in lake and pool swimming, relaxing in hot tubs, boating (rentals are available), and fishing. Both summer and winter are busy here, as the crowds return after snowfall for cross country and downhill skiing and snowboarding. There are 170 sites, all with hookups. Families should note that this is not a campground in the strictest sense. No tent camping is allowed, and campers built on trucks are not accepted either. Reservations are mandatory.

*Big Bear Shores RV Resort & Yacht Club, 40751 North Shore Dr., Box 1572, Big Bear Lake, CA 92315, tel. 909/866–4151. Year-round: $49–$69 per night.*

### Joshua Tree National Park

**ALL**

Joshua Tree National Park, in California, is most appealing in what is off-season for many other areas: Because of extreme weather conditions (heat and wind), the best times to visit are from February to April and from October to December. The park, about 140 mi east of Los Angeles, covers 1,238 square mi and preserves sections of two deserts—the Mojave and the Colorado. Rock climbers from all over the world test their skills on mountains that rise from the desert to heights of from 1,000 ft to 6,000 ft (see Rock Climbing), and hikers can explore many magnificent trails. Joshua Tree is a natural for an RV adventure: The only way to cover most of this vast area is by private vehicle, and there's no better means of transport for family exploration than an RV.

**FOR FAMILIES.** Five of the eight campgrounds are free and available on a first-come, first-served basis. The park charges a fee for Indian Cove, Cottonwood Springs, and Black Rock Canyon campgrounds, and only Indian Cove and Black Rock take reservations. All the campgrounds have access to the trees, trails, and rocks that make the monument unique. Campers must have their own water (except at Cottonwood and Black Rock, where water is available) and their own firewood, so fill your RV's water tank before arriving, and check your propane tanks if you're planning on cooking inside instead of using firewood.

You can pick up trail maps and other information at the visitor center, just north of the Twentynine Palms entrance. Guided hikes and campfire programs are scheduled in spring and fall. Families with young children should check out the Hidden Valley Nature Trail, a mile-long loop enclosed by a wall of rocks; the trail starts near Hidden Valley Campground. Other easy trails begin near the White Tank, Cottonwood Springs, and Black Rock Canyon campgrounds. Fortynine Palms Canyon (not far from the Twentynine Palms entrance) and Lost Palms Oasis (near the Cottonwood Springs campground) are reached by way of mostly moderate trails; allow several hours for these hikes.

*Joshua Tree National Park, Superintendent, 74455 Park Dr., Twentynine Palms, CA, 92277, tel. 760/367–5500 or 800/365–CAMP for reservations. Year-round: $8–$10 per night plus $10 per vehicle park entrance fees.*

## *Alaska*

### Denali National Park

ALL

For many travelers Denali is synonymous with Alaska—huge, untamed, and full of adventure. Within the park's 6 million acres is 20,320-ft Mt. McKinley, or Denali, as the native people call it; yet the moose, grizzly bears, and caribou may seem even more impressive to young visitors. If your family is ready to brave the wildness that makes Denali so awesome, camp inside the park and let its spirit seep into your soul.

**FOR FAMILIES.** Wildlife viewing, hiking, interpretive walks and talks, cross-country skiing, and dogsledding are all possible in Denali, though these activities are appropriate for different ages and abilities. Camping in the park, however, is an experience for children and adults alike as long as you're not looking for services and amenities. Riley Creek (101 sites), Savage River (33 sites), and Teklanika (53 sites) are the only three campgrounds accessible by private vehicle. Riley Creek has the best facilities, including a store, but none of the campgrounds has hookups. Reservations are strongly recommended.

*Denali National Park, Superintendent, Box 9, Denali Park, AK 99755, tel. 907/683–2294 or 800/622–7275 for reservations. Year-round (all facilities not open all year): $12 per night plus $4 one time per campground reservations fee and $10 per family entrance fee.*

### McKinley RV and Campground

ALL

A trip to Alaska doesn't have to mean primitive backcountry camping, and in such a rugged area you may have several reasons to choose an organized campground with full facilities rather than a remote, primitive site. Families traveling with very young children or grandparents and those with little camping experience may do better with the comfort and security of private campgrounds. Perhaps most important, you can make reservations at private campgrounds so you'll never end up stranded. However, many families enjoy both wilderness campsites and organized, private campgrounds. There's a place for both—often on the same trip.

**FOR FAMILIES.** McKinley RV and Campground, about 10 mi north of the park entrance, is surrounded by all the beauty Denali has to offer. You'll spend most days in the park, then return in the evenings to hot showers, a store, flush toilets, firewood, and good company. If you want to take a day off from exploring the park, you can book a tour at the campground—rafting, horseback riding, and helicopter flightseeing trips among them. There are 90 sites; reservations are highly recommended.

*McKinley RV and Campground, Mile 248.5, Rte. 3, Box 340, Healy, AK 99743, tel. 907/683–2379 or 800/478–2562. May–Sept: $19–$28 per night, children under 12 free.*

## *Canada*

### Burnaby Cariboo RV Park

ALL

Many adventure-oriented families use urban campgrounds such as this one as convenient meeting places for groups preparing to travel into wilderness areas. Vancouver is particularly appealing because it has easy access to many Canadian adventures, as well as outdoor activities within the city limits. The famous Capilano Suspension Bridge, for example, stretches 450 ft across and 230 ft above the Capilano River. Lynn Canyon Park, in North Vancouver, has miles of easy and rugged hiking trails as well as a suspension bridge of its own, hanging some 20 stories above Lynn Creek. Grouse Mountain, just 15 minutes from downtown, has hiking trails, a tram that hikers can ride to alpine meadows, rivers for gold panning, and, in winter, sleigh rides and skiing. Vancouver Island, much of it unpopulated wilderness area, is popular for many outdoor activities and is easily accessible by ferry from the city of Vancouver.

**FOR FAMILIES.** Burnaby Cariboo RV Park, a private RV park with 217 sites, lies within greater Vancouver and yet is surrounded by the 400-acre Burnaby Lake Regional Park, where bird-watching and walking are favorite pastimes. This park has an equestrian center and a nature center with activities for families, too. A full-service, first-class facility, Burnaby Cariboo has a pool, hot tub, playground, and other amenities; it also has a tour service that will help you book guided fishing tours and other adventures. Because it's on a public transit route, you can park your RV and not have to move it to see the sights.

*Burnaby Cariboo RV Park, 8765 Cariboo Pl., Burnaby, British Columbia, Canada V3N 4T2, tel. 604/420–1722. Year-round: $21–$31 per night.*

# Resources

## Organizations

**National Park Service** (Office of Public Inquiries, National Park Service, Department of the Interior, 1849 C St., Room 1013, Washington, DC 20240, tel. 202/208–4747) will send a general information kit on the parks and monuments. The **U.S. Forest Service** (Office of Communication, Box 96090, Washington, DC 20090-6090, tel. 877/444–6777 for information and reservations) strongly recommends using two Web sites to plan your trip. The National Recreation Reservation Service site (www.reserveusa.com) has information and reservation booking services for everything from cabins to wilderness adventures. On the Recreational Opportunities on Federal Lands site (www.recreation.gov), you can pinpoint your options in each state by choosing specific activities and facilities.

**Pat Dickerman's Adventure Guides, Inc.** (7550 E. McDonald Dr., Suite M, Scottsdale, AZ 85250, tel. 602/596–0226 or 800/252–7899) creates customized driving vacations in the U.S. and the Canadian west, complete with reservations, directions, and maps. Trips are designed according to your interests and budget. They can include adventures such as rafting, hiking, and more.

**Go RVing Coalition** (Box 2999, Dept. P, Reston, VA 20195-0999, tel. 888/467–8464) will send you a free introduction to RVing video with rental and travel tips, plus a list of dealers and campgrounds. You can also request more detailed written information on RV campgrounds, rentals, and trip planning.

The **Good Sam Club** (2575 Vista del Mar, Ventura, CA 93001, tel. 805/667–4100 or 800/234–3450) offers services for RVers, including road service, mail forwarding, insurance, travel information, and organized trips.

The **Recreation Vehicle Rental Association** (3930 University Dr., Fairfax, VA 22030, tel. 703/591–7130 or 800/336–0355) has a directory with more than 300 listings of American and Canadian rental outlets. RVRA recommends getting the directory free from its frequently updated Web site (www.RVRA.org). For a printed version call

800/872–1074, ext. 3. However, this version won't be as current and costs $10 in the U.S., $15 for international mailing. **Cruise America** (11 W. Hampton Ave., Mesa, AZ 85210, tel. 602/262–9611 or 800/327–7799 for reservations only) is a nationwide rental organization. It has fly-and-drive options that allow you to pick up your rental in the area where you'll be traveling. In Canada, **CanaDream** (2508 24th Ave. NE, Calgary, Alberta, Canada T1Y 6R8, tel. 403/250–3209) puts together RV vacation packages through its rental division, Canada Campers.

Each of the three major campground chains will send you a directory of its member campgrounds: **Best Holiday Trav-L-Park Association** (1310 Jarvis Ave., Elk Grove Village, IL 60007, tel. 800/323–8899), **Kampgrounds of America** (KOA; Box 30558, Billings, MT 59114, tel. 406/248–7444; also ask about purchasing a KOA Value Kard, which gives you a 10% discount on all registration fees), and **Leisure Systems, Inc./Yogi Bear's Jellystone Park Camp-Resorts** (6201 Kellogg Ave., Cincinnati, OH 45228-1118, tel. 513/232–6800 or 800/626–3720). In Canada, **Alberta Country Vacations** (Box 396, San Gudo, Alberta, Canada T0E 2A0, tel. 780/785–3700) will send you a free brochure listing its member ranches and farms, some of which have RV sites.

## Periodicals

Don't leave home without a pile of campground directories in your RV. *Trailer Life Campground & RV Services Directory* (2575 Vista del Mar, Ventura, CA 93001, tel. 805/667–4100) comes from the Good Sam Club and includes discounts for club members. *Wheelers Recreational Vehicle Resort & Campground Guide* (1310 Jarvis Ave., Elk Grove Village, IL 60007, tel. 847/981–0100) rates the various campgrounds, giving them from one to five stars, with three being standard. *Woodall's Campground Directories* (13975 W. Polo Trail Dr., Lake Forest, IL 60045, tel. 847/362–6700 or 800/323–9076) publishes a North American edition and smaller eastern and western editions. Woodall's awards from one to five diamonds for facilities and recreation at each campground.

## Books

Millbrook Press publishes two excellent books for school-age children: Michael Weber's *Our National Parks* and Eleanor Ayer's *Our National Monuments.* Both have color photographs and interesting facts.

## Also See

Families that like the idea of an adventure that's a movable feast—and bed and bathroom—should look at the Houseboating *and* Sailing chapters. Keep in mind, too, that many trips in Archaeology Adventures, Digging for Dinosaur Bones and Other Fossils, Kayaking, *and* Rock Climbing require participants to arrange their own accommodations, often at nearby campgrounds; RVs are perfect for these.

# SAILING

Sailing is about teamwork, whether you are learning the basics as a family or working together as a crew. That's a skill that will benefit both parents and children long after they've left a sailing school or vacation behind. Sailing isn't all about work, though. These adventures by their very nature are the stuff of fantasy: uninhabited islands; intriguing wildlife; turquoise waters and coral reefs teeming with exotic fish; interesting cultures—you and your family with the wind and the wide-open sea and nothing but time on your hands. How much you'll work depends on whether you choose a school or a sailing vacation. Either way you will join a long and honored heritage of seagoing families that have come to believe there is no better way to strengthen ties and explore the world than by boat.

## Questions to Ask

**Is the trip safe—and fun—for kids?** Thousands of young children have spent time on boats, but not every boat is right for every child or family. Open railings and slippery decks, for example, are dangerous for young children who are left to play on their own; parents must ask themselves if they are prepared to be on constant watch. Some courses include the deliberate capsizing of a boat so students can learn how to handle that situation. Will your child be overly frightened by this? If so, perhaps he or she is too young to take the course, regardless of whether the school allows it. By asking questions about courses and about the layout of the boat, you'll be able to make a knowledgeable decision.

**Are there life jackets on board, and will they fit my children?** This is crucial: If a school or ship does not have a life jacket to fit your child, you must get one. Go to a marine supply store or reputable outdoor store, and pick a Coast Guard–approved life vest made for the type of water and area in which you will be. Read the labels carefully. A life vest intended for use in calm inland water will not protect your child on the open seas.

**How many years of experience does the captain have sailing in this area?** When you go on a sailing vacation, ideally you want a skipper and crew who know the area well—both so you'll be safe and so they'll be able to give you interesting stories and facts about the history of the land and the waters near which you'll be sailing, about its plant and animal life, and about the local people.

**Are your captains licensed?** In the United States boat captains—and other sailors carrying passengers for hire—must be licensed by the Coast Guard. Other countries have corresponding licensing agencies; before you charter a boat with a captain, make sure he or she is, in fact, licensed.

**Are your instructors certified, and what are their qualifications?** There are organizations with certification criteria for instructors: the United States Sailing Association (US Sailing) and the American Sailing Association (ASA). These competing organizations have differing criteria, resulting in no universal standard for instructors in this country, particularly with regard to recreational sailing. Some very good instructors may not have joined or been tested by either organization. If you're looking for quality instruction, certification is just one measure. Experience is an equally valid measure, so ask how long instructors have been teaching (bad teachers don't last long with a school or company), and how long they've been sailing. This is a sport in which qualifications definitely improve with experience. If, however, you're taking bareboat cruising courses and other advanced classes for sailing boats with engines because your goal is to captain and crew your own boat, your instructor should have a Coast Guard license. When you're taking day sailing courses, Coast Guard licensing is not an issue.

**Will I be certified when I finish this course?** There are no universally accepted criteria for certifying students. Some schools offer their own certificate; some offer their own and one from US Sailing or ASA. A school's certificate has limited importance. On the one hand, if you were to go to the Caribbean to charter a boat, the company probably would not even ask for certification. If, however, you could not prove sailing competence based on experience, it would require you to take a licensed captain with you at your own expense—but you could still charter the boat. On the other hand, a certificate proves you've learned a certain number of things and sailed a certain number of hours, and it tells instructors you're ready to move on to the next level. And it's nice to hang on your wall.

**Can we help crew?** If you're joining a sailing expedition or chartering a boat, and if learning is important to your family, choose a ship on which guests are allowed and encouraged to help out and learn the fundamentals of sailing. If your children are interested in learning, make certain the captain and crew want to teach children and have some experience doing so.

**Do you carry snorkeling or other recreational gear for children?** Snorkeling is an ideal activity for families on boats; so is fishing. Many charters carry snorkel and fishing equipment—but not always in children's sizes. Ask ahead of time because you can't generally buy child-size gear in exotic locations.

**Is any other recreational equipment available?** Some boats carry kayaks or canoes; some have dinghies and inflatables. You may be able to windsurf or scuba dive from some boats. If you are interested in a particular water sport, make a request well in advance of your sailing date.

**What's included in the cost?** If you sign up with a sailing school, courses are usually instruction only, with no meals or accommodations included; that's the case with most of the courses listed here. If you take a course during which you live on the boat, however, accommodations and meals on board are included, unless otherwise noted. There are also resort courses, which combine sailing school with lodging and the use of facilities at the school's resort location. When you charter a boat or join a scheduled trip on a sailing vessel, accommodations, meals, activities, sailing instruction, and sightseeing are included. Airport pickup may also be part of the trip fee. Alcohol is usually extra, as is dive equipment.

### Instruction

Sailing schools, of course, are mostly instruction, though they often combine learning with playing in some of the world's most popular vacation spots. Charters and sailing adventures, on the other hand, generally give live-aboard guests the option of working alongside the crew or doing nothing at all. Although relaxing is great, why not use some of the time for hands-on learning from real sailors—people who have a unique experience and perspective to share. Learning to sail this way is just too good an opportunity to miss.

### Finding the Fun

**Northeast:** North End Shipyard Schooners, Offshore Sailing School, Outward Bound. **Mid-Atlantic:** Annapolis Sailing School, Offshore Sailing School, Outward Bound. **South:** Annapolis Sailing School, Ocean Voyages, Offshore Sailing School, Outward Bound, VYC Charters and Sailing School. **Midwest**: Offshore Sailing School. **West Coast:** Ocean Voyages, Outward Bound. **Alaska:** American Wilderness Experience/GORP Travel, Ocean Voyages, Rascals in Paradise. **Hawaii:** Ocean Voyages. **Caribbean:** Annapolis Sailing School, Bitter End Yacht Club, Ocean Voyages, Offshore Sailing School. **Mexico:** Ocean Voyages. **Central America, South America:** Ocean Voyages, Rascals in Paradise. **Europe, Africa, Asia, Australia, New Zealand:** Ocean Voyages, Rascals in Paradise. **South Pacific:** Ocean Voyages, Rascals in Paradise.

## Favorite Schools and Charters

### American Wilderness Experience/GORP Travel

ALL

Small boats traveling along the 1,000 mi of protected waterway in Alaska's Inside Passage can bring visitors closer to the real Alaska than large cruise ships could ever do. The passage is marked by deep fjords and magnificent snowy peaks, and there are hundreds of islands, small villages, and extensive forested areas that provide food and shelter for black and brown bears and bald eagles. Along the coast are otters, seals, and sea lions; in the deeper waters orcas and humpbacks leap and glide. Sound Sailing, the operator the company contracts with for this adventure, has two 50-ft sloops and a wealth of experience to share with families in America's great northern frontier. You can embark in Petersburg or Sitka.

**FOR FAMILIES.** Each boat has three private cabins to accommodate a family of five or six (three small children could share one double berth). You don't need any sailing experience, and all family members are welcome to help or to learn to crew under the guidance of a licensed captain. The pace and itinerary are flexible. You can take the dinghy ashore for beachcombing and inland hiking or relax in a natural hot spring. You can learn about natural history as well as Tlingit native history and culture. There's first-rate fishing equipment on board, so plan on testing your skills against Pacific halibut or salmon.

*American Wilderness Experience/GORP Travel, Box 1486, Boulder, CO 80306, tel. 303/444–2622 or 800/444–0099. Apr.–Oct.: 7 days, $1,255–$1,655, depending on season.*

## Annapolis Sailing School

5+

Annapolis Sailing School is one of the oldest and largest sailing schools in the country. Its main campus is on Chesapeake Bay in Maryland, but it has branch schools in St. Petersburg, Florida, based at the Marina Beach Resort Hotel, and in Christiansted, St. Croix in the U.S. Virgin Islands. All Annapolis Sailing School courses are primarily hands-on. With the exception of about four hours of lecture time, classes take place in boats on the water.

**FOR FAMILIES.** Become a Sailing Family is the popular course in which parents and children work together to master the sailing of 30-ft sloops. Offered only at the Annapolis campus, this is one of the few courses that includes lodging. It combines the beginner weekend course with five days of cruising. Families spend three nights at hotels in Annapolis, then four nights on a boat in Chesapeake Bay. An instructor is on board each day.

If you want to vacation together but learn separately, the school suggests you combine adult courses with Kid Ship, for ages five and up. Kid Ship, also scheduled only in Annapolis, coincides with the school's adult courses. While parents are learning on 24-ft sloops, children are on 12-ft Holder Hawk sailboats, which most youngsters find manageable and unintimidating. These are not live-aboard courses; families are out on the water from about 9 to 4, then on their own in the evenings.

*Annapolis Sailing School, Box 3334, Annapolis, MD 21403, tel. 410/267–7205 or 800/638–9192. Mar.–Oct.: 2–5 days, $280–$550 adults, $180–$350 children (Kid Ship); 7 days, $2,660–$4,065 for 2–6 students in the family course.*

## Bitter End Yacht Club

6+

The Bitter End Yacht Club is for both sailors and sailor wannabes. The resort is tucked into the flowering hills of Virgin Gorda in the British Virgin Islands, its beach a dazzling sweep of white against the clear turquoise waters of North Sound. The location is remote; the only way to get here is by boat. Families can stay at the resort or in live-aboard yachts moored in the harbor—or do a little of each. There's nothing pretentious about the resort; barefoot and casual is the norm. It's an incredible place for family connecting and rejuvenating. And because the resort is family-owned and operated, by the end of your trip you'll feel like part of the Bitter End family, too.

**FOR FAMILIES.** The Bitter End has more than 100 watercraft, with windsurfers, kayaks, and Boston Whalers in addition to the many types of sailboats—including Lasers, Rhodes 19s, Escapes, and Optimists. All guests can take the free Sailing 101 course offered by an experienced staff of instructors. The pros at the Nick Trotter Sailing and Windsurfing School, which is based at the resort, also teach beginner to advanced sailing clinics (at an additional charge), as well as windsurfing, which even young children can try. Youngsters ages 7 to 12 can join the Junior Sailing Program, offered five days a week, year round, with complementary lessons during summer months and some school holidays. Learn to Sail weeks are scheduled periodically, ideal for adults and teens who want to immerse themselves in the sport.

While sailing is the focus here, there are plenty of other activities. Snorkel day trips leave from the resort to various reefs and coves, and there's fishing and hiking, too. Or just borrow one of the Boston Whaler skiffs and motor out to an island of your own for a family picnic away from it all.

Thanksgiving is Family Fun Week at the Bitter End. Not only are children ages 6 to 18 half price, but there are special activities including Sail Caribbean, a traveling sailing program for ages six and up, and the Junior Program, which includes storytelling, beach games, sand painting, nature walks, and an introduction to sailing, windsurfing, and snorkeling. Families can also team up to race in the Turkey Day Regatta. Between April and December (called Celebration Season) the resort offers a seven-night Admiral's Family Package that includes lodging with two adjoining rooms for two adults and two children, all meals, all water sports, an introductory sailing course, daily excursions, and airport transfers (the airport is across the water on the island of Tortola).

*Bitter End Yacht Club, North Sound, Virgin Gorda, British Virgin Islands. U.S. sales and reservations office, 875 N. Michigan Ave., Chicago, IL 60611, tel. 312/944–5855 or 800/872–2392. Year-round: 8–15 days, Admiral's Inclusive Package $3,850–$10,800 per room; Celebration Season 8-day family package $5,600 for a family of 4.*

## North End Shipyard Schooners

**12+**

North End Shipyard Schooners consists of two owner-operated vessels working cooperatively and sailing from North End Shipyard Wharf in Rockland, Maine. The *American Eagle,* built in 1931, has been designated a National Historic Landmark. The *Heritage* was built at the shipyard in 1983. The ships have no set itineraries; they go with the prevailing winds, anchoring in a different scenic harbor each night. There are hundreds of islands to sail around and explore along Maine's rocky midcoast.

**FOR FAMILIES.** Both the *Heritage,* a 95-ft schooner for 30 passengers, and the *American Eagle,* a 92-ft schooner for 28 passengers, welcome families with children at least 12 years old on all cruises. Families are encouraged but not required to help around the ships. Activities include whale-watching, stargazing, swimming, and exploring the small coves where the ships anchor. The captains and crew are adept at telling salty tales of the sea, and they may even teach some sailing skills such as knot tying and rowing. Every cruise includes an old-fashioned Maine lobster bake.

Only two sailors can fit in a cabin, so a family of four needs two separate cabins. If there are just three of you, your child will probably bunk with another passenger of the same sex and age unless one of the single cabins is available.

*North End Shipyard Schooners, Box 482, Rockland, ME 14841, tel. 207/594–8007 or 800/648–4544. Late May–early Oct.: 3–6 days, $395–$745.*

## Ocean Voyages

**ALL**

For 20 years Ocean Voyages has arranged small group sailings and maritime adventures for all kinds of sea lovers, including families. Founder Mary Crowley, an accomplished sailor, introduced her daughter Colleen to sailing as a toddler. Since then they've sailed most of the world's oceans together. Whether your family is looking for a charter or a scheduled sailing, whether you want to sail in the Pacific, the Caribbean, the Mediterranean, or around the world, Ocean Voyages will find a boat and a crew to give you the oceangoing vacation of a lifetime.

**FOR FAMILIES.** When you call, ask for the Family Sailing information sheet. It lists 50 yachts in 11 parts of the world—all are ships that Ocean Voyages knows will welcome families. There's a 72-ft yacht crewed by a New Zealand couple sailing throughout the Pacific islands. If Greece and Turkey appeal, an eight-passenger yacht sails around the Greek islands and along Turkey's Turquoise Coast. A 10-passenger, 71-ft yacht and its family-of-four crew will take you on a nature-oriented trip around Fiji, Vanuatu, the Solomon Islands, New Guinea, and Australia. See the Hawaiian Islands—and snorkel, swim, whale-watch, and surf while you're doing it—via a six-passenger boat or a large schooner that accommodates family groups of between 12 and 22. The Australian crew of *Ocean Leopard,* an 87-ft yacht on its way around the world, invites you to join part of its voyage in Indonesia, Thailand, the Indian Ocean, Africa, or beyond; *Ocean Leopard* sleeps four to eight guests.

For families that want to sail in Darwin's wake, Ocean Voyages can arrange yachts accommodating from 6 to 30 passengers in the Galápagos Islands. You can sail for a week around the islands, then stay for a week at a small family-owned inn on Isla Santa Cruz Galápagos. If time allows, the company will also arrange land excursions for those who want to explore more of Ecuador.

Ships also sail off California, Florida and the Bahamas, the Pacific Northwest, Alaska, Mexico, Tahiti, the Marquesas, Tonga, Fiji, and Vanuatu, among other places. The majority accommodate family groups of from 3 to 16 people. Most charters are for one week, but if you want to sail for six weeks or the entire summer, that can also be arranged. And Ocean Voyages can coordinate sailing family reunions as well.

*Ocean Voyages, 1709 Bridgeway, Sausalito, CA 94965, tel. 415/332–4681. Year-round (all ships not available all months): 7 days, $875–$2,850 adults, $420–$1,600 children; rates depend on location and group size; typically children under 12 receive 50% discount, some vessels take infants free of charge, and many ships offer special family rates.*

## Offshore Sailing School

8+

Steve Colgate, America's Cup and Olympic sailor, has always believed that sailing is for everyone. Since he founded Offshore Sailing School in 1964, the school has taught more than 80,500 people of all ages and backgrounds. Offshore has schools in Jersey City and Barnegat Bay, New Jersey; Chicago, Illinois; and Stamford, Connecticut; besides branches at five first-class resort areas: South Seas Plantation on Captiva Island, Florida; Prospect Reef Resort, Tortola, British Virgin Islands; Admiral Farragut Inn, Newport, Rhode Island; Hawk's Cay Resort, Duck Key, Florida, and St. Petersburg, Florida.

**FOR FAMILIES.** Families with children 12 and up can join any of the school's courses. If you have at least four family members—enough to fill one boat—the school is flexible on the minimum age but feels the instruction is most appropriate for children eight and older. A family of four participating in the same course also gets a discount. There are five basic courses, which you can take at the school sites or in some cases as part of a resort package.

Learn to Sail, with three-, four-, and eight-day versions, is for beginners and intermediate sailors; it's taught on 26-ft Colgates, with no more than four students to a boat. The extensive list of topics covered includes nautical terminology, hull speed, mechanics of wind and sail, crew overboard recovery—even backward sailing. More experienced sailors can take such courses as performance sailing, bareboat cruising preparation, live-aboard cruising, and sailboat racing.

The South Seas Resort branch on Captiva offers six-day family packages that combine the sailing school with use of the resort's well-regarded children's program. Accommodations at the resort are included in these packages. Children ages 8 through 12 can take Offshore's Junior Sailor's program; instruction is aboard 12-ft Escapes and daily hours coincide with parents' on-water instruction courses. For families with children not taking a sailing course, South Seas Plantation offers a supervised children's program and baby-sitting services.

Finally, families might consider Fast Track to Cruising, which combines Learn to Sail and Live-Aboard Cruising in a 10- to 14-day course at several of the school's vacation destinations. At the end of this course, you'll crew your own boat—without instructors—on a 24-hour minicharter.
*Offshore Sailing School, 16731 McGregor Blvd., Fort Myers, FL 33908, tel. 941/454–1700 or 800/221–4326. Year-round (all locations not available all months): 3–14 days, $595–$995 for courses only, $995–$2,995 for resort packages, depending on accommodations and season; 6 days, $1,445–$1,666 per person for Captiva family package; discounts for children on some packages.*

## Outward Bound

14+

For more than 30 years Outward Bound has challenged novice and experienced sailors alike to master the skills to navigate Maine's rugged coast and waters. According to the organization's philosophy, a weeklong course develops not only strong sailing skills for you and your child but bonds that will strengthen relationships on and off the water.

**FOR FAMILIES.** The parent-child course, which is generally offered a couple of times each summer, starts and ends in Rockland, Maine; participants spend about six days sailing in Penobscot Bay and two days on land activities on a few of the 3,500 islands in the area. Usually from 10 to 12 people share one boat; to a large extent the weather dictates your schedule. Your family will focus on teamwork, leadership, and seamanship skills while working on a 30-ft open ketch. The entire group rotates responsibilities throughout the course, and among the skills you master are sail handling (including tacking and jibing), navigation (chart and compass use and course plotting), and boat handling, which means helmsmanship as well as such fundamentals as anchoring and rowing. During the island stays, you try rock climbing, rappelling, and a ropes course.

At night you camp out on islands in platform tents for about half the course and sleep on the boat the rest of the time. The boat does not have berths or cover; guests need to bring their own sleeping bags. In the Outward Bound tradition, you will learn how to construct a shelter over the boat if the weather demands it.

In addition to the parent-child courses aimed at parents with children age 14 and older, the regular Outward Bound sailing courses for teens age 16 and older are appropriate for parents and teens to take together. These courses, which run 8, 14, or 26 days, are available in the winter, spring, and fall in Florida and generally May through September or October in Maryland, Maine, and Washington's San Juan Islands.
*Outward Bound, 100 Mystery Point Rd., Garrison, NY 10524, tel. 914/424–4000 or*

*800/243–8520. June–Aug.: 8–26 days, $995–$2,195 adults, $695 children in the parent-child course.*

## Rascals in Paradise

3+

Rascals represents several yachts around the world that are ideal for one family or for two families to charter together. Like all the outfitters, hotels, and resorts with which Rascals contracts, the charter owners and captains are chosen not only for their sailing expertise and knowledge of the areas in which they work but for their love of sharing their world with children and parents.

**FOR FAMILIES.** Typical of a Rascals charter is the *Discovery,* a 65-ft yacht owned and operated by Dean Rand, with help from his four young daughters. Dean tries to match his children with the children on each sailing: If older children are coming, he brings his older girls along; when families have young children, the younger daughters sail, too. The *Discovery,* which explores Alaska's Prince William Sound, has six cabins for 12 passengers; families can help out with ship chores if they wish.

Although the exact itinerary depends on the weather, the group's interests, and the location of wildlife, the boat usually sails to Barry Arm and Harriman Fjord, past the expansive Columbia Glacier with its 300-ft-high walls of blue ice, and through Orca Bay. Families can see where the *Exxon Valdez* ran aground and watch sea lions and puffins. There are several opportunities to go ashore via inflatable Zodiak rafts; if you like, you can hike to a waterfall. The food—freshly baked goods, seafood, steaks, salads, vegetables, and wine—will please children and parents. At night the ship anchors in protected coves. On the six- and eight-day voyages you spend two nights at a family-friendly bed-and-breakfast in the Rands' small hometown of Cordova, on Prince William Sound. There you can meet local families and explore a glacier and other sights away from the coast.

If Alaska is not for your family, consider sailing the coast of Turkey. Rascals has several ships from which to choose, some large enough to accommodate a family reunion. If you wish, you can tour Istanbul and Cappadocia in addition to cruising. Another voyage is in Central America, where besides diving and exploring the San Blas Islands of Panama, families have an opportunity to interact with Cuna Indians, the last full-blooded Carib people left in the Caribbean. Ask Rascals about charters in Fiji, Australia, Tonga, Tahiti, Papua New Guinea, Vanuatu, and the Solomon Islands, as well.

*Rascals in Paradise, 650 5th St., Suite 505, San Francisco, CA 94107, tel. 415/978–9800 or 800/872–7225. Alaska, May–Sept.: 3–7 days, $2,050–$2,750; 50% discount for children 8–15; children under 8, $400–$600. Months vary for other charters: Turkey starts at $600 per day for a family of 6, with all meals and activities; Panama, $5,600 per week for a family of up to 5, including diving and excursions.*

## VYC Charters and Sailing School

16+

Situated at the Renaissance Vinoy Resort in St. Petersburg, Florida, VYC offers five courses: basic sailing, bareboat chartering, basic-to-bareboat, coastal navigation, and advanced coastal cruising. Classes are available seven days a week, year-round, and the schedule is flexible so families can fit classes into their resort stay. The school uses the American Sailing Association curriculum, and all class work takes place on 31- or 34-ft Hunters. Each sailboat is fully equipped for both safety and comfort, with shade and refrigerators for snacks and lunches. Once your group is ready to leave the docks, you'll head out into the protected waters of

Tampa Bay or, in the more advanced courses, the Gulf of Mexico. All successfully completed courses result in a certificate from the American Sailing Association.

**FOR FAMILIES.** Parents and teens can sail together in any of the courses; the school will consider children of 14 or 15 with a real interest in sailing, but talk to instructors first (a younger teen not ready for the course-work may be allowed to sail with you while you learn). The school has a minimum of four students per class. Families in the beginner classes learn all about sailing terminology, equipment, theory, points of sail, crew communication, crew overboard recovery, knots, traffic rules, and more, with an emphasis on docking and safety. No experience is required. In the more advanced courses, which have prerequisites of basic course work, the focus changes to learning troubleshooting, increasing technical (as in how cooling and electrical systems work) and safety knowledge, and accomplishing more advanced sailing techniques. The six-day basic-to-bareboat course includes one night on board the sailboat.

Originally built in 1925 as the Vinoy Park Hotel, the Renaissance Vinoy Resort has been completely renovated with careful attention to historical detail. When you're not sailing, take the hotel's history tour and luncheon. Staff members at the hotel can also help you get to all of the area's best museums and amusements. There's a supervised children's program from June through August. If you have a young child and sign up for a sailing course at another time of year, the hotel will help arrange child care.

*VYC Charters and Sailing School, 1421 Bay St. SE, Suite 4, St. Petersburg, FL 33701, tel. 800/879–2244 (school), 727/894–1000 (resort only). Year-round: 2–6 days, $325–$995, 10% discount for 2nd, 3rd, and 4th person in your group.*

# Resources

## Organizations

The **American Sailing Association** (13922 Marquesas Way, Marina del Rey, CA 90292, tel. 310/822–7171) and **United States Sailing Association** (Box 1260, Portsmouth, RI 02871, tel. 401/683–0800) are the major sailing organizations in this country. Call ASA for a list of affiliate members or schools in your area that teach ASA courses. US Sailing has a "Where to Sail" pamphlet listing rentals, schools, and US Sailing programs across the country. Both organizations have books and other materials available for sale.

## Periodicals

*Cruising World* (The Sailing Company, 5 John Clark Rd., Newport, RI 02840, tel. 401/847–1588) is a monthly magazine for sailors who cruise the world in their own sailboats; it's also interesting reading for novice sailors. Some issues include articles that discuss family sailing and educating children about cruising. An annual special section on chartering that lists and rates companies is a must for anyone considering a charter vacation. The classified ads have opportunities for crewing, too.

## Also See

If you can't decide between sailing and taking an animal-encounter vacation, see Wildlife Encounters; some of these adventures include both. If you want to be on and *under* the water, see Snorkeling and Diving.

# SNORKELING AND DIVING

The ocean is like a circus—a place where brilliant colors, balletic grace, and heart-in-your- mouth thrills exist in a swirling world unto itself. Or perhaps it's more like a vast, watery classroom, filled with fascinating creatures that tell us not only about life under the sea but sometimes about ourselves as well. Children, of course, know about the underwater world from myths and fairy tales as well as from science and nonfiction books. Seeing underwater life firsthand is both intriguing and educational at any age.

Families have several options for exploring underwater. Snorkelers float face down in the water and look at the sea below. Almost any child who can swim and is comfortable in the water can snorkel, though some young children don't like wearing a mask over their face or breathing through a tube. Scuba diving is more complicated. You must be certified (pass written and practical tests) or take a certification course on-site before you can dive with a licensed dive operator. The minimum age for certification is 12.

Because both snorkeling and diving are often particularly good around reef areas, many of the places listed here are ideal for both activities. Parents, however, should be aware that snorkelers and divers don't always depart together. A number of resorts with children's activity programs are included because these allow parents and teens to dive while younger children snorkel or play and explore with peers and counselors.

This chapter presents a cross section of snorkeling and diving experiences. All of these entries, like those in the chapter on Wildlife Encounters, are away from the mainland United States. Most are in other countries—places where you are not likely to encounter crowds or cloudy waters and where sea life is unusual in some way. These resorts or operators are all known for their work with children and families as well as for their expertise around the water. The selections are truly adventure vacations, which is not to say you can't don a mask and fins for half-day and day trips at many resorts in Florida, California, or even Michigan.

Of the more than 30 dive and snorkel trips here, some are based on ships, some are resort-based, and others are for adventurers who want to aid in scientific research while snorkeling or diving. The choices are for a variety of ages, abilities, and interests. Most are in places where families can learn the sports or where already certified divers can share their passion with other members of their family.

## Questions to Ask

**What kind of equipment is used for snorkeling and diving?** Snorkelers need a mask to see clearly in the water, fins on their feet for easier swimming, and a snorkel tube through which to breathe. Young children will require some time to get used to this equipment. Divers use the same equipment as snorkelers (some carry a snorkel so that if they surface far from the boat, they can swim back easily); this is often referred to as personal equipment. They also use dive gear. The most important pieces of gear are regulators and BCDs (buoyancy control devices), which you inflate and deflate depending on whether you want to go up or down. Serious divers usually own their own. Divers also need weight belts to help them dive down, as well as two gauges, one to measure depth and one to measure the air in the tanks. A tank or tanks, generally carried in a backpack, provide air. Some divers wear wet suits.

**Is snorkeling equipment available for rent? What about diving equipment?** If you don't have snorkeling equipment and don't want to borrow or buy it, make certain rentals are available on the boat or at the resort—and in the right sizes. You'll need properly fitting masks and fins as well as snorkels small enough for your children. Also, if anyone in your family wears glasses, you may want to ask a dive shop about purchasing a prescription mask. Dive packages and dive operators generally supply the necessary diving equipment but not personal gear.

**Do we have to be certified in advance to dive?** At some resorts and on some boats, instruction is not an option; you must be certified and have your C-card (certification card) with you in order to dive. Be clear about this beforehand if you are not yet certified.

**Do you have diving certification courses?** Many resorts and resort areas have certification courses. The main certification organizations in this country are the National Association of Underwater Instructors (NAUI) and the Professional Association of Dive Instructors (PADI). Resorts and resort areas are likely to offer courses from these organizations. NAUI and PADI teach basically the same skills, although their instructional methods differ. Courses generally combine anywhere from 25 to 32 hours of instruction divided between classroom and pool work, plus checkout dives (a real dive in fairly shallow water on which your instructor tests your skills). Children ages 12 through 15 can take the same course with parents and receive junior certification; the only difference for someone with such certification is he or she must be accompanied by an adult on dives. If you want to devote more of your vacation time to actual diving, you can take the classroom and pool portion near your home and finish up at a resort or with a dive operator in the location of your choice. If you do this, make sure the resort or operator accepts the type of certification whose process you have begun at home.

**Do you have a resort course?** If you don't want to commit to full certification, most resorts offer a less expensive resort course, with anywhere from 6 to 20 hours of instruction, pool work, and dive time over one to five days. Resort courses certify you to dive only at that resort and only during that stay. The minimum age is 12.

**Can snorkelers go out with divers?** Sometimes snorkelers and divers visit the same site together. Even operators that allow this, however, may change their minds if the weather or sea is rough or if the boat is full. If you have children who are not old enough to dive and who plan to snorkel, be aware you may not be able to go out together.

**Is there snorkeling right from shore?** Resorts that have snorkeling from their shores, or boats that take snorkelers to the shores of cays and islands, make life easy for parents with young children. It's much less intimidating for children to learn to snorkel in water they can stand in.

**What happens with ear pressure?** Diving creates the same kind of pressure as on airplane flights and other activities at high altitudes. If your preteen or teen is prone to ear pain in these situations, discuss ahead of time how to clear your ears by holding your nose and blowing out. Talk to your pediatrician, too.

**Are shots or other health precautions necessary?** Some diving trips take place in foreign countries that require inoculations and other kinds of preventive medication. Check far in advance and ask a pediatrician or the local health department about health precautions in foreign countries, especially as they relate to children. Always pack basic children's medication—acetaminophen, an antihistamine, cough syrup, motion-sickness pills, and antidiarrheal pills; these can be hard to find abroad. If your child is prone to ear infections or any other ailments, you may want to ask your pediatrician for an antibiotic that doesn't need to be refrigerated.

**What's included in the cost?** Certification courses generally include class materials (such as a manual), instruction, gear with which to learn, transportation to dive sites, and checkout dives. Equipment for checkout dives is often an extra charge. Dive packages at resorts typically give you one or two dives daily, transportation to dive sites, and lodging. Some cover meals; this is noted in individual listings. You often get dive equipment, such as tanks, weights, and belts, as part of the deal. Personal gear—snorkels, masks, fins—is usually not included. Dedicated dive-boat vacations are pretty much all-inclusive: equipment, gear, dives, local transportation, accommodations, and meals. Snorkel equipment for adults, though not for children, is often available. Diving instruction, however, is generally not provided on these boats. Any exceptions in pricing for these various experiences are noted in the individual listings.

## Instruction

Depending on the resort or boat from which you're diving, you will already have had all your instruction—and a certification card to prove it—or you'll need to sign up for a resort or certification course before you can dive. Any good snorkel boat operator will give basic instruction on snorkeling if your family needs it, though practice is what will make you comfortable in the water.

## A Note About Diving

When making travel plans, remember that you cannot fly within 24 hours after scuba diving.

## Finding the Fun

**Hawaii:** Denver Museum of Natural History, Ocean Voyages. **Mexico:** Rascals in Paradise. **Central America:** American Wilderness Experience/GORP Travel, Ocean Voyages, Rascals in Paradise. **Caribbean:** Earthwatch Institute, Hyatt Regency Grand Cayman, Ocean Voyages, Rascals in Paradise. **Bermuda:** Earthwatch Institute. **Around the Pacific:** Earthwatch Institute, Ocean Voyages, Rascals in Paradise, World of Adventure.

# Favorite Places to Snorkel and Dive

## American Wilderness Experience/GORP Travel

8+

Roatán is 35 mi off the coast of Honduras, in the Islas de la Bahía. On a palm-covered island near Roatán, the private bungalows of Anthony's Key Resort blend into a lush tropical hillside or overlook a quiet lagoon. The longest barrier reef in the Americas lies under the clear, warm Caribbean waters—a diving and snorkeling site of astonishing beauty. Several times between June and August the company has special weeks for families at Anthony's Key, with some activities beyond the usual ones.

**FOR FAMILIES.** Divers or anyone coming here to learn to dive will not be disappointed. Three boats leave daily from the resort, and there is shore diving both day and night. Boats go out twice weekly for night dives, too. The waters just offshore are great for snorkeling, too; the resort organizes special guided outings.

Anthony's Key Resort has a special relationship with the Institute for Marine Sciences, which is based in the area and runs the popular Dolphin Discovery programs. Participants in the program learn about and interact with the institute's dolphins. A special Dolphin Discovery Camp for children ages 8 through 14 coincides with dive and/or snorkel weeks for parents booking through American Wilderness Experience/GORP Travel (*see* Wildlife Encounters), so whether or not the whole family dives, everyone can experience the resort's abundant marine life and natural beauty. Certified divers don't miss out on close encounters either: Many wild dolphins live in these waters and frequently visit with divers.

Nondivers can ride horses on the beach, paddle in canoes, and explore nature trails. During each family week, the resort organizes children's and family activities and arranges baby-sitting, too. Meals, diving, riding, and most resort activities are included in the price of the all-inclusive package.
*American Wilderness Experience/GORP Travel, Box 1486, Boulder, CO 80306, tel. 303/444–2622 or 800/444–0099. Resort, year-round: 8 days, $750–$975 for a dive package, $625–$900 for a snorkel package.*

## Denver Museum of Natural History

**8+**

A recent addition to the museum's list of family learning adventure trips (*see* Canoeing, Native American Experiences, Rafting, *and* Wildlife Encounters) is one to Hawaii, where study of marine biology, volcanology, geology, nature sciences, and Hawaiian culture is mixed with snorkeling, hiking, swimming, craftmaking, and other activities. A 'Young Naturalists Education Team,' local educators, and Hawaiian elders work with children to present an all-encompassing view of these Pacific islands, from their fiery formation to their current development as a tourist destination, from the native flora and fauna to the complex, multicultural history of Hawaii's human inhabitants. The program was developed in conjunction with the University of Hawaii.

The 10-day trip starts and ends in San Francisco and includes stays on two islands: Kauai and Hawaii, the Big Island. Throughout the trip, families stay in comfortable, modern hotels. On Kauai, the group explores impressive Waimea Canyon and Koke'e State Park. High in Kauai's interior, you hike near the wettest place on earth and get bird's-eye views of the awesome Na Pali coast. In the lowlands, naturalists help children uncover the mysteries of tide pools. The whole group is taught the fundamentals of snorkeling and given plenty of time to practice or renew snorkeling skills.

From Kauai it's on to the Big Island, with the first stop on the Hilo side. Here the group visits an ocean park for exploration of marine systems and snorkeling. You'll have dinner with local Hawaiian families, who will introduce you to traditional music and dancing. Hilo's elders share island lore and teach native crafts; the Hilo Bay Canoe Club takes the group on a canoe outing in the bay. One of the island's most dramatic sights is Kilauea, the most active volcano in the world, along with the trails, craters, calderas, rims, and lava tubes that make up Hawaii Volcano National Park. Later, you gather for a traditional Japanese dinner and an origami demonstration, and learn how Japanese culture has added to Hawaii's diversity. Moving to the Kona coast, you'll visit archaeological sites to learn about the ancient Hawaiians. There's also a snorkel cruise to Kealakekua Bay, one of the Hawaiian islands' best snorkeling spots. The trip winds down with a luau and a farewell party at which all the hula lessons will be put to good use in a final performance.
*Denver Museum of Natural History, 2001 Colorado Blvd., Denver, CO 80205-5798, tel. 303/370–6304. June: 10 days, $3,695 adults, $2,495 children age 17 and under, $1,995 3rd person sharing the same room.*

## Earthwatch Institute

**16+**

With Earthwatch, a nonprofit organization, your family can satisfy both a love of snorkeling or diving and a desire to contribute to scientific research. From the Caribbean to Indonesia, researchers on Earthwatch-supported projects are working to better understand marine life or to protect endangered species and threatened environments. Snorkelers and divers aid scientists by observing, photographing, and tagging fish and marine animals. If you have teenagers, pick a place or pick a species—the Earthwatch world is your oyster, so to speak.

**FOR FAMILIES.** You must be a certified diver to work at Earthwatch dive sites; plan on two dives a day, which means two to four hours in the water. Snorkelers average three to five hours a day in the water. Participants also do much related work on land: cataloging, marking, sketching, and sometimes working with electronic equipment. Some sites are for divers or snorkelers only; at others both groups work together. Volunteers on these projects stay in everything from campsites and field stations to houses and hotels. Lodging is generally included in the cost (though campers may need to bring their own camping equipment), and volunteers usually take turns with food preparation.

Not surprisingly, the Caribbean offers several opportunities. Bimini in the Bahamas is home to spotted eagle rays and to marine biologist William Stillman. Snorkelers assist him in studying how the graceful, intelligent eagle rays—with an average 'wing' span of 1½ meters (5 ft)—affect one of the Bahamas' most precious natural resources, the endangered queen conch. The conch's two principal predators are humans and the spotted eagle rays; while the effect of human influence on the conch population is well documented, less is known about the behavior and ecology of rays, and how they impact the conch. Also in the Bahamas, a project on the island of San Salvador uses snorkelers to study reef damage.

If you've dreamed of diving to explore a shipwreck, your destination is Bermuda, where anthropologists are studying a 570-gross-ton Scottish sailing ship that sank on Chub Reef, off the south coast of Bermuda, in 1880. The researchers are interested in what the ship can tell us about Victorian society and the Industrial Revolution, based on such factors as its construction and technological sophistication.

Earthwatch volunteers help marine researchers study reefs in many different sites and habitats. Typical is the project on Balicasag Island in the Philippines, where the underwater visibility is astonishing. Here diving and snorkeling volunteers document the state of the coral, surrounding rock, rubble, sand, algae, and seagrass, and count the numbers of butterfly fish and other inhabitants. Filipinos depend on fish for 60% of their animal protein, yet through current practices of dynamiting fish and careless anchoring of fishing and tourist boats, the Filipinos have been decimating the marine life they depend on. The goal of the research on Balicasag is to provide data to encourage the maintenance of the islands' ecosystems.

*Earthwatch Institute, 680 Mt. Auburn St., Box 403BO, Watertown, MA 02471-9104, tel. 617/926–8200 or 800/776–0188. Year-round (all sites not available at all times): 8–11 days, $1,495–$2,295.*

## Hyatt Regency Grand Cayman

3+

The Cayman Islands deserve their reputation as one of the world's top dive spots, and neither divers nor snorkelers will be disappointed in the clarity of the water or the abundance of sea life. The Caymans, however, are a popular destination, which means this adventure is in well-developed surroundings. Nevertheless, the Caymans—and particularly the Hyatt on Grand Cayman—are a good choice for families because few other places in the world offer the same quality of diving *and* a full-service, supervised activity program for very young children. Parents and older children can venture into the deep while those too young to do so can explore on land.

**FOR FAMILIES.** Red Sail Sports operates at the Hyatt and has both resort and full-certification courses for would-be divers. The resort course includes two hours of instruction followed by a test; pass the test, and you can dive in the afternoon with an instructor. Boats leave twice daily for a number of spots around the islands. Lodging, a sunset cruise, a round of golf, and a Red Sail T-shirt are part of Hyatt dive and learn-to-dive packages.

One of the all-time great snorkeling experiences for children (they should be comfortable with the sport in advance) and adults alike is the catamaran trip to Stingray City; the extra charge for this includes lunch. In an area of open water swim some two dozen stingrays; these rays are so used to human companions that you can touch them and swim among them with no fear. If you want to see the rays from a deeper perspective, dive boats stop here, too.

On land children can take nature walks, learn traditional Caymanian crafts and Caribbean dancing, and visit local museums with Camp Hyatt, the resort's supervised program for youngsters ages 3 through 12. The program runs daily year-round, with both day and evening programs available. All campers take snorkel lessons in the pool. Families that want a land destination to explore together can travel to the Turtle Farm in West Bay to look at turtles of all sizes and ages.

*Hyatt Regency Grand Cayman, Box 1588, Grand Cayman, tel. 345/949–1234 or 800/553–1300. Year-round: 4–8 days, $545–$1,819 for dive and scuba school packages; a portion can be deducted for a nondiving adult in the same room. Children under 18 stay free in room with parents.*

## Ocean Voyages

10+

It would be difficult to find a company more dedicated to the concept of getting families onto boats and into the waters of the world than this one. Ocean Voyages takes pride in its association with vessels and dive masters who love welcoming families on board—and they have many for snorkelers and divers to choose from. Pick an ocean or sea you want to explore, and Ocean Voyages can put together a vacation for you.

**FOR FAMILIES.** The 145-ft Dutch schooner *Modriaan* attracts families and others who want to explore the bountiful reefs and isolated cays and islets off the coast of Belize, which has the second-longest barrier reef in the world. Serenity, solitude, and first-class diving and snorkeling are the draws here. Sailing on this two-masted tall ship, which uses both wind and motor power, is an adventure in itself.

The *Modriaan* sleeps just 20 guests in air-conditioned cabins that have double beds or upper and lower twins, as well as private bathrooms and showers. One cabin accommodates a family of three. The ship is equipped for diving, including a dive master or guide, but you must be certified before your trip. Bring your own snorkel gear for the family. There are two Zodiac landing craft for expeditions to uninhabited islands and cays.

Sailings start and end in Belize City, and Ocean Voyages will help arrange airfare, though it's not part of the charter price. Also ask about land stays before or after sailing. Hidden Valley, in a jungle setting, has cottages, lots of wildlife, and natural pools and waterfalls; it's near Maya ruins, too. The staff of an environmental institute at the resort leads nature walks and studies.

The sleek, 55-ft sloop *Sunyata* also sails around Belize, Guatemala, and Honduras; its

American captain runs excellent family trips. The *Sunyata* sleeps six, but if you have a larger group (up to 12) the captain can arrange to have another boat sail in tandem with him. The 121-ft schooner *Regina Chatarina* sails the Caribbean waters around Guadeloupe, St. Lucia, St. Vincent, and Grenada. Captain Anton Jacobsen's two children are on board, and he welcomes families enthusiastically. The vessel is equipped with a compressor and tanks, and diving for certified divers is available with advance notice. There's plenty of snorkeling for all ages. This is the boat on which to have a family reunion—a special weekly rate of $17,500 for 16–22 people (with at least six children among them) includes all meals. If your group isn't that large, your family can join scheduled sailings.

In Hawaii a Gulfstar 50 sails along the Kona Coast of the Big Island—the Hawaiian island with the best snorkeling, according to some aficionados. Scuba can be arranged. This is an intimate vessel with room for just four to six people. A larger schooner accommodates 12–22 guests and is equipped for scuba diving.

Ocean Voyages also has family-friendly ships throughout the Pacific and in the Galápagos, in many superb snorkeling and diving destinations.

*Ocean Voyages, 1709 Bridgeway, Sausalito, CA 94965, tel. 415/332–4681. Year-round: 8 days, $800–$2,400 adults, discounts for children and families on some ships.*

## Rascals in Paradise

**ALL**

Rascals is a tour company exclusively devoted to family vacations, whether you book custom trips or join scheduled family weeks. Rascals works with many high-end resorts around the world, but its trip list has bargains, too. On scheduled family departures, an escort arranges activities of all kinds for children and families. Because Theresa Detchemendy and Debbie Baratta, the company's owners, believe children should learn something about where they are traveling, a cultural component—such as visits with local families—is part of each trip. Although only a small portion of its family weeks qualifies as adventure, this company has many trips, and few people in the travel business know as much about traveling families as the professionals at Rascals.

**FOR FAMILIES.** The Divers with Kids program lists 10 resorts that are great for both divers and younger children. Most hotels offer resort and certification courses. Some allow children to snorkel at the same sites at which parents are diving, though that's never guaranteed. Still, parents and children should have plenty of time to enjoy both the marine life and each other at all these resorts. Regardless of your destination, Rascals is a full-service agency that can book your air travel (not included in prices) and anything else you need. Most trips include at least two meals a day, sometimes three, and airport transfers are almost always part of the package. Diving is often, but not always, extra, depending on the resort.

In the Caribbean you can choose from such family diving resorts as Bird Rock Beach Hotel on St. Kitts, where teens and new divers get a complimentary scuba lesson and everyone can explore the island's rain forests, and South Ocean Beach in the Bahamas, known for its reef walls, drop-offs, and caves. Tortola's Prospect Reef has its own harbor and peaceful lagoons, along with a wide variety of services for divers and nondivers alike. Families that opt for the Sand Dollar Condominiums in Bonaire can explore caves and tidal pools or sail as an alternative to viewing the marine life in the reef just offshore. Unspoiled and uncrowded, Grenada offers diversity in its diving, snorkeling, and hiking. The longest wreck in the Caribbean is here—the *Bianca C*, an Italian passenger ship that sank in 1965; it draws experienced divers from around the world. But this is a fine place to learn, too, and the resort here has a special deal for teens: a $99 certification course (of course, teens must be accompanied by adults).

Far to the west but still in the Caribbean are resorts in Mexico, Belize, and Honduras. Mexico has one of the best and most affordable hotels for families with young snorkelers, the Club Akumal Caribe. Although Akumal is not far south of Cancún, it is everything that city is not: uncrowded, noncommercial, peaceful. You can snorkel right from the beach or take in Palancar Reef, across the water in Cozumel. There are brilliantly colored fish and exotic coral formations, along with sunken Spanish galleons. Don't miss a chance to visit nearby Tulum, the only Maya ruin on the coast. On Ambergris Cay in Belize, Journey's End Club has family snorkel and picnic trips as well as lots of water and land sports. Most important, you can explore the second-largest barrier reef in the world along with intriguing coral atolls. Rascals also has family-week departures to Anthony's Key Resort, off the island of Roatán in Honduras. Youngsters can take advantage of some of the children's and family activities at the resort, but the Rascals escort sets up special experiences and programs.

Beyond the Caribbean—way beyond in some cases—are more choices for the most adventurous families. Vatulele Island Resort on Fiji is a luxury hotel that gives equal importance to romance and family time. You dive and snorkel in shimmering aqua waters and hike through rain forests during the day. At night parents can dine together in one of the world's most beautiful spots while children visit with peers. Rascals also schedules a summer family week at Palau Pacific Resort in a Micronesian diving paradise, the Republic of Palau. Palau has world-class diving and snorkeling, and a Rascals escort works with the resort to keep young ones busy with children's activities throughout the day.

*Rascals in Paradise, 650 5th St., #505, San Francisco, CA 94107, tel. 415/978–9800 or 800/872–7225. Year-round: 8–11 days, $1,120–$10,950 for family of 4; dive costs vary.*

## World of Adventure Vacations

**ALL**

This company deals specifically with the countries of Micronesia. One of these, the Republic of Palau (also known as Belau), is 550 mi east of the Philippines—a nine-hour flight from Hawaii. Palau comprises 343 islands spread over 100 mi and is one of the world's top dive sites. Jacques Cousteau named Palau's Ngemelis Wall the world's best wall dive, and CEDAM International, an organization whose acronym comes from its dedication to conservation, education, diving, archaeology, and museums, nominated Palau as number one of the seven diving wonders of the world.

This is a destination for diving and snorkeling families that love to visit the hot new spots before much of the rest of the world even knows they exist. A first-rate hotel, Palau Pacific Resort, caters to families, even those with infants. With one call to World of Adventure Vacations, you can book airfare, lodging, dive and snorkel packages, museum visits, rental cars, and sightseeing.

**FOR FAMILIES.** Palau Pacific Resort, a 20-minute drive from Koror, Palau's capital, has family resort amenities that are unusually extensive for this part of the world. Snorkeling is excellent right from the beach—perfect for young children—and child-size equipment can be rented. Fascinating creatures, such as 2-ft giant clams, can be glimpsed along the reef close to shore. The resort also has a pool, a nature trail, and lots of water-sports equipment for rent, including underwater cameras. The recreation staff can arrange a family snorkeling instructor, guided nature hikes, or kayaking lessons—all free of charge, except for equipment rental fees.

Independent tour operators have desks at the hotel for booking tours; in some cases you can even prebook through World of Adventure. One operator, Sam's Dive Tours, leads hiking tours to the Ngardmau Waterfall and to Palau's stone monoliths. You can also rent a car at the resort and drive to the Palau National Museum in Koror, where Palauan history, legends, and culture are interpreted through artifacts and traditional carved storyboards.

Palau's waters, however, with huge caverns, unspoiled reefs, and live coral formations, are what make it a world-class destination. No one should leave without taking a boat tour of the famous rock islands, which appear to float above the surface of the water. You can snorkel and dive from these boats. Among the most compelling attractions is Jellyfish Lake, filled with thousands of these eerily translucent, non-stinging creatures. Snorkelers come from all over the world to float among them; others study the jellyfish from a raft. One company, Adventure Kayaking, has kayaking tours from 1 to 10 days for those who want to see Palau from the vantage point of a hard-shell, sit-on-top kayak—boats easy enough for children to master quickly. And of course there's the diving. In order for you to dive with them, many operators require you to be age 16, certified, and in possession of your certification card. Splash, operating at Palau Pacific Resort, has both resort and certification courses.

Palauans are very family oriented, which makes the country a wonderful place to travel with children. It also helps that the main language in Palau is English and the currency is the U.S. dollar. Everyone in the family does need a passport, though. *World of Adventure Vacations, 301 Main St., El Segundo, CA 90245, tel. 310/322–8100 or 800/945–9955. Year-round: 7 days, Palau Pacific Resort, $598–$1,227 for lodging, depending on room and season; children under 18 free in room with parents. Children under 6 eat free at breakfast, lunch, and dinner buffet when families are on meal plan; ages 6–12 eat for half-price. Most tours are half-price for ages 5–12; children under 5 are usually free. Diving packages through World of Adventure run $105 per day; airfare is $900–$1,500 per person from Los Angeles or San Francisco; add-ons from other gateways average $270; 33% discount on airfare for children 2–11.*

# Resources

## Organizations

Contact the following organizations for information about certification, for the locations of retail shops and resorts from which you can get instruction and gear, and for written material on great dive destinations around the world: **National Association of Underwater Instructors** (9942 Currie Davis Dr., Suite H, Tampa, FL 33619, tel. 800/553–6284) and **Professional Association of Dive Instructors** (30151 Tomas St., Rancho Santa Margarita, CA 92688-2125, tel. 949/858–7234 or 800/729–7234, ext. 565). Known as NAUI and PADI, respectively, these are *the* certification organizations in the United States. They can also tell you about snorkeling.

The **Handicapped Scuba Association International** (1104 El Prado, San Clemente, CA 92672, tel. 949/498–6128) is a certification agency for instructors who work with people with special needs. It also has a Dive Buddy program for family members of physically challenged individuals. If you have a special-needs teen, for example, you can learn what you need to know to dive with your child. Send $2 and a stamped, self-addressed envelope for more information.

# TREKKING WITH LLAMAS AND BURROS

Children, especially young ones, require lots of gear that parents invariably end up hauling around. This system can be a problem in the world of long-distance and backcountry hiking. Parents with packs can't also carry infants and toddlers in a backpack-style child carrier, and adding another person's gear to an already heavy pack may be an impossibility. The end result: Many families feel they can't trek into remote areas or hike longer, more difficult trails until their children are old enough—about 11 or 12—to walk a good distance and carry their own gear.

Fortunately, there is another way: trekking with animals. Most children are happy to help lead and care for their four-footed hiking friends, an arrangement with the added bonus of occupying them on the trail and in camp. And even though they think they're just having fun, children who hike with animals are learning responsibility and patience as well.

Perhaps best of all, trekking with animals literally takes the load off parents, freeing them up to carry nonwalkers or preschoolers into some of North America's most beautiful terrain. Animal trekking opens backcountry areas up to school-age children, too—six- to eight-year-olds who can walk (and run and leap and dawdle) over several miles of rugged trails each day, but not with a heavy pack.

Families have several choices of animal companions. Llamas are the most popular; these smart, agile South American natives have been domesticated beasts of burden for more than 5,000 years. Although they don't like a lot of petting, llamas are gentle, good-natured souls. They're among the most environmentally friendly of pack animals because of the leathery padding on their two-toed feet; they make about the same impact on the wilderness as a deer. As for burros, they're gentle, strong, surefooted, and particularly well suited to the High Sierra in California, where they've been used as pack animals for years.

## Questions to Ask

**Does each hiker get to lead an animal?** On some treks this is the case; on others two hikers share an animal. Sometimes the animals may be tied together in a group, with the guide leading the whole gang. Depending on the age of your children, one of these styles will probably suit you best. Find out how things work so your children won't be either disappointed or overwhelmed.

**Can my children or I help care for the animals?** This is a learning experience as well as a fun one, and tending to the animals can make the difference between a good and a great trip for some families. If animal care interests you, pick an outfitter that encourages you to join in.

**How many miles will we walk each day?** These treks average from 4 to 6 mi in a day, though some cover as little as 1½ mi and others as many as 10. Make sure your children can walk the distance or that you can carry them in a backpack, because riding the pack animals is never allowed.

**On what kind of terrain will we hike?** As important as the number of miles covered is the difficulty of the trail. One mile through a level forested area may be doable for a five-year-old, but a mile on a steep canyon trail is not. Most outfitters rate their trips easy, moderate, or strenuous based on the difficulty of the terrain; check the classifications and ask specific questions.

**Which trip is best for families?** Even among the easy or moderate treks, some are better for families than others, and some are better for younger children. The outfitters listed here named their best family trips without hesitation because they've seen lots of families out in the wilderness. Listen to their advice. Even when llamas or burros are carrying the gear, children still have to be able to negotiate the trails safely and in a reasonable amount of time.

**How much personal gear can we bring?** Many outfitters have a limit—frequently about 20 pounds per person—depending on whether the animals will be carrying gear for one person or two. This is a good opportunity to teach your children how to economize on equipment and gear, weigh things, and set priorities. Of course, if they choose a second stuffed animal over a warm jacket, you'll have to convince them to choose again.

**What gear must we bring?** Only some outfitters supply sleeping bags. Read equipment lists carefully and ask if you are uncertain. Also, many treks are in mountainous areas, where the weather can change drastically in a matter of minutes and the temperature can fluctuate significantly from daytime to evening. Clothes that can be layered and that dry quickly are best for everyone.

**Will there be other activities on the trip?** A few treks include wildlife viewing, nature studies, fishing, geology lessons, and hikes without the animals as part of the itinerary. Depending on the ages and interests of your children, such activities might be almost as important to you as the main event.

**Do you offer tours of your farm or ranch?** Some llama outfitters, especially those specializing in day hikes, will give minitours so your family can see babies and other llamas that will not be on your trip. These tours are usually, but not always, free. This can be a very special treat for children, so don't be shy about asking. If you're staying at the outfitter's headquarters, a tour is probably part of the package.

**What's included in the cost of the trip?** Outfitters provide animals, guides, food, tents, and sleeping pads, unless noted otherwise. Gourmet meals are common—one outfitter even wakes you up with hot towels and coffee. Sleeping bags are not usually included, but there are some exceptions. Local transportation varies: You may meet at company headquarters and then be taken with your group to the trailhead; in other cases you must get to the trailhead on your own. Most outfitters will give you some help finding accommodations in the area before and after a trip, though they don't usually provide lodging themselves.

## Instruction

Animal trekking involves minimal instruction, although before the trip you will be given information on how to lead an animal properly (if you will be doing that), how to move around them safely (for the animals' protection and your family's), and what you can expect in terms of their personality and behavior. If caring for and feeding the animals is part of the trip, you will learn as you go. Your children must listen to these instructions, too.

## A Note About Ages

The age mentioned in each listing is the outfitter's suggested minimum age for children to be able to hike on their own. When two ages or ranges are given, it means the outfitter will allow children on the trip who are young enough for parents to carry in a backpack. The younger range is generally one through three; however, you know your children and your capacity for carrying them.

## Finding the Fun

**Northeast:** Appalachian Mountain Club, Northern Vermont Llama Company, Telemark Inn. **Mid-Atlantic:** Virginia Highlands Llamas. **South:** WindDancers Lodging & Llama Treks. **Rockies:** American Wilderness Experience/GORP Travel, Off the Beaten Path. **West Coast:** Hurricane Creek Llama Treks, Sierra Club, Wallowa Llamas. **Canada:** Strider Adventures.

# Favorite Packers

### American Wilderness Experience/GORP Travel

**10+**

Although American Wilderness Experience/GORP Travel is not an outfitter itself, it works with some of the country's best outfitters to bring adventures of all kinds to people who want to experience the solitude and beauty of life in the wilderness. It offers two llama trips in Wyoming and Montana. Ten is the recommended minimum age for both these treks, but the company may make exceptions for families with hiking and wilderness experience. Discuss this first before booking a trip.

**FOR FAMILIES.** For the Wyoming location, choose from three- to six-day treks of varying difficulty in the peaks and backcountry surrounding the Jackson Hole valley. An easy trek winds along the Snake River and the southern part of Yellowstone National Park. For a more challenging hike, try the trip into the Green Lakes–Jedediah Smith Wilderness area; the 5- to 6-mi hike to base camp ascends 2,000 ft. For experienced hikers, there's the guides' favorite trip: an autumn adventure to Alaska Basin–Jedediah Smith Wilderness (rated strenuous). Talk to the company's experts to determine the trek that's right for your family's abilities and time frame. The town of Jackson, your starting and ending point, is a terrific place to spend an extra day or two; check out the famous antler arches in the town square. In summer you can also take in the rodeo.

If Montana is where you want to meet your llama, start your trip in Missoula, where guides David and Amy Rubin Harmon will pick you up at your hotel. From there you travel into the Clark Fork River valley and then into the spectacular terrain of western Montana. The Hoodoo Pass trailhead, at 6,000 ft in the Bitterroot Range, is your destination. In spite of the rugged land, the trail is fairly gentle—suitable for beginner and advanced hikers. The hike goes through alpine meadows and glacial bowls, down to the first base camp on the shores of Trio Lakes. On Day three it's off to Dalton and Pearl lakes, then on to the shores of Heart Lake, where the second camp will be established. During the day families leave the base camps for a variety of activities: hiking, swimming, fishing, wildlife viewing, taking pictures, or just lolling around in the sun. Before or after your trek, spend time in Missoula. A ride on the restored carousel is a must, and if you're there on a Saturday, check out the farmer's market down by the depot.

Whichever trek you choose, the guides will welcome your family's help with your llama companions and around camp. You'll need to bring a good sleeping bag or reserve one through the company for an additional $30.

*American Wilderness Experience/GORP Travel, Box 1486, Boulder, CO 80306, tel. 303/444–2622 or 800/444–0099. July–Sept.: 3–6 days, $550–$1,295.*

## Appalachian Mountain Club

13+

Join this venerable organization, and you'll meet other families, guides, naturalists, and a host of other people who love the wilderness and respect nature. Members get a discount on trips and courses. The Appalachian Mountain Club (AMC) has llama trekking in New York at its Catskill Mountains center in the High Peaks region.

**FOR FAMILIES.** The focus of this weekend trip is really to teach novices all about llamas and give them a chance to spend time around the animals. Participants arrive Friday night and stay in the Valley View Lodge. Saturday morning everyone learns a bit about their four-footed hiking companions before the group takes off for a 6- to 8-mi hike on mountain trails. Return to the lodge Saturday evening for dinner, videotapes, and discussions about caring for, showing, and breeding llamas. Sunday morning is spent at the lodge playing games with the llamas and finding out more about them.

*Appalachian Mountain Club, Box 366, Long Lake, NY 12847, tel. 518/624–2056 for reservations at the Catskills center or 603/466–2727 for general AMC information and a full catalog. Sept.: 2 days, $180; 10% discount for members.*

## Hurricane Creek Llama Treks

6+

Twelve thousand years ago glaciers carved what is now the Eagle Cap Wilderness out of northeastern Oregon's landscape. Today rugged granite and marble peaks rise from flower-filled alpine meadows and pine forests; clear streams and lakes teem with rainbow and brook trout. Elk, bighorn sheep, mountain goats, and mule deer are often seen on the ridges and in high valleys. People, however, are harder to find. Eagle Cap remains uncrowded and unspoiled, a terrific place to trek with children and llamas. You could not be in better hands than with Stanlynn Daugherty, owner of Hurricane Creek Llama Treks and the person who wrote the book on llama trekking—literally (*see* Resources, *below*).

**FOR FAMILIES.** Stanlynn recommends three of her 10 trips for families with younger children. Eagle Cap Wildflowers, a six-day trek in mid-July, takes hikers along the lower reaches of Hurricane Creek when the wildflowers are nearing their peak. You can fish along the way, too. Brownie Basin Base Camp, in midsummer, is ideal for six- and seven-year-olds or those with limited hiking experience. You hike to several alpine lakes where the fishing is surpassed only by the scenery. These two trips coincide with Chief Joseph Days rodeo weekend, which is generally in late July, so arrive in Joseph early to catch the action.

Parents with older children and hiking and wilderness experience might opt for the Hells Canyon Base Camp in the remote Hells Canyon National Recreation Area. On this trip you look across North America's deepest gorge to the mountains of Idaho and hike canyons and rims high over the Snake River.

All Hurricane Creek trips include a night at the Bed, Bread and Trail Inn in Joseph, Oregon, before and after the trip, as well as dinner and breakfast at the inn before the start of your adventure. The outfitter also supplies transportation between the inn and the trailhead.

*Hurricane Creek Llama Treks, 63366 Pine Tree Rd., Enterprise, OR 97828, tel. 541/432–4455 or 800/528–9609. July–Aug.: 6–7 days, $710–$825 adults; 20% discount for children 6–18.*

## Northern Vermont Llama Company

**1–3, 4+**

Your family can trek with llamas through the Green Mountains of Vermont near the resort areas of Smugglers' Notch and Stowe. Although this company offers day trips only, Vermont and the Green Mountains are the setting for so many family adventures—kayaking, canoeing, and rock climbing, to name a few—you could easily spend a week here and not try the same activity twice.

**FOR FAMILIES.** The cross-country ski trails of Smugglers' Notch, a year-round family resort, make ideal llama trekking trails in spring, summer, and fall. All treks meet at Smugglers', but you don't have to be a guest there to join up with Lindsay and Geoff Chandler of Northern Vermont Llama Company. Half-day, full-day, and sunset treks are all good choices for families with babies and toddlers in backpacks or for parents with preschoolers. Walks are leisurely, with ample break time to meet the needs of the littlest explorers. On a typical full-day hike, you walk for 1¼ hours and then take a morning break, followed by an hour-long hike. After lunch and rest time of an hour or so, the hike back to Smugglers' is about 1½ hours. All treks include fresh fruit, Lindsay's baked goods, and Vermont's own Ben & Jerry's ice cream.

If you have time at the end of your hike, follow Lindsay 10 mi back to the farm in your car. Most of the 10 to 15 babies born each year at the 35-acre llama and Christmas tree farm arrive in summer, so there's a good chance you'll get to see a few.

*Northern Vermont Llama Company, 766 Lapland Rd., Waterville, VT 05492, tel. 802/644–2257. May–Oct.: ½–1 day, $30–$60 adults, $15–$30 children age 12 and under.*

## Off the Beaten Path

1+

Off the Beaten Path (OBP) specializes in customized vacations in the Rockies, Southwest, and Alaska and works only with experienced outfitters that provide the highest-quality service. Once you arrange a trip, OBP takes care of every detail. Although custom can mean expensive, OBP is also dedicated to helping families plan the trip of a lifetime—even when budget is a consideration.

**FOR FAMILIES.** OBP works with llama packers in the Rockies. There are trips in the towering Tetons of Wyoming, in Colorado, and around West Yellowstone in southern Montana, among other spectacular places. Treks vary in terms of length and difficulty. When you ask about a family llama trek, OBP takes down extensive information about your family: ages, experience, budget, vacation needs and dreams, where you most want to go and what you most want to see, and how much time you have. OBP then makes suggestions about the outfitter and trip it believes will give you the best experience.

*Off the Beaten Path, 27 E. Main St., Bozeman, MT 59715, tel. 406/586–1311 or 800/445–2995. June–Sept.: $150–$225 per day; some trips offer children's discounts.*

## Sierra Club

7+

Gentle, strong, friendly, and occasionally confounding, burros make ideal trekking companions for families hiking the High Sierra in California. The Sierra Club's burro-assisted hikes are extremely popular, so if you want to go along, sign up early. Leading and caring for the burros is somewhat demanding, so families should be prepared for a little work as well as a lot of fun. Good physical condition is a must.

**FOR FAMILIES.** Traditionally, two or three of the weeklong burro trips each summer are designated as family departures, each one accommodating about 12 people. You camp overnight on all trips, and will need to bring your own sleeping bags and tents (though you can rent tents on some trips). The Cottonwood Lakes Basin trip takes families into the southern Sierra Nevada and Inyo National Forest. Numerous lakes, home of the rare golden trout, are wonderful settings for campsites; on several layover days there's time for relaxing and fishing. The Miter Basin and Sequoia National Park trip follows a moderate route across ridges and glaciated Sierra landscape. Fishing, day hikes, and just lounging around are all part of the agenda. Those who join the Mt. Langley trip will visit Inyo National Forest and Sequoia National Park, hike over Cottonwood Pass and onto the northern edge of the Kern Plateau, fish, and explore the High Sierra timberline.

Sierra Club does not offer burro treks every year; call for a full catalog to see when these trips are next available. And because the club uses llamas on several of its adult trips, it's also possible that some family treks include llama packing. Call to ask.

*Sierra Club, 85 2nd St., 2nd floor, San Francisco, CA 94105, tel. 415/977–5522. July–Aug.: 7 days, $695 adults, $595 children age 16 and under. All participants 18 and up must be Sierra Club members; application and fees ($35 per person, $42 per couple) can be sent in with the trip reservation form.*

## Strider Adventures

6+

If llama trekking with a small group in British Columbia's backcountry sounds like an adventure your family is ready for, contact Dan Hunter at Strider. You can choose treks through the alpine meadows, lakes, and high country of the majestic Canadian Rockies or the Cariboo Mountains. The company also has trips along the glaciers and rivers of Kakwa Recreation Area. If you're lucky, you'll see the magical northern lights in addition to vast star-filled skies, wildlife, waterfalls, and unforgettable panoramic views.

**FOR FAMILIES.** Families are welcomed on all Strider llama treks. There are two-, three-, five-, and seven-day scheduled adventures, or you can opt for a custom trip of any length. Treks vary in distance. Typical for families is the two- or three-day Fang Mountain trek, good for children age six and older, with its round-trip hike of 10 km (a little more than 6 mi) and walks along alpine lakes and meadows, ridges and bluffs. The Kakwa Adventure is a five- or seven-day, 80-km (50-mi) trek into the Canadian Rockies and up a long, gentle grade over the Continental Divide. It's best for hikers at least 10 years old. All treks are suitable not only for children but also for senior citizens, which makes Strider a good outfitter for multigenerational adventures. With llamas carrying the load, hikers of all ages have a chance to access Canada's superb mountain backcountry.

You have to bring your own high-quality, warm sleeping bag, but Strider supplies all other camping and trekking equipment in addition to transportation to and from the trailhead in Prince George. The trip price also includes traveler's insurance and Canada's goods and services tax.

*Strider Adventures, 17075 Perry Rd. E, Prince George, British Columbia, Canada V2K 5E3, tel. 250/963–9542 or 800/665–7752. July–Sept.: 2–7 days, C$337.65–C$1061.71 adults; 50% discount for children under 16 and additional 10% discount for family groups of 4 or more and seniors.*

## Telemark Inn

3½+

This Maine inn at the base of Caribou Mountain, on the edge of White Mountain National Forest, was built in 1900 as a private wilderness retreat. Today Telemark Inn accommodates from 12 to 14 people, who come for the serenity of the wilderness and to trek with llamas, among other activities (see Cross-Country Skiing). An appreciation for nature is at the heart of what Telemark offers; llama trekkers learn not only about the animals but about alpine ecology, local geology, and the area's wildlife. On these treks all those who want to can lead their own llama.

**FOR FAMILIES.** One-, three-, and four-day llama treks take you into the surrounding White Mountain National Forest, to beaver ponds (where moose and raptors congregate) and rivers, and into magnificent mountain settings. These are Himalayan-style treks, meaning guides go ahead and set up everything before your party arrives in camp each afternoon. You're awakened with hot towels and coffee brought to your roomy dome tent. Yes, it's pampering, but this doesn't detract from the emphasis on nature. Inn owner Steve Crone is an alpine ecologist, and his guides are geologists, botanists, and outdoor educators. But don't think they aren't also fun. Throughout the trek there's time to swim, hike without the llamas, and relax. There's also bound to be good wildlife viewing; moose, coyotes, and black bears inhabit the area.

Not a camper? You can have your adventure and your cozy New England inn, too. Telemark offers three-, five-, and seven-day adventure activity packages during which you stay in rooms at the inn and go out each day for a variety of activities, including a chance to see bald eagles and to visit a peregrine falcon nesting site. The three-day package includes a day each of llama trekking, canoeing, and guided hiking. On the five-day package families can add a day of mountain biking or a swimming-hole day. The five-day option includes one free day, the seven-day option, two free days on which families can relax around the inn and enjoy its setting and amenities. There's one more choice: If your family can't decide between a canoe adventure and a llama trek, ask about the six-day combo trip: three days each of llama trekking and Maine lakes canoeing. Steve will take children as young as 3½ on any llama trek, but talk to him first about the trip and your child's personality and abilities.

Not all llama-trekking guests stay at the inn before or after a trip, but if you have the time, it's well worth a visit.

*Telemark Inn, R.F.D. 2, Box 800, Bethel, ME 04217, tel. 207/836–2703. June–mid-Sept.: 1–7 days, $75–$795 adults, $50–$575 children.*

## Virginia Highlands Llamas

5+

The ancient, rolling terrain of the Appalachians beckons hikers of all ages and abilities. This company in Virginia's southwestern corner leads day hikes of varying difficulty, one of which is perfect for young hikers who need time to play as they go.

**FOR FAMILIES.** The journey doesn't sound like much—just 1½ mi—but when you add in time for eating lunch, wading in the creek, and inspecting a natural spring that pumps out 350 gallons of water a minute, it's a full day of llama trekking and an excellent summer choice for children age five and up. Virginia Highlands is somewhat flexible about age, but ask before bringing a younger child.

In the spring and fall, when it's a little cooler, you and your older children—those age eight and up—might choose to climb Big Walker Mountain. This trek is a strenuous 3 mi out and 3 mi back on steep, rugged trails, so be prepared.

*Virginia Highlands Llamas, Rte. 1, Box 41, Bland, VA 24315, tel. 540/688–4464. Apr.–Nov. (all treks not available all months): 1 day, $60.*

## Wallowa Llamas

1–3, 6+

Although most people who have never been to Oregon think it has only fir forests and green valleys, the state also has cliff-lined coasts, high volcanic mountain ranges, red-rock desert, and areas where wheat fields sweep all the way to the horizon. Oregon's northeast corner is primarily high desert, mountains, and wilderness—the perfect setting for llama trekking.

Wallowa Llamas usually takes 10 trekkers and 8 llamas, equally divided into two strings. Hikers don't usually lead their own llama; however, the guides might let you lead a string of four as you get accustomed to working with the animals during the trip. You are always welcome to help feed and water the llamas in camp and to help bring them in when it's time to break camp.

**FOR FAMILIES.** Like Hurricane Creek Llama Treks (*see above*), Wallowa Llamas has easy treks for families into the Eagle Cap Wilderness in the Wallowa Mountains, not far from the Idaho border. Infants and toddlers have made this four-day trip in backpacks, and most six-year-olds are capable of walking it.

Beyond that, Wallowa Llamas offers a whole range of treks and destinations, from an easy three-day adventure to Imnaha Falls (a 16-mi round-trip trek) to a moderately difficult 23-mi hike in the high meadows of Sugarloaf Mountain with views of the ridges of Red Mountain. There are also moderate three- to seven-day treks into the Wallowas near Pine and Crater lakes. Expect to cover about 7 mi on five- and seven-day treks; the three-day adventure covers a little less ground. You can swim in the lakes, but the water is definitely cool. Teens and their parents who are ready for a seven-day mountain adventure can choose Across the Rugged Wallowas, the company's fairly strenuous 32-mi trek. U.S. Forest Service regulations allow only four guests and two guides on this trip, so sign up early if this one is for you.

*Wallowa Llamas, 36678 Allstead La., Halfway, OR 97834, tel. 541/742–2961. Apr.–Oct.: 3–7 days, $350–$990; discounts if you carry some of your own gear.*

## WindDancers Lodging & Llama Treks

ALL

Set on 270 acres of wilderness in the Smoky Mountains, WindDancers is a working llama ranch and bed-and-breakfast. Though the establishment is relatively new, the folks at WindDancers are experienced, having put hikers and llamas together for 10 years, formerly under the name Windsong Llama Treks. Their current wilderness retreat has three log lodges with nine guest rooms or suites. Each lodge room is decorated in the style of a country, state, or region: Peru, Kenya, and New Mexico among them. Some have decks while others have fireplaces; some are tucked high in the hills, others sit beside a stream. Organized llama treks explore the woodland trails snaking across the ranch's land.

**FOR FAMILIES.** If your family is taking a Far Camp Overnight, the llamas and guides will pick you up at the door of your lodge. The forest trail leads you to a tent campsite with a 60-mi view of Great Smoky Mountain National Park, where you'll have dinner around a campfire. In the morning, you'll head back to the lodge, then perhaps on to other adventures in the Smoky Mountain region.

It's precisely because the region offers so much—RV adventures, canoeing, kayaking, rock climbing, mountain biking, and more—that families may wish to take only a short llama trek. A good option is one of WindDancers' day trips: lunch treks that combine a scenic hike with a fresh lunch, and dinner treks where dinner is served at a table by a brook up on the mountain. And because WindDancers combines adventure with a luxury B&B, this is the ideal place to come to after you've gotten an adrenaline rush on some of North Carolina's other adventures. (The inn is open year-round.)

All ages are welcome on any of the llama treks; however, parents should be willing and able to carry very young adventurers in a child backpack. Ask ahead of time about the length and difficulty of the trail to the overnight site to determine if your child can do it alone or would need to be carried. The company provides all equipment, including sleeping bags.

*WindDancers Lodging & Llama Treks, 1966 Martins Creek Rd., Clyde, NC 28721, tel. 828/627–6986. Mar.–Oct: Overnights $150 per person; lunch and dinner treks $40 adults, $30 children under 8.*

# Resources

## Organizations

Contact the **International Llama Association** (Box 1891, Kalispell, MT 59903, tel. 406/257–0282 ) for a catalog with a variety of material: information about llamas; a list of reference materials; and a list of packers and breeders across the nation.

## Books

Stanlynn Daugherty, owner of Hurricane Creek Llama Treks, is the author of the informative *Packing with Llamas* (Clay Press).

## Also See

If your family loves traveling with four-footed friends, consider the trips in Horse Packing, Covered Wagon Adventures, and Cattle Drives. The chapter on Ranches also describes vacations in which you can get to know horses and other animals. For up-close meetings with more exotic creatures, turn to Wildlife Encounters.

# WILDLIFE ENCOUNTERS

Almost from birth children show immense joy in sharing this planet with finned, winged, and four-footed creatures. Although the benefits of teaching children about animals and giving them a chance to meet the creatures of the world up close and personal are clear, there is another reason for seeking out this type of trip: Wildlife encounters are also good for adults. They bring out the child in us, taking us back to a time when we saw the world as full of wonder. I have seen this transformation take place among adults on all the animal-encounter trips I've taken. In the Galápagos, adults and children vied for the sea lions' attention and made faces at the somber-eyed iguanas. When the captain of our boat announced that a troop of dolphins was leaping off our bow, the adults were the first ones to the railing.

Whether you choose a vacation on which you actually hug a wild creature (as is possible in Baja California and on the ice floes in the Gulf of St. Lawrence) or one on which you only observe them at close range, the rewards are immediate and long-lasting. Some animal encounters benefit the animals, too, because tourist dollars provide important funding or because tourists themselves provide research assistance.

It's worth noting that some outfitters and tour operators—not, of course, those described here—may be more interested in the bottom line than in the protection of animals. By choosing a trip carefully, you're ensuring that future generations will be able to experience the magic of these encounters, too. However, it's important to point out that scientists have different opinions about how close humans should come to animals in their native habitat. Some scientists feel direct contact with wildlife is not a good idea, while others believe long-term benefits outweigh potential negatives, as long as the animals engage in contact of their own volition and are not cornered, teased, or fed. If you're concerned about this, talk to outfitters to be sure that the animals' welfare is always top priority.

Unlike other family adventures, all but a few of the wildlife encounters in this chapter take place outside the United States. Of course, many adventures, such as kayaking and hiking, in various parts of this country afford you the opportunity to see wildlife, and individual trip descriptions will highlight that aspect. The encounters in this chapter, however, were chosen because they focus on the animals, many unique to the habitat you will be exploring. A family's contact with these creatures great and small can be the experience of a lifetime, with the power to change a child's perceptions not only of the world's animals but of our place in the universe.

## Questions to Ask

**How long will we be watching for animals each day, and is there an option to cut it short if my children get fidgety?** As much as children love animals, few enjoy the long trips and dragged-out waits that many animal encounters require. That's why trips planned just for families are designed to move quickly, without unnecessarily long waiting periods and delays. Still, even on nonfamily trips, outfitters do their best to accommodate everyone, so you may be able to make special arrangements. Some trips, however, cannot be altered; when you're flying to ice floes by helicopter, for example, you're bound to a strict schedule. Study your itinerary carefully. If there are morning and afternoon encounters, you will probably have the option of going on just one. Ask about the possibility of child care while you're away from camp. Find a trip that's right for your child's age, temperament, and capacity for sitting.

**Are shots or other health precautions necessary?** Many animal encounter trips take place in foreign countries that require inoculations and other kinds of preventive medication. Check far in advance and ask a pediatrician or the local health department about health precautions in foreign countries, especially as they relate to children. Always pack basic children's medication—acetaminophen, an antihistamine, cough syrup, motion-sickness pills, and antidiarrhea pills; these are often hard to find in foreign countries. If your child is prone to ear infections or any other ailments, you may want to ask your pediatrician for an antibiotic that doesn't need to be refrigerated.

**Is any special clothing required?** On some trips, such as those to the Arctic, special cold-weather apparel is crucial. Although outfitters often provide outerwear that will fit children, they may not have all that's necessary. Finding extreme-weather clothing for youngsters can be difficult in the United States, let alone in foreign destinations, so plan ahead.

**What kind of luggage and gear should we pack?** Almost all flights on small planes in the Arctic or Africa have limited capacity for luggage. Because many of these adventures have lodging in small quarters anyway—tents and ship cabins, for example—it's a good idea to pack lightly. Attire for adventure is always casual; keep in mind that you'll be getting dirty. Some African safari camps offer laundry service.

**What's the primary language where we're going?** If you're lucky enough to travel to a foreign land, take advantage of the opportunity to expose your children—and yourself—to a new language. Buy a phrase book before you leave so your family can learn to say basic phrases and the names of animals in the local language. Audiotapes for adults and children can also help you make language part of the travel experience.

**Should we tip our guides?** Your guide or naturalist is your window onto a world you've paid a great deal to see. A good guide can make the difference between a mediocre trip and an incredible one. When it comes to children, good guides work extra hard to bring the world to life for them, too—not always an easy task. Parents may show appreciation for guides' efforts in the form of tips. On trips of this sort, $10 per adult per day is appropriate; an extra few dollars for the children is a good way to encourage your guides to keep up the good work. In addition, I like to have my children give their favorite guides a note, a picture, a Polaroid shot, or any other small token of their appreciation.

**What's included in the cost?** Lodging, most meals, transportation throughout the expedition, entrance fees to sites included in the itinerary, all group equipment, and the services of qualified guides and naturalists are part of the package, unless otherwise noted. On some camping trips you must bring your own sleeping bags. In some cases, as with those tour operators running African safaris, airfare to and from certain cities in the United States is also included. When airfare is not part of the trip cost, outfitters and operators can usually arrange it for you, often at a better rate than you could get on your own. Hotel stays may be required before and after trips because of flight schedules; these are generally an additional expense.

## Instruction

Much of the instruction in preparation for these trips is about safety—both yours and the animals'—and about teaching visitors how to minimize human impact on the earth's fragile environments. In areas where the weather and conditions are extreme, you must follow instructions about proper clothing and emergency procedures. To make this process fun for children, rather than a chore, enlist their help. They can help ensure that your family follows all the guidelines.

## Finding the Fun

**West Coast:** Sea Quest Expeditions. **Alaska:** Alaska Wildland Adventures. **Canada:** Arctic Odysseys, Blue Loon Adventures, Natural Habitat Adventures. **Caribbean:** Natural Habitat Adventures. **Mexico:** Baja Discovery, Baja Expeditions. **Central America:** American Wilderness Experience/GORP Travel, Cross Country International, Temptress Adventures, Thomson Family Adventures. **South America:** Galápagos Network, Lindblad Special Expeditions, Thomson Family Adventures. **Europe:** Natural Habitat Adventures, Thomson Family Adventures. **Africa:** Big Five Tours & Expeditions, Rascals in Paradise, Thomson Family Adventures. **Asia, Australia:** Thomson Family Adventures.

# Favorite Outfitters

## Alaska Wildland Adventures

(6+)

Alaska Wildland Adventures believes that Alaska should be experienced personally, "not passively viewed through the windows of a tour bus or via the endless buffet of a luxury cruise liner." The company, however, also understands the needs of both children and senior citizens; trips specifically for these groups explore the real Alaska at a comfortable, easy pace.

**FOR FAMILIES.** Every summer special Family Safari departures cater to parents with children ages 6 to 12. On these trips you might see moose, bald eagles, and spawning salmon in the Kenai Mountains; sea otters, puffins, seals, sea lions, and maybe even whales during a wildlife cruise in Kenai Fjords National Park. There are hikes, nature walks, drives, and a train ride back to Anchorage at the end of the nine-day adventure. Accommodations are in hotels and wilderness lodges. This is the perfect action adventure for parents, children, and grandparents to share together.

If you'd rather stay put in one place for your whole vacation or even just a part of it, consider booking a few nights at Denali Backcountry Lodge, which is managed by Alaska Wildland Adventures. Because of the level of hikes typically offered at the lodge, as well as the long bus ride required to get there, this place is best for families with children eight and up. The lodge lies deep within Denali National Park, in Kantinsha along spectacular Denali Park Road. Grizzlies, moose, caribou, wolves, fox, Dall sheep, and golden eagles are commonly seen on the park road and on adventures that depart from the lodge each day. Transportation to and from the park entrance is included in the cost of a lodge stay.

*Alaska Wildland Adventures, Box 389, Girdwood, AK 99587, tel. 907/783–2928 or 800/334–8730. June–Sept.: 1–9 days, $315–$3,595 adults, $275–$3,395 children age 12 and under; discounts for groups of 3 or 4 sharing accommodations.*

## American Wilderness Experience/GORP Travel

(8+)

Although some dolphin-encounter programs have been accused of disregarding the dolphins' health and well-being, not all such programs are problematic. When reputable marine scientists are able to care for the dolphins and to teach humans about these remarkable animals, the programs have long-term beneficial effects for both groups. The experts at the Institute of Marine Sciences on the Bay Islands off the coast of Honduras have developed a program at nearby Anthony's Key Resort that practically guarantees a transcendent experience for all involved. American Wilderness Experience/GORP Travel, a specialist in environmentally friendly vacations with outfitters and tour operators that are ecologically responsible, is the U.S. agent through which you can book such encounters.

**FOR FAMILIES.** Dolphin Discovery Camp, for children ages 8 through 14, centers on the world of the Atlantic bottle-nosed dolphin. Under the supervision of the Institute of Marine Sciences staff, children have outdoor sessions on snorkeling, dolphin feeding and training, swimming, and marine experiments, as well as short classroom slide shows and discussions. When not working with the scientists, campers go horseback riding, take nature hikes, view the awesomely clear waters and coral reefs by glass-bottom boat, and otherwise play in what can only be described as paradise. Parents are welcome to join their children for some activities, and families take all meals together. The program is designed, however, to give parents (and older teens) time to do what most adults come here to do—scuba diving or snorkeling in water with visibility that ranges from 75 to 100 ft (see Snorkeling and Diving). Accommodations are in private bungalows set around the lush island.

*American Wilderness Experience/GORP Travel, Box 1486, Boulder, CO 80306, tel. 303/444–2622 or 800/444–0099. June–Aug.: 8 days, $625–$975 adults, $500 children's camp; discount for more than 1 child in camp.*

## Arctic Odysseys

12+

Arctic Odysseys has been taking adventurers to the North Pole and the area around it for more than 20 years. The Polar Bear Odyssey may be the star in this outfitter's trip list, but families have other treks from which to choose (see Native American Experiences), all of which provide unsurpassed access to the north country.

**FOR FAMILIES.** One trip goes to Wager Bay, which is some 30 mi south of the Arctic Circle in Canada and has one of the world's greatest concentrations of polar bears. Because the bay can be reached only by chartered aircraft, you view these white giants unhindered by crowds of other wildlife watchers. Boats take you amazingly close for a look at the paddling bears (if they didn't paddle, they would sink). Although polar bears are the reason most people come here, they are by no means the only wildlife in the area. On the way to and from Winnipeg, Manitoba, where the trip begins and ends, and on hikes around Wager Bay, you may see beluga whales, caribou, arctic wolves and hares, seals, gyrfalcons, peregrine falcons, and a host of other north-country birds. Accommodations at the bay are in an Inuit-owned and -operated lodge; Inuit guides lead the boat trips and hikes as well. Because of the group dynamics of this trip, participants should be at least 12 years old—but owner Robin Duberow will consider slightly younger children on an individual basis.

The Discover the Worlds of the High Arctic itinerary gives families insight into the fascinating history of the Arctic and a glimpse into the native cultures of the region. Caribou, snow geese, beluga whales, narwhals, polar bears, and bowhead whales are all likely to be seen from the low-flying planes that provide most of your transportation. From boats off Cape Dorset on Baffin Island in Canada, seals are a common sight, and if you hike around the Eureka Weather Station on Ellesmere Island, you're likely to see arctic wolves, foxes, and musk oxen. Most nights are spent in hotels, and you'll stay at the Eureka Weather Station as well. The trips starts and ends in Ottawa.

Families considering either of these trips should keep two things in mind. First, the unpredictable arctic weather and tides often cause delays or force leaders to change itineraries altogether. If your family doesn't want to be flexible, look for a different adventure. Second, Arctic Odysseys uses native guides and stops at small out-of-the-way towns and villages. You have wonderful opportunities to meet native people and learn about their unique culture.

*Arctic Odysseys, 2000 McGilvra Blvd., Seattle, WA 98112, tel. 206/325–1977. July–Aug.: 8–10 days, $4,550–$6,800; ask about family discounts.*

## Baja Discovery

5+

With red rock and gold sand set against deep blue seas, Mexico's Baja California is as incomparably beautiful as it is remote. Moreover, Baja is an extremely child-friendly place; local boatmen and crews on the Baja Discovery tours will make your children feel welcome and loved. The two trips specifically for families begin and end in San Diego.

**FOR FAMILIES.** The Gray Whale Discovery at San Ignacio Lagoon takes families to the only place on earth where whales regularly swim up to boats and seek human contact. Known as friendlies, these whales stick their heads up next to skiffs half their size and look whale-watchers directly in the eye. Wild and under no obligation or enticement to stay (Mexican law forbids humans from chasing, feeding, or harassing the whales in any way), friendlies love having their heads patted and their backs rubbed. They also have an incredible sense of humor; it's not unusual for one to push the skiff around and splash the humans on board for as much as an hour. Much of this trip is a waiting game—whale lovers may spend hours circling the waters in vain—so patience and the ability to sit for long periods of time are a must; the age minimum is eight.

Accommodations for this five-day trip are at the company's tented campsite on a point overlooking the lagoon. Families can choose a departure date from January through March, when the grays come to San Ignacio to mate and give birth to their young. The price includes everything except one breakfast from the time you leave San Diego until you return.

The La Unica and Sea of Cortez Islands trip is the best way to see the heart of Baja—wind-sculpted boulders, cactus "forests," wine-producing and agricultural regions, and the rich and varied flora and fauna of the central desert. You travel in a van for two days—stopping to look at things that will be engaging to even very young travelers (minimum age is five) and spending the night at hotels. On the way down to La Unica on the Sea of Cortez (also known as the Gulf of California), you visit a park, towns, a museum, a turtle research station, and more.

At the coast participants board 28-ft *pangas* (Mexican fishing skiffs) that travel to La Unica Island. Days three–five are spent exploring the remote desert islands and emerald waters of the Sea of Cortez, home to whales, dolphins, sea lions, and countless marine birds. There's snorkeling, fishing, hiking, and relaxing by day; at night families sleep in cabins, each with cots and personal bath and shower facilities. On Day six you have time for a final swim, followed by a leisurely drive up through Baja to San Diego. This trip runs in May and October and includes everything but meals at the two hotels during the van trip.

*Baja Discovery, Box 15257, San Diego, CA 92195, tel. 619/262–0700 or 800/829–2252. Jan.–Mar., May, late Sept.–Oct.: 5–8 days, $1,395–$1,725; family discounts may be available on some trips.*

## Baja Expeditions

5+

In business for 26 years, this company has been taking adventurers to Mexico's Baja California longer than any other. Baja Expeditions' trips are learning oriented, with a special emphasis on the fragile and unique environment of the Baja land and seas; lectures and slide shows are daily events.

**FOR FAMILIES.** On the San Ignacio Lagoon Gray Whale Adventure, the outfitter sends boats out several times daily in search of friendlies. When the whales choose to come up to your boat and look you in the eye, it's an experience unlike any other. Participants sleep at a desert campsite on the lagoon, with roomy dome tents, comfortable cots, and fluffy sleeping bags. There's a shower with solar-heated water, and the food cooked by the Mexican staff is hearty and delicious.

Children are treated with extra love and care by the crew, but adults outnumber children by far on these trips; try to book a departure on which another family has signed up. Parents are responsible for their children at all times. When you sign up for the trip, you will be asked whether your child can swim and how you feel your child will function in a primarily adult environment. Also, remember that you may have to wait patiently for hours before the whales appear. This five-day trip starts and ends in San Diego and includes charter flights between San Diego and San Ignacio.

Baja Expeditions has other whale-encounter trips, such as an eight-day voyage to see blue whales, the largest creatures on earth. The trip takes place aboard an 80-ft motor vessel, and you may spot dolphins and six kinds of whales in addition to blues. About two-thirds of each day is spent cruising, but the trip allows time for hiking, snorkeling, and exploring—a combination that's ideal for children and teens. Overnights are spent on the boat. Families can also choose a 10-day adventure that brings you close to the whales, dolphins, mantas, and whale sharks of the Sea of Cortez, or a seven-day trip on Magdalena Bay—calmer than San Ignacio—to encounter Baja's magnificent gray whales. All these trips start and end in the Baja California city of La Paz.

*Baja Expeditions, 2625 Garnet Ave., San Diego, CA 92100, tel. 619/581–3311 or 800/843–6967. Jan.–Nov.: 5–10 days, $1,200–$1,895; some family discounts available.*

## Big Five Tours & Expeditions

ALL

Africa remains the ultimate destination for those seeking an exotic animal encounter and a cultural experience that most people can only dream about. The animals of this huge continent fill children's books, making them recognizable and, in some ways, surprisingly accessible to children. Not too long ago only hard-core adventurers traveled to Africa. Now it attracts all kinds of people, including families. Big Five Tours & Expeditions is one of the tour operators that have made it possible for children, even very young ones, to discover this amazing land.

**FOR FAMILIES.** Big Five has special 15-day family safaris to Kenya throughout the year. There is no minimum age, but children older than four are likely to appreciate and retain the experience in a way younger children cannot. Besides wildlife viewing, the rich itinerary includes visits to museums and a crafts and cultural center. All children receive daily lessons in Swahili and participate in sing-along sessions. Stops include the famous Masai Mara Game Reserve (where much of *Out of Africa* was filmed), Sweetwaters Game Reserve, Samburu National Reserve, the Aberdare Mountains, and Lake Nakuru National Park. You'll see giraffes, zebras, elands, oryx, flamingos and eagles, and, of course, lions, leopards, elephants, and rhinos.

Big Five makes a point of getting off the beaten path, even in this wild land, to spend time at private ranches and wildlife sanctuaries in addition to wild game viewing areas. Accommodations are at deluxe hotels and luxury camps; prices include airfare via Swissair between several U.S. cities and Nairobi.

*Big Five Tours & Expeditions, 819 S. Federal Hwy., Suite 103, Stuart, FL 34994, tel. 407/287–7995 or 800/244–3483. Year-round: 15 days, $4,395–$5,195 adults, from New York depending on season; $3,295–$4,895 children, depending on age and season. Moderate add-on fares from other U.S. cities.*

## Blue Loon Adventures

3+

Tanya Wheeler and Laura McLennan are two biologists whose work has focused on the birds of northwest Ontario. While their research keeps them busy, they also wanted to share their expertise with families. Blue Loon Adventures was born, and come summer they make it possible for families to work side by side with researchers, banding and monitoring birds on the northern shore of Lake Superior.

**FOR FAMILIES.** At Blue Loon Bird Camp, families can help biologists and naturalists study song birds, raptors, water fowl, and a variety of migratory species. The camp is based at Thunder Cape Bird Observatory, on a peninsula connected to Sleeping Giant Provincial Park, not far from the city of Thunder Bay. The peninsula itself is a sort of travel marker for migratory birds, and is one of the great flyways of North America. Families participate in much of the biologists' work. Birds are captured in mist nets (fine, almost invisible nets that don't harm the birds). They're then removed from the nets and banded if they haven't been banded before. After research data is recorded, they're sent on their way. Best of all, you have the rare and thrilling opportunity to hold wild birds in your hands. Blue Loon is an experience that stays with you for a long time. More than a year after our trip, my family still talks about the purple finch Hutch held and the black capped chickadee Molly banded.

Accommodations are in cabins and large army surplus tents outfitted with cots, pillows, and all you need for comfortable camping. On request, Blue Loon can take families out to its own wilderness base camp, about 30 mi from Thunder Bay. The focus there is on song birds only. Blue Loon can also help arrange other adventures in the area, such as kayaking, canoeing, or visiting an amethyst mine. If you don't have your own camping gear, you can rent it in town. Fly into Thunder Bay; Blue Loon will arrange transportation to camp. Longer and shorter stays can be arranged.
*Blue Loon Adventures, Box 4398, Hwy.61, R.R. #7, Blake Township, Thunder Bay, Ontario, Canada P7C 5V5, tel. 888/846–0066. Late June–Aug.: 3 days, C$720 per family of 3 or 4.*

## Cross Country International

8+

Cross Country International (CCI) has wonderful walking adventures (see Hiking and Backpacking), but it's also one of the few companies to specialize in equestrian vacations as well. Though domesticated horses certainly don't count as wildlife, equestrian vacations do provide a close-up animal experience, and CCI has one horseback trip which brings you face to face with some of Costa Rica's most colorful wildlife.

**FOR FAMILIES.** The Costa Rica Trail is a five-day, six-night trek along Costa Rica's west coast in the sparsely populated province of Guanacaste. Formed by volcanic eruptions more than 60 million years ago, this is an area where mountains meet the sea, where pirates once hid treasure, and where iguanas, macaws, and sea turtles are found in abundance. You'll ride along magnificent white beaches and on country trails lined with exotic trees (keep an eye out for howler monkeys and parrots). You'll pass mango and teak plantations by day and sleep in beachfront hotels and guest houses by night. One of the best experiences of the trip is a swim in the rolling Pacific with your horse. Trip leaders Christina Rahm and David Clark are longtime residents of Costa Rica; Christina is Swedish and David is American.

The most important prerequisite is that riders of all ages must be able to walk, trot, and canter, feel comfortable on a horse, and happily spend much of the vacation in the saddle, as you'll be riding four to five hours a day. CCI will consider younger children who are good riders, but talk to them before booking. Non-riders are welcome to come along; there are several nature/wildlife tours to take from hotels while the rest of the group is out riding. Cars or vans shuttle non-riders between hotels. You can also pre-arrange a local sitter to care for younger children; the going rate is about $20 for a full day.
*Cross Country International, Box 1170 Millbrook, NY 12545, tel. 914/677–6000 or 800/828–8768. Nov.–May: 5 days, $1,500 adults, 25% discount for children under 12.*

## Galápagos Network

7+

Nature, history, and science come together on the Galápagos Islands as they do nowhere else on earth. Scattered across 17,000 square mi of the Pacific Ocean about 600 mi off the coast of Ecuador, this archipelago is home to the only marine iguanas in the world, as well as to sea lions, giant tortoises, penguins, and seals. The 13 major islands and 17 islets have more birds than most people see in a lifetime: blue-footed boobies, pink flamingos, hawks, doves, pelicans, warblers, mockingbirds, herons, ducks, cormorants, flycatchers, and, of course, Darwin's finches, the little birds that helped inspire Darwin's theory of evolution. A visit to the Galápagos, now a national park of Ecuador, will help families understand what a fragile world we live in.

**FOR FAMILIES.** Children ages seven and up are welcome on all four Galápagos Network ships. The 48-passenger, 195-ft *Corinthian* is a luxury expedition ship and the largest of the Network ships, with a 1,000-square-ft observation lounge, Jacuzzi, and solarium. The *Letty, Eric,* and *Flamingo* are identical 20-passenger, 85-ft motor yachts. The ships depart from San Cristóbal island; guests fly in from Quito or Guayaquil. All accommodations are in outside cabins; most sleep only two, though two cabins have room for three. Polished wood and superb service allow passengers to feel pampered. Rates vary by ship, cabin, and itinerary. Your choice of four- to eight-day excursions determines the number of islands you visit. Most trips give you a chance to snorkel with sea lions, and national park regulations require a stop at Darwin Station on the island of Santa Cruz (one of the only islands where you can purchase souvenirs, T-shirts, and some supplies).

All cruises have at least two naturalist-guides on board to lead hikes and provide information about the natural and cultural history of the archipelago. Guides work well with children, interspersing lectures with other activities so that even young children remain intrigued. Everyone can use the snorkeling gear and sea kayaks on board and swim at expansive white-sand beaches on various islands. (Some snorkeling gear is available in children's sizes, but parents should ask ahead.)

A trip to the Galápagos Islands will not be a solitary wilderness experience; several groups often visit the same islands at once. Fortunately, permits to sail the islands are severely limited by national park administrators, and guides are good at leading groups on different paths. Not included in the price of the cruise is the national park tax of about $100 per adult ($50 per child), payable in U.S. dollars on arrival in the Galápagos Islands.

*Galápagos Network, 7200 Corporate Center Dr., Suite 510, Miami, FL 33126, tel. 305/262–6264 or 800/633–7972. Year-round: 4–8 days, $550–$1,950; 50% discount for children 7–11 on the cruise and on Saeta Airlines, owned by the same parent company. Call 800/827–2382 to book your airfare.*

## Lindblad Special Expeditions

6+

Founded in 1979, Lindblad Special Expeditions is a leader not only in expedition travel but in environmentally responsible travel. It's got quite a pedigree; Lars-Eric Lindblad organized one of the first tourist expeditions to the Galápagos Islands back in 1967. The staff included the vice president of the National Audubon Society, a director of the World Wildlife Fund, and one of the world's best-known ornithologists. Today the Lindblad name is still associated with such pioneering partnerships, and it continues its altruistic efforts. For instance, in the Galápagos, under the direction of Sven-Olaf (Lars-Eric's son), Lindblad and its guests have raised nearly $400,000, which has been channeled directly into island conservation projects.

**FOR FAMILIES.** There are special family departures to the Galápagos each month from June to August. In addition to the expedition leader and naturalist staff, these trips include a Family Coordinator who organizes activities for families and children. Educational activities are planned throughout the seven-day voyage, both on land and on the ship. They cover the origin of species, island formation, plant and animal identification, and stargazing, among other topics.

*Polaris*, the 80-passenger ship that's home for this adventure, is big enough to be stable and comfortable, yet small enough to enter ports and inlets inaccessible to larger ships. While the itinerary can vary, the ship generally makes stops at eight islands, each one with its own unique environment. Isabela is home to the Galápagos penguin, northernmost of the world's penguins, while Florean is famous for its flamingos. Sea lions and blue-footed boobies are found on several of the islands, and on Santa Cruz you stop at the Darwin Research Station, home to Lonesome George the tortoise, the last of his particular kind. *Polaris* carries Zodiac landing craft for easy access to coastlines and a glass-bottom boat for remarkable, close-up underwater views. On board, families will find a specially developed activity kit with material for children and parents to use throughout the trip. There are also talks and nightly recaps geared to the entire family; children are encouraged to ask questions. Meals include child-friendly food, and all young passengers receive a pre-voyage reading list to help them prepare for this incredible journey.

*Lindblad Special Expeditions, 720 Fifth Ave., New York, NY 10019, tel. 212/765–7740 or 800/397–3348. June–Aug.: 7 days, $3,970–$5,990 adults, $750 discount for ages 6–14.*

## Natural Habitat Adventures

6+

Letting you get close to animals in their natural habitat is what this outfitter is all about. Starting with a profound respect for nature and a belief that people don't have to sacrifice every comfort to take part in the world's greatest nature vacations, Natural Habitat Adventures has become one of the premier companies of its kind. Whether you are on a pure vacation or on a trip in which you help researchers and scientists, the result is the same: an unforgettable encounter with some of the world's most intriguing inhabitants. Besides its scheduled tours, the company will customize a trip for a single family or even several families together.

**FOR FAMILIES.** The top family trip is indisputably the five- or six-day Seal Watch in Canada, with four departure dates in March. During that month, some 250,000 doe-eyed harp seals give birth to their fuzzy white offspring on the massive floating ice fields just west of the Magdalen Islands in the Gulf of St. Lawrence. Adorable and unafraid, some of the babies even allow visitors to pet them. These treks were begun as part of a plan to provide tourist dollars to the local community so selling seal skins would no longer be the only way to make a living there. As a result, participation in this trip may ultimately help save future seals from death. The trip begins and ends in Halifax, Nova Scotia, with additional family activities such as tubing, sledding, and cross-country skiing. Accommodations are in a cozy hotel. Natural Habitat Adventures will take children as young as age six on the seal watch, but consider carefully whether your child can handle the elements, the helicopter flights out on the ice floes, the proximity of the animals, and the travel.

You can also ask about joining any of their other regularly scheduled trips. These range from riding Tundra Buggies out to visit the polar bears in Churchill, Manitoba, to swimming with wild Atlantic spotted dolphins in the Bahamas and Caribbean humpback whales off the coast of the Dominican Republic. If research appeals to your family, you can help scientists with a variety of projects, such as observing puffins in Scotland at the Fair Isle Bird Observatory. Different trips are appropriate for different ages, so talk to the staff to determine the best adventure for your family.

*Natural Habitat Adventures, 2945 Center Green Ct., Boulder, CO 80301, tel. 303/449–3711 or 800/543–8917. Year-round (all trips not available all months): 5–12 days, $1,895–$6,895.*

## Rascals in Paradise

7+

Rascals in Paradise, a tour company just for families, works with outfitters and hotels worldwide that are especially accommodating to children. Trips with Rascals are cultural adventures in which all participants not only see new places but truly experience the people and heritage of that country. A special escort educates and entertains the children and provides support for parents. Storytelling, activities, and face-to-face contact with interesting people help families learn about the destination.

**FOR FAMILIES.** The 13-day Family Safari begins and ends in Nairobi, Kenya, home of the famous Giraffe Centre, where you study these elegant animals from a treetop aerie. Leaving the city, you stay in a mix of game lodges and deluxe tented camps. The itinerary includes watching the water hole at Ark Lodge in the Aberdare Forest and visiting Solio Game Ranch and Samburu Lodge, where crocodiles come up on the lawn for dinner. The Masai Mara Game Reserve with its vast herds of African wildlife perhaps best defines the animal viewing on this trek. It's not all four-footed beasts, though. One trip highlight is an immense flock of coral-color flamingos on Lake Elmenteita. You can also opt for a hot-air balloon ride and a fishing excursion on Lake Victoria. Once back in Nairobi, families can visit the home and museum of writer Karen Blixen (whose life story was portrayed in *Out of Africa*) before heading home.

Besides the standard inclusions (see Questions to Ask), the fee for this trip covers a baby-sitter, airport transfers, and $2,300 trip-cancellation insurance per family booking. Airfare is extra.

*Rascals in Paradise, 650 5th St., #505, San Francisco, CA 94107, tel. 415/978–9800 or 800/872–7225. Year-round: 13 days, $10,890–$13,792 for family of 4 with 2 adults and 2 children 7–11.*

## Sea Quest Expeditions

5+

Kayaking is the mode of travel for Sea Quest's San Juan Archipelago adventure in Washington, but the trip's focus is whale-watching. These islands, straddling the border with British Columbia, provide opportunities for families to observe orcas—sometimes up close—especially in summer. Besides orcas, visitors to the wildlife-rich San Juans can also spot eagles, minke whales, Dall's porpoises and harbor porpoises, and seals. There is no better way to approach these creatures than in a sea kayak. You can skirt the islands and camp in areas inaccessible to land-based travelers.

**FOR FAMILIES.** Children age five and up are welcome on one-day trips, provided they travel in a three-person kayak with two adults. For the multi-day adventures children must be at least eight years old. Youngsters who weigh a minimum of 100 pounds and are in good health and condition can participate in paddling a two-person kayak. Sea Quest's San Juan trips begin and end in Friday Harbor on San Juan Island (accessible via Seattle, Washington, or Vancouver and Victoria in British Columbia).

Families concerned about kayaking near orcas should be aware that these intelligent animals have never injured a human in the wild. Moreover, the orcas living within the San Juan Islands are used to boaters and are among the most studied and well-known whales in the world. On these expeditions learning and adventure go hand in hand. A biologist accompanies all Sea Quest's San Juan groups, so your family's questions about the whales and other aspects of life in these islands can be answered. The trip involves kayaking between about four and five hours daily, mostly with prevailing currents. No previous paddling experience is necessary, though you must be in good physical condition. No Eskimo rolls—upside-down flips—are performed in the state-of-the-art sea kayaks; the boats are extremely stable. The group receives instruction in basic paddling techniques.

*Sea Quest Expeditions, Box 2424, Friday Harbor, WA 98250, tel. 360/378–5767. May–Oct.: 1–5 days, $59–$549.*

## Temptress Adventures

2+

In recent years Costa Rica has become a major family-vacation destination, primarily because of easy access to startlingly beautiful wildlife and vegetation. Politically stable and safe for tourists, Costa Rica has jungles, beaches, mountains, and most important, incredible animals to observe. For families that want to see a lot of the country with a minimum of packing and unpacking, a cruise with Temptress Adventures is ideal.

**FOR FAMILIES.** Over the course of seven nights and eight days the *Temptress Explorer* takes 99 passengers along Costa Rica's Pacific coastline (three-and four-night cruises are also available). The ship sails at night; during the day you hike through verdant rain forests, where children keep track of numerous wildlife sightings. There are four kinds of monkeys to be discovered: howler, spider, whiteface, and squirrel. You'll also see toucans, macaws, and sloths, both the two- and three-toed varieties. Iguanas and lizards abound, including the popularly named Jesus Christ lizard, which walks on water. Butterflies are ubiquitous, and snakes are easy to find. You may spot a fer-de-lance snake, one of the deadliest in Costa Rica. (You needn't worry about being bitten by snakes; they are shy, and the ship naturalists who always accompany you will watch for them.) If you're really lucky, a poison dart frog may cross your path. Dolphins play offshore, and whales occasionally surface as well.

In July and August, the company has a supervised program for children ages 2 through 12. A youth director is on board, and more counselors are added if the number of families requires it. One of the three guided hikes at every stop is designed specifically for children, though adults are welcome, too. Special nature briefings use language children will understand. Youngsters also picnic on Costa Rica's stunning beaches (children's menus are available), and the ship carries enough water-sports paraphernalia to keep preteens and teens occupied when they aren't hiking. Waterskiing, snorkeling, and kayaking are all options. This flexible program generally runs from 9 to 9; children can spend all or part of that time with the children's group, and parents can spend as much time as they wish with the children's group. It should be noted, however, that guides aren't baby-sitters, and while you can put very young children in the program, those who will get the most out of it are school-age children.

*Temptress Adventures, 351 N.W. LeJeune Rd., Penthouse 6, Miami, FL 33126, tel. 305/643–4040 or 800/336–8423. Year-round: 4–8 days, $830–$2,695 adults, 50% discount for ages 11 and under in summer, 25% discount for ages 12–17 in summer.*

## Thomson Family Adventures

6+

Rick Thomson and Judi Wineland have been in the adventure travel business for more than 20 years. They're also seasoned family travelers; their two daughters have accompanied them on trips since they were infants. They know from personal experience how to tailor a trip to a family's needs and expectations. Thomson runs family trips throughout the world, visiting Tanzania, Turkey, Costa Rica, Nepal, the Galapagos and Peru, and Australia.

**FOR FAMILIES.** Cosmopolitan cities and vast stretches of desolate outback, homeland of aboriginal peoples, habitat of curious creatures, and, of course, site of the largest barrier reef in the world—all these attributes make Australia a terrific family destination. Thomson's Australia's Outback, Reefs & Rainforests itinerary covers everything from the isolated Red Centre to sophisticated Sydney. As with most of the company's family departures, your group is accompanied by an adventure mentor, a certified teaching professional who leads hands-on activities and games. The group stays two days at each of six destinations, with transfers by van and airplane kept to a minimum amount of time so kids won't get restless. Accommodations range from a modern beach hotel to a rustic rain forest lodge. You can search for koalas near Noosa, explore the rain forests and sand dunes of Fraser Island, and snorkel the Great Barrier Reef accompanied by a marine biologist. On a nighttime naturalist-led walk you might see some of Australia's nocturnal residents—brushtailed bettongs, pademelons, quolls, owls, opossums, and the rare Lunholtz tree kangaroo. During a stay on a working farm in the MacDonnell Mountain Range, you can opt to ride horses or camels. You'll also travel to the sacred site of Uluru (otherwise known as Ayers Rock) and to Uluru and Blue Mountains national parks. The final day is spent in Sydney, where you'll tour the much-photographed harbor.

Throughout the trip you and your children can tackle several ancillary activities, such as surfing, swimming, hiking, bushwalking, even boomerang throwing. Afterward, children can keep the adventure alive in the company's Young Adventurers Club, with its newsletter, Web site, and photo contest. The trip's price includes airfare from Los Angeles or San Francisco into Brisbane and out of Sydney; you can fly from other cities for moderate add-on fares.

*Thomson Family Adventures, 347 Broadway, Cambridge, MA 02139, tel. 617/864–4803 or 800/262–6255. Year-round (all trips not available all months): 16 days, $5,890–$6,990 adults, $1,000 discount for children 11 and under, $500 discount for children 12–17.*

# Resources

## Organizations

Many organizations protect animals and encourage membership and participation by families and children. These groups don't sponsor trips, but they can help foster an interest in the world's wildlife. The **International Fund for Animal Welfare** (IFAW; 411 Main St., Yarmouth Port, MA 02675, tel. 508/362–6268 or 800/932–4329) has worked particularly hard to stop both Canadian seal hunts and whaling by Japanese and Norwegian hunters. It sends out literature to schoolchildren and others, tries to answer questions, and accepts monetary support for its efforts. You can adopt an orca through **Save the Whales** (Box 2397, Venice, CA 90291, tel. 831/899–9957 or 800/942–5365), which also has an excellent educational program that goes to schools. If you'd rather adopt a finback whale, contact **Allied Whale** (College of the Atlantic, 105 Eden St., Bar Harbor, ME 04609, tel. 207/

288–5644); the adoption program funds research. **Friends of the Sea Otter** (2150 Garden Rd., Suite A3, Monterey, CA 93940, tel. 831/373–2747) has information about otters, a map of where to spot them on the Monterey Peninsula, and a catalog of otter-related items you can buy. Ask for the Educational Packet for Children (or first check the packet out online at www.seaotters.org); money goes to support educational programs and research. **Wolf Haven International** (3111 Offut Lake Rd., Tenino, WA 98589, tel. 360/264–4695 or 800/448–9653) is the organization through which you can adopt a wolf. Adoption and membership include a subscription to its quarterly magazine, *WolfTracks*. You can visit Wolf Haven's facility near Olympia, Washington, and take a tour to see the wolves the organization has rescued.

## Books

*Swimming with Sea Lions and Other Adventures in the Galápagos Islands* (Scholastic), by Ann McGovern, describes a young traveler's 15-day boat trip around the islands. There are also numerous children's books about Darwin and his discoveries; many of the best are now out of print but still available in libraries. Look for *A Visit to Galápagos* (Abrams), by Katie Lee, an excellent picture book with paintings and drawings of many of the islands' most famous inhabitants, as well as informative text. Another good choice is Piero Ventura's 70-page *Darwin: Nature Reinterpreted* (Houghton Mifflin), which tracks Darwin's entire *Beagle* voyage and takes a look at his theories and writings.

Patricia Arrigoni's *Harpo, the Baby Harp Seal* (Travel Publishers International, tel. 415/456–2697 or 800/942–7760) is a beautifully photographed story about a baby seal on the ice floes off the Magdalen Islands (where Natural Habitat Adventures' trip takes place). The book is aimed at children ages 7–10 but has appeal for all ages.

## Also See

There are many other ways and places to meet animals up close. Snorkeling and Diving lists adventures with amazing marine-life encounters. Horse Packing, Cattle Drives, *and* Covered Wagon Adventures have trips that involve horses, and Ranches includes encounters with horses, mules, farm animals, and, in one case (the Y.O. Ranch in Texas), exotic wildlife.

# APPENDIX: FINDING THE ADVENTURES

Here is a geographical list of activities, outfitters, and schools in this book. Descriptions of the outfitters and schools appear alphabetically in the chapter on each activity.

## IN THE U.S.

### ALASKA

**Biking**
Backcountry

**Dogsledding**
American Wilderness Experience/GORP Travel

**Hiking and Backpacking**
Alaska Wildland Adventures
Camp Denali
REI Adventures

**Kayaking**
Kayak & Canoe Institute
Nantahala Outdoor Center
REI Adventures

**Native American Experiences**
Athabasca Cultural Journeys

**Rafting**
Wilderness River Outfitters

**RV Adventures**
Denali National Park
McKinley RV and Campground

**Sailing**
American Wilderness Experience/GORP Travel
Ocean Voyages
Rascals in Paradise

**Trekking with Llamas and Burros**
Off the Beaten Path

**Wildlife Encounters**
Alaska Wildland Adventures

### ARIZONA

**Archaeology Adventures**
Earthwatch
White Mountain Archaeological Center

**Biking**
Backcountry
Escape the City Streets

**Digging for Dinosaur Bones**
Dinamation International Society

**Hiking and Backpacking**
Sierra Club
Southwest Trekking

**Horse Packing**
American Wilderness Experience/GORP Travel

**Houseboating**
Forever Resorts
Lake Powell Resorts & Marinas
Seven Crown Resorts

**Native American Experiences**
Crow Canyon Archaeological Center
Grandtravel
Off the Beaten Path

**Rafting**
Arizona Raft Adventures
Far Flung Adventures
Grand Canyon Dories/O.A.R.S. Dories

**Ranches**
White Stallion Ranch

**RV Adventures**
Lake Powell Resorts & Marinas

### ARKANSAS

**Ranches**
Scott Valley Resort & Guest Ranch

### CALIFORNIA

**Cattle Drives**
Hunewill Circle H Guest Ranch

**Fishing**
Fly-Fishing Outfitters Clinics
Trinity Canyon Fly Fishing Workshops

**Hiking and Backpacking**
Backroads
REI Adventures
Sierra Club

**Horse Packing**
Mammoth Lakes Pack Outfit

**Houseboating**
Forever Resorts
Seven Crown Resorts

**Kayaking**
Cutting Edge Adventures

**Rafting**
American River Touring Association
Cutting Edge Adventures
O.A.R.S.
Outdoor Adventures

**Ranches**
Coffee Creek Ranch
Rankin Ranch

**Rock Climbing**
Alpine Skills International
Eastern Mountain Sports Climbing School
Joshua Tree Rock Climbing School

**RV Adventures**
Big Bear Shores RV Resort & Yacht Club
Joshua Tree National Park

**Sailing**
Ocean Voyages

**Trekking with Llamas and Burros**
Sierra Club

### COLORADO

**Archaeology Adventures**
Crow Canyon Archaeological Center

**Canoeing**
Boulder Outdoor Center
Denver Museum of Natural History

**Cross-Country Skiing**
Adventures to the Edge
C Lazy U
Off the Beaten Path

**Digging for Dinosaur Bones**
Dinamation International Society

**Dogsledding**
Telluride Outside

**Fishing**
Orvis Fly Fishing School
Telluride Outside

**Hiking and Backpacking**
Sierra Club

**Horse Packing**
Adventure Specialists
Fantasy Ranch
Vista Verde Ranch

**Kayaking**
Boulder Outdoor Center
Dvorak's Kayak & Rafting Expeditions

**Native American Experiences**
Crow Canyon Archaeological Center
Grandtravel
Off the Beaten Path

**Rafting**
American Wilderness Experience/GORP Travel
Canyonlands Field Institute
Dvorak's Kayak & Rafting Expeditions
Far Flung Adventures
Holiday Expeditions
O.A.R.S.

**Ranches**
Aspen Canyon Ranch
Cherokee Park Dude Ranch
Colorado Trails Ranch
Drowsy Water Ranch
Elk Mountain Ranch
Lake Mancos Ranch
North Fork Guest Ranch
Rainbow Trout Ranch
Sky Corral
Skyline Guest Ranch

**Rock Climbing**
Adventures to the Edge
Colorado Mountain School
Eastern Mountain Sports Climbing School
Fantasy Ridge Mountain Guides

**RV Adventures**
Colorado National Monument
Great Sand Dunes National Monument

**Trekking with Llamas and Burros**
Off the Beaten Path

## CONNECTICUT

**Rock Climbing**
Eastern Mountain Sports Climbing School

**Sailing**
Offshore Sailing School

## FLORIDA

**Fishing**
Orvis Fly Fishing School

**Kayaking**
Nantahala Outdoor Center
Outward Bound

**RV Adventures**
Everglades National Park

**Sailing**
Annapolis Sailing School
Ocean Voyages
Offshore Sailing School
Outward Bound
VYC Charters and Sailing School

## GEORGIA

**Canoeing**
Nantahala Outdoor Center

**Houseboating**
Forever Resorts

**Kayaking**
Nantahala Outdoor Center

**RV Adventures**
Chattahoochee National Forest

## HAWAII

**Hiking and Backpacking**
American Wilderness Experience/GORP Travel
REI Adventures
Sierra Club

**Snorkeling and Diving**
Denver Museum of Natural History
Ocean Voyages

## IDAHO

**Fishing**
Orvis Fly Fishing School

**Rafting**
American River Touring Association
Echo
Grand Canyon Dories/O.A.R.S. Dories
Holiday Expeditions
Hughes River Expeditions
Idaho Afloat
O.A.R.S.
Outdoor Adventures
Ouzel Outfitters
River Odysseys West
Salmon River Outfitters
Wilderness River Outfitters

**Ranches**
Hidden Creek Ranch

## ILLINOIS

**Houseboating**
Seeser's Mississippi Rent-a-Cruise

**Sailing**
Offshore Sailing School

## INDIANA

**Hiking and Backpacking**
Sierra Club

## IOWA

**Houseboating**
Seeser's Mississippi Rent-a-Cruise

## KENTUCKY

**RV Adventures**
Mammoth Cave National Park

## MAINE

### Canoeing
L.L. Bean
Sunrise County Canoe Expeditions

### Cross-Country Skiing
L.L. Bean
Telemark Inn

### Fishing
L.L. Bean

### Hiking and Backpacking
Backroads
Sierra Club

### Kayaking
Maine Island Kayak Company
Outward Bound
Paddleways
Wilderness Expeditions & The Birches

### Rafting
Northern Outdoors
Unicorn Outdoor Adventures

### Sailing
North End Shipyard Schooners
Outward Bound

### Trekking with Llamas and Burros
Telemark Inn

## MARYLAND

### Canoeing
Outward Bound

### Fishing
Orvis Fly Fishing School

### Sailing
Annapolis Sailing School
Outward Bound

## MASSACHUSETTS

### Biking
VBT Bicycling Vacations

### Fishing
Orvis Fly Fishing School

### Hiking and Backpacking
Appalachian Mountain Club

### Kayaking
Zoar Outdoor

### Rock Climbing
Zoar Outdoor

## MICHIGAN

### Biking
Michigan Bicycle Touring

### Kayaking
Wilderness Inquiry

### RV Adventures
Porcupine Mountains Wilderness State Park

## MINNESOTA

### Canoeing
Boundary Country Trekking
Gunflint Northwoods Outfitters/ Gunflint Lodge
Kayak & Canoe Institute
Outward Bound
Wilderness Inquiry

### Cross-Country Skiing
Gunflint Northwoods Outfitters/ Gunflint Lodge

### Dogsledding
Boundary Country Trekking
Gunflint Northwoods Outfitters/ Gunflint Lodge
Outward Bound
Wilderness Inquiry

### Fishing
Gunflint Northwoods Outfitters/ Gunflint Lodge

### Kayaking
Kayak & Canoe Institute
Outward Bound

## MISSISSIPPI

### Canoeing
Wolf River Canoes

## MISSOURI

### Houseboating
Forever Resorts

## MONTANA

### Biking
Backcountry
Wilderness River Outfitters

### Cattle Drives
American Wilderness Experience/GORP Travel
Cowboy Crossing
Hargrave Cattle & Guest Ranch
Laredo Enterprises
Montana High Country Cattle Drive
Off the Beaten Path

### Covered Wagon Adventures
Myers Ranch Wagon Trains

### Cross-Country Skiing
Izaak Walton Inn
Lone Mountain Ranch

### Fishing
L.L. Bean
Montana River Outfitters

### Hiking and Backpacking
Backroads

### Horse Packing
Great Divide Guiding & Outfitters
WTR Outfitters/White Tail Ranch

### Native American Experiences
Journeys into American Indian Territory
Off the Beaten Path

### Rafting
American Wilderness Experience/GORP Travel
Glacier Wilderness Guides/ Montana Raft Company
Wilderness River Outfitters

### Ranches
Lone Mountain Ranch

### Trekking with Llamas and Burros
American Wilderness Experience/GORP Travel
Off the Beaten Path

## NEBRASKA

### Covered Wagon Adventures
Oregon Trail Wagon Train

## NEVADA

**Biking**
Escape the City Streets

**Cattle Drives**
Cottonwood Ranch
Hunewill Circle H Guest Ranch

**Horse Packing**
Cottonwood Ranch

**Houseboating**
Forever Resorts
Seven Crown Resorts

**Rock Climbing**
Eastern Mountain Sports Climbing School

## NEW HAMPSHIRE

**Biking**
Bike Vermont

**Hiking and Backpacking**
Appalachian Mountain Club

**Rock Climbing**
Appalachian Mountain Club
Eastern Mountain Sports Climbing School

## NEW JERSEY

**Rock Climbing**
Appalachian Mountain Club

**Sailing**
Offshore Sailing School

## NEW MEXICO

**Archaeology Adventures**
Denver Museum of Natural History

**Horse Packing**
American Wilderness Experience/GORP Travel

**Native American Experiences**
Grandtravel
Journeys into American Indian Territory

**Rafting**
Dvorak's Kayak & Rafting Expeditions
Far Flung Adventures

## NEW YORK

**Biking**
Brooks Country Cycling & Hiking Tours

**Canoeing**
Bear Cub Adventure Tours

**Cross-Country Skiing**
Appalachian Mountain Club

**Fishing**
Appalachian Mountain Club
Orvis Fly Fishing School

**Hiking and Backpacking**
Appalachian Mountain Club

**Houseboating**
Collar City Charters
Mid-Lakes Navigation Company
Remar Rentals

**Kayaking**
Paddleways
Zoar Outdoor

**Native American Experiences**
Journeys into American Indian Territory

**Ranches**
Pinegrove Ranch Resort
Rocking Horse Ranch
Timberlock

**Rock Climbing**
Adirondack Rock & River Guide Service
Appalachian Mountain Club
Eastern Mountain Sports Climbing School

**RV Adventures**
Lake Placid/Whiteface Mountain KOA

**Trekking with Llamas and Burros**
Appalachian Mountain Club

## NORTH CAROLINA

**Biking**
Nantahala Outdoor Center

**Canoeing**
Nantahala Outdoor Center

**Hiking and Backpacking**
Backroads

**Kayaking**
Nantahala Outdoor Center

**Rock Climbing**
Outward Bound

**RV Adventures**
Cherokee/Great Smokies KOA

**Trekking with Llamas and Burros**
WindDancers Lodging & Llama Treks

## OKLAHOMA

**Native American Experiences**
Journeys into American Indian Territory

## OREGON

**Kayaking**
Outward Bound

**Rafting**
American River Touring Association
Echo
Hughes River Expeditions
O.A.R.S.
Ouzel Outfitters
Rogue River Raft Trips

**Ranches**
Rock Springs

**Trekking with Llamas and Burros**
Hurricane Creek Llama Treks
Wallowa Llamas

## PENNSYLVANIA

**Hiking and Backpacking**
Appalachian Mountain Club

**Rock Climbing**
Appalachian Mountain Club

## RHODE ISLAND

**Sailing**
Offshore Sailing School

## SOUTH DAKOTA

**Covered Wagon Adventures**
Grandtravel

**Digging for Dinosaur Bones**
Earthwatch
The Mammoth Site

**Horse Packing**
Dakota Badlands Outfitters

**Native American Experiences**
Journeys into American Indian Territory

**Rock Climbing**
Sylvan Rocks Climbing School & Guide Service

**RV Adventures**
Rafter J Bar Ranch Campground

## TENNESSEE

**Canoeing**
Nantahala Outdoor Center

**RV Adventures**
Great Smoky Mountains National Park

## TEXAS

**Canoeing**
Outward Bound

**Houseboating**
Forever Resorts

**Native American Experiences**
Journeys into American Indian Territory

**Rafting**
Far Flung Adventures

**Ranches**
Mayan Dude Ranch
Y.O. Ranch

**RV Adventures**
Palo Duro Canyon State Park

## UTAH

**Biking**
Escape the City Streets

**Canoeing**
Kayak & Canoe Institute

**Cattle Drives**
Off the Beaten Path
Rockin' R Ranch

**Digging for Dinosaur Bones**
Dinamation International Society

**Hiking and Backpacking**
Sierra Club

**Horse Packing**
American Wilderness Experience/GORP Travel
Rockin' R Ranch

**Houseboating**
Lake Powell Resorts & Marinas

**Native American Experiences**
Crow Canyon Archaeological Center

**Rafting**
American River Touring Association
Arizona Raft Adventures
Canyonlands Field Institute
Denver Museum of Natural History
Dvorak's Kayak & Rafting Expeditions
Holiday Expeditions
Sheri Griffith Expeditions
Tag-A-Long Expeditions

**Rock Climbing**
Eastern Mountain Sports Climbing School
Fantasy Ridge Mountain Guides

**RV Adventures**
Lake Powell Resorts & Marinas

## VERMONT

**Biking**
Bike Vermont
VBT Bicycling Vacations

**Canoeing**
Adventure Quest

**Dogsledding**
Adventure Guides of Vermont

**Fishing**
Orvis Fly Fishing School

**Hiking and Backpacking**
Sierra Club

**Kayaking**
Adventure Quest
Paddleways
Zoar Outdoor

**Rock Climbing**
Adventure Quest

**Trekking with Llamas and Burros**
Northern Vermont Llama Company

## VIRGINIA

**Biking**
VBT Bicycling Vacations

**RV Adventures**
Shenandoah National Park

**Trekking with Llamas and Burros**
Virginia Highlands Llamas

## WASHINGTON

**Biking**
Backcountry

**Hiking and Backpacking**
Backroads
REI Adventures
Sierra Club

**Kayaking**
Outward Bound
REI Adventures

**Rock Climbing**
American Alpine Institute

**Sailing**
Outward Bound

**Wildlife Encounters**
Sea Quest Expeditions

## WEST VIRGINIA

**Rafting**
Class VI River Runners

## WISCONSIN

**Dogsledding**
Trek & Trail

### Kayaking
Kayak & Canoe Institute
Trek & Trail
Wilderness Inquiry

## WYOMING

### Biking
Backcountry

### Cattle Drives
American Wilderness Experience/GORP Travel
Cheyenne River Ranch
Cowboy Crossing
High Island Ranch and Cattle Company
Off the Beaten Path

### Covered Wagon Adventures
American Wilderness Experience/GORP Travel
Grandtravel
Teton Wagon Train and Horse Adventure

### Cross-Country Skiing
Lone Mountain Ranch
Off the Beaten Path

### Digging for Dinosaur Bones
Dinamation International Society
Wyoming Dinosaur Center

### Hiking and Backpacking
Backroads

### Horse Packing
American Wilderness Experience/GORP Travel
Skinner Brothers

### Native American Experiences
Journeys into American Indian Territory

### Rafting
Dvorak's Kayak & Rafting Expeditions
O.A.R.S.

### Ranches
Breteche Creek
Paradise Guest Ranch
Red Rock Ranch
Seven D Ranch

### Rock Climbing
Exum Mountain Guides
Sylvan Rocks Climbing School & Guide Service

### Trekking with Llamas and Burros
American Wilderness Experience/GORP Travel
Off the Beaten Path

# OUTSIDE THE U.S.

## AFRICA

### Rafting
Cutting Edge Adventures

### Sailing
Ocean Voyages

### Wildlife Encounters
Big Five Tours & Expeditions
Rascals in Paradise
Thomson Family Adventures

## ASIA

### Archaeology Adventures
Earthwatch

### Sailing
Ocean Voyages

### Wildlife Encounters
Thomson Family Adventures

## AUSTRALIA AND NEW ZEALAND

### Sailing
Ocean Voyages
Rascals in Paradise

### Wildlife Encounters
Thomson Family Adventures

## CANADA

### Biking
Backcountry

### Canoeing
Kayak & Canoe Institute
Sunrise County Canoe Expeditions
Wells Gray Chalets & Wilderness Adventures

### Cross-Country Skiing
Backroads
Off the Beaten Path
Wells Gray Chalets & Wilderness Adventures

### Digging for Dinosaur Bones
Royal Tyrrell Museum

### Dogsledding
Arctic Odysseys
Boundary Country Trekking
Kanata Wilderness Adventures/Wells Gray Ranch

### Fishing
Babine Norlakes Lodge

### Hiking and Backpacking
American Wilderness Experience/GORP Travel
Backroads
Canadian Mountain Holidays
REI Adventures
Sila Sojourns
Wells Gray Park Backcountry Chalets

### Horse Packing
American Wilderness Experience/GORP Travel
Spatsizi Wilderness Vacations

### Houseboating
Remar Rentals
Waterway Houseboat Vacations

### Kayaking
Outward Bound
Paddleways
REI Adventures
Wilderness Inquiry

### Native American Experiences
Arctic Odysseys
Off the Beaten Path

### Rafting
Canadian River Expeditions
Wilderness River Outfitters

### Rock Climbing
American Alpine Institute
Yamnuska, Inc.

### RV Adventures
Burnaby Cariboo RV Park

**Trekking with Llamas and Burros**
Strider Adventures

**Wildlife Encounters**
Arctic Odysseys
Blue Loon Adventures
Natural Habitat Adventures

## CARIBBEAN

**Archaeology Adventures**
Earthwatch

**Sailing**
Annapolis Sailing School
Bitter End Yacht Club
Ocean Voyages
Offshore Sailing School
Rascals in Paradise

**Snorkeling and Diving**
Earthwatch
Hyatt Regency Grand Cayman
Ocean Voyages
Rascals in Paradise

## CENTRAL AMERICA

**Archaeology Adventures**
Earthwatch

**Digging for Dinosaur Bones**
Earthwatch

**Hiking and Backpacking**
Backroads

**Sailing**
Rascals in Paradise

**Snorkeling and Diving**
American Wilderness Experience/GORP Travel
Ocean Voyages
Rascals in Paradise

**Wildlife Encounters**
American Wilderness Experience/GORP Travel
Cross Country International
Natural Habitat Adventures
Temptress Adventures
Thomson Family Adventures

## EUROPE

**Archaeology Adventures**
Earthwatch

**Biking**
Backroads
Brooks Country Cycling & Hiking Tours
Butterfield & Robinson
Ciclismo Classico

**Hiking and Backpacking**
Backroads
Butterfield & Robinson
Ciclismo Classico
Cross Country International

**Horse Packing**
Adventure Specialists

**Sailing**
Ocean Voyages
Rascals in Paradise

**Wildlife Encounters**
Natural Habitat Adventures

## MEXICO

**Digging for Dinosaur Bones**
Dinamation International Society
Earthwatch

**Hiking and Backpacking**
Southwest Trekking

**Horse Packing**
Adventure Specialists

**Houseboating**
Forever Resorts

**Kayaking**
Cutting Edge Adventures
Paddleways

**Native American Experiences**
Crow Canyon Archaeological Center

**Rafting**
Cutting Edge Adventures
Far Flung Adventures

**Sailing**
Ocean Voyages

**Snorkeling and Diving**
Rascals in Paradise

**Wildlife Encounters**
Baja Discovery
Baja Expeditions

## THE PACIFIC

*(Fiji, French Polynesia, Indonesia, Micronesia, New Guinea, Palau, Philippines)*

**Sailing**
Ocean Voyages
Rascals in Paradise

**Snorkeling and Diving**
Earthwatch
Ocean Voyages
Rascals in Paradise
World of Adventure Vacations

## SOUTH AMERICA

**Digging for Dinosaur Bones**
Earthwatch

**Horse Packing**
Adventure Specialists

**Rock Climbing**
Eastern Mountain Sports Climbing School

**Sailing**
Ocean Voyages

**Snorkeling and Diving**
Ocean Voyages

**Wildlife Encounters**
Galápagos Network
Lindblad Special Expeditions
Thomson Family Adventures

# INDEX

# Notes

# Notes

# Notes

# Notes

# Notes

# Notes